FORMAL SEMANTICS AND PRAGMATICS
FOR NATURAL LANGUAGES

FORMAL SEMANTICS
AND PRAGMATICS
FOR
NATURAL LANGUAGES

Edited by

F. GUENTHNER

Universität Tübingen, Seminar für Englische Philologie, Tübingen, B.R.D.

and

S. J. SCHMIDT

Universität Bielefeld, B.R.D.

D. REIDEL PUBLISHING COMPANY

DORDRECHT : HOLLAND / BOSTON : U.S.A.
LONDON : ENGLAND

Library of Congress Cataloging in Publication Data

Main entry under title:

Formal semantics and pragmatics for natural languages.

    (Synthese language library; v. 4)
    "Essays in this collection are the outgrowth of a workshop held in June 1976."
    Includes bibliographies and index.
    1. Languages — Philosophy. 2. Semantics. 3. Pragmatics. 4. Predicate calculus. 5. Tense (Logic). 6. Grammar, Comparative and general. I. Guenthner, Franz. II. Schmidt, S. J., 1941–
III. Series.
P106.F66   401   78–13180
ISBN 90–277–0778–2
ISBN 90–277–0930–0 pbk.

Published by D. Reidel Publishing Company,
P.O. Box 17, Dordrecht, Holland

Sold and distributed in the U.S.A., Canada, and Mexico
by D. Reidel Publishing Company, Inc.
Lincoln Building, 160 Old Derby Street, Hingham,
Mass. 02043, U.S.A.

CONTENTS

v

PREFACE

The essays in this collection are the outgrowth of a workshop, held in June 1976, on formal approaches to the semantics and pragmatics of natural languages. They document in an astoundingly uniform way the developments in the formal analysis of natural languages since the late sixties. The avowed aim of the workshop was in fact to assess the progress made in the application of formal methods to semantics, to confront different approaches to essentially the same problems on the one hand, and, on the other, to show the way in relating semantic and pragmatic explanations of linguistic phenomena. Several of these papers can in fact be regarded as attempts to close the 'semiotic circle' by bringing together the syntactic, semantic *and* pragmatic properties of certain constructions in an explanatory framework thereby making it more than obvious that these three components of an integrated linguistic theory cannot be as neatly separated as one would have liked to believe. In other words, not only can we not elaborate a syntactic description of (a fragment of) a language and then proceed to the semantics (as Montague pointed out already forcefully in 1968), we cannot hope to achieve an adequate integrated syntax and semantics without paying heed to the pragmatic aspects of the constructions involved. The behavior of polarity items, 'quantifiers' like *any*, conditionals or even logical particles like *and* and *or* in non-indicative sentences is clear-cut evidence for the need to let each component of the grammar inform the other.

The papers are arranged according to the three major topics discussed at the workshop: the analysis of quantification, and pronominalization, temporal constructions, and the relation between semantics and pragmatics.

Since Montague's 'Proper Treatment of Quantification' linguists and logicians alike have paid more attention to quantificational problems and questions of cross-reference, i.e., pronominalization, than ever before. At the workshop five quite different — yet logically oriented — ways of dealing with quantification in natural languages were discussed. These are presented in the first five papers; they constitute basic references for further work in this area.

F. Guenthner and S. J. Schmidt (eds.), Formal Semantics and Pragmatics
for Natural Languages, vii–viii. All Rights Reserved.
Copyright © 1978 by D. Reidel Publishing Company, Dordrecht, Holland.

The next group of papers deals with a variety of temporal expressions in English. These are of interest in several respects not only because they contain novel and detailed analyses of temporal adverbs and tenses in a natural language but also because they are theoretical contributions to the area of tense logic.

The last group of papers — with the exception of the treatment of truth-predicates in predicate logic — discusses the intricate relations between semantics and pragmatics already mentioned above.

These papers, we expect, lead us to rethink our views on the nature of the way syntax, semantics and pragmatics interact. They address themselves not only to readers already versed in the formal analysis of natural languages and who are interested in comparing different logical frameworks but also to readers who — having little or no previous acquaintance with logical semantics — are looking for an overview of the kinds of problems and results in that field.

It is a pleasure to acknowledge the wonderful hospitality of the Werner-Reimers-Stiftung (Bad Homburg v.d.H.) as well as their material support of the workshop.

F. GUENTHNER
S. J. SCHMIDT

JAAKKO HINTIKKA AND LAURI CARLSON

CONDITIONALS, GENERIC QUANTIFIERS, AND OTHER APPLICATIONS OF SUBGAMES

In examining the interrelations of use and meaning, one of the most promising testing grounds is constituted by the theory of conditional sentences in natural languages. On this ground the differences between different approaches to meaning and those between the several uses of 'use' have clashed dramatically, and yet left many of the principal problems unresolved. The truth-functional analysis of 'if–then' sentences is as interesting an example of an approach to meaning by means of recursive truth-characterizations as one can hope to find. Yet it has run into a sharp criticism from those philosophers of language whose paradigm of meaning–giving use is usage, i.e., intralinguistic use. These philosophers are sometimes misleadingly called ordinary-language philosophers. However, they have likewise failed to solve many of the most interesting questions concerning the actual behavior of conditionals in natural languages. The initial problems we shall be dealing with in this work (see below) are cases in point. Hence the field is wide open for new approaches.

In order to avoid misunderstandings, it is important to realize that there are reasons of two different kinds why the truth-functional treatment of natural-language conditionals is inadequate. Here we shall confine our attention to those problems that are caused by the conditional character of if–then sentences. This is not what has primarily occupied most philosophers of language, however, when they have been considering conditionals. What has caught their fancy is usually the stronger logical tie that binds the antecedent and the consequent of a natural-language conditional as compared with purely truth-functional conditionals. This extra force is seen in problems about counterfactuals, paradoxes of 'material' implication, and so on.

This extra force of natural-language conditionals is a much less subtle problem than the conditional character of if–then sentences in (say) English. A suitable modal analysis of conditionals goes a long way toward solving the problems of extra force. Furthermore, these problems are also amenable to a treatment in terms of conversational forces. However, they will not be treated in the present essay, which focuses exclusively on the conditional nature of conditionals. The phenomena caused by this nature are quite

1

F. Guenthner and S. J. Schmidt (eds.), Formal Semantics and Pragmatics
for Natural Languages, 1–36. All Rights Reserved.

different from the problems of extra (non-truth-functional) force of natural-language conditionals. They are considerably subtler than these, and cannot be treated in the same way.

How can they be treated, then? One promising approach — not necessarily a completely new one, though — can be reached by taking the use that figures in the famous identification of meaning and use to be, not usage or intralinguistic use (use in language) but use in the sense of those rule-governed activities ('language-games') which link a language, or a part of it, to the world it enables us to describe or to interact with. Some such language-games happily turn out to be games also in the strict sense of the mathematical theory of games. Such language-games have been studied by the authors of this essay and by their associates in what they have called 'game-theoretical semantics'. In this work, game-theoretical semantics is brought to bear on a number of apparently unrelated semantical (linguistic, logical) phenomena. They include certain 'generic' (i.e., universal-quantifier) use of words like 'a(n)' and 'some', certain difficult types of pronominalization, and the semantics of conditionals. They all turn out to be closely related to each other and to admit of very natural explanations which all involve the same basic idea. The most prominent one of these problems is precisely the semantics of conditionals just mentioned.

For the fundamentals of game-theoretical semantics, the reader is referred to Hintikka (1974), (1975), and (1976). The main idea underlying our semantical games may be said to be to consider each such game as an attempted verification of a sentence S against the schemes of a malevolent Nature who is trying to defeat me. These games are thus games against Nature. Their two players will be called 'myself' and 'Nature'. The former wins if the game ends with a true atomic sentence, while the latter wins if it ends with a false one. The rules of these games can be gathered without much difficulty from what has been said. For instance, to verify a sentence of the form

$$X — \text{some } Y \text{ who } Z — W$$

(where the 'who' in 'who Z' is for simplicity assumed to occupy the subject position and to be singular) I clearly will have to choose a person, say b, such that in the rest of the game I can verify

$$X — b — W, b \text{ is a(n) } Y, \text{ and } b \text{ } Z.$$

The game rule for 'some' whose special case this recipe is will be called (G.some).

In order to verify the sentence

$$X — \text{every } Y \text{ who } Z — W$$

(with the same proviso concerning 'who Z') I will have to verify

$$X — d — W \text{ if } d \text{ is a(n) } Y \text{ and } d Z$$

for any individual d Nature might choose. This can be generalized into a game rule (G.every) for the English quantifier word 'every'.

To verify 'S_1 or S_2' I will have to verify S_1 or verify S_2, i.e., choose one of them for the rest of the game to deal with, and to verify 'S_1 and S_2' I will have to verify whichever conjunct Nature chooses. (Special attention will have to be paid here to anaphoric relations between S_1 and S_2.)

These examples will suffice to illustrate how our games are played. The rule for truth and falsity embodies an improved version of the old idea that a sentence S is true if it can (in principle) be verified. This is now taken to mean that S is true iff I have a winning strategy in the correlated game $\bar{G}(S)$, false iff Nature has a winning strategy in $G(S)$. If $G(S)$ is indeterminate (if neither player has a winning strategy), S is neither true nor false.

As a starting-point, let us recall the obvious simple-minded game-theoretic treatment of if-conditionals. In earlier game-theoretical treatments, they were handled by means of the following rule:

(G.if) When the game has reached a sentence of one of the forms

> If X, Y
>
> or
>
> Y if X

then I may choose either neg $+ [X]$ or Y, and the game is continued with respect to it.

Here 'neg $+$' refers to the process of forming the (semantical) negation (contradictory) of a given sentence. Its analysis presents a separate problem. This problem is not the reason why (G.if) is not wholly satisfactory. The rules for semantical negation will have to be discussed in game-theoretic semantics anyway. (Cf. Hintikka, forthcoming.) Indeed, the rule (G.if) is in many respects a good first approximation. For instance, it enables us to discuss the important principles that govern the order in which the game rules are applied. (Cf. Hintikka (1975).)

The problem with (G.if) is connected with its purely truth-functional character. As was already indicated, ordinary-language philosophers have time and again claimed that a conditional like

(1)   If X, Y

is not equivalent with the disjunction

(2) $neg + [X]$ or Y.

In asserting the conditional (1) one does not assert the disjunction (2). One somehow makes, rather, a purely conditional assertion whose force does not come to the play at all until its antecedent clause X is verified or otherwise asserted. However, these ordinary-language philosophers also have totally failed to spell out the precise logical and semantical difference between (1) and (2).

If anything, the game-theoretic approach encourages an emphasis on the differences between (1) and (2). One reason is what happens in the case that a semantical game $G(X)$ connected with X turns out to be indeterminate. (It is trivially true that both players cannot have a winning strategy in one of our semantical games. However, there is no general guarantee that either of them must have one.) If the game is indeterminate, the associated logic is a non-classical three-valued one. It is well known that in such a three-valued logic it is unnatural to define (1) as (2). Hence the possibility of indeterminacy makes the putative game rule (G.if) unnatural, for it has precisely the force of assimilating (1) to (2).

The purely truth-functional character of (G.if) is also seen from the fact that this rule is virtually identical with the game rule (G. ⊃) for material implication (horseshoe) in the semantical games connected with formal first-order languages. In fact, in the sequel we shall treat (G.if) and (G. ⊃) as being essentially identical. The inadequacies of (G.if) as an explication of the semantics of natural-language conditionals are to some extent paralleled by the criticism presented by certain philosophers of mathematics and of logic who prefer non-classical logic to the classical one.

It is also clear that rules like (G.if) do not do justice to the way in which speakers process a conditional sentence like (1) semantically. In some sense, we process (1) by first processing X and only then — depending on the outcome of the first stage — processing Y. Insofar as our rules of semantical games are supposed to approximate the way in which we actually deal with ordinary-language sentences semantically — insofar as they capture the *dynamics* of natural-language semantics, we might say — insofar they fail to deal with (1) in a realisting fashion.

How can our game rule for 'if' be improved on? In order to answer this question, let us go back to the idea of (1) as a genuine conditional which only becomes operative if and when its antecedent X is found to be true. Then, and only then, must I be able to show that Y is true, too.

Now the different attempted ways of verifying X can be understood as the different strategies I have available to me in the associated game $G(X)$, and the attempted ways of verifying Y are my strategies in $G(Y)$. For, as it was already indicated above, the basic crude but useful intuitive interpretation of our semantical games $G(Z)$ is that they are my attempts to verify Z against the schemes of a malicious Nature. What I undertake to do in defending (1) is therefore naturally understood to be to correlate to each winning strategy ζ of mine in $G(X)$ a winning strategy $\Phi(\zeta)$ of mine in $G(Y)$. The force of (1) itself is to assert the existence of a functional Φ which carries out this correlation. This simple idea captures very well the notion of conditionalization, and we shall argue that it leads us to an eminently natural game rule for if-sentences.

First we have to develop it a little further, however. One trouble is that the concept of a *winning* strategy is not an absolute one, but relative to an opponent's strategy set. This makes it awkward to speak of a mapping of my *winning* strategies in $G(X)$ on my *winning* strategies in $G(Y)$. The natural thing is to consider mappings of *all* my strategies in $G(X)$ into *all* my strategies in $G(Y)$.

The natural way to realize this idea through actual game rules is to have the two players carry out a play of the game $G(X)$ first, fought to the bitter end. For it is part and parcel of the basic ideas of game theory that to play a game is to choose a strategy. To play a game to the end is thus naturally interpreted as divulging one's strategy in it. Since these strategies are (or are represented by) functions, the strategies of the two players at the later stages of the game will have functions as their arguments and hence be higher-order functions (functionals). For their moves at these later stages will depend on their already divulged strategies in a completed subgame. Thus it is the idea of a concluded *subgame* that leads us to consider strategies representable by *functionals* rather than (first-order) *functions*.

In order to force myself to consider all of my strategies in $G(X)$, as required for the purpose of speaking of a function on the set of all such strategies, the two players must exchange roles in $G(X)$: Nature chooses one of the strategies that would ordinarily be mine, and *vice versa*. If I win in $G(X)$, I have in effect falsified X, and no need to consider Y arises. Hence we might declare myself a winner in this case.

However, if Nature wins, she has verified X and hence forced myself to consider Y. In this case, the players must move on to carry out a play of $G(Y)$. The fact that the game is continued only if one of 'my' strategies, as chosen by Nature, wins in $G(X)$ is the precise technical counterpart of the earlier crude and inaccurate idea that in a conditional 'If X, Y' we are dealing with a mapping of my *winning* strategies in $G(X)$ into my *winning* strategies in $G(Y)$.

My strategy in $G(Y)$ will now depend on the way in which X was verified, i.e., on Nature's choice of 'my' strategy in $G(X)$. Nature, in contrast, clearly does not enjoy any comparable privilege. The outcome of this play will decide the outcome of the overall game $G(\text{If } X, Y)$.

Thus the game rule for $G(\text{If } X, Y)$ can be represented by means of the following 'flow chart'.

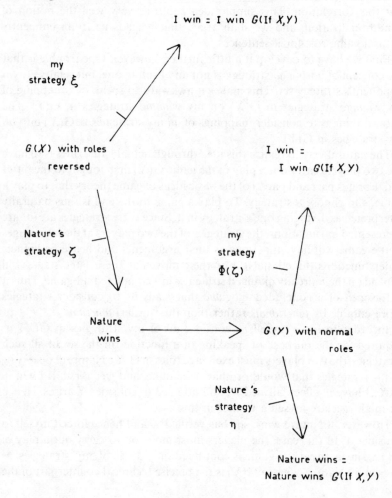

Hence 'If X, Y' is true iff there is a functional Φ and a function ξ such that they win against any strategy of Nature's represented by the functions ζ and η.

We shall call a game rule defined by the flowchart (G.cond$_1$). If this game rule strikes the reader as being rather complicated, we would like to counter by asking whether he really feels entitled to expect a simple rule here in view of all the complicated problems ('difficulties') about natural-language conditionals. Moreover, we doubt that (G.cond$_1$) is felt to be very complicated when its precise import is appreciated.

But why are not both players asked to divulge their strategies in $G(X)$? In other words, why does not Nature's strategy η in $G(Y)$ depend on my strategy ξ in $G(X)$? Why is ξ as it were forgotten in $G(Y)$? The answer is implicit in the intuitive motivation given above for the game rule (G.cond$_1$) It was intimated there that Y comes into play only when and after X has been verified, and its role will hence naturally depend on the way in which X turned out to be true. Now this way of turning out to be true is what ζ codifies. In contrast, ξ represents merely a hypothetical attempt to falsify X. Intuitively, we must therefore require that $G(Y)$ should be played so as to disregard ξ. It may be recalled here that initially we tried to establish only a mapping of *my* winning strategies in $G(X)$ into my winning strategies in $G(Y)$.

Thus the point of the game rule (G.cond$_1$) is not really to add much to the intuitive ideas it is based on. Rather, what (G.cond$_1$) does is to show how the precise dependencies such as the roles of η and ξ in $G(Y)$ serve as objective counterparts to our intuitive ideas of conditionality. An even more explicit way of spelling out the same basic idea would be to say that $G(Y)$ is played with full knowledge of ζ but in ignorance of ξ.

The formulation of (G.cond$_1$) in terms of subgames implies that in an important respect the new rule does not change the character of our semantical games. Before replacing (G.$\supset$) by (G.cond$_1$), our game-theoretical semantics could have been said to effect a translation of each first-order sentence into a second-order sentence of the form

(3) $(\exists f_1)(\exists f_2)\ldots(\exists f_m)(x_1)(x_2)\ldots(x_n)F(f_1, f_2, \ldots, f_m, x_1, x_2, \ldots, x_n)$

where $f_1, f_2, \ldots, f_m$ are such Skolem functions as serve to define my strategies insofar as quantifier rules are concerned, and $(x_1), \ldots, (x_n)$ are all the universal quantifiers of the original sentence (assuming that all negation-signs were first driven in so as to precede immediately atomic formulas). Furthermore, in (3) F is the original sentence with quantifiers omitted and with each existentially quantified variable y replaced by a different term of the form $f(x_i, x_j, \ldots, x_k)$ where $(x_i), (x_j), \ldots, (x_k)$ are all the universal quantifiers within the scope of which $(\exists y)$ occurs in the original sentence. The universal quantifiers $(x_1), (x_2), \ldots, (x_n)$ in effect embody Nature's strategies as far as her quantificational moves are concerned. The import of (3) thus comes very close to saying just that I have a winning strategy in the game correlated with the original sentence.

The replacement of (G. $\supset$) by (G.cond) has the effect of replacing some of the function and individual variables $f_1, f_2, \ldots, x_1, x_2, \ldots$ by variables for functionals, i.e., higher-type functions (or for functions in the case of universal quantifiers), plus adding to their number. Since nested occurrences of '$\supset$' serve to push the types of these functionals higher and higher, we must in principle be prepared to use functionals of any finite type.

We can in fact obtain a kind of formalized expression of (G.cond$_1$) by hanging on each subordinate clause X and Y two argument places, indicating respectively my strategy and Nature's in the correlated games. Then the game rule (G.cond$_1$) corresponds to a translation rule which takes us from 'If X, Y' to

$$(4) \qquad (\exists \Phi)(\exists \xi)(\zeta)(\eta)(X(\zeta, \xi) \supset Y(\Phi(\zeta), \eta)).$$

Our new game rule (G.cond$_1$) calls for a few comments. First, the idea it incorporates is obviously related very closely to the ideas of the intuitionists. According to them, a conditional asserts that there is a way of obtaining a 'proof' (verification) of the consequent from any given 'proof' (verification) of the antecedent. This is very closely related to what (4) says. For basically what it asserts is just the existence of a functional Φ which takes us from a successful strategy in verifying X to a successful strategy in verifying Y.

Secondly, it is worth noting how the subgame idea which led us to (G.cond$_1$) helps us to capture some of the dynamics of one's natural semantical processing of a conditional sentence which was mentioned above. Intuitively speaking, we first process the antecedent. This corresponds to the complete playing off of the game $G(X)$ correlated with the antecedent. (This is what brings in subgames or, as we really ought to call them, *completed* or *closed* subgames.) Only after we have made clear to ourselves what the world would be like if the antecedent is true do we move on to consider what the consequent says on this assumption. This second stage corresponds to playing the game $G(Y)$, and its conditionality is reflected by the dependence of my strategy $\Phi(\zeta)$ in $G(Y)$ on Nature's strategy ζ in $G(X)$, played with reversed roles.

This insight into the dynamics of first-order semantics will be put to use later by considering the behavior of pronominalization in a context involving subgames. Conversely, what we shall find about those types of pronominalization will support the diagnosis we have built into the rule $(G.cond_1)$.

At this point, a skeptical reader may very well wonder how much real difference the replacement of $(G.if)$ (or $(G. \supset)$) by $(G.cond_1)$ really makes. There are in fact some *prima facie* reasons for skepticism here. It can easily be seen that on purely classical assumptions, including prominently the stipulation that all function variables (of any type) range over *all* functions of the appropriate type, the interchange of $(G. \supset)$ and $(G.cond_1)$ does not in fact make any difference to the truth of the sentences of formal first-order languages. For purely classically (i.e., if myself is declared the winner if I win $G(X)$ with roles reversed) $X \supset Y$ is true iff $\sim X$ or Y is true, i.e., iff I have a winning strategy either in $G(Y)$ (call it ξ_0) or else in $G(\sim X)$ (call it ζ_0). Then I can respectively put either $\xi = \xi_0$ or (identically) $\Phi(\zeta) = \zeta_0$ in (4). Conversely, suppose that there are ξ and Φ in (4) such as to guarantee my win. Then either I have a winning strategy in $G(\sim X)$ or else for each winning strategy ζ in $G(X)$ there is λ such that I win in $G(Y)$ by playing λ against any strategy η of Nature's. But I can have as much as one such strategy classically only if Y is true.

However, even though formally and classically speaking there is little to choose between $(G.if)$ (or $G. \supset$)) and $(G.cond_1)$, there are further possibilities that might seem to serve to drive a wedge between the two. In fact there are two entirely different openings for a distinction here.

(a) The game-theoretical viewpoint strongly suggests that we restrict the strategy sets of the two players to *computable* functions and functionals. More accurately, we can restrict the strategies represented, in (4) by functions and functionals to computable ones.

This modification immediately changes the whole situation. It does so already in the otherwise classical first-order case. The set of true sentences will be affected by the change.

More generally, we might be inclined to admit suitable nonstandard models in the sense of Henkin (1950) (see also the correction in Andrews, 1972), that is to say, allow function quantifiers to range over suitable subsets of all arbitrary functions of the appropriate type. The most liberal policy here is to require merely that these subsets be closed with respect to Boolean operations and projective operations.

It turns out, however, as Laurence Nemirow first pointed out to us, that after a restriction to computable functions and functionals has been carried out, the distinction between $(G. \supset)$ and $(G.cond_1)$ does not make any difference. By modifying slightly the argument for the classical case, on this restriction $(G. \supset)$ and $(G.cond_1)$ can be shown to be equivalent. This equivalence may perhaps be considered a partial reason for the relative success of a purely truth-functional analysis of conditionals — and for the absence of any viable alternative in the earlier literature.

It also shows that the main reasons for the greater naturalness of $(G.cond_1)$ as compared with $(G. \supset)$ have to be sought for elsewhere.

There is a major change, however, that can result from restrictions imposed on strategy sets. Such a restriction may imply that neither player has a winning strategy in some of the semantical games. Then there will be a difference between asserting that a sentence is true, i.e., that I have a winning strategy in the correlated game, and asserting that it is not false, i.e., that Nature does not have a winning strategy in it. This in turn generates a certain ambiguity, as the sentence can be thought of as asserting either.

If a conditional like 'If X, Y' is given the latter of these two interpretations, its force will be that of

$$(\zeta)(\eta)(\exists \Phi)(\exists \xi)(X(\zeta, \xi) \supset Y(\Phi(\zeta), \eta))$$

which is the same as that of

$$(\zeta)(\eta)(\exists \varphi)(\exists \xi)(X(\zeta, \xi) \supset Y(\varphi, \eta)).$$

This is related very closely to the so-called no-counterexample interpretation. (For it, see Mostowski (1966), Chapter V; Per Martin-Löf (1970), p. 12.)

(b) In natural language, there are certain phenomena which become explainable as soon as the rule $(G.cond_1)$ (or some other rule which likewise involves subgames) is adopted. In order to see what they are, let us consider an example. What kind of pronominalization do we have in the following simple conditional?

(5)   If Bill owns a donkey, he beats it.

Here 'it' cannot refer to any particular donkey referred to earlier, for taken as a whole (5) does not speak any more of one of Bill's donkeys than of another one of them. Hence we do not have here an instance of the usual function of pronouns (pronominal anaphora), viz. to recover an earlier reference to a particular individual. Nor does the 'it' in (5) serve as a so-called 'pronoun of laziness', that is, merely as a placeholder for its grammatical antecedent 'a donkey', for (5) is not synonymous with

(6)   If Bill owns a donkey, he beats a donkey.

Sometimes it is said, in view of these facts and of the intended meaning of (4), that in (5) 'a' has a 'generic' function, i.e., serves as a universal quantifier rather than as an existential one. (We shall not try to criticize here this use of the term 'generic', even though it is in certain respects a misleading one.) Why should 'a' be generic in sentences like (5) has not been explained, however, even though such an explanation is made highly desirable by the fact that in many contexts the indefinite article 'a(n)' must be construed as a genuinely existential quantifier.

Moreover, the explanatory force of a mere postulation of a new sense of 'a(n)' with a 'generic' force is greatly reduced by the fact that the truly universal quantifier 'every' is not admissible in the same context, for we cannot say

(7)   *If Bill owns every donkey, he beats it.

The inadmissibility of (7) may have a partial explanation in terms of the relative order of the game rules for 'every' and 'if'. However, that this explanation is not completely satisfactory is seen by turning (5) around. For we can say

(8)   Bill beats every donkey if he owns it.

Moreover,

(9)   Bill beats a donkey if he owns it,

is perhaps a little less natural than (5). Moreover, insofar as (9) is acceptable, it seems ambiguous between an existential-quantifier and a universal-quantifier reading, again unlike (5). In fact, a slight change in the example makes the existential-quantifier reading almost mandatory as, e.g., in

Bill will beat a donkey if he finds it.

Hence we have in our hands a problem both about the behavior of 'a' in (5) and (9) and about the behavior of 'every' in (7) and (8), over and above the question of the nature and conditions of pronominalization in all these different sentences.

The more general problem we are facing here concerns the conditions on which a quantifier phrase can be the antecedent of a singular pronoun. What we have just seen suggests that a satisfactory answer cannot be given, e.g., in terms of definiteness, for presumably 'every' is more definite than 'a', and is equally definite in (7) and (8). (Here we have one more indication of the unsystematic and frequently misleading character of linguists' concept of definiteness.)

It is not surprising that more complicated versions of these examples, such as

(10)   If Bill owns a donkey that he likes, he beats it,

have caused not inconsiderable difficulties in Montague-type grammars.

Further examples similar to (5), (7)–(9) are easily found. Here is one bunch:

(11)   If a member contributes, he will be praised.
(12)   *If every member contributes, he will be praised.
(13)   A member will be praised if he contributes.
(14)   Every member will be praised if he contributes.

Notice also that the conversion which takes us from (5) to (9) and from (7) to (8) might very well be expected to preserve not only meaning but acceptability. After all, all that happens in this conversion is the replacement of a sentence of the form 'If X, Y' by 'Y if X', together with a reversal of the relations of pronominalization between X and Y. It is hard to think of an operation which *prima facie* would seem likelier to preserve meaning and acceptability (including degree of acceptability). Yet we have seen that the latter sometimes changes in the operation, and later we shall find an example in which the preferred reading of the sentence in question is also affected. All this requires an explanation.

In order to begin to solve these problems, let us consider first (5). How do we get hold of the individual donkey that is supposed to be picked out in some sense by 'it'? This question is well-nigh impossible to answer as long as we think of conditionals along the lines of as semantically indivisible wholes as in (G.if). However, the basic idea underlying (G.cond$_1$) at once throws new light on the situation. This basic idea is that in the game connected with the conditional (1) I have to correlate with each of my strategies in $G(X)$, say ζ, a similar strategy of mine in $G(Y)$. This correlation is needed in the game iff ζ wins in the subgame $G(X)$ (cf. our flowchart for $G(\text{If } X, Y)$). What does such a strategy look like in (5)? Here $X = $ 'Bill owns a donkey'. Understanding 'a' in the most straightforward way as an *existential* quantifier, such strategies in

(15)   G(Bill owns a donkey)

are simply the different choices of a donkey owned by Bill. Thus in the antecedent of the conditional (5) we are as it were considering Bill's donkeys one by one. And this is obviously just what semantically speaking gives us the foothold for pronominalization in (5). After we have chosen to consider some one winning strategy of mine in (15), i.e., to consider a donkey owned by Bill, we can in the consequent (5) refer pronominally to that very donkey and say something about *it*. And *this is just what happens in* (5). It is precisely the consideration of my several strategies in (15) that leads us to consider a particular beast which in the consequent of (5) can be recovered by a pronominal reference.

Thus we see how it is that the subgame idea serves to explain why certain quantifier phrases can serve as pronominal antecedents. They represent choices made in an earlier, already concluded subgame.

Several further observations can be made here which support our diagnosis. First, let us note that what we just saw is in effect *an explanation why the indefinite article 'a(n)' comes to have a 'generic' (universal-quantifier) sense in conditionals like (5)*. This explanation has the merit of turning on the assumption that the basic force of 'a' in (5) is that of an *existential* quantifier (in the precise game-theoretical sense marking *my* move in our semantical games). It thus dispenses with all assumptions of irreducibly different senses or uses of the indefinite article in English.

We must hasten to add that there are other generic uses of the indefinite article 'a' which are not explainable in this way — at least not without a great deal of further argument. A case in point is, e.g.,

(16)   A cat loves comfort.

However, there is further evidence to support our diagnosis of cases like (5). The only thing we assumed of 'a' in (15) was that it expresses existential quantification (i.e., marks my move). But so does 'some'. Hence, by the same token, there ought to be a kind of generic sense to the sentence with 'some' instead of 'a' otherwise analogous with (5), i.e., to

(17)   If Bill owns some donkey, he beats it.

The acceptability of this sentence is not obvious, but insofar as it is acceptable, 'some' in it clearly has a 'generic' (*prima facie* universal) force, just like (5). The acceptability of (17) may in fact be improved greatly by changing it into

(18)   If Bill owns some donkey or other, he beats it.

Here we have an interesting indication of the strength of our explanation why 'a' has a generic force in (5). If it is replaced there by 'some', which normally does not exhibit any predilection for a generic sense, it is likewise forced to the role of a generic quantifier, albeit a little awkwardly.

Although we have not yet uncovered the mechanics of the conversion from (5) to (9) or from (7) to (8), it is of interest to see that 'some' follows here roughly the same pattern as 'a(n)'. Applied to (17) the conversion yields

(19)   Bill beats some donkey if he owns it.

It is not clear whether this is acceptable, but insofar as it is, its preferred reading is clearly different from that of (17). Insofar (19) is acceptable, it seems to allege Bill's animus against some particular beast. Hence in (19) 'some' seems to have the force of an initial existential quantifier, not that of a universal quantifier. This point is even clearer if we change the example to read

Bill will beat some donkey if he finds it.

The explanation we gave above for the possibility of pronominalization in (5) serves to explain also why (7) is not acceptable. The idea was that (G.cond$_1$) invited the players to consider my different strategies in $G(X)$. Insofar as certain individuals are produced in a play of the game by such a strategy, they can be referred to again pronominally. Now the individuals so produced (selected for special attention) are the ones that an *existential* quantifier prompts me to select. In contrast, my strategy does not specify which individuals Nature perhaps chooses as the values of a universally quantified variable. Hence our theory yields the prediction that only an existential-quantifier phrase can serve as an antecedent of a singular pronoun in the kind of pronominalization (i.e., from the antecedent of a conditional to its consequent) we have in (5).

This prediction is confirmed on its negative side by the unacceptability of (7). (The acceptability of the analogous sentence

(20)   If Bill owns any donkey, he beats it

causes no problems here in view of the well-established ordering principle

(*O*.any) which among other things gives the game rule (G.any) a priority over the rule for 'if'. (See Hintikka (1975).)

Our predictions concerning the conditions of admissible pronominalization are confirmed by many examples on the positive side, too. Perhaps the most interesting ones are those conditionals whose antecedent contains an existential quantifier within the scope of a universal quantifier. The following example is due essentially to Lauri Karttunen.

(24)   If you give every child a present for Christmas, some child will open it the same day.

Here a winning strategy of mine for the antecedent assigns to every child a present. Hence when 'some child' in the consequent invites us to pick out one, he or she comes already with an associated present, recoverable by the pronoun 'it' in the consequent of (24).

Further explanation is needed to account for the unacceptability of the corresponding plural sentence

(24)'   *If you give every child presents for Christmas, some child will open it the same day.

The explanation does not lie in any requirement of uniqueness, for the following is an acceptable sentence.

(24)"   If you give every child at least one present for Christmas, some child will open it the same day.

The right explanation seems to lie in some sort of congruence requirement between the pronoun and its antecedent. This requirement is not satisfied in (24)' where the pronoun is singular but its antecedent is in the plural. In contrast, the acceptability of (24)" is predicted by our theory, and so is the acceptability of the following sentence.

(24)'''   If you give every child presents for Christmas, some child will open at least one of them the same day.

Notice that 'them' does not refer here to the gifts given to different children, but to those given to that child intended by 'some'.

As a word of warning, it must be pointed out that there does not seem to be any hard-and-fast connection between the subgame idea and the direction of pronominalization.

But why should a conversion from (5) to (9) make a difference here? An answer is not hard to find. It leads to an interesting generalization, however.

We have seen that the clause-by-clause semantic unfolding which is characteristic of conditionals in natural language is captured by the subgame idea. Now how is the order of the different subgames determined? *A priori*, this order could be determined in many different ways. However, it is not difficult to guess that *ceteris paribus* it proceeds from the left to the right (from the earlier to the later in speech). This generalization we shall call the *Progression Principle*. It is in keeping without psycholinguistic intuitions as to how the understanding of a sentence actually proceeds. It is closely connected with the linearization phenomena studied in text linguistics.

From the Progression Principle it follows that the game rule for 'Y if X' cannot be the same as the game rule (G.cond$_1$) for 'If X, Y'. For in (G.cond$_1$) the subgame $G(X)$ connected with X is played before the subgame $G(Y)$ connected with Y, and the latter subgame depends on the former. In the case of 'Y if X' this order is ruled out by the Progression Principle. In its stead, we have the rule embodied in the following flow chart (next page). We shall call this rule (G.cond$_2$).

The translational counterpart to (G.cond$_2$) can be seen to be

$$(25) \qquad (\exists \Phi)(\exists \xi)(\zeta)(\eta)(X(\eta, \Phi(\zeta)) \supset Y(\xi, \zeta)).$$

This is different from (4). We therefore obtain the interesting result that 'If X, Y' and 'Y if X' are not completely synonymous in English. The difference is due to the dynamic left-to-right preference expressed by the Progression Principle.

A comparison between (G.cond$_1$) and (G.cond$_2$) may be instructive at this point. It is easily seen from the flow charts that the intuitive situation is somewhat different with the two. In our first flow chart, my strategy in $G(Y)$ was seen to depend only on ζ but not on ξ. It is easily seen that the corresponding reasons are somewhat weaker in the case of (G.cond$_2$). In other words, there may be some reasons for making my strategy (in Nature's original role) in $G(X)$ dependent on ξ and not only on ζ. Then the representation would be, not (25) but

$$(26) \qquad (\exists \Phi)(\exists \xi)(\zeta)(\eta)(X(\eta, \Phi(\xi, \zeta)) \supset Y(\xi, \zeta)).$$

However, (25) clearly is still more natural than (26). Even so, this observation serves to explain why such sentences as (9) and (13) are acceptable even with a universal-quantifier reading. For what (26) means is that in the $G(X)$ both a strategy of Nature's and a strategy of mine in $G(Y)$ are as it were known. Hence pronominal reference can recover also

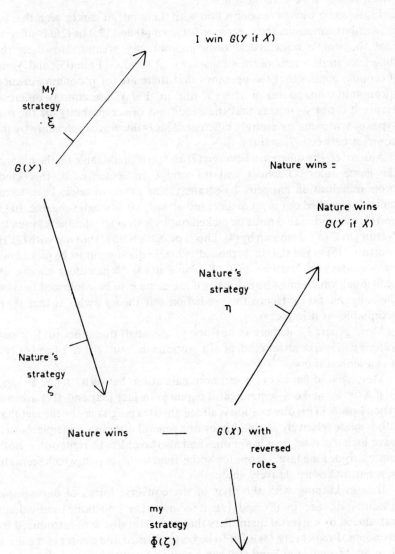

$(G. \; cond_2)$

I win =

I win $G(Y$ if $X)$

My
strategy
$\cdot \xi$

$G(Y)$

Nature wins =

Nature wins
$G(Y$ if $X)$

Nature's
strategy
η

Nature's
strategy
ζ

Nature wins ——— $G(X)$ with
reversed
roles

my
strategy
$\Phi(\zeta)$

I win = I win $G(Y$ if $X)$

individuals specified by the latter and not only these specified by the former. This is what happens in (9) and (13) on their universal-quantifier reading, which seems to be a viable one.

In the same way as in connection with (G.cond$_1$) it can be seen that on classical assumptions the difference between (4) and (25) or (26) is nil, and that the simple nonclassical ones are not any greater. However, the difference in the order of the subgames $G(X)$ and $G(Y)$ in (G.cond$_1$) and (G.cond$_2$) implies that the openings that there are for pronominalization (pronominal anaphora) in 'If X, Y' and in 'Y if X' are entirely different. Hence it is not surprising that the conditions of acceptability for the two types of sentences are entirely different. This is illustrated forcefully by the contrast between (7) and (8).

Moreover, the difference between (7) and (8) is predictable on the basis of the game rules (G.cond$_1$) and (G.cond$_2$). In sentences of this kind, pronominalization happens 'by strategy': the pronoun refers back to an individual picked out in an earlier (and already concluded) subgame. In (5) and (7), this individual must be picked out by a strategy of mine (chosen by Nature) in $G(X)$, as shown by (4). This is possible with (5) but not with (7). In contrast, (25) shows that in (8) the individual in question must be picked out by a strategy of Nature's in $G(Y)$. Now in (8) Nature does choose an individual, which must be a donkey if the game is to be continued beyond the subgame $G(Y)$. Hence the prediction our theory yields is that (8) is acceptable, as it in fact is.

More generally, if there is just one (unnegated) quantifier in Y, it can (*ceteris paribus*) be an antecedent of a pronoun in X (in 'Y if X') if and only if it is a *universal* one.

Moreover, differences in pronominalization between 'If X, Y' and 'Y if X' may make a semantical difference. In fact (18) and (19) are not synonymous. (This observation is added an extra poignancy by the fact that (19) is made relatively acceptable by our general ordering principles which favor higher clauses over lower ones and also favor left-to-right order. Both factors argue for a larger scope for 'some' than for 'if' in (19), which seems to be what makes it relatively acceptable.)

It is in keeping with this that in the converse forms of our sample conditionals, i.e., in (8) and (9), it is now the 'indefinite' individuals introduced by universal quantifiers that can naturally be re-introduced by pronouns. Predictably, (8) is felt to be better formed and clearer in meaning than (9). Moreover, (9) and (19) can be given some semblance of meaning not so much by the kind of 'pronominalization by strategy' we have been studying as by assuming that the existential quantifier 'a' or 'some' has an exceptionally wide scope comprising the whole conditional (9) or (19) respectively. The reason why this effect is less marked in the case of (9) than in the case of (19) is that in (9) the other generic uses of the indefinite article 'a(n)' than those we can explain are also operative.

Another fact that now can be explained is that mirror-image examples dual to (24) are acceptable, i.e., examples in which existential and universal quantifiers exchange roles over and above the reversal of order of X and Y. The following is a case in point.

(27)   Some man will seduce every girl if she does not watch out.

At the same time we obtain an explanation of the fact — it seems to us an unmistakable fact — that (8) is perceptibly less natural than (5). The explanation lies in the fact that the strategies which make pronominalization possible in (5) are as many choices of donkeys owned by Bill. These are the individuals (5) intuitively speaking is *about*. They are of course just the individuals whose choice by Nature in $G(X)$ leads us to play $G(Y)$.

In contrast to this, the 'right' choices in (8) are donkeys *not* beaten by Bill. This accounts for the 'contrapositive' feeling we seem to have in trying to understand (8) and also for the intuitive unclarity as to (8) is 'about' donkeys beaten by Bill or about those not beaten by Bill or about those owned by him — or about each and every donkey. It is as if we in (8) first said something about all donkeys and the subsequently qualified it by excluding those donkeys not owned by Bill. It is amusing to see how neatly this feeling matches what happens in a play of the game connected with (8). (Here we can incidentally also see how elusive and unsystematic a notion 'aboutness' is.)

Along these lines we can hence solve all the problems concerning (5)–(10), (18)–(19) and their ilk. These problems include the following.

(i)   The possibility of pronominalization in sentences like (5).

(ii)   The universal-quantifier sense of 'a' or 'some' in examples like (5) and (18), respectively.

(iii)   The asymmetry between existential and universal quantifiers *vis-à-vis* the kind of pronominalization illustrated by (5).

(iv)   The sweeping effects of the *prima facie* innocuous conversion of (5) to (9), (7) to (8), or (18) to (19).

(v)   The (small but unmistakable) difference in the degree of acceptability between (5) and (8).

(vi)   The possibility of a universal-quantifier reading in sentences like (9) and (13).

Our solution to these problems can be extended in several different directions, thus gaining further support. One such direction is the treatment of other English particles that can be used in conditionalization. As an example, we shall consider here the particle 'unless'. The extension is as straightforward as it is obvious. Sentences of the form

(28) Z unless Y

are treated essentially in the same way as the sentences

If neg + (Z), Y.

The difference as compared with the plain 'if' is that in the game rule for 'unless' Nature's strategies in $G(Z)$ play the same role as my strategies in $G(X)$ played in the game rule for 'if'.

The relevant game rules — we shall call them (G.unless$_1$) and (G.unless$_2$) — appear from the diagrams on the following pages.

Of these rules, the former is parallel to (G.cond$_2$) and hence straightforward. The latter is not parallel with (G.cond$_1$), and hence may require an explanation.

The leading idea on which (G.unless$_2$) is based is that when I say,

Unless Y, Z

what I have in mind is a dependence of the way in which Z fails to be true depending on how Y turns out to be true. For instance, if I say,

Unless you give him a gift, he is unhappy,

the intended way of avoiding his unhappiness depends the way in which the antecedent 'you give him a gift' is made true. This dependence is what (G.unless$_2$) codifies.

The corresponding translations are

(29) $(\exists \xi)(\exists \Phi)(\zeta)(\eta)(\sim Z(\zeta, \xi) \supset Y(\Phi(\zeta), \eta))$

and respectively,

(30) $(\exists \xi)(\exists \eta)(\zeta)(\Phi)(\sim Y(\xi, \zeta) \supset Z(\eta, \Phi(\xi)))$.

If we check what these rules imply for our theory, we can see that they

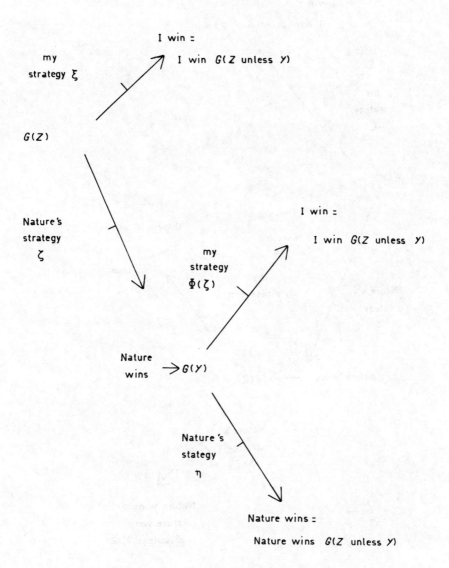

$(G. \text{ unless}_1)$

my
strategy ξ

I win =
   I win $G(Z \text{ unless } Y)$

$G(Z)$

Nature's
strategy
ζ

my
strategy
$\Phi(\zeta)$

I win =
   I win $G(Z \text{ unless } Y)$

Nature
wins $\quad \to G(Y)$

Nature's
stategy
η

Nature wins =
   Nature wins $G(Z \text{ unless } Y)$

$(G. \text{ unless}_2)$

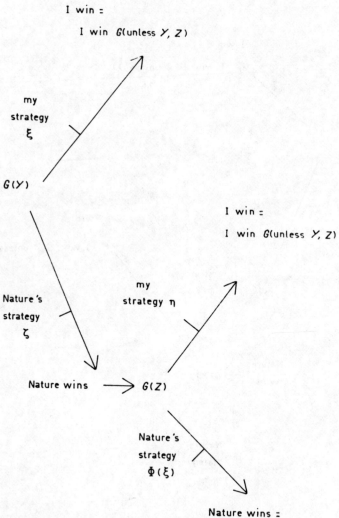

I win =
I win $G(\text{unless } Y, Z)$

my
strategy
ξ

$G(Y)$

Nature's
strategy
ζ

my
strategy η

I win =
I win $G(\text{unless } Y, Z)$

Nature wins $\longrightarrow$ $G(Z)$

Nature's
strategy
$\Phi(\xi)$

Nature wins =
Nature wins
$G(\text{unless } Y, Z)$

preserve the roles of existential and universal quantifiers. Thus our explanations will automatically cover the corresponding sentences with 'unless', too. Examples show that this is precisely what happens. For comparison, we repeat at the same time some of the earlier ones.

(5)   If Bill owns a donkey, he beats it.
(31)   Unless Bill likes a donkey, he beats it.
(8)   Bill beats every donkey if he owns it.
(32)   Bill beats every donkey unless he likes it.
(7)   *If Bill owns every donkey, he beats it.
(33)   *Unless Bill owns every donkey, he beats it.
(9)   ?Bill beats a donkey if he owns it,
(34)   ?Bill beats a donkey unless he owns it.
(17)   If Bill owns some donkey or other, he beats it.
(35)   Unless Bill likes some donkey or other, he beats it.
(19)   Bill beats some donkey if he owns it.
(36)   Bill beats some donkey unless he likes it.

Here the acceptability of the last six examples is not clear, and the precise meaning of (9) and (34) is likewise problematic. What is absolutely clear, however, is the parallelism between 'if' and 'unless'. Notice in particular that we have a very natural explanation here for the universal-quantifier force of 'a' in (31) and (34) and for the similar force (such as it is) of 'some' in (35).

Prima facie, our theory does not square very well with the fact that the presence of negation in the antecedent of a conditional does not reverse the conditions of acceptability, as our explanation might seem to presuppose. For instance, we can say

(37)   If Bill doesn't like a donkey, he beats it

and perhaps also

(38)   If Bill doesn't like some donkey or other, he beats it

but not

(39)   *If Bill doesn't like every donkey, he beats it.

Again we can say

(40)   Bill beats every donkey if he doesn't like it

with roughly the same meaning as (34), whereas

(41)   Bill beats some donkey if he doesn't like it

is either unacceptable or else clearly nonsynonymous with (37).

This all seems wrong, for negation changes my strategies into Nature's and *vice versa*. Hence one might *prima facie* expect (39) to be acceptable but not (37). Yet the converse was just found to be the case.

It is nevertheless clear that some additional account of (37)–(41) will have to be given in any case. For one thing, the antecedent of (37), viz.

(42)   Bill doesn't like a donkey

has on one of its readings an entirely different force alone and in (37). Alone, it says (on this particular reading) that Bill has no affection for any one donkey. Presumably its having a different role in (37) is what also makes pronominalization possible there.

The explanation for these facts lies in the fact that the ordering principles (scope conventions) governing the English indefinite article 'a(n)' are exceptionally fluid. This holds for instance for the relative order of the game rules (G.an) and (G.not) (or (G.neg)) for 'a(n)' and for negation, respectively. It also holds for the relative order of (G.an) and epistemic rules.

The latter fact is illustrated by the ubiquity of the *de dicto–de re* ambiguity. (This ambiguity typically concerns just the relative order of a quantifier rule like (G.an) and an epistemic rule.) The former fact is illustrated by the fact that sentences like (42) have two readings, on which it has the logical force of

(43) $(\exists x)(x$ is a donkey $\wedge$ Bill does not like $x)$

or the force of

(44) $\sim (\exists x)(x$ is a donkey $\wedge$ Bill likes $x)$.

It is the second of these two readings that was commented on briefly above.

This ambiguity of 'a(n)' is one of the main sources of its universal-quantifier uses.

What happens in problematical conditionals like (37) is that only one of the two *a priori* possible rule orderings (in connection with the antecedent of (37)) enables us to interpret the pronominalization in (37). If the reading adopted is (44), which in other circumstances is perhaps the preferred one, it follows from our earlier arguments that pronominalization in (37) cannot be given a reasonable semantical interpretation. On this reading, (37) will be in the same boat with (7). No wonder, therefore, that this is not how (37) is ordinarily understood.

However, if the other ordering is adopted (corresponding to the reading (43) of the antecedent taken alone), (37) can be analyzed semantically just like (5). The resulting reading has the same logical force as

(45) $(x)(x$ is a donkey $\supset$ ($\sim$ Bill likes $x \supset$ Bill beats x)).

And this is in fact the force of (37) in English. Now we can see how it comes about. The restraints on the semantical interpretation of pronouns filter out one of the two ways of processing the antecedent of (37). The remaining order of the game rules yields (45).

In this particular case, the impossibility of the other, filtered-out reading is also illustrated by the impossibility of expressing it in the usual logical notation. In fact, it would have to be written out as something like the following

(46) $(\exists x)(x$ is a donkey $\wedge$ Bill does not like $x) \supset$ Bill beats x

which is either ill-formed or has the last 'x' dangling.

This line of thought receives further support from supplementary observations. One of them is that our treatment of (37) extends in a predictable way to a large number of conditionals with an epistemic operator in their antecedent. Consider, as an example, the following sentence

(47)   If Bill believes that a thief has stolen one of his horses, Bill will at once pursue him.

Here the 'a' in 'a thief' clearly has the force of a universal quantifier. Moreover, the belief-context in (47) must clearly be understood *de re*, for how else can we make sense of Bill's pursuing some one putative thief? (If Bill merely opines as a purely existential judgment that someone or other has stolen a horse, it is nonsense to suggest that Bill undertakes to pursue the thief. For then there would not be any answer to the question: whom is he pursuing?) Nevertheless the antecedent of (47) admits also a *de dicto* reading. Why should the latter be filtered out in (47)? The answer lies in precisely the same mechanism as served to explain the peculiarities of (37). Because of this mechanism, only the *de re* reading of the antecedent of (47) makes it possible to interpret the pronoun 'it' in (47).

What was just said is not incompatible with saying that there is a reading of (47) on which its antecedent has merely the force of an existential judgment. From what has been said it follows that then the pronoun in the consequent must be interpreted as a 'pronoun of laziness'. This reading

49605

assigns to (47) roughly the same force as

(48)   If Bill believes that a thief has stolen one of his horses, Bill will at once pursue such a thief.

It is interesting to see that if one wants to paraphrase (47) by reversing the order of the (logical) antecedent and consequent one will end up making the *de re* character of the belief-construction blatant, over and above having to switch from an existential into a universal quantifier:

(49)   Bill will at once pursue every thief if Bill believes that he has stolen one of Bill's horses.

Another apparent counter-example to our theory may be seen by comparing the following two sentences.

(50)   If some student did not flunk the test, he must have been studying hard.

(51)   *If not every student flunked the test, he must have been studying hard.

Now my strategies in (50) and (51) are the same, except for a temporary exchange of roles. This is reflected by the logical equivalence of (50) and (51). Accordingly, it might be thought that any explanation why the anaphora in (50) is a happy one which (like ours) turns on 'pronominalization by strategy' would yield a wrong prediction here. For it would apparently have to predict that the anaphora in (51) is quite as happy as in (50). Yet (51) clearly is unacceptable.

This is the same problem we were confronted by earlier when we noted the unacceptability of (39).

A clue to an explanation of the unacceptability of (51) is seen from our remarks above on the requirement of congruence between a pronoun and its grammatical antecedent. These observations can be extended by requiring that there be a coreferential antecedent for each pronoun in the first place. This requirement is in some sense not satisfied by (51), for 'every student' there is not coreferential with 'he' in (51).

It is not quite easy to see how this idea can be incorporated in our actual treatment of sentences like (51). For the unanalyzed notion of coreference the requirement just formulated relies on is not automatically available to us, and in the actual game associated with (51) the individual whose name replaces 'every student' will in fact be also referred to by 'he'. So how can we do justice to the observation which seemed to solve our problem?

It seems to us that the key to a solution of these problems lies in the need of a nonclassical game rule for negation. An explicitly negated sentence, say `neg + [X]`, does not just describe a world in which X fails to be true. It first describes a world in which X is true, and then says that this is *not* what the world is like. In spite of being subsequently cancelled, the description of a world in which X is true may open the door to pronominalization.

The game-theoretical counterpart to this idea is as follows. What happens when $G(neg + X)$ is true that every one of my attempts to win in $G(X)$ by means of a strategy ξ must give rise, through a constant functional Φ, to a winning strategy $\zeta = \Phi(\xi)$ of mine in $G(neg + X)$.

In terms of the subgame idea this can be expressed as follows. When the game has reached $neg + X$, play of $G(X)$ is undertaken with roles reversed. If I win it (playing what originally was Nature's role), I win $G(neg + [X])$. If Nature wins (playing for myself, as it were), the game is continued. After Nature has divulged her strategy ξ in $G(X)$, a new play of the same game $G(X)$ is undertaken, again with the roles of the two players reversed. Since I now know Nature's original strategy ξ, my new strategy is a function $\Phi(\xi)$ of ξ. In the new game Nature must again use ξ. If I win this new subgame, I win the whole game, and *vice versa*.

The flow chart that goes together with this game rule is shown overleaf.

The corresponding translation rule is

(52) $(\exists \Phi)(\exists \zeta)(\xi)(X(\xi, \zeta) \supset \sim X(\xi, \Phi(\xi))$

which can be seen to be equivalent with

(53) $(\exists \Phi)(\xi) \sim X(\xi, \Phi(\xi))$.

Now when this rule is being used, the first and only individual chosen in the game connected with (51) is selected by Nature trying to falsify the antecedent of (51). As was pointed out earlier, strategies on which such moves are based are not 'remembered' in the game connected with the consequent of a conditional, and hence cannot support a pronoun occurring there. Hence our theory predicts that the pronoun is out of place in (51), as we have found it to be.

This confirmed prediction further supports our theory, and certainly does not amount to a counterexample to it. It is perhaps worth observing that there is some independent evidence for the uncertainty as to whether the 'he' in (51) is supposed to pick out an arbitrary student who flunked or an arbitrarily selected student who did not. This uncertainty is a consequence of our explanation for the unacceptability of (51) in that the

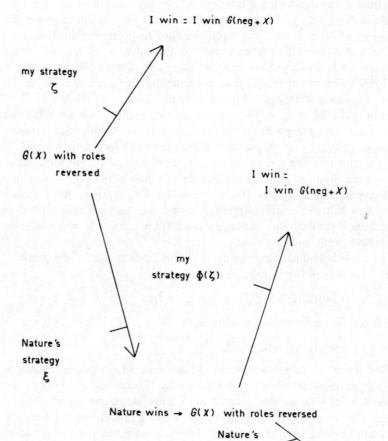

arbitrarily selected student in (51) only serves to highlight the speaker's comment on what not all students are like. The same uncertainty shows up in another way in the fact that it is not clear on linguistic grounds alone whether the following sentences speak of flunking or nonflunking students or of students *simpliciter*.

(54)   If not all students flunked, they must have studied quite hard.
(55)   Even if not all students flunked, they cannot have studied very hard.

This strengthens further our explanation for the unacceptability of (51).

Our treatment of pronominalization in sentences like (6) is immediately extended to a large class of relative clauses. The following are cases in point.

(56)   Everyone who owns a donkey beats it.
(57)   Everyone who owns a donkey that he likes beats it.
(58)   Everyone who doesn't like a donkey beats it.

In all similar cases, we can explain why 'a' has in them a universal-quantifier sense. Again, this sense is not a separate meaning or separate use of the indefinite article, but an inevitable consequence of the way it occurs in such sentences as (56)–(58).

It is important to realize, furthermore, that the relevance of the subgame idea is not restricted to conditionals. Changes similar to the transition from (G.if) to (G.cond) are needed also in (G.and) and (G.or). For instance, and quite importantly, in the game $G(X$ and $Y)$ the players first play $G(X)$. Only if the winner is myself do they move on to play $G(Y)$. The winner of this second subgame wins $G(X$ and $Y)$.

Thus a pronoun in the second conjunct Y of 'X and Y' with a quantifier phrase as its antecedent in X is admissible in essentially the same circumstances as in the consequent Y of 'If X, Y'. For instance, when there is just one unnegated quantifier in the antecedent of the pronoun, we have an acceptable conjunction if and only if this single quantifier is an existential one. Thus we have examples like the following.

(59)   Some soldier was given a rifle, and he immediately fired it.
(60)   *Every soldier was given a rifle, and he immediately fired it.

Since the modification of (G.and) seems to be only a preferential one, some speakers might want to have a question mark instead of an asterisk in (60). This would not tell against our theory, however.

This theory also explains why the indefinite article is an existential one and not a universal (generic) one in conjunctions like the following.

(61)   Bill owns a donkey, and he beats it.

We have already explained why the pronoun is grammatical in (61). It picks out an individual earlier chosen by a strategy of mine, just as in (5). However, in (5) this strategy is chosen by Nature while playing what originally was my role, whereas in (61) it is chosen by myself. Since it is Nature's role here that turns a quantifier into a universal one, our theory predicts that the indefinite article is generic in (5) but not in (61), as it obviously is. Once again we see that the so-called generic force of 'a(n)', is not always an irreducible phenomenon but can often be predicted by means of a suitable semantical theory.

In contrast to (61), the following sentence is not grammatical, just as our theory predicts that it is not.

Bill owns every donkey, and he beats it.

Likewise, the subgame idea has often to be brought in to account for pronominalization across disjuncts.

Although we shall not discuss the syntactical problems of pro-nominalization in this essay, some light may be thrown on them by our observations. Our account of the possibility of certain types of pronominalization turns entirely on semantical concepts and semantical conceptualizations, such as the subgame idea which forms the gist of (G.cond$_1$) — (G.cond$_2$) and (G.neg). This heavy reliance on semantics suggests rather strongly, albeit somewhat obliquely, that a full account of pronominalization is impossible along purely syntactical (generative) lines.

This suggestion is reinforced further when counterparts to some of the problems of pronominalization within a sentence are found in text semantics (in sentence-to-sentence pronominalization). A full solution to such problems cannot very well be expected in terms of the generation process of individual sentences. We shall in fact turn our attention to these problems next.

For the most sweeping extensions of our results we have to go back to the basic idea of our new rules like (G.cond) and (G.neg). This idea is that sometimes the semantical behavior of a word or phrase in a certain context has to be accounted for in terms of suitable semantical games which are supposed to have been played to the end already when we come to interpret this word or phrase. Often, these critical words are pronouns. In the case of the pronouns in (4) and (27) the games that are needed to understand them are subgames, that is, games occurring as parts of the more comprehensive supergame associated with the sentence in which the pronoun occurs. However, this is not the only case of its kind. Perhaps the most interesting repercussions of one basic idea are the text-semantical ones. One of the most important phenomena of text semantics and text grammar is that the semantical interpretation of a text proceeds in order from sentence to sentence. When we come to a given one, we can assume the semantical games connected with the earlier sentences to have already been carried out. And since the different sentences of a text are normally thought of as being combined conjunctively, the earlier sentences are to be assumed to be true, for only if I win in the earlier games do the players proceed to later ones.

These observations are but further applications of our *Progression Principle* formulated earlier. It is obviously relevant to many interesting phenomena in text grammar and text semantics. Its main bite is in fact found here, it seems to us. Only a part of its force is brought to bear on sentence grammar and sentence semantics in the form of the subgame idea which we have been exploiting in this essay.

As was already hinted at, one of the most obvious applications of the Progression Principle is to explain the semantical possibility of certain kinds of sentence-to-sentence pronominalization. Many of these kinds of intersentence pronominalization are closely related to similarly problematic varieties of intrasentence pronominalization. The following examples illustrate this.

(62)   John just gave every child a present for Christmas. Some child or other will open it already to-day.

(63)   Every soldier has a loaded rifle. Some of them will fire it before they are ordered to do so.

The great variety of sentence types creates of course an almost corresponding variety of similar examples of text-grammatical pronominalization. For instance, the second sentences of (62) and (63) could equally well be, respectively,

(64)   I forbid any child to open it until Christmas Eve.

(65)   Has any soldier fired it?

The examples (64) and (65) (and their ilk) are especially interesting in that they show that sentence-to-sentence pronominalization problems cannot be reduced to intrasentential problems by the mere trivial device of conjoining the different sentences in question. This becomes very unnatural when the different sentences are of different kinds (declaratives, imperatives, questions, etc.), and it becomes completely impossible when the sentences in question are uttered by different speakers, as in the following example.

(66)   Does every soldier have a rifle? Yes, even though some of them received it only yesterday.

More complicated examples combine a modification to one of our game rules with sentence-to-sentence pronominalization. Here is an example which turns on the difference between (G.neg) and (G.not).

(67)   John did not after all marry a girl who has lots of money. She is quite pretty, however.

All these examples (62)–(67) allow for an explanation by means of the Progression Principle. The full implications of the principle nevertheless need a separate investigation. Let us note here only that some of the uses of our theory are negative ones, to explain (at least partly) why certain types of sentence-to-sentence pronominalizations are not feasible.

In order to find such applications, an observation supplementary to our earlier ones is needed. Even though we cannot syntactically speaking conjoin the different bits and pieces of a text into one long conjunction, semantically speaking a text usually proceeds conjunctively: the successive sentences are all intended to be true. If so, the conditions of sentence-to-sentence pronominalization will normally be the same as those of pronominalization between conjuncts. Even though this explanatory schema needs qualifications, it has plenty of explanatory bite. For instance, witness the difference in acceptability between the following pairs of sentences.

(68)   Some soldier has been given a rifle. Has he fired it?
(69)   *Every soldier has been given a rifle. Has he fired it?

The relationship between (66) and (67) is not obvious unless we assume the Progression Principle. *Prima facie*, one might even expect that a universal quantifier has a more definite reference than an existential one, and would therefore be a better candidate for an antecedent of a pronoun. Yet a comparison between (66) and (67) shows that the opposite is the case.

In fact, this observation can be generalized. An earlier quantifier phrase marking my move, e.g., 'some X' or 'a(n) Y' can *ceteris paribus* serve as an antecedent of a pronoun in a later sentence, while a similar universal-quantifier phrase usually cannot. What we have said serves as an explanation for this phenomenon.

The explanatory force of our theory can be illustrated further by reference to the following example.

(70)   Every student held a tray. A girl had laden it with fruit.

Here either the tray of each student had been filled by a girl who need not be a student, or else the second half speaks of only one girl and *her* tray. In the latter case, the girl must clearly be one of the students. Why? Where does this implication come from? It comes from the need of having an antecedent for 'it'. According to our theory, this pronoun relies on a strategy of mine, and it is readily seen that such a strategy provides an individual reference for 'it' only if the girl in question is one of the students.

Another phenomenon which becomes understandable is the use of the-phrases anaphorically, that is to say, to pick out individuals introduced earlier in the same text, perhaps even rather indefinitely. Such the-phrases need not have a unique reference absolutely, only given certain plays of the games associated with earlier sentences of the same text. Here is a sample narrative:

(71)   A tall stranger appeared on the road. The stranger approached a farmhouse. He came to a door of the farmhouse. The tall stranger knocked on the door . . . .

This illustrates an important difference between logicians' theories of definite descriptions and their actual use in ordinary discourse (text). For any account of the semantics of 'the' which is like Russell's famous theory of definite descriptions requires that the-phrases exhibit uniqueness absolutely, and not just in relation to a given play of a certain game. At the same time, it suggests that logicians' idea of unique reference has something to recommend itself, if developed and applied appropriately.

Again, we can note that the individual which has been introduced earlier in the text and to which a the-phrase ('definite description') refers can typically be introduced by an existential-quantifier phrase but not by a universal-quantifier phrase. Our subgame idea again explains why this should be the case.

We cannot resist the temptation of casting a side glance here at attempts to explain pronominalization in terms of definitization. What we have been discussing is a type of context where the possibility of either process requires an explanation. However much progress is achieved by reducing one to the other, such a reduction accordingly cannot solve all the problems of pronominalization.

These sample applications of our theory of subgames are probably enough to whet the reader's appetite for further ones.

A general comment on what we have been doing in this essay may be in order by way of conclusion. Some of the pronominalization phenomena we have studied have been assimilated in the literature to the so-called 'pronouns of laziness', that is, to pronouns which merely serve as placeholders for their antecedents, irrespective of questions of coreference. It should be obvious by this time that the pronouns studied in this essay are not pronouns of laziness. On the contrary, they serve to recover a reference to an individual which has somehow been introduced earlier. Their peculiarity lies rather in the fact that the antecedently introduced individual is somehow an 'arbitrarily chosen' or otherwise underdetermined individual. Thus a better slogan for the phenomena studied here would be 'coreference without reference'. This label is partly metaphoric, of course, and what we have been doing here is to spell out what it really covers, without using the dubious notion of coreference. Hintikka has pointed out earlier that some instances of 'coreference without reference' are essentially modal, that is, involve tracing one and the same individual from one possible world to another. Here we have been discussing instances of 'coreference without reference' that arise in apparently completely nonmodal contexts.

Another interesting general remark prompted by our observations is the following. We have offered an account of the reasons for the acceptability and unacceptability for certain types of expressions in English. This account is in terms of certain semantical regularities of English, indeed regularites which can be generalized from sentence semantics to text semantics. It is therefore in sharp contrast to the whole tenor of generative grammar, where acceptability, unacceptability, and differences in the degree of acceptability are (hopefully) accounted for by means of the generation process of different kinds of sentences. What are we to say of this contrast?

What has been said does not exclude a generative account of the same phenomena. But what would such an account look like? Basically, it would in the paradigm case of conditionals have to deal with the restraints on forming 'If X, Y' and 'Y if X' from X and Y. It is not obvious that these restraints can be incorporated in an effective (recursive) generative rule. However, even if they can, what would a theoretical motivation of the resulting rule look like? It is quite obvious that there cannot be any purely syntactical motivation forthcoming. For one thing, the governing regularity we have found extends also to text grammar, and hence cannot conceivably be accounted for in its full generality in terms of the way in which individual sentences are generated.

We have noted, moreover, that the relevant text-semantical principle cannot be reduced to its sentence-semantical counterpart by the tempting device of thinking of a text as a conjunction of its constituent sentences.

In contrast, our account ensues perfectly naturally from certain semantical ideas which are forced on us in any case by the non-truth-functional character of conditionals, quite independently of any problems of pronominalization. Moreover, in some obvious sense our account is also closely related to the way in which we in fact process a sentence semantically. When a speaker rejects (7) but accepts (8), he is scarcely relying, however implicitly, on the processes by means of which these two strings could perhaps be generated. Rather, he perceives what happens when he tries to analyse these two strings semantically. In (7), but not in (8), he is confronted by a pronoun whose reference has not yet been fixed in the context of our semantical games at the time he comes to it. This explanation is in keeping with the basic idea of our approach: to understand a sentence S is to know what happens in the correlated game $G(S)$.

Hence we have found an example of an essentially semantical explanation of the facts which in the generative approach are paradigmatically explained (insofar as they can be explained) in syntactical (generative) terms. This casts serious doubts, not on the soundness of the research strategy of the generativists, but on its scope.

One example perhaps does not carry much persuasion in this respect. However, Hintikka has found another striking example to the same effect in the any–every contrast in English. (Hintikka (1975).) Nor is this the only interesting recent example of interesting interplay between semantics and syntax. It seems to us in fact that the interaction of semantics and (what is usually taken to be) syntax is a much deeper and subtler phenomenon than linguists have recently realized.

Academy of Finland

BIBLIOGRAPHY

Andrews, Peter (1972), 'General Models and Extensionality', *Journal of Symbolic Logic*, Vol. 37, pp. 395–397.

Henkin, Leon (1950), 'Completeness in the Theory of Types', *Journal of Symbolic Logic*, Vol. 15, pp. 81–91.

Hintikka, Jaakko (1974), 'Quantifiers vs. Quantification Theory', *Linguistic Inquiry*, Vol. 5, No. 2, pp. 153–177.

Hintikka, Jaakko (1975), 'On the Limitations of Generative Grammar', in the *Proceedings of the Scandinavian Seminar on Philosophy of Language (Uppsala, Nov. 8–9, 1974)*, Filosofiska Studier utgivna av Filosofiska förening och filosofiska institutionen vid Uppsala Universitet, Vol. 26, Uppsala, pp. 1–92.

Hintikka, Jaakko (1976), 'Quantifiers in Logic and Quantifiers in Natural Languages', in *Philosophy of Logic*, S. Körner (ed.), Basil Blackwell, Oxford, pp. 208–232.

Hintikka, Jaakko, forthcoming, 'Negation and Semantical Games'.

Martin-Löf, Per (1970), *Notes on Constructive Mathematics*, Almqvist & Wiksell, Stockholm.

Mostowski, Andrzej (1966), *Thirty Years of Foundational Studies*, Acta Philosophica Fennica, Vol. 17, Basil Blackwell, Oxford.

RICHARD M. SMABY

AMBIGUOUS COREFERENCE WITH QUANTIFIERS

A semantics of informing provides a good framework for formalizing descriptions of coreference systems in natural languages, especially for capturing the ambiguity so natural to such systems. Pronouns are clearly ambiguous when taken out of context. The sentence

(1)   He is tall.

asserts different things depending on the interpretation of *he*. However, it is insufficient to close the topic with such an observation; for there appears to be a quite systematic procedure for resolving coreferential ambiguities. The syntactic form of the context is part of the procedure, as comparing the preferred understandings of the following two texts shows.

(2)   Bill is next to John. He is tall.

(3)   John is next to Bill. He is tall.

In both texts coreference of *he* is to the subject of the preceding sentence. In addition, knowledge of the world plays a part, as illustrated by the text:

(4)   Bill tickled John. He squirmed.

Crucial to the interpretation of the pronoun in this case is the knowledge that it is the tickled person that has reason to squirm; that is, John's squirming is a relevant issue, Bill's squirming is not. Informally speaking, the syntactic form of the context prepares the hearer for interpreting pronouns by providing a ranking of possible interpretations, from which the hearer selects the highest ranked interpretation which provides a relevant reading of the sentence. A model-theoretic formalization of such an interaction of syntax and knowledge is the purpose of the present paper.

Many quantifiers have variable domains, as seen clearly in the domain of *everyone* in the following two texts.

(5)   John invited Bill and Sam and George to a party at his house. Everyone had a good time.

(6)   John invited Bill and Sam and George to a party at his house. Everyone arrived before eight o'clock.

37

F. Guenthner and S. J. Schmidt (eds.), Formal Semantics and Pragmatics for Natural Languages, 37–75. All Rights Reserved.

In (5) *everyone's* domain is everyone whose having a good time is relevant, namely, John, Bill, Sam, and George. In (6) *everyone's* domain is everyone whose arrival before eight is relevant, namely, Bill, Sam, and George.

A quantifier like *some* or *a* can provide a coreferent for a singular pronoun later in the text, as in the example:

(7)   Someone left. He went home.

The above topics will be treated in turn in an expanding application of the basic concept of ambiguity in an informing semantics.

1. INFORMING SEMANTICS

Informing semantics as employed here is an application of model-theoretic semantics, augmented perhaps with syntactic information. The philosophical idea behind informing semantics is that communicants use a language to construct a common knowledge or belief base, which can be used for various purposes. A set of communicants at a given time have a given agreed upon (if only for the sake of argument) belief base, which I will call information state. The utterance of a sentence or text by one of the communicants then (in the simplest case) expands the common belief base to a new base, that is, to a new information state. This concept of informing suggests that each sentence or text of the language can be assigned an informing function as its meaning. A sentence is assigned a partial function on the set of information states.

In the simplest case an information state consists exclusively of an information content; in more complex cases, various additional factors may be present. An information content is merely a set of models (model structures) appropriate to the language. Indeed, for the present explication in which intensional and deictic considerations are ignored, the models are just models of a first-order language: $\langle U, V \rangle$ where U is a set of individuals and V evaluates each predicate of the language as a relation of the appropriate arity. The universe remains fixed, as spatial, temporal, and modal variation is not discussed; thus, an information content k, relative to a fixed universe U, can be taken as a set of valuations V. The sets of valuations form a complete lattice with the ordering: superset precedes subset:

(8) $k_1 \sqsubseteq k_2$ iff $k_2 \subseteq k_1$.

The philosophical understanding is that a set of valuations corresponds to an information content in the informal sense by consisting of those states of the world (or better, complete state descriptions of the world) which could obtain based on the information given. Thus, the set V of all valuations corresponds to zero information. Singletons correspond to complete information. And the null set corresponds to contradictory information. See Fig. 1.

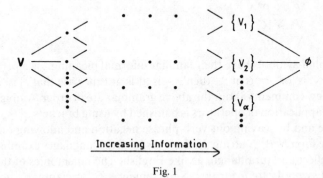

Increasing Information

Fig. 1

We will also make use of undefined entities of various kinds, such as the undefined individual $u_\perp$ and the undefined information content $k_\perp$. These are technical conveniences for ease of precise statement of when a text fails to inform, that is, is undefined. The convention is that the value of a function applied to an undefined argument is the undefined element of the type of the value of the function.

Let us now begin with a simple example of a language with transitive and intransitive predicates or verbs, proper names, and the usual assortment of sentential connectives. For the purposes of later development we will take the elements of the universe U as proper names of themselves. Doing this means we will be unable to discuss the concept of proper name (Smaby, 1976); however, proper names are a complex topic and a discussion of them would obscure the present discussion of quantifiers.

The following context-free grammar describes the expressions of the language.

(9) $T \to S\ T$

(10) $T \to \#$

(11) $S \to C$

(12) $C \to C_\wedge$

$$(13) \quad C \rightarrow C_{\bar{\pi}}$$
$$(14) \quad C_{\wedge} \rightarrow [C_{\bar{\pi}} \wedge C]$$
$$(15) \quad C_{\bar{\pi}} \rightarrow N \vee^p$$
$$(16) \quad C_{\bar{\pi}} \rightarrow \sim C$$
$$(17) \quad C_{\bar{\pi}} \rightarrow [C \vee C]$$
$$(18) \quad C_{\bar{\pi}} \rightarrow [C \supset C]$$
$$(19) \quad \vee^p \rightarrow P_j^1$$
$$(20) \quad \vee^p \rightarrow P_j^2 N$$
$$(21) \quad \vee^p \rightarrow |C$$
$$(22) \quad N \rightarrow u_j.$$

The familiar symbols have their familiar informal meaning. . is a period. $\wedge$ is 'and'. $\vee$ is 'or'. $\supset$ is 'if . . . then'. $\sim$ is 'it is not the case that'. | is 'is such that'. A few comments about the above grammar are in order. Ambiguity of order of application of operators is banished by using brackets in the object language and by leaving out verb-phrase negation and allowing only one structure for a $N \ P_j^2 \ N$ string. In these respects the languages examined will fail to reflect a natural language like English. The mnemonics of the non-terminal symbols are T for text, S for sentence, C for clause, $C_{\wedge}$ for and-clause, $C_{\bar{\pi}}$ for non-and-clause, $\vee^p$ for verb-phrase, N for noun. The purpose of $C_{\wedge}$ and $C_{\bar{\pi}}$ rules is to have n-ary conjunctions. A sample text with its derivation tree (omitting brackets) is given in Fig. 2.

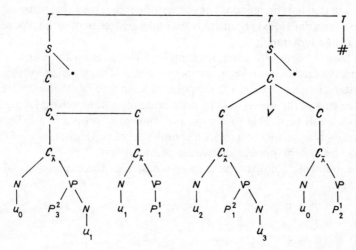

Fig. 2

I will take some liberties in varying the drawing of trees to emphasize certain points. For example, in the above Fig. 2 some dominance relations are drawn horizontally to indicate the intent of an n-ary sequence of sentences or n-ary conjunction. In the Appendix a set-theoretical definition of tree will be given, so that these vagaries will not really matter and heuristics can dictate.

Now an inductive definition of informing can be given for this simple language. An information state i in this case will merely be an information content, that is, a set of valuations. t is a string of category T; s is one of category S, and c_j are of category C, $C_\wedge$, or C_π.

(23) $\quad \text{INF}(st)(i) = \text{INF}(t)(\text{INF}(s)(i))$

(24) $\quad \text{INF}(c_.)(i) = \text{INF}(c)(i)$

(25) $\quad \text{INF}(c_1 \wedge c_2)(i) = \text{INF}(c_2)(\text{INF}(c_1)(i))$

(26) $\quad \text{INF}(c_1 \vee c_2)(i) = \text{INF}(c_1)(i) \cup \text{INF}(c_2)(i)$

(27) $\quad \text{INF}(\sim c)(i) = i - \text{INF}(c)(i)$

(28) $\quad \text{INF}(c_1 \supset c_2)(i) = i - (\text{INF}(c_1)(i) - \text{INF}(c_2)(\text{INF}(c_1)(i)))$.

For the present case there are obvious alternative definitions. The ones chosen are in preparation for later definitions in more complex cases of informing. Using composition of functions in clauses (23), (25), and (28) will be useful in describing pronominal coreference where an antecedent can be created in the prior string for a referential in the later string.

The elementary clauses will be handled with parameters; a predicate can inform only relative to an assignment of arguments. $\wp$ is a $\vee^p$.

(29) $\quad \text{INF}(u \wp) = \text{INF}(\wp)(u)$

(30) $\quad \text{INF}(P_j^2 u) = \text{INF}(P_j^2)(u)$

where

(31) $\quad \text{INF}(P_j^1)(u)(i) = \{V \in i : \langle u \rangle \in V(P_j^1)\}$

(32) $\quad \text{INF}(P_j^2)(u_2)(u_1)(i) = \{V \in i : \langle u_1, u_2 \rangle \in V(P_j^2)\}$

(33) $\quad \text{INF}(|c)(u) = \text{INF}(c)$

(34) $\quad \text{INF}(\#)(i) = i$.

The informing function associated with a clause, sentence, or text is an increasing function:

(35) $\quad i \sqsubseteq \text{INF}(\alpha)(i)$.

The relation to classical truth-semantics is quite direct in this simple case: if $\text{SAT}(\alpha)$ is the set of valuations that satisfy α according to the obvious classical definition of 'satisfy', then

$$(36) \qquad \text{INF}(\alpha)(i) = i \cap \text{SAT}(\alpha).$$

2. PRONOUNS

We will now enrich the set of nouns of the language with a pronoun x, by adding the rule

$$(37) \qquad N \rightarrow x.$$

Be forewarned that x is not an individual variable as in classical logic; the coreference of an occurrence of x with other occurrences of x or other nouns cannot be determined by the syntactic structure of the context alone. The syntactic context provides a well-ordering of possible interpretations of x according to a strategy of interpretation. The interpretation of an occurrence of x is then the least element of the well-ordering which provides a relevant interpretation of x. An interpretation of an occurrence of x is relevant if it results in information which is relevant relative to the input information.

Consider as a simple example the text

$$(38) \qquad u_0 P_1^2 u_1. \; x P_1^1. \; \#$$

which when translated into English reads

$$(39) \qquad \text{John tickled Bill. He squirmed.}$$

The syntactic context is depictable by the tree

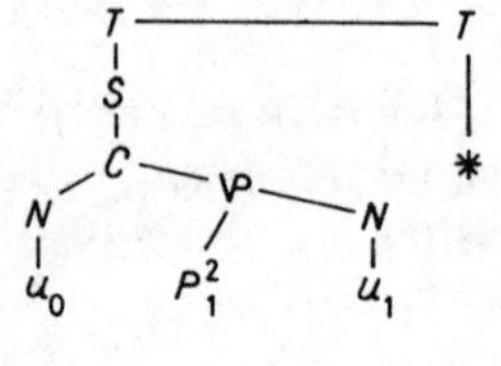

Fig. 3

where ∗ indicates the location at which the informing with $x P_1^1$. takes place. If the strategy is like that of English, it will operate on the context to produce the well-ordering: $u_0 < u_1$.

Interpreting the occurrence of x as the least element of the well-ordering

u_0 would result in informing as with $u_0 P_1^1.$, translated *John squirmed*. However, since the squirming of the tickler is not really relevant, the next element u_1 of the well-ordering must be considered. Informing with $u_1 P_1^1.$ would result in relevant information, since the squirming of the tickled is clearly relevant.

I note that the informal concept of relevance is more appropriate than that, say, of expectation, as can be seen from the example above and

(40) $u_0 P_1^2 u_1. \sim x P_1^1. \#$

translated as

(41)   John tickled Bill. He didn't squirm.

Certainly one would expect that the tickler would have no reason to squirm. Thus, choosing an interpretation according to expectation would result in x interpreted as u_0, John the tickler, which is incorrect. On the other hand, the tickler's not squirming is no more relevant than his squirming, so the tickler is again passed over in favor of the tickled.

We now have two concepts to formalize: relevance and context.

Let us consider relevance first. Given an information content k, there is a set of information contents which are greater than k and are also relevant to k. Thus, a relevance function R will overlay the structure K of information contents. It is a function from K to its power-set $\mathscr{P}K$. For any $k \in K$, let

(42) $G(k) = \{k' \in K : k \sqsubseteq k'\},$

the set generated by k.

Then R is subject to the restriction: for any $k \in K$,

(43) $R(k) \subseteq G(k),$

the relevant information contents are among the greater information contents. In case someone decides to order the undefined information content $k_\perp$ among other information contents, let us also require explicitly:

(44) $k_\perp \notin R(k)$, for any $k \in K$.

We must consider other restrictions on R, e.g., whether for every k,

(45) $k \in R(k)$

and whether for every $k \neq \phi$,

(46) $\phi \in R(k).$

We will assume here without argument that (45) holds; we will leave (46) out.

Let us consider how a relevance function R is specified. We must state specifically which elements of $G(k)$ are in $R(k)$. This is most easily accomplished by viewing R as a binary relation on K rather than a function from K to $\mathscr{P}K$. The two views of R are readily interchangeable by the equivalence:

(47) $R(k_0, k_1)$ if and only if $k_1 \in R(k_0)$.

For example, to capture the informal generalization that it is the ticklee and not the tickler whose squirming is relevant, we require for all u_0 and u_1 and for all k_0 and k_1 in $G(k_0)$:

(48)   if P_1^2 holds of $\langle u_0, u_1 \rangle$ at k_0 and $k_1 = \{V \in k_0 : \langle u_1 \rangle \in V(P_1^2)\}$, then $R(k_0, k_1)$;

where we say

(49) P_j^n holds of an n-tuple $\langle u_0, u_1, \ldots, u_{n-1} \rangle$ at a content k if and only if for all $V \in k$, $\langle u_0, u_1, \ldots, u_{n-1} \rangle \in V(P_j^n)$.

The requirement (48) ensures that the ticklee's squirming is relevant, but it does not yet exclude the tickler's squirming. We do not want to exclude the tickler's squirming in a wholesale manner. What if a particular individual has the habit of squirming whenever he tickles other people? We might place a particular requirement on R for that kind of individual. Or it might automatically result as in this case, from a general requirement on R that for all k,

(50) $R(k, k)$

We might also want to require for all k,

(51) $R(k, \phi)$;

that is, a contradiction is always relevant. After enumerating all the requirements on R, we define R in the usual fashion as the smallest relation on K satisfying these requirements. This automatically excludes, for example, the tickler's squirming, except in cases where it is induced by other requirements on R.

Including syntactic context will lead us to complicate the notion of information state. An information state will now consist of information content and interpreted syntactic context. The sense in which the context is interpreted is that occurrences of *x* are replaced by their interpretations in syntactic trees.

I will state the definition of informing using pictures of trees, overlayed with functions on information content, with the functions written in reverse functional notation. Thus a picture such as in Fig. 4 describes the tree in Fig. 5 together with information content $INF(\varphi)(u)(k)$, where τ' is the tree resulting from informing with φ. The convention is that the edges of the graph are attached to the main functor of the description of the tree to be attached to the edge. The precise formalization of the definition of informing would be in the manner of that given in the appendix for the case with quantifiers. Information states would be triples of a set-theoretical tree, a location on the tree, and an information content. The pictures are, I hope, heuristically superior.

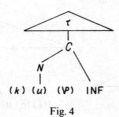

Fig. 4

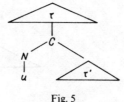

Fig. 5

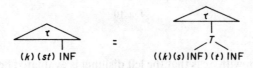

Fig. 6

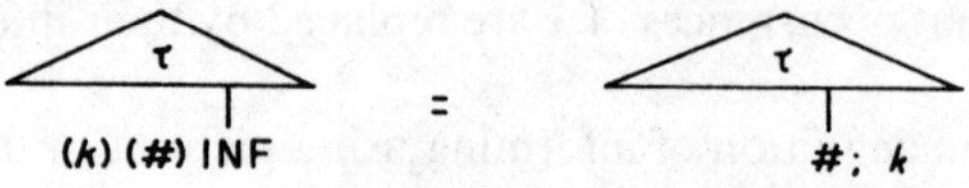

Fig. 7

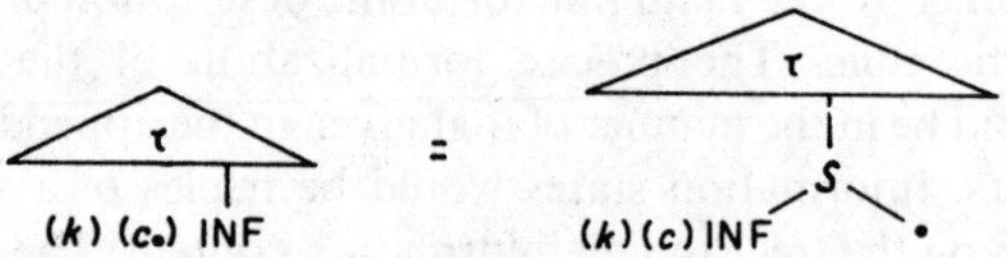

Fig. 8

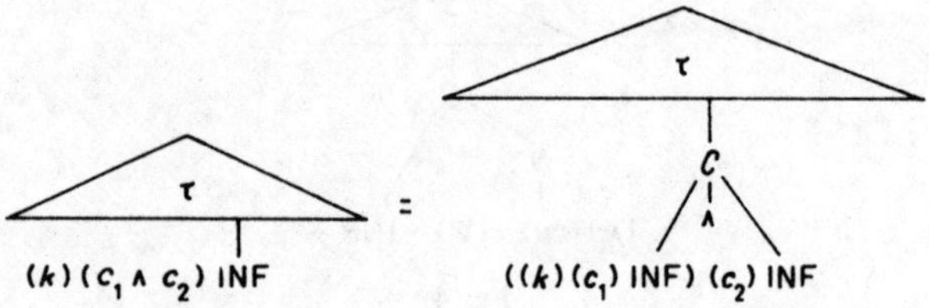

Fig. 9

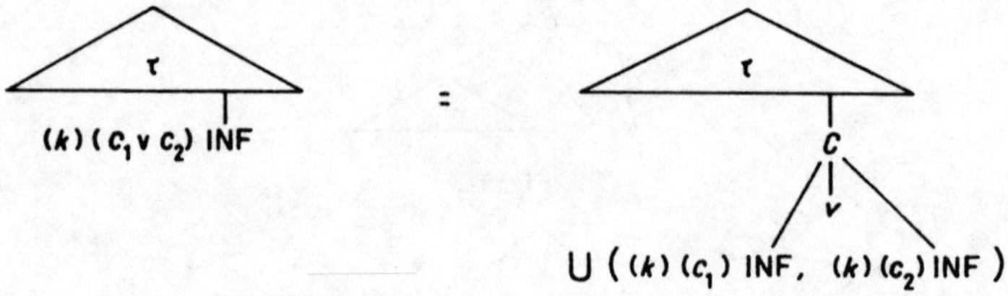

Fig. 10

The convention with $\vee$ is that the left disjunct is evaluated before the right and thus provides context for the right disjunct.

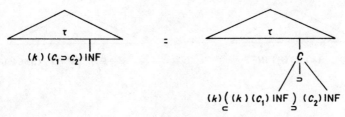

$(k)\,(C_1 \supset C_2)\,\mathrm{INF}$ $=$ $(k)\,\big(\,(k)\,(C_1)\,\mathrm{INF}\,\big)\,(C_2)\,\mathrm{INF}$

Fig. 11

where $\mathrm{INF}(c)\ (k')(k) = k - (k' - \mathrm{INF}(c)(k'))$.

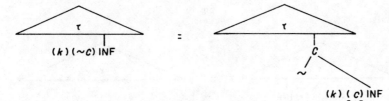

$(k)\,(\sim c)\,\mathrm{INF}$ $=$ $(k)\,(\underline{c})\,\mathrm{INF}$

Fig. 12

where $\mathrm{INF}(\underline{c})(k) = k - \mathrm{INF}(c)(k)$.

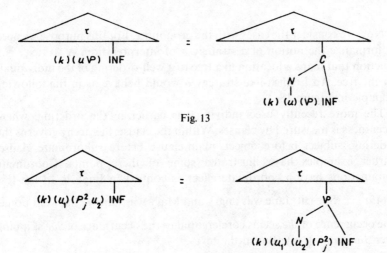

$(k)\,(u \vee P)\,\mathrm{INF}$ $=$ $(k)\,(u)\,(\vee P)\,\mathrm{INF}$

Fig. 13

$(k)\,(u_1)\,(P_j^2\,u_2)\,\mathrm{INF}$ $=$ $(k)\,(u_1)\,(u_2)\,(P_j^2)\,\mathrm{INF}$

Fig. 14

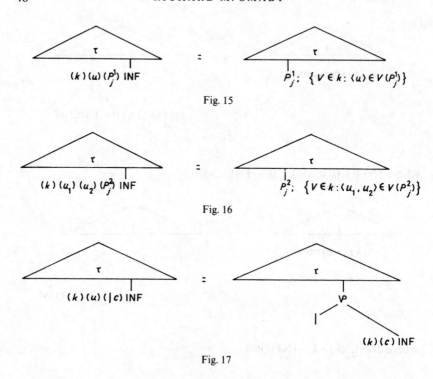

Fig. 15

Fig. 16

Fig. 17

Now we consider the cases with the pronoun x. For this purpose we need to formalize the notion of a strategy σ of interpretation. A strategy is a function that maps a location in a tree to a well-ordering of the individuals on the tree. An English-like strategy σ would behave as in the following example in Figure 18.

The more recently used individual is earlier in the ordering, where recentness is measured by clauses. Within the clause, hierarchy governs the ordering, subject before object, main-clause before subordinate clause. Earlier examples have illustrated some of these points. Coordinate conjunctions have a coordinate effect as context in English. In the text

(45)   Sue left. Jane was angry and Mary was happy. She went home.

The occurrence of *she* seems coreferential to the occurrence of *Sue* skipping over *Jane* and *Mary*. But in the text

(46)   Sue left. Jane was angry. And Mary was happy. She went home.

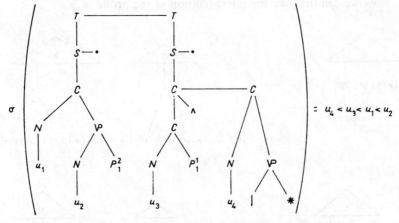

Fig. 18

She seems coreferential to *Mary*, the most recent antecedent. Prosodic features are important in distinguishing true coordinate constructions as in (45) from sequential constructions as in (46); and I have used conventional punctuation to convey these prosodic features. Now consider one more example of a coordinate construction:

(47)   Sue left. Jane was angry and she complained. She went home.

Here the lost *she* is coreferential with *Jane* and *she* of the coordinate construction. The two coordinate examples suggest that the well-ordering derived from a coordinate construction is the intersection of the two well-orderings derived from the conjuncts. I will allow such sketchy deliberations to suffice and merely assume we have formulated a strategy for the language. (More details on this are in Smaby (1976).)

Let L be the least element function on well-orderings. That is,

(48) $L(u_0 < u_1 < \ldots) = u_0$
$L(\phi) = u_\perp$, the undefined individual.

Recall that all functions return the undefined value for undefined arguments.

Let ω be a well-ordering and Y a subset of the universe U. Then $\omega \restriction Y$ is the well-ordering ω restricted to Y.

Now we can describe the interpretation of the pronoun x.

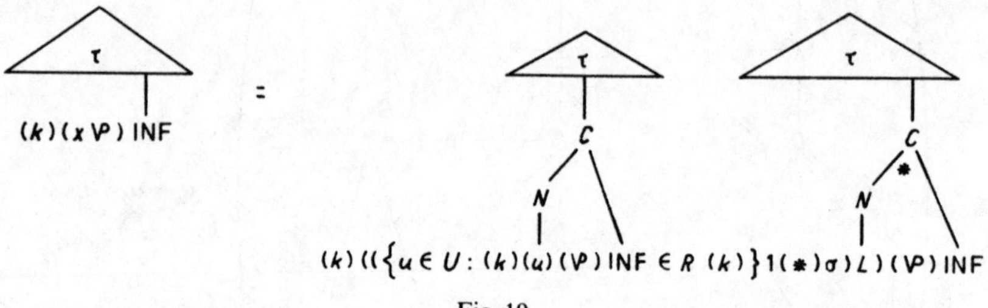

$$(k)((\{u \in U: (k)(u)(\mathcal{P})\,\mathrm{INF} \in R\,(k)\}1\,(*)\sigma)L\,)\,(\mathcal{P})\,\mathrm{INF}$$

Fig. 19

$$(k)(u_1)((\{u_2 \in U: (k)(u_1)(u_2)(P^2)\,\mathrm{INF} \in R(k)\}1\,(*)\sigma)L\,)(P_j^2)\,\mathrm{INF}$$

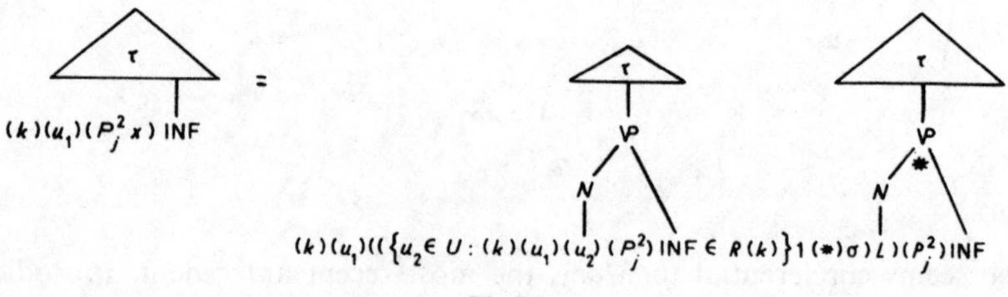

Fig. 20

The $*$'s on the trees indicate the location on the tree at which the strategy σ operates.

Consider again the text:

(36) $u_0 P_1^2 u_1.\ xP_1^1.\ \#$

as a simple example to illustrate the informing definition.

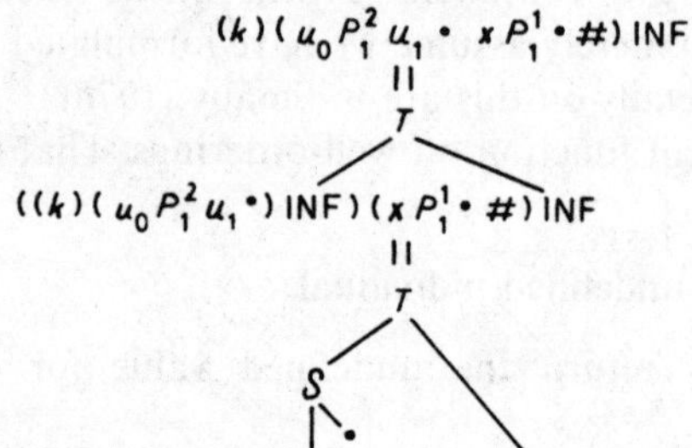

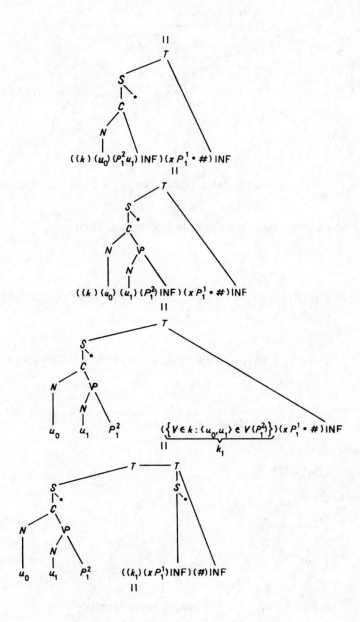

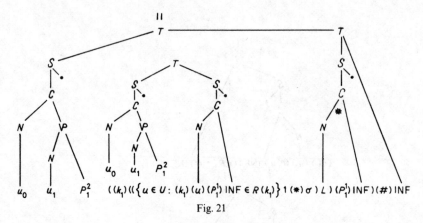

Fig. 21

Now let us assume σ is such as indicated before. Then

(49) $\sigma(*) = u_0 < u_1.$

But

(50) $\mathrm{INF}(P_1^1)(u_0)(k_1) = \{V \in k: \langle u_0, u_1 \rangle \in V(P_1^2) \ \& \ \langle u_0 \rangle \in V(P_1^1)\}$
         $\notin R(k_1)$

and

(51) $\mathrm{INF}(P_1^1)(u_1)(k_1) = \{V \in k: \langle u_0, u_1 \rangle \in V(P_1^2) \ \& \ \langle u_1 \rangle \in V(P_1^1)\}$
         $\notin R(k_1).$

Thus,

(52) $\sigma(*) \upharpoonright \{u \in U: \mathrm{INF}(P_1^1)(u)(k_1) \in R(k_1)\} = u_1.$

And then

(53) $L(u_1) = u_1.$

So now we have

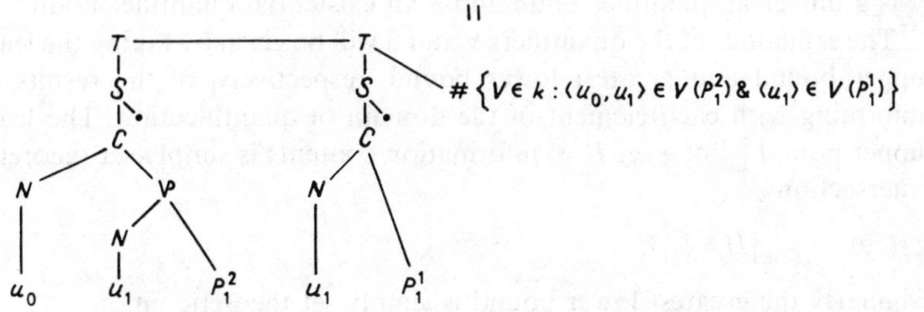

$$\# \left\{ v \in k : \langle u_0, u_1 \rangle \in V(P_1^2) \,\&\, \langle u_1 \rangle \in V(P_1^1) \right\}$$

Fig. 22

This treatment of a pronoun is not meant to capture all the nuances of English, but merely to illustrate a framework in which a description of a language with pronouns, such as English, could be carried out.

3. QUANTIFIERS AND COREFERENCE

There are two features of quantifiers in English which I would like to fit onto the framework already developed. One is the variable domain of quantifiers. The sentence

(54)   Everyone left.

is understood as saying that everyone of a certain group of people left, which group depends on context and whose leaving is relevant. The second feature of English quantifiers I wish to treat is the difference in scope between *everyone* and *someone*. In the text

(55)   Someone left. He went home.

the occurrence of *he* is understood as bound by *someone*, while in

(56)   Everyone left. He went home.

the occurrence of *he* is not understood as bound by *everyone*. *Someone's* scope is open to the end of the text; while *everyone's* scope is the clause of which it is subject or the verb-phrase of which it is object. It is *someone* that will require enriching the concept of information state.

The language is augmented with two more nouns

(57) $N \rightarrow \forall$

(58) $N \rightarrow \exists$

$\forall$ is a universal quantifier noun and $\exists$ an existential quantifier noun.

The semantics of the quantifiers $\forall$ and $\exists$ will be given by taking the least upper bound and greatest lower bound, respectively, of the results of informing with each element of the domain of quantification. The least upper bound $\bigsqcup$ of a set H of information contents is simply set theoretic intersection:

$$(59) \qquad \bigsqcup H = \bigcap H.$$

Similarly the greatest lower bound is simply set theoretic union:

$$(60) \qquad \bigsqcap H = \bigcup H.$$

However, as in the case of informing with a singular pronoun, information states will consist of syntactic context along with information content. What then is the least upper bound or greatest lower bound of a set of syntactic contexts? Fortunately, we don't need to develop a general theory of ordering of syntactic contexts, since we need only to use the concepts in the case of quantification. In this case the elements of the set Z should vary according to the pattern:

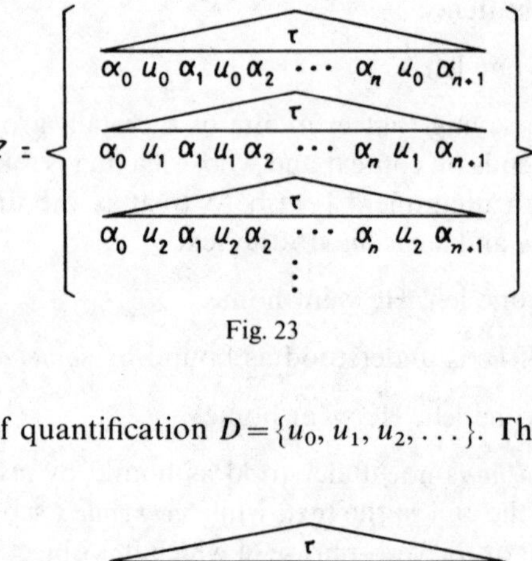

Fig. 23

for the domain of quantification $D = \{u_0, u_1, u_2, \ldots\}$. Then

Fig. 24

and

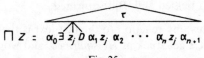

$$\sqcap Z = \alpha_0 \exists z_j D \alpha_1 z_j \alpha_2 \cdots \alpha_n z_j \alpha_{n+1}$$

Fig. 25

where z_j is the first of the sequence $\langle z_0, z_1, z_2, \ldots \rangle$ of meta-variables, which doesn't occur in any of $\alpha_0, \alpha_1, \alpha_2, \ldots \alpha_n, \alpha_{n+1}$. I note that the use of least upper bound and greatest lower bound here is parallel to that in the Lindenbaum algebra of formulae of first order logic.

Now consider some English examples.

(61)   Sam and George and Bill were playing. Someone tickled Bill. He squirmed.

A plausible informal semantic analysis of the above text is that with a universe of Sam, George, and Bill, out of the possible combinations

(62) α Sam tickled Bill. Sam squirmed.
(63) α Sam tickled Bill. Bill squirmed.
(64) α George tickled Bill. George squirmed.
(65) α George tickled Bill. Bill squirmed.
(66) α Bill tickled Bill. Bill squirmed.   (with α the first sentence of the text)

only the second and the fourth are relevant. Those two provide a uniform set of syntactic structures whose greatest lower bound is

(67)   Sam and George and Bill were playing. $\exists z_0 \{$Sam, George$\}$ tickled Bill. Bill squirmed.

Suppose, however, the text were

(68)   Sam and George and Bill were playing. Sam is the kind of guy that squirms when tickling other people. Someone tickled Bill. He squirmed.

Then out of the possible combinations listed above, with α now the first two sentences of this last text, the first, second, and fourth are relevant. But this set:

(69)   Sam tickled Bill. Sam squirmed.
(70)   Sam tickled Bill. Bill squirmed.

(71)   George tickled Bill. Bill squirmed.

is not uniform. Now, my reaction to the last text is that it is unresolvably ambiguous; that is, I get stuck at *He squirmed.* and would have to inquire who *he* referred to. Such a brief self-examination is hardly empirical research; however, I will use it as a guide in the matter of choice of domain of quantification.

The least upper bound and greatest lower bound of a non-uniform set will be an information state with the undefined information content $k_\perp$. I can say information state here, since in the actual definition to follow, $\bigsqcup$ and $\bigsqcap$ will operate on context–content combinations, that is, information states. As with the undefined individual $u_\perp$, the undefined content $k_\perp$ as argument yields undefined values of functions. $k_\perp$ is never relevant. Thus, symbolically, if

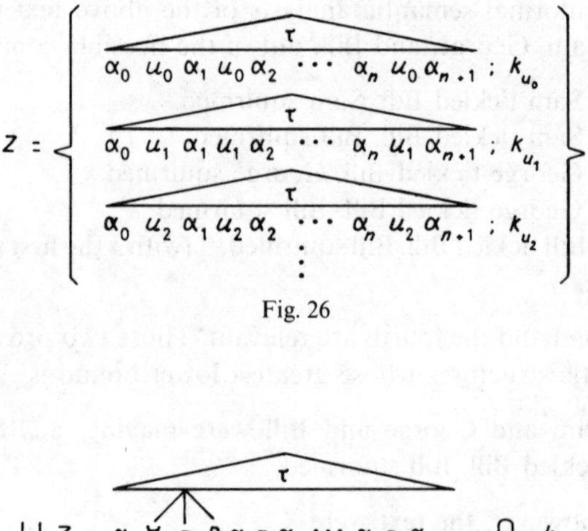

$$Z = \left\{ \begin{array}{l} \overbrace{\alpha_0 \, u_0 \, \alpha_1 \, u_0 \, \alpha_2 \, \cdots \, \alpha_n \, u_0 \, \alpha_{n+1}}^{\tau} : k_{u_0} \\ \overbrace{\alpha_0 \, u_1 \, \alpha_1 \, u_1 \, \alpha_2 \, \cdots \, \alpha_n \, u_1 \, \alpha_{n+1}}^{\tau} : k_{u_1} \\ \overbrace{\alpha_0 \, u_2 \, \alpha_1 \, u_2 \, \alpha_2 \, \cdots \, \alpha_n \, u_2 \, \alpha_{n+1}}^{\tau} : k_{u_2} \\ \vdots \end{array} \right\}$$

Fig. 26

then

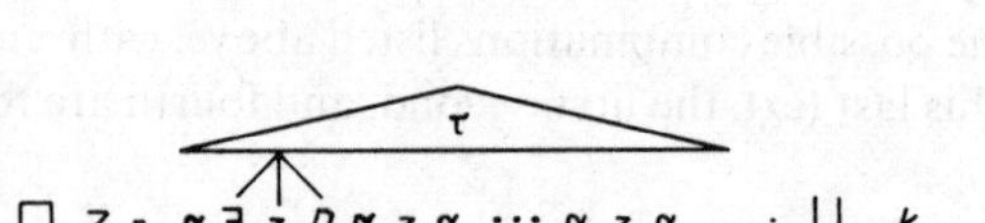

$$\bigsqcup Z = \overbrace{\alpha_0 \, \forall \, z_j \, D \, \alpha_1 \, z_j \, \alpha_2 \, \cdots \, \alpha_n \, z_j \, \alpha_{n+1}}^{\tau} : \bigcap_{u_m \in D} k_{u_m}$$

Fig. 27

and

$$\bigsqcap Z = \overbrace{\alpha_0 \, \exists \, z_j \, D \, \alpha_1 \, z_j \, \alpha_2 \, \cdots \, \alpha_n \, z_j \, \alpha_{n+1}}^{\tau} : \bigcup_{u_m \in D} k_{u_m}$$

Fig. 28

where D is the set of individuals whose substitutions produce the set Z, and z_j is the first of the sequence $\langle z_0, z_1, z_2, \ldots \rangle$ of meta-variables, which doesn't occur in any of $\alpha_0, \alpha_1, \alpha_2, \ldots \alpha_n, \alpha_{n+1}$. If Z is not of the form above, then

(72) $\bigsqcup Z = \bigsqcap Z = i_\perp.$

I have not spelled out the concept of a uniform set of information states. For now let it suffice to say it is a set of cardinality strictly greater than one and which has a pattern as in Fig. 26. A formal definition is given in the Appendix.

Now in the uses of $\bigsqcup$ and $\bigsqcap$, information states will vary as functions of individuals of U:

(73) $i(u) = \langle \tau(u), k(u) \rangle,$ enabling us to write

(74) $\bigsqcup_{u \in D} i(u)$ and

(75) $\bigsqcap_{u \in D} i(u)$

as abbreviations for

(76) $\bigsqcup \{i(u): u \in D\}$ and

(77) $\bigsqcap \{i(u): u \in D\},$

respectively.

Actually, we will need to calculate D as a function of information content. D will be the set of uniformly relevant individuals for informing with an expression at an information state. We unpack this bit of jargon as follows.

We derivatively call an information state relevant if its information content k is relevant: thus, for any information content k, we define

(78) $R'(k) = \{\langle \tau, k' \rangle : k' \in R(k)\}.$

Using $R'(k)$ we can extract from any set Z of information states, those which are relevant to k:

(79) $\mathrm{REL}(k)(Z) = \{i \in Z: i \in R'(k)\}.$

I note that states $\langle \tau, k_\perp \rangle \in Z$, where $k_\perp$ is the undefined information content, are always excluded from $\mathrm{REL}(k)(Z)$ for any k.

Now we define the function D on sets of information states to sets of individuals as

(80) $D(Z) = \begin{cases} \{u_0, u_1, \dots\} & \text{if } Z \text{ is uniform as in Fig. 25} \\ \{u_\perp\} & \text{if } Z \text{ is not uniform} \end{cases}$

The uniformly relevant set of individuals for a function i from individuals to information states, relative to an information content k, is

(81) $D(\text{REL}(k)(\{i(u): u \in U\}))$.

Least upper bounds and greatest lower bounds will then typically take the form

(82) $\displaystyle\bigsqcup_{u \in D(\text{REL}(k)(\{i(u): u \in U\}))} i(u)$ and

(83) $\displaystyle\bigsqcap_{u \in D(\text{REL}(k)(\{i(u): u \in U\}))} i(u)$.

Let us now turn to the difference in scope between *everyone* and *someone* as represented by $\forall$ and $\exists$, respectively. As mentioned earlier, I am taking the difference to be that the scope of $\forall$ is the verb-phrase of which it is the subject or the predicate of which it is the object, while the scope of $\exists$ extends beyond, to succeeding clauses and sentences. The scope of $\forall$ is automatically provided for in the construction of the preceding paragraph. The scope of $\exists$, however, requires extending the construction. So let us examine *someone* in English for some guidance.

The unifying observation about the scope of *someone* is that it extends to the right to the end of a sequence of *and*-conjuncts:

(84)   someone left and he went home and he cooked supper

This can occur at the level of a sentence or at the level of the scope of a negation:

(85)   it is not the case that someone left and he went home and he cooked supper

However, in such a case it does not extend beyond the scope of the negation: the text

(86)   It is not the case that someone left. He stayed.

does not have the occurrence of *he* bound by the occurrence of *someone*. A similar situation arises with *or*-disjuncts.

(87)   Either someone left and Bill saw him or Bill is lying.

The scope of *someone* is limited to the disjunct in which it occurs. So, for

example, in

(88)   Either someone left or he stayed.

the occurrence of *he* is not bound to the occurrence of *someone*, leaving *he* with no antecedent.

The scope of *someone* is limited to the scope of *everyone*. Thus, we have easy coreference in

(89)   Everyone was such that someone liked him and he invited him to supper.

but not in

(90)   Everyone was such that he invited someone to supper. He arrived late.

The case of *if . . . then* is slightly more complex, since it is what one could call conditional *and*:

(91)   If someone comes, he will be surprised.

I take the above to be the facts of English I wish to imitate in the formalized language we are discussing. The extra-scope of ∃ I will accommodate by 'saving' the remainder of the sequence of *and*-conjuncts after the occurrence of ∃ in question.

Again I will avail myself of pictures to facilitate presentation, leaving the precise formalization to the appendix. The new feature of the pictures is the indication of 'saved' right context which will appear as

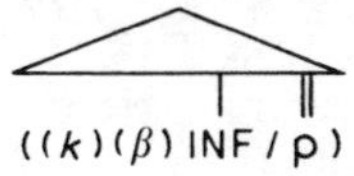

$$((k)(\beta) \text{ INF } / \rho)$$

Fig. 29

The understanding of such an element is that β is informing with right contexts ρ, possibly multiple, possibly null, at the locations indicated. In the formal definitions right context will never be actually null, though when it is #, it is essentially null in that informing with # is the identity function. The parentheses are crucial, as they indicate extent of right context for a given evaluation. As mentioned above, the importance of saved right context is to widen the scope of ∃. Thus, the crucial cases of right context are

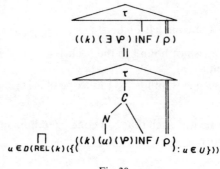

Fig. 30

and

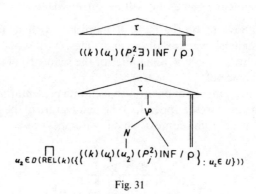

Fig. 31

where the extended parentheses save copying the tree over again.

As a simple example consider the text

(92) $\exists P_1^1. \; x P_2^1. \; \#$

translating, say,

(93)   Someone left. He went home.

After a few steps the computation with input information k is

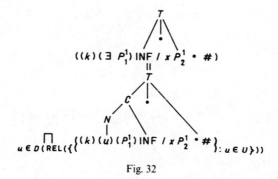

Fig. 32

The scope of ∃ thus extends over the entire text. To make this completely clear we need to consider how P_j^1 and P_j^2 inform with right context:

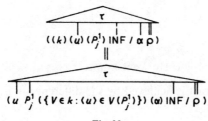

Fig. 33

and

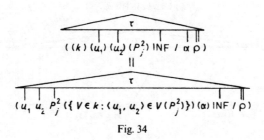

Fig. 34

Thus, one can informally characterize / as indicating delayed composition of functions.

Now returning to the above example, we have

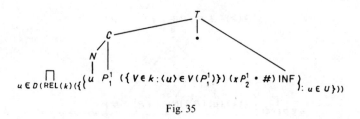

Fig. 35

We see that the pronoun strategy sketched in the preceding section will suggest the subject of the preceding sentence as a possible interpretation of the pronoun x.

This example contrasts with

(94) $\forall P_1^1. \, xP_2^1. \, \#$

which glosses as

(95)   Everyone left. He went home.

The formal contrast is achieved by the difference in informing with the universal quantifier $\forall$:

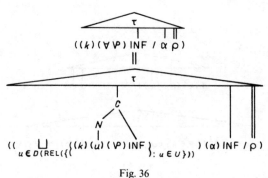

Fig. 36

and

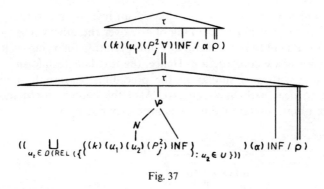

Fig. 37

Our example with ∀ after a few steps of computation is

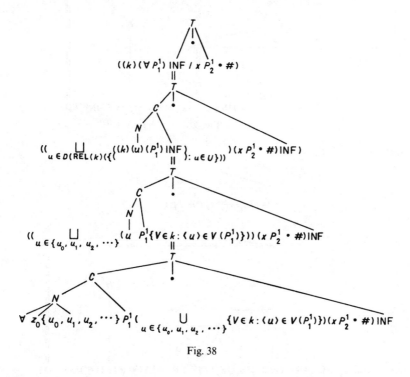

Fig. 38

The contrast is now evident. The subject of the context is not a single element which a singular pronoun like x can refer to, but rather a set of elements, with no syntactic ranking of one over the others. The pronoun strategy would fail to recommend any interpretation for x, just as it would for any coordinate construction. Hence, the text fails to inform.

Informing with x is similar to the preceding paragraph. σ must be adjusted to deal with new contexts. Also the context for determining relevance of interpretations of x has been expanded.

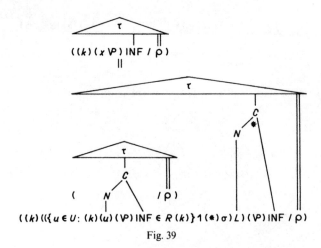

Fig. 39

and

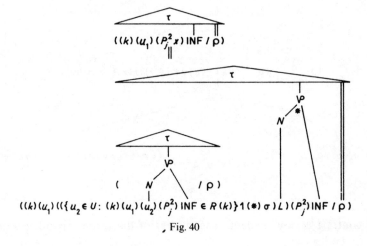

Fig. 40

Remaining clauses of the definition of informing differ from those of the preceding paragraph primarily in establishing sufficient scope for ∃ by placing it as right context. For informing with a text we have the following two equations.

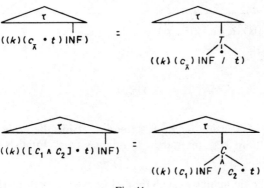

Fig. 41

Schematically the resulting syntactic context in the above manner of informing with a text is

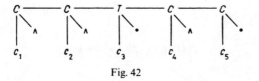

Fig. 42

for a text of the form

(96) $[c_1 \wedge [c_2 \wedge c_3]]. [c_4 \wedge c_5]. \#$

provided c_3 and c_5 are c_π, i.e. not $c_\wedge$. The grammar's yielding only n-ary conjunction, rather than say $[c_1 \wedge c_2] \wedge c_3$ as well, is profited from here. The text $\#$ is merely the identity function.

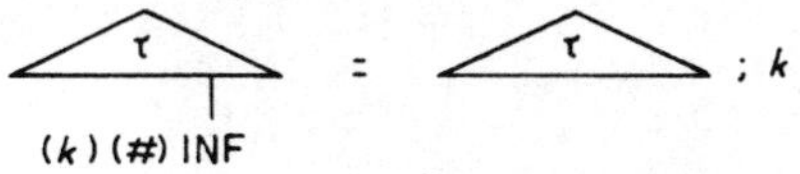

Fig. 43

In embedded contexts informing with a $c_\wedge$ will occur and is similar to the text case.

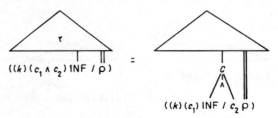

$$((k)(c_1 \wedge c_2) \text{ INF } / \rho) \quad = \quad ((k)(c_1) \text{ INF } / c_2 \rho)$$

Fig. 44

The scope of $\exists$ inside $|$-clauses extends outside the embedded clause, provided nothing else interferes. Guidance from English comes from examples such as

(97)   The elephant was such that it knocked something over. It broke.

where *it* refers to the thing knocked over.

Let the text in our sample language be

(98) $u_1|xP_1^2 \exists. \, xP_1^1. \, \#$

Then

$$(k)(u_1 | x P_1^2 \exists \bullet x P_1^1 \bullet \#) \text{INF}$$
$$\| \quad T$$
$$((k)(u_1 | x P_1^2 \exists) \text{INF} / x P_1^1 \bullet \#)$$
$$\| \quad T$$
$$(k)(u_1)(| x P_1^2 \exists) \text{INF} / x P_1^1 \bullet \#)$$

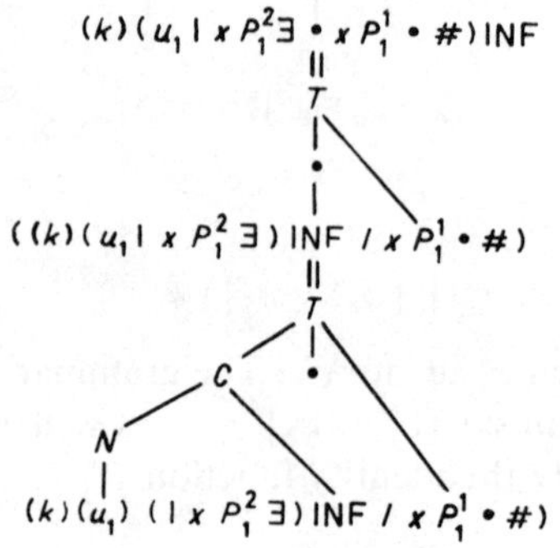

Fig. 45

Now we need the clause of the definition for $|c$.

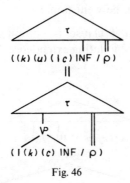

$$((k)(u)(1c)\,\text{INF}\,/\,\rho)$$

$$\|$$

$$(1(k)(c)\,\text{INF}\,/\,\rho)$$

Fig. 46

So now our example evaluates to

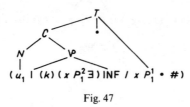

$$(u_1\,1\,(k)(x\,P_1^2\,\exists)\,\text{INF}\,/\,x\,P_1^1\,\bullet\,\#)$$

Fig. 47

Skipping deliberations about the interpretation of the first x we have

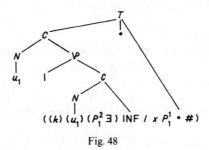

$$((k)(u_1)(P_1^2\,\exists)\,\text{INF}\,/\,x\,P_1^1\,\bullet\,\#)$$

Fig. 48

which as in previous examples allows the scope of $\exists$ to extend over the right context xP_1. # as desired.

We can also follow the guidance of *if–then* examples of English:

(99)   If someone left, he went home.

The content of a $[c_1 \supset c_2]$ clause is computed as in the preceding paragraph, but with accommodating extended scope of $\exists$. The treatment of $\supset$ is similar to . in the case of a text.

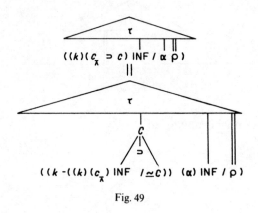

Fig. 49

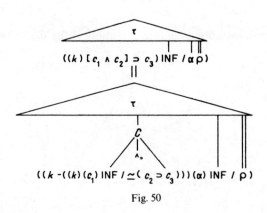

Fig. 50

Consider the example

(100) $[\exists P_1^1 \supset x P_2^1]$. #

glossed as (99) above.

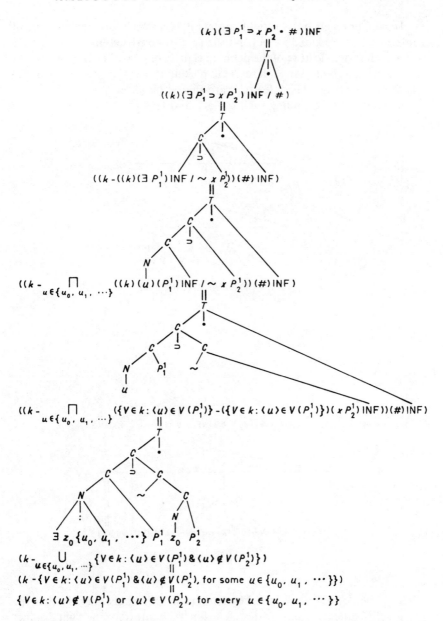

Fig. 51

$[c \supset c]$ brackets its own right context if any, which forbids the scope of internal $\exists$ from extending beyond the $[c \supset c]$ construction.

An additional feature of the defining clauses of $[c \supset c]$ is the discharging of the nearest right context. It serves to pick up the right context for a higher level computation. These features are shared by all $c_{\bar{\pi}}$.

We have two remaining such $c_{\bar{\pi}}$: $\sim c$ and $[c \vee c]$.

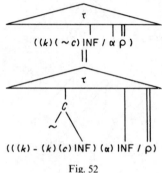

Fig. 52

and

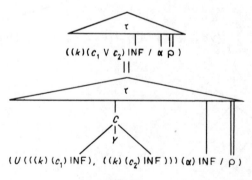

Fig. 53

where the convention of the last paragraph still holds, namely that the syntactic context created by the left disjunct is context for the right disjunct and not the reverse.

There are many features of English pronominal coreference which are not modelled by this language. For example, English has a plural pronoun. It would be straight-forward to add a plural pronoun; the real work and interest here would be in spelling out the plural strategy, which is complementary to the singular strategy. More difficult is the real variety of English quantifiers and variation of scope of a single quantifier in context. For example, in

(101)　　Each boy left. He went home.

the scope of *each* clearly extends beyond its clause, which contrasts with

(102)　　Every boy left. He went home.

On the other hand, there is a contrast between *each* and *any* in *if–then* contexts. In

(103)　　If any boy left, he went home.

the scope of *any* extends to the consequent clause, while in

(104)　　If each boy left, he went home.

the scope of *each* does not extend to the consequent clause.

There is also the problem of ambiguity of order of application of operators:

(105)　　everyone loves someone
(106)　　everyone didn't leave

Before adding such cases one would like to have a general account of ambiguity of order of application.

That is, there remains much work to do. Perhaps, the above framework will suggest to others how to describe more than I have been able to so far.

APPENDIX

The above pictorial presentation of informing can be made mathematically precise. The concept of an information content k as a set of valuations is precise enough. What needs to be made more precise is the concept of a tree and operations on trees.

We take a tree η to be a finite set of finite sequences of natural numbers such that the empty sequence $\langle\ \rangle \in \eta$, if $\langle\alpha, \beta\rangle \in \eta$, then $\langle\alpha\rangle \in \eta$, and if $\langle\alpha, \beta +1\rangle \in \eta$, then $\langle\alpha, \beta\rangle \in \eta$. The pictorial idea is that $\langle\ \rangle$ is the root node, $\langle\alpha\rangle$

dominates $\langle \alpha, \beta \rangle$, and descendent nodes of $\langle \alpha \rangle$ are ordered left to right consecutively starting from $\langle \alpha, 0 \rangle$. An example is

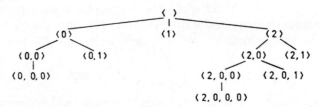

Fig. 54

In the definitions of informing I will leave out the brackets and commas for ease of reading; and the empty sequence I will write $\diamond$.

A labelled tree τ is a function, formalized as a set of ordered pairs, from a tree into the set of labels: T, C, $\vee^{\!P}$, N, $.$, $\wedge$, $\vee$, $\supset$, $\sim$, $\#$, P_j^1, P_j^2, u_j, x, $\forall$, $\exists$, $D \subseteq U$. For example, a labelling of the tree of Fig. 54:

(107) $\{ \langle \diamond, T \rangle, \langle 0, C \rangle, \langle 1, . \rangle, \langle 2, T \rangle, \langle 00, N \rangle, \langle 01, P_1^1 \rangle, \langle 000, u_0 \rangle,$
$\langle 20, C \rangle, \langle 21, . \rangle, \langle 200, N \rangle, \langle 201, P_2^1 \rangle, \langle 2000, u_1 \rangle \}$

corresponds to the picture of Fig. 55.

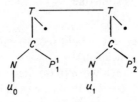

Fig. 55

Recall that we also referred to informing at a location in a tree. Hence, we will need to distinguish a node λ.

In order to handle right context ρ we need an additional parameter which will consist of a sequence of ordered pairs of a tree location and object-language textual material: $\langle \langle \lambda_0, \alpha_0 \rangle, \langle \lambda_1, \alpha_1 \rangle, \ldots \rangle$.

Thus, altogether an information state is a 4-tuple: $\langle \tau, \lambda, \rho, k \rangle$ of a labelled tree τ, a node λ, a right context ρ, and an information content k.

Now we need to consider operations on information states.
A few are rather mechanical.

(108) $SUB_2(\lambda')(\tau, \lambda, \rho, k) = \langle \tau, \lambda', \rho, k \rangle$

(109) $SUB_3(\rho')(\tau, \lambda, \rho, k) = \langle \tau, \lambda, \rho', k \rangle$

(110) $PROJ_4(\tau, \lambda, \rho, k) = k; \ PROJ_1(\tau, \lambda, \rho, k) = \tau$

(111) $-(k')(\tau, \lambda, \rho, k) = \langle \tau, \lambda, \rho, k' - k \rangle$

(112) $\langle \tau_1, \lambda_1, \rho_1, k_1 \rangle \cup \langle \tau_2, \lambda_2, \rho_2, k_2 \rangle = \langle \tau_1 \cup \tau_2, \lambda_2, \rho_2, k_1 \cup k_2 \rangle.$

More substantial operations are $\bigsqcup$ and $\bigsqcap$. Recall that these operations referred to the concept of a uniform set of information states.

A set $Z = \{\langle \tau_j, \lambda_j, \rho_j, k_j \rangle : j \in J\}$ is uniform iff its cardinality is greater than one, all $\lambda_j = \lambda_0$, for some λ_0, all $\rho_j = \rho_0$, for some ρ_0, and there is a set of nodes Y and a function $f: J \to U$ such that
$\langle \tau_j, \ \lambda_j, \ \rho_j, \ k_j \rangle = \langle \tau_j \cup \{\langle \lambda 0, \ f(j) \rangle : \lambda \in Y \}, \ \lambda_j, \ \rho_j, \ k_j \rangle$,
that is, altering τ_j by adding the label $f(j)$ at each node $\lambda 0$ for λ in Y produces no change in τ_j, which is to say that those nodes were already labelled that way.

Now we can define $\bigsqcup$ and $\bigsqcap$:

(113) $\bigsqcup Z = \langle \bigcup\limits_{j \in J} (((\tau_j - \{\langle \lambda 0, \tau_j(\lambda 0) \rangle : \lambda \in Y\}) \cup \{\langle \lambda 0, z_m \rangle : \lambda \in Y \ \&$
$\lambda \neq \lambda' \}) \cup \{\langle \lambda'0, \forall \rangle, \langle \lambda'1, z_m \rangle, \langle \lambda'2, D(Z) \rangle\}), \lambda_0, \rho_0, \bigcap\limits_{j \in J} k_j \rangle$

(114) $\bigsqcap Z = \langle \bigcup\limits_{j \in J} (((\tau_j - \{\langle \lambda_0, \tau_j(\lambda 0) \rangle : \lambda \in Y) \cup \{\langle \lambda 0, z_m \rangle : \lambda \in Y \ \&$
$\lambda \neq \lambda' \}) \cup \{\langle \lambda'0, \exists \rangle, \langle \lambda'1, z_m \rangle, \langle \lambda'2, D(Z) \rangle\}), \lambda_0, \rho_0, \bigcup\limits_{j \in J} k_j \rangle$

where

(115) $D(Z) = \begin{cases} \{f(j) : j \in J\} & \text{if } Z \text{ is uniform} \\ \{u_\perp\} & \text{otherwise} \end{cases}$

λ' is the left-most λ_j, i.e. λ' occurs prior to any other λ_j in the lexicographical ordering of finite sequences, and z_m is the first in the sequence of meta-variables $\langle z_0, z_1, z_2, \ldots \rangle$ which does not occur as a label in any τ_j.

We generally assume that informing starts with a state of the form: $\langle \phi, \diamondsuit, \langle \diamondsuit, \# \rangle, k \rangle$.

Now we can precisely define informing for the language with quantifiers and a pronoun.

(116) $\text{INF}([c_1 \wedge c_2].t)(\tau, \lambda, \rho, k)$
   $= \text{INF}(c_1)(\tau \cup \langle \lambda, C \rangle \cup \langle \lambda 1, \wedge \rangle, \lambda 0, \langle \lambda 2, c_2.t \rangle \hat{\ } \rho, k)$

(117) $\text{INF}(c_{\pi}.t)(\tau, \lambda, \rho, k)$
   $= \text{INF}(c_{\pi})(\tau \cup \langle \lambda, T \rangle \cup \langle \lambda 1, . \rangle, \lambda 0, \langle \lambda 2, t \rangle \hat{\ } \rho, k)$

(118) $\text{INF}(c_1 \wedge c_2)(\tau, \lambda, \rho, k)$
   $= \text{INF}(c_1)(\tau \cup \langle \lambda, C \rangle \cup \langle \lambda 1, \wedge \rangle, \lambda 0, \langle \lambda 2, c_2 \rangle \hat{\ } \rho, k)$

(119) $\text{INF}(\sim c)(\tau, \lambda, \langle \lambda', \alpha \rangle \hat{\ } \rho, k)$
   $= \text{INF}(\alpha)(\text{SUB}_2(\lambda'))(\text{SUB}_3(\rho)(-(k)$
   $(\text{INF}(c)(\tau \cup \langle \lambda, C \rangle \cup \langle \lambda 0, \sim \rangle, \lambda 1, \langle \diamond, \# \rangle, k)))))$

(120) $\text{INF}(c_1 \vee c_2)(\tau, \lambda, \langle \lambda', \alpha \rangle \hat{\ } \rho, k)$
   $= \text{INF}(\alpha)(\text{SUB}_2(\lambda'))(\text{SUB}_3(\rho)(\text{INF}(c_1)(\tau \cup \langle \lambda, C \rangle, \lambda 0,$
   $\langle \diamond, \# \rangle, k) \cup$
   $\text{INF}(c_2)(\text{PROJ}_1(\text{INF}(c_1)(\tau \cup \langle \lambda, C \rangle, \lambda 0, \langle \diamond, \# \rangle, k))$
   $\cup \langle \lambda 1, \vee \rangle, \lambda 2, \langle \diamond, \# \rangle, k))))$

(121) $\text{INF}([c_1 \wedge c_2] \supset c_3)(\tau, \lambda, \langle \lambda', \alpha \rangle \hat{\ } \rho, k)$
   $= \text{INF}(\alpha)(\text{SUB}_2(\lambda'))(\text{SUB}_3(\rho)(-(k)$
   $(\text{INF}(c_1)(\tau \cup \langle \lambda, C \rangle \cup \langle \lambda 1, \wedge \rangle, \lambda 0, \langle \lambda 2, \sim (c_2 \supset c_3) \rangle, k)))))$

(122) $\text{INF}(c_{\pi} \supset c)(\tau, \lambda, \langle \lambda', \alpha \rangle \hat{\ } \rho, k)$
   $= \text{INF}(\alpha)(\text{SUB}_2(\lambda'))(\text{SUB}_3(\rho)(-(k)$
   $(\text{INF}(c_{\pi})(\tau \cup \langle \lambda, C \rangle \cup \langle \lambda 1, \supset \rangle, \lambda 0, \langle \lambda 2, \sim c \rangle, k)))))$

(123) $\text{INF}(\#)(\tau, \lambda, \rho, k) = \langle \tau, \lambda, \rho, k \rangle$

(124) $\text{INF}(u \vee\!\!\!\vee)(\tau, \lambda, \rho, k)$
   $= \text{INF}(\vee\!\!\!\vee)(u)(\tau \cup \langle \lambda, C \rangle \cup \langle \lambda 0, N \rangle \cup \langle \lambda 00, u \rangle, \lambda 1, \rho, k)$

(125) $\text{INF}(\exists \vee\!\!\!\vee)(\tau, \lambda, \rho, k)$
   $=$
$$\prod_{u \in D(\text{REL}(k)(\{\text{INF}(\vee\!\!\!\vee)(u)(\tau \cup \langle \lambda, C \rangle \cup \langle \lambda 0, N \rangle \cup \langle \lambda 00, u \rangle, \lambda 1, \rho, k); u \in U\}))}$$
   $\text{INF}(\vee\!\!\!\vee)(u)(\tau \cup \langle \lambda, C \rangle \cup \langle \lambda 0, N \rangle \cup \langle \lambda 00, u \rangle, \lambda 1, \rho, k)$

(126) $\text{INF}(\forall \vee\!\!\!\vee)(\tau, \lambda, \langle \lambda', \alpha \rangle \hat{\ } \rho, k)$
   $= \text{INF}(\alpha)(\text{SUB}_2(\lambda'))(\text{SUB}_3(\rho)$
$$\bigsqcup_{u \in D(\text{REL}(k)(\{\text{INF}(\vee\!\!\!\vee)(u)(\tau \cup \langle \lambda, C \rangle \cup \langle \lambda 0, N \rangle \cup \langle \lambda 00, u \rangle, \lambda 1, \langle \diamond, \# \rangle, k); u \in U\})}$$
   $\text{INF}(\vee\!\!\!\vee)(u)(\tau \cup \langle \lambda, C \rangle \cup \langle \lambda 0, N \rangle \cup \langle \lambda 00, u \rangle, \lambda 1, \langle \diamond, \# \rangle, k))))$

(127) $\text{INF}(x \vee\!\!\!\vee)(\tau, \lambda, \rho, k)$
   $= \text{INF}(\vee\!\!\!\vee)(u_0)(\tau \cup \langle \lambda, C \rangle \cup \langle \lambda 0, N \rangle \cup \langle \lambda 00, u_0 \rangle, \lambda 1, \rho, k)$
   where
   $u_0 = L(\sigma(\tau) \upharpoonright \{u \in U; \text{INF}(\vee\!\!\!\vee)(u)(\tau \cup \langle \lambda, C \rangle \cup \langle \lambda 0, N \rangle \cup \langle \lambda 00, u \rangle,$
   $\lambda 1, \rho_1, k) \in R'(k)\})$

(128) $\text{INF}(P_j^2 u_2)(u_1)(\tau, \lambda, \rho, k)$
   $= \text{INF}(P_j^2)(u_2)(u_1)(\tau \cup \langle \lambda, \vee\!\!\!\vee \rangle \cup \langle \lambda 0, N \rangle \cup \langle \lambda 00, u \rangle, \lambda 1, \rho, k)$

(129) $\text{INF}(P_j^2 \exists)(u_1)(\tau, \lambda, \rho, k)$

$$= \prod_{u_2 \in D(\text{REL}(k)(\{\text{INF}(P_j^2)(u_2)(u_1)(\tau \cup \langle \lambda, \vee^\rho \rangle \cup \langle \lambda 0, N \rangle \cup \langle \lambda 00, u_2 \rangle, \lambda 1, \rho, k): u_2 \in U\}))}$$

$$\text{INF}(P_j^2)(u_2)(u_1)(\tau \cup \langle \lambda, \vee^\rho \rangle \cup \langle \lambda 0, N \rangle \cup \langle \lambda 00, u_2 \rangle, \lambda 1, \rho, k)$$

(130) $\text{INF}(P_j^2 \forall)(u_1)(\tau, \lambda, \langle \lambda', \alpha \rangle^\frown \rho, k)$

$= \text{INF}(\alpha)(\text{SUB}_2(\lambda')(\text{SUB}_3(\rho)$

$$\left(\bigsqcup_{u_2 \in D(\text{REL}(k)(\{\text{INF}(P_j^2)(u_2)(u_1)(\tau \cup \langle \lambda, \vee^\rho \rangle \cup \langle \lambda 0, N \rangle \cup \langle \lambda 00, u_2 \rangle, \lambda 1, \langle \diamond, \# \rangle, k): u_2 \in U\}))} \right.$$

$$\text{INF}(P_j^2)(u_2)(u_1)(\tau \cup \langle \lambda, \vee^\rho \rangle \cup \langle \lambda 0, N \rangle \cup \langle \lambda 00, u_2 \rangle, \lambda 1, \langle \diamond, \# \rangle, k))))$$

(131) $\text{INF}(P_j^2 x)(u_1)(\tau, \lambda, \rho, k)$

$= \text{INF}(P_j^2)(u_2)(u_1)(\tau \cup \langle \lambda, \vee^\rho \rangle \cup \langle \lambda 0, N \rangle \cup \langle \lambda 00, u_2 \rangle, \lambda 1, \rho, k)$

where

$u_2 = L(\sigma(\tau) \upharpoonright \{u: \text{INF}(P_j^2)(u)(u_1)(\tau \cup \langle \lambda, \vee^\rho \rangle \cup \langle \lambda 0, N \rangle \cup \langle \lambda 00, u_2 \rangle, \lambda 1, \rho, k) \in R'(k)\})$

(132) $\text{INF}(| c)(u)(\tau, \lambda, \rho, k)$

$= \text{INF}(c)(\tau \cup \langle \lambda, \vee^\rho \rangle \cup \langle \lambda 0, 1 \rangle, \lambda 1, \rho, k)$

(133) $\text{INF}(P_j^1)(u)(\tau, \lambda, \langle \lambda', \alpha \rangle^\frown \rho, k)$

$= \text{INF}(\alpha)(\tau \cup \langle \lambda, P_j^1 \rangle, \lambda', \rho, \{V \in k: \langle u_1 \rangle \in V(P_j^1)\})$

(134) $\text{INF}(P_j^2)(u_2)(u_1)(\tau_1, \lambda, \langle \lambda', \alpha \rangle^\frown \rho, k)$

$= \text{INF}(\alpha)(\tau \cup \langle \lambda, P_j^2 \rangle, \lambda', \rho, \{V \in k: \langle u_1, u_2 \rangle \in V(P_j^2)\})$

Linguistics Program
University Park, Pa., U.S.A.

BIBLIOGRAPHY

Karttunen, Lauri (1975), 'Presupposition and Linguistic Context', *Theoretical Linguistics*.
Scott, Dana and Strachey, Christopher (1972), 'Toward a Mathematical Semantics for Computer Languages', *Symposium on Computers and Automata*, Brooklyn Polytechnic, pp. 19–46.
Smaby, Richard (1976), 'Ambiguity of Pronouns' (manuscript).
Smaby, Richard (1974), 'Subordinate Clauses and Asymmetry in English', *Journal of Linguistics*, pp. 235–269.

EDWARD KEENAN

NEGATIVE COREFERENCE:
GENERALIZING QUANTIFICATION FOR
NATURAL LANGUAGE

I shall argue here that standard logic is not sufficiently rich to represent the means natural languages use to restrict the coreference of noun phrases. I will propose to extend standard logic by adding a class of *reference restricting operators*[1] which can represent the required properties of natural language.

In Section 1 below I summarize several criteria that the structures which represent the logical properties of natural language (henceforth Natural Logic), should satisfy. In Section 2 I employ these criteria to justify the addition of reference restricting operators (RROs) to standard logic. And in Section 3 I provide a partial formalization of Natural Logic and mention a few unsolved problems that the RROs, despite appearances, are not adequate to handle.

1. ADEQUACY CRITERIA FOR NATURAL LOGIC

1.1. *The generality criterion*

Natural Logic should define the class of logical structures which we need to represent the logical properties of any particular natural language. It may be the case, as is argued in Keenan (1975a), that natural languages vary with regard to their logical expressive power and hence with regard to the class of logical structures needed to represent them. Thus Natural Logic will define the class of possible logical structures from which the logic for any particular language may be chosen. If natural languages are logically distinct then an additional component of Natural Logic would be the description of how a possible human language can choose the logical structures it expresses from the set of possibilities afforded by Natural Logic. Although we do not discuss the nature of such a component here, we will argue that certain logical structures are 'harder' to express in natural language than others in the sense that if a language can express them it must be able to express the others as well. That is, a language is not free to choose at random from among the set of possible logical structures but rather certain choices are constrained by the prior choice of other options.

77

F. Guenthner and S. J. Schmidt (eds.), Formal Semantics and Pragmatics for Natural Languages, 77–105. All Rights Reserved.

1.2. *The criterion of logical adequacy*

For a set of logical structures to be logically adequate for a natural language it must correctly represent the logical properties of each sentence (and more generally each linguistic structure) of the language, and more generally it must correctly determine the logical relations which obtain among the sentences of the language. Being *logically true* is an example of a logical property of sentences, being a *logical consequence of*, a *logical pre-supposition of*, a *true answer to*, etc., are examples of logical relations. We shall not attempt a general definition of *logical property/relation* here, although the ones we consider are all ones which depend on the *truth* relation — a relation between a sentence and the world. Thus a sentence is *true* in a given state of the world if indeed the world is the way the sentence says it is. We cannot hope of course to characterize the actual truth conditions of every sentence in every language — this would require far more knowledge than we are ever likely to have. We can however characterize dependencies of truth conditions of sentences. Thus while we cannot say what the world must be like for *John loves Mary* to be true, we can say unequivocally that whatever the world is like, if it is such that *it is John who loves Mary* is true then it is also such that *John loves Mary* is true. And in general, whenever the truth of one sentence is sufficient for the truth of another we say that the first *logically implies* (*entails, has as a logical consequence*) the other.

We shall be particularly concerned in this paper with the relative truth conditions of negative sentences. Since it is clear that the truth of a negative sentence depends, at least in part, on the truth conditions of the sentence of which it is the negation, it is clear that the meaning of natural language negation is one of the things we want to characterize in Natural Logic. What is of particular interest here is that in natural language not all the information in an affirmative sentence is affected by negating it. Thus, to take the classic example, the natural denial of *the king of France is bald*, namely *No, he isn't* (*No, the king of France is not bald*) does not deny that France has a king, it only denies that that king is bald. Thus for the negative sentence to be true, as well as the affirmative one, it must be the case that France has a king. And thus we have a non-trivial sentence which is a logical consequence of an affirmative sentence as well as its negation. Such sentences we shall call *logical presuppositions* of the affirmative sentence, and in general any information in a sentence which is not affected by denying it we shall call *logically presupposed*. Information which is affected by negation will be called *logically asserted*. For example, consequences of a given sentence which are not presuppositions of it are *assertions* of it.[2]

To account for the consequence relation in natural language then Natural Logic must represent the notion *true in a state of the world*, which standard logic does in various well known model theoretic ways. Given such a representation for the logical structures of a given natural language then, we can determine whether the set of such structures is logically adequate by, in principle, investigating each pair of sentences in the language, and whenever the truth of one sentence is judged by native speakers to be sufficient to guarantee the truth of another it must be the case that the logical structure we assign to the second is true in every state of the world in which the logical structure we assign to the first is true. Otherwise the logical structures are not adequate for that language.

Similarly Natural Logic must assign a meaning to negation which is such that, at the very least, a negative sentence is never true when its non-negative counterpart is true. How to distinguish the presuppositions of a sentence from those consequences which are merely assertions however is less well understood. The approach we adopt here is to assign value *false* to an affirmative sentence only in those cases where the negative sentence is assigned value *true* and conversely. If, in a given state of affairs, a presupposition of a given sentence fails, then neither it nor its negation will be true, and the given sentence will be left without a truth value (or alternatively, assigned a third value). We adopt this approach for ease of presentation only. Other means of characterizing presuppositions are available (cf. Van Fraassen, 1969). For our purposes here it is sufficient that some means is adopted for distinguishing assertions from presuppositions. Once we adopt some means of doing this formally then again we can evaluate, now with respect to presupposition, the adequacy of a given set of logical structures for a given language. Namely, if native speakers judge that both some sentence and its natural denial logically imply another sentence, then the logical structure we assign to that other sentence must be true in any state of affairs in which the logical structure of the first sentence or its negation is true. Otherwise the set of logical structures is inadequate in this respect.

1.3. *Naturalness conditions*

Basically we would like the logical structure of a sentence (or any other linguistic structure) to have as many structural properties in common with that sentence *as possible*. This is natural since it is in fact on the basis of those structural properties that we do infer consequences and pre-suppositions, and in Natural Logic we do want to characterize as directly as possible those properties of natural language which speakers actually avail themselves of in making inferences. An ideal form of this condition, which cannot in principle be realized in natural language, is given below as the Correspondence Principle:

THE CORRESPONDENCE PRINCIPLE (CP)

Each linguistic structure in a language (sentence, noun phrase, etc.) is isomorphic to its logical structure. So, e.g., there is a function from the structures of a language to the set of logical structures such that each structure s is associated with its logical structure $l(s)$ in such a way that each distinct constituent of s corresponds, or is associated with, a distinct constituent of $l(s)$ and conversely.

If the CP held however it would be possible to define logical relations like consequence directly on the sentences of the language itself. But this clearly is not possible. The reason is that natural language sentences are quite generally ambiguous, that is they have more than one distinct meaning and hence can be both true and not true in the same state of affairs, depending upon which meaning we consider the sentence in. If this is the case for some sentence S then we cannot even argue that S logically implies itself, since it is not necessarily true in every state of affairs in which it is true! Logical structures then must be semantically unambiguous and receive only one semantic interpretation in each state of the world. And a natural language sentence which is ambiguous must be associated with a set of logical structures each of which represents exactly one of its meanings. We can expect then that any of the logical structures for a given sentence (noun phrase, etc.) will differ in structure from it to some extent. Accepting the existence of such differences we can still offer the following version of the Naturalness Condition:

THE NATURALNESS CONDITION

Given two sets of logical structures for a given language, choose that set which in general yields the closest correspondence between sentences (noun phrases, etc.) and their logical structures.

We have, at the moment, no general procedure to compute the degree of correspondence between logical structures and natural language structures, but some cases are clear enough pretheoretically to serve as limiting cases of a definition for such a procedure. For example, (b) below clearly corresponds better to (a) than does (c).

(a)   Socrates is mortal
(b)   Mortal(s)
(c)   Mortal(s) & $((\exists x)\text{Horse}(x) \lor -(\exists x)\text{Horse}(x))$

Furthermore we can suggest the following constraints that a reasonably good correspondence should satisfy:

CORRESPONDENCE CONSTRAINTS (CCs)

1. There are only a finite number of ways any of the logical structures for a given natural language structure may differ from it. Thus there should be a computable function (relative to the structures of the language) which associates natural language structures with their logical structures.
2. If two natural language structures S and T are logically distinct, e.g., have different consequences, presuppositions etc., then any logical structure for S corresponds more closely to S than it does to T. This is a kind of rationality condition, in effect. If it were to fail then, e.g., the structure of T would be a more natural way to express the logical meaning of S than S itself!
3. Logical structures for S and T are structurally similar to the same extent that S and T are themselves structurally similar. Thus for example if two sentences in a language have the same syntactic form (not just the same surface form) then their logical structures should also have the same syntactic form.
4. If the syntactic structure of S is a function of that of T then the logical structure of S is a function of that of the logical structure of T. This is, in effect, a slight generalization of the Fregean condition that the meaning of the whole is a function of the meaning of the parts. It is a generalization in the sense that what we count as a part of, say, a sentence S does not have to appear in surface as a constituent of it. Thus, e.g., we want to say that the logical meaning of a negative sentence in natural language is a function of the meaning of the affirmative one, although the affirmative one will often not appear as a constituent in surface of the negative one.

Perhaps needless to say, the Naturalness Condition and the Correspondence Constraints are very much the subject of further research.

Nonetheless they are stated with enough precision to be useful in the discussion to follow.

2. REFERENCE RESTRICTING OPERATORS (RROs) IN NATURAL LOGIC

We now justify extending standard logic by the addition of a class of RROs. These operators, like quantifiers in standard logic, are operators which form formulas from formulas [3] and are introduced by a rule of the following form:

(i)   if F is a formula in Natural Logic then $(Rx, y)F$ is a formula in Natural Logic, where y is variable occuring free [4] in F, x is some referential expression (variable, proper noun, common noun phrase) and R is any of a class of symbols expressing the way in which the reference of y is constrained relative to the reference of x.

For example, (1b) below would be (roughly) the logical structure assigned to (1a) in standard logic. (1c) is our proposal for Natural Logic.

(1a)   he criticized himself
(1b) xCx
(1c) $(I\ x,y)(xCy)$.

(1b) might be read out as 'x criticized x', whereas (1c) might be read out as 'Identifying y with x, x criticized y'. Thus in standard logic the identity of reference of the subject and object phrases in (1a) is expressed by using occurences of the same referential expression in both argument positions of the logical predicate. On our proposal however distinct referential expressions are used and an overt operator is added which constrains them to be interpreted as the same object. The identity operator, I, is but one of several RROs we will include in natural logic.

In the simple case cited above there is no difference in logical adequacy between standard logic and natural logic. Our primary motivation for adding the class of RROs to Natural Logic is that many languages present ways of constraining the reference of referential positions which cannot be captured by using occurences of the same referential expression (or variable bound by a quantifier phrase). Thus many languages present overt operators which constrain one referential position to be different in reference from that of another. Consider for example the following sentence

from Mojave, a Yuman Indian language, kindly provided to me by Pamela
Munro (see also Munro (1974) for further discussion).

(2a)	$n^y a$- iva:-		k	$yaamo$:m-		k
(2b)	$n^y a$- iva:-		m	$yaamo$:m-		k
	'when- arrive + 3sg-			drunk 3sg-past'.		

The sentences in (2) differ solely by the presence of -k or -m as the final suffix
on the subordinate verb 'arrive'. Either sentence might be translated into
English as *when he arrived he was drunk*. However in (2a) the suffix -k
unequivocally indicates that the person who arrived and the person who
was drunk are the same. It thus forces the identity of reference of subject
pronouns (contained in the verb form) of the two verbs. In (2b) however, the
use of the suffix -m means that the subject phrases of the two verbs refer to
different individuals. We note that either of the two suffixes may be present
if either of the two verbs has a full NP subject.

Logically the same subject suffix -k is similar to a reflexive marker, such
as a reflexive pronoun, in that it constrains two referential positions to refer
to the same thing. The difference between same-subject marking in Mojave
and reflexivity in English is in the choice of NP positions whose coreference
they can constrain. Reflexivity in English is largely restricted to constrain
the reference of positions which are arguments of the same predicate,
whereas the same-subject or different-subject marking in Mojave
constrains the reference of a main clause subject and the subject of a clause
subordinate to the main clause.

Further, same-subject marking is like reflexivity in English in that the
stipulation of coreference is not affected by negation. That is, if we deny
that, e.g., *John criticized himself* it is still understood that the person who
we are denying that John criticized is John himself. Similarly if we deny (2a)
in Mojave it still must be the case that the one who was drunk were the
same. All that is denied is that that individual was drunk when he arrived.

Different-subject marking in Mojave patterns morphologically like
same-subject marking in that the different-subject affix goes in the same
position on the verb as the same-subject affix. Logically they are similar in
that they both constrain the reference of what are otherwise independently
referring positions. The different-subject marker however constrains them
to be different in reference. Further, this constraint is presuppositional in
the sense that it is not affected by negation. Thus for (2b) to be true it must
be the case that two distinct individuals are referred to, and when the one
arrived the other was drunk. Similarly the natural (full) denial of (2b),

namely (3) below, still requires that the one who arrived and the one asserted to be drunk are different. It only denies that in fact the person in question was drunk.

(3) $n^y a$- iva:- m $yaamo$:m- $mpotč$
         when- arrive + 3sg ds drunk + 3sg-neg
         'When he arrived he wasn't drunk'.

We can easily represent this negative constraint on coreference using a negative RRO. Thus the rough logical structure for (2b) would be (4).

(4) $(N\ x, y)$ (when x arrived, y was drunk).

And in general, where F is any formula in Natural Logic in which y occurs free, $(N\ x, y)F$ will be a formula. The semantics of such formulas is given in (5).

(5) $(N\ x, y)F$ is true in an interpretation just in case:
                        1. x and y are interpreted as different members of the universe of discourse, and
                        2. F is true.
         $(N\ x, y)F$ is false in an interpretation just in case:
                        1. x and y are interpreted as different members of the universe of discourse, and
                        2. F is false.
         $(N\ x, y)F$ is valueless (or third valued) in an interpretation just in case it is neither true nor false in that interpretation.

It is clear then that for a negatively restricted formula to be either true or false, and hence for either it or its negation to be true, it must be the case that the negatively restricted positions refer to different individuals, and in this sense then the coreference constraint is presupposed.

We see no natural way to express such negative constraints in standard logic. Obviously a logical structure like (6), in which distinct, unbound, variables are used is not sufficient, since distinct unbound variables may always be interpreted, by accident so to speak, as the same individual, yet the logical structure for sentences like (2b) in Mojave must require that the positions refer to distinct individuals.

(6)   when x arrived, y was drunk.

Another alternative in standard logic might be a logical structure like (7) in which we overtly require that x and y refer differently.

(7)   (when x arrived, y was drunk) & $(x \neq y)$

Such a structure however fails to be logically adequate since it *asserts* the distinctness of x and y. That is, (7) may be merely false, and hence its negation true, if x and y refer to the same individual but that individual was not drunk when he arrived. But this does not adequately represent, as we have seen, the case in which the negation (of 2b) in Mojave is true.

Consequently we feel that for reasons of logical adequacy and generality, negative RROs should be added to Natural Logic.

We should perhaps point out that negative coreference is not an aberrant fact about some little spoken American Indian language. Such restrictions are, it appears, rather widely distributed. Thus many languages of the Yuman group present such operators. See Jacobsen (1967) for some discussion. In addition some Uto-Aztecan languages like Hopi present such negative RROs. See Keenan (1975a, 1975b) for some examples. In addition such negative RROs are a typological trait of the Eastern New Guinea Highlands languages. The example below from Fore (Scott, 1973) is illustrative.

(8a)   *kana-ogà-*   *na wa-tà-*   *y-   e*
         come-*ds* 3*sg* past   3*sg* go-past-   3*sg*-indic
         'He came and he (different) went'

(8b)   *kana-nta*   *na wa-tà-*   *y-   e*
         come-*ss* 3*sg* past   3*sg* go-past-   3*sg*-indic
         'He came and he (same) went'.

Thus many languages require logical structures with negative RROs, so this is clearly an option that Natural Logic should make available. On the other hand, it does not seem likely that all languages express such operators. English, in particular, does not have at least an obvious need of such operators. The transformational literature (see, e.g., Reinhart (1976) and references cited there) does discuss certain syntactic patterns which appear to force a disjoint reference of two referential expressions. Thus in distinction to (9a) below, in which the subject and object phrases must be coreferential, it appears in (9b) that they are naturally judged to be different in reference.

(9a)   John criticized himself
(9b)   John criticized him.

The judgments of negative coreference in (9b) however have, in our opinion, a different logical status from those which obtain for the negative RROs in, e.g., Mojave and Fore. In our opinion, all we can infer from (9b) on a 'normal' occasion of its use, is that the speaker does not intend to indicate that the person criticized and the criticizer are the same. It might well be the case that in a normal assertion of (9b) *John* and *him* do in fact refer to the same individual — it is sufficient for the use of (9b) that the speaker does not know this. It is of course a pragmatic condition on the 'normal' uses of proper nouns and definite pronouns that the speaker can identify their referents in a socially acceptable way. Thus most usually one who asserts (9b) will know if they refer to the same individual, and if they do the most normal way to express the thought would be to use the reflexive pronoun, as in (9a). Hence pragmatically we can typically infer from the absence of the reflexive form that the referents of the two referential expressions are different. This is perhaps easier to see in a sentence like (10).

(10)   One of the athletes criticized him but the others were indifferent.

Imagine (10) as a report of an interview with the athletes competing say at an international tennis match. They are asked to comment on the much publicized unusual court behavior of, e.g., the Romanian contender. Clearly someone might summarize the results of the interviews by using (10), and he clearly need not know whether the athlete who criticized the Romanian contender was the Romanian contender or not.

Similarly in a sentence like (9b) in which the subject phrase is a proper noun. Imagine for example that Mr. Glenn is the recently appointed bank manager of a local bank, and as such is obligated to adhere to the bank's policy of not giving loans to students, even though he himself is strongly in favor of such loans. So he writes an article in the local paper criticizing the bank and the mercenary actions of its manager. Glenn however does not identify himself in the article as the bank manager. Someone reporting on the article might use (11).

(11)   Perhaps the bank manager will begin to give loans to students since *Mr. Glenn has criticized him* in a recent article.

Clearly in our example *Mr. Glenn* and *him* do in fact refer to the same individual, although the speaker presumably, does not know this. If the identity of the two is pointed out to him he might be surprised (or he might not, if he knows Glenn to be a clever politician) but the truth value of the original claim, (11), does not change. (11) is still true in that state of affairs.

Thus the truth of a sentence like (9b) does not require that the two referential expressions refer to different individuals. Compare this, e.g., with the judgment of sameness of reference of the subject and object expressions in (9a) *John criticized himself.* Here if we point out, contrary to the speaker's intention, that the person John criticized was not in fact John himself then we have more than the speaker's surprise to contend with: The sentence is clearly untrue in such a state of affairs.

Now, with regard to the negatively restricted sentences in Mojave and Fore we feel that their truth value status is like that of the reflexive usage in (9a) rather than the non-reflexive usage in (9b). That is the speaker of such sentences unequivocally intends that the reference of the two expressions be different rather than merely being non-committal as to the identity of their referents. The reason is that pragmatically speaking, the purpose or use of what we have called negative RROs is to indicate that the speaker is changing the topic of discussion. That is, such restrictions primarily apply to the subject positions of adjacent clauses. If, at the end of the first clause, the speaker is going to maintain his topic in the next one he uses a same-subject marker. But if he is going to change his topic of discussion he uses a different-subject marker. There is then a subtle, but logically important difference between intending that the referents be different and merely not intending that they be the same. For other possible candidates of negative RROs in natural languages see Keenan (1975b). And again, perhaps needless to say, the relative inaccessibility of the languages which seem to evidence the clearest cases of such operators does mean that their nature and use are not completely well understood.

Given the existence of negative RROs in Natural Logic it is natural to wonder if natural languages possess other restrictions on the reference of NPs which can be captured by the use of such operators. The most obvious candidate of course is the stipulation of positive coreference, evidenced in our English examples by the use of reflexive pronouns and in Mojave and Fore by the use of same-subject markers. We may easily represent positive coreference in Natural Logic by the addition of an identity RRO as follows: If F is a formula in Natural Logic then $(I\ x, y)F$ is a formula in Natural Logic. The semantics for these formulas is given below:

(12)　　$(I\ x, y)F$ is true in an interpretation i just in case letting y denote the same thing as x, F is true.

　　　　$(I\ x, y)F$ is false in i if F is false when y is interpreted identical in reference to x. Otherwise $(I\ x, y)F$ is third valued or valueless.

The case for adding the identity RRO to Natural Logic appears less compelling than for the negative RRO. Basically the truth and falsehood conditions represented in (12), and hence the consequences and presuppositions of formulas having that form, would be the same if the identity of reference were expressed by using the same variable in the relevant referential positions. Thus the truth conditions of $(I\ x, y)F$ above are the same as those of F', where F' results from F by replacing each free occurrence of y by an occurrence of x. Analogous claims hold for the falsehood conditions in (12).

However, even on the basis of the limited data so far presented we do have a naturalness argument in support of adding the identity operator to natural logic. Namely, if we compare the sentences in Mojave (2a, b) and in Fore (8a, b) which differ only by stipulating positive or negative coreference on the two referential positions we see that the surface forms of those sentences are almost identical, they differ solely by the choice of morpheme which gives the reference restrictions. Thus by the third Correspondence Constraint, syntactically similar sentences have syntactically similar logical structures, the logical structures we assign to such sentences appear natural, since they also are identical except at one point — namely the choice RRO. Note that if we took perhaps the most plausible means of representing these pairs of sentences in standard logic, namely the one where positive coreference is indicated by using identical variables and the negative one by using distinct variables and conjoining a sentence which states that the variables are different in reference, the third Correspondence Constraint would be less well satisfied since the surface forms would differ only by a single choice of morpheme but the logical structures would differ by the addition of an entire sentence. The case is quite similar to the Socrates-is-mortal one we used to support the Naturalness Condition in the first place. Further, we shall consider other types of reference restrictions in natural language which interact with the identity operator and yield naturalness arguments applied directly to English.

First however we would like to point out an advantage of having both positive and negative RROs in Natural Logic which is not included in our general adequacy criteria, but which depends directly on the motivation for formulating Natural Logic in the first place. Namely, we want to know what logical structures for natural language look like not solely because we want to explicitly represent notions like consequence and presupposition but also because we want to make generalizations concerning the logical expressive power of natural languages. To give just one example, we have argued in Keenan (1975c) that languages which form relative clauses by presenting in surface a personal pronoun in the position relativized (e.g., they say *the girl that John saw her* rather than *the girl that John saw*) permit the formation of a larger class of relative clauses (which they do) *because* they present in surface form of the logical structure of relative clauses. That is, they present in surface more of what we need to know to understand the reference of a relative clause. We obviously cannot make such generalizations without knowing what the logical structures for relative clauses look like.

Another type of generalization we are interested in making in universal grammar concerns the distribution of syntactic or semantic properties. For example, we know that (Greenburg, 1963) if verbs agree with subjects in gender in a given language they will also agree in number. Thus among the class of possible verb agreement features (like person, number, gender, definiteness), certain features in a language require the presence of others. Thus in defining the class of possible human languages we can state a non-trivial constraint on the form of such languages by saying that we may only have gender agreement if we have number agreement.

Similarly the positive and negative RROs we have posited also belong to the same logical class of operators and we might expect to make such generalizations on members of this class. And we can, as (13) illustrates.

(13a)   If a language can express a negative restriction between two referential positions, then it can in general express a positive restriction between.

(13b)   If a language has means of restricting the reference of NP positions at all, then in general it can restrict the reference of NPs relative to the main clause subject NP.[5]

(13a) says in effect that it is harder to express negative coreference than positive coreference and thus in designing a possible human language if we endow the language with negative RROs then we must also endow it with positive ones which cover the same ground. We may however expect to find languages, very possibly English, which have positive RROs but no negative RROs.

(13b) states that main clause subjects are the primary controllers of reference restrictions, regardless of whether the restriction is positive or negative. Thus we could not have a human language in which, e.g., only direct objects but not subjects could control the reference of reflexive pronouns (assuming that is the only means in that language of stipulating positive coreference).

The generalization in (13a) in fact suggests a simplification of our logical notation. We may consider that expressing positive coreference is the most usual or least marked type of reference restriction. Thus if we do not overtly indicate the reference restriction between two restricted referential expressions we will assume it to be the identity restriction. Thus instead of expressing (14a) by (14b) we shall usually merely write (14c).

(14a)   he criticized himself
(14b) $(I\ x, y)\ (xCy)$
(14c) $(x, y)\ (xCy)$.

We consider now a further application of the RROs we have discussed. RROs form logical structures of the form $(R\ x, y)F$, as we have seen, where y is constrained to be an unbound variable occurring in F. x may be any of a large variety of referential expressions. We have so far only considered the case where x was itself a variable distinct from y occurring free in F. Now we consider cases in which x is a *definite noun phrase* such as *John, the man who left early*, etc. (15b) and (16b) illustrate the logical structures we propose for the English sentences in (15a) and (16a) respectively (ignoring those aspects of logical structure which do not directly pertain to coreference).

(15a)   John drinks
(15b) $(J, x)\ (x\ drink)$
(16a)   The man who left early drinks
(16b)   (the man who left early, $x)\ (x\ drink)$.

We might read out (15b) for example as 'Identifying John with x, x drinks'. Our intuition here is that (15a) is not the simple sentence it appears to be, but rather consists of a simpler sentence *he drink* in which the pronoun *he* is overtly constrained to refer to John. Thus proper nouns, and definite noun phrases in general do not directly occur in the argument positions of predicates, rather pronouns, or more exactly variables since we are speaking of logical structures, occur in the argument slots, and definite noun phrases express restrictions on the reference of the variable. The restriction is of course the identity restriction, expressed in (15) and (16) using the abbreviated notation discussed above. Notice now the logical structure we propose for (17a).

(17a)   John criticized himself
(17b) $(J, x)\ (x, y)\ (xCy)$.

(17b) might be read as 'Identifying x with John, and y with x, x criticized y'. Note then that the formulas formed from RROs the x position remains unbound and so may have its reference restricted by the addition of further operators.

At this point the reader may object that logical structures like (17b) appear rather unnatural by our criteria since the correspondence between (17a) and (17b) does not appear very close to one-to-one. And we would agree that there is a significant disparity. Note however that the disparity evidenced in (17) is merely the result of iterating the application of operators for which we already have some motivation. Thus it is conformity with the first Correspondence Principle which requires that logical structures differ in only a finite number of ways from the sentences they represent. The number of ways in which (17b) differs from (17a) is no greater than the number of ways that, e.g., (15b) differs from (15a).

Furthermore, as regards naturalness, consider the usual logical structure for (17a), namely (18).

(18) jCj.

The coreference is expressed by the use of the same referential expressions in the two positions. But this appears universally unnatural in that no natural language normally expresses coreference between subject and object of a verb by repeating the subject phrase. That is, no language would ever as a norm, express the idea in (17a) by something like *John hit John*. In fact the most natural interpretation of this latter sentence is that there are two individuals, both named John, and that the one hit the other. In other words, the most natural interpretation is one in which coreference of the two positions does not obtain.

In terms of naturalness conditions then (18) looks unnatural in at least two respects. First, the direct correspondence between (18) and (17a) is not good since in (18) there are identical expressions, the two occurrences of the individual constant j, which correspond to constitutents of the English sentence which are not identical, namely *John* and *himself*. And second, it appears that the fourth Correspondence Principle (the logical structure of a sentence S should correspond more closely to it than to any other sentence not logically equivalent to it) has been violated since (18) clearly corresponds more closely to *John criticized John* than it does to *John criticized himself*, yet it is the latter whose logical properties it is supposed to represent. It is not obvious then that the lack of correspondence between (17b) and (17a) is worse than between (18) and (17a). We are inclined to prefer our proposal over (18) since the violation of the fourth Correspondence Principle seems to us more serious than the repeated but systematic differences which result from our proposal. Furthermore, we shall argue that in terms of the Generality Criterion the type of miscorrespondence exhibited in (17) is much less severe in a great many languages than it is in English.

Consider for example the following sentence from Swahili (Alexander Kimenyi, personal communication) and the logical structure we assign it.

> (19a)   wa- naume wa- li-   m- piga m- ke
>   they- man   they- past- her- hit she- woman
>   'The men hit the woman'
> (19b)   (the men, x) (the woman, y) (xHy).

Note first that the two noun phrases in (19a), *wanaume* and *mke* present prefixes *wa-* and *m-* respectively which we have glossed as pronouns (although they would more normally be called noun class markers) and that these prefixes also both occur within what appears to be the verb. Further, within the 'verb' these morphemes clearly have a pronominal, that is referential, function. Thus in a situation in which a woman and a group of men had been identified, the normal way to say *they hit her* would be as in (20).

> (20)   wa- li-   m- piga
>   they- past- her- hit
>   'They hit her'.

(20) is as much a sentence in Swahili as is its English translation. The prefixes *wa-* and *m-* then clearly have a referential function so we are justified in calling them pronouns. And of course such pronouns correspond very well with our use of variables in the logical structure for (19a). In fact, ignoring the past tense marker in (19a) there is a one-to-one correspondence between (19a) and (19b).

Further this type of correspondence recurs in many unrelated languages. (21)–(23) illustrate this.

> (21)   *Genoese* (Vattuone, 1975)
>   *a Kataynin a   vende i   pesi*
>   she Catherine she sells they fish
>   'Catherine sells fish'.

(22)   *Avar* (Anderson, 1975)[6]
         v- as v- eker- ula
         he- boy he- run- present
         'The boy runs'.
(23)   *Hebrew*
         anaxnu katav-nu
         we   wrote-we
         'We wrote'

(For further examples see Keenan, 1972.)

It appears then that, at least for a fair range of simple sentences, the logical structures we propose do present a reasonably good correspondence to sentences in natural language. At the very least such a correspondence must be regarded as natural, even if it is not realized in all languages.

Even more important, our logical structures enable us to explain why structures like (20) in Swahili ('They hit her') do function as sentences, that is, are the kind of structure which has a truth value in a given state of affairs. The reason is that (20), on our analysis, expresses a logical structure which contains a binary predicate symbol and two referential expressions, expressed by pronominal forms in surface. On the other hand, the structures proved by standard logic would, in effect, have the phrases *the men* and *the woman* occurring directly in the argument positions of (19), and consequently (20) should simply express the predicate *hit* without any argument expressions, and hence should not be the sort of linguistic object which carries a truth value. On our analysis, (19), 'The men hit the woman' contains, in effect, the sentence 'They hit her' but supplies the additional restrictions that *they* must refer to the men, and *her* must refer to the woman. It appears then that our logical structures conform to the fourth correspondence constraint (if the form of S is a function of that of T then the logical structure of S is a function of the logical structure of T) since formally (19) contains (20) as a subpart and differs from it merely by the addition of full noun phrases. And our logical structures for (20) contain the logical structure of (19) as a subpart, differing from it by the addition of the RROs which represent the full noun phrases.

Our logical structures enable us to explain an additional fact which is unexplained in terms of standard logical structures and not even adequately represented syntactically in current linguistic theory. Namely, it is possible within our framework that the variable whose reference is restricted by some operator may still express information about the referent which is not contained within the restriction. Within our framework pronouns correspond in general to variables in logical structure but it is clearly not the case that a given pronoun can, in principle refer to any object in the universe of discourse. Pronouns like *he* can only refer to masculine objects for example, *she* to feminine ones and so on. To represent these facts we will require that Natural Logic have several different *sorts* of variables, such as ones that can only refer to masculine objects, others that can only refer to feminine objects, etc. Different languages of course will avail themselves of these sortal distinctions to a greater or lesser extent. Restricting ourselves for sake of example to third person pronouns logical structures for English might need four sorts of variables — those expressed by *he*, *she*, *it*, and *they* for example. Languages like Malagasy would only need one sort of variable (see Keenan, 1976a for some discussion of Malagasy pronouns) and Bantu languages like Swahili would typically need about 20 sorts.

Given the addition of sortal variables to Natural Logic it is clear that our RROs do not require that the expression which restricts the reference of a variable is necessarily interpreted in isolation from a particular formula, as an object within the domain of reference of any particular variable of some sort. Thus it would be natural within our logic to find languages in which for example the pronominal elements on verbs are restricted to refer to objects of a certain sort even though the definite noun phrase with which they are coreferential does not *have* to be interpreted as an object of that sort. And this is in fact the case.

Thus in (24) from Avar (Don Stilo, personal communication) the independent object pronoun *mun* 'me' could refer to either a male or female speaker. But the pronominal form on the verb must distinquish male from female reference.

(24a)	*dos-*	*ta*	*mun*	*vi-*		*xula*
	3*sg-*	*erg*	*lsg*	*me* masc-		see
	'He saw me (masculine)'					
	dos-	*ta*	*mun*	*yi-*		*xula*
	3*sg-*	*erg*	*lsg*	*me* fem-		see
	'He saw me (feminine)'.					

Similarly in Russian the name *Sasha* might name either a boy or a girl, but in *Sasha pil* 'Sasha drank' the verb form tells us that Sasha must be male, whereas in *Sasha pila* 'Sasha drank' *Sasha* must be female. Similarly in Hebrew *Tal medaber* 'Tal is speaking' presupposes that Tal is a male, whereas *Tal medaberet* presupposes that Tal is female. And note the following example from Spanish (Alfredo Hurtado, personal communication).

(25)   *las mujeres protesta- mos pero los hombres ...*
    the women complain- we but the men ...
    'We women complain but the men ...'

Here the restricting expression, *las mujeres* 'the women' does not, obviously, have to include the speaker of the sentence among the set women it refers to, but the pronominal form on the verb does require this.

These examples serve as well to refute the standard linguistic account of pronominal forms on verbs. On that approach, such pronominal forms are not present in the underlying syntactic structure of sentences.

Full noun phrases occupy the subject and object positions of the verb. A rule of verb agreement, which is sensitive to certain semantic or syntactic features of full noun phrases then copies some of these features onto the verb, and then these are realized phonologically in language particular ways. But the examples above show that the pronominal forms on the verb may have features which are not present in the full noun phrases and hence which could not be obtained by copying. In addition of course this approach cannot generate the purely pronominal sentences like (20) 'They hit her' in Swahili, since there are no full noun phrases from which the pronominal forms on the verb could have been copied.

We consider now an additional class of RROs. In these cases the restricting expression x (in a formula of the form $(R\ x, y)F$) is a common noun phrase like *man, men, men who drink beer*, etc. Such noun phrases are semantically interpreted (in the simplest cases) as sets of objects from the universe of discourse, and y, the free variable in F, is restricted in any of several ways, to refer to an object within the set x.

Perhaps the simplest case of such an operator, whose existence in any natural language is problematic, is what we shall call the Specific-Indefinite operator, which yields formulas of the form $(\text{Spec}\ x, y)F$. Here y is interpreted as a member of the universe of discourse which is also within that subset denoted by x. Somewhat more formally we have:

(26) $(\text{Spec}\ x, y)F$ is true in i just in case
        1. y is interpreted as a member of the set of things x is interpreted as, and
        2. F is true.

(Spec x, y)F is false in i just in case 1 above holds but F is false
in i. Otherwise the whole formula is third valued
(or undefined).

If such operators are expressed in English it is probably in sentences like
(27).

(27)   — *A student* in my class refused to sign the petition.
        — No *he* didn't, he just didn't have a pen.

The intuition here, which we will not argue for, is that the phrase *a student* in
(27) is somehow understood to refer to some particular student who did
something rather than merely asserting the existence of such a student. To
the extent that we can deny it naturally by using a definite pronoun, as we
have above, (27) for example will be false if the specific student referred to
didn't have the property in question even though other students may have.
Thus formulas of the form (26) will contrast sharply in falsehood conditions
with the Existential operator, where the falsehood conditions require that
no member of the restricting set x have the property in question and the
truth conditions of those formulas merely require the existence of a member
of the restricting set which has the property in question. More formally the
truth conditions of the Existential operator are:

(28)   (E x, y)F is true in i just in case there is some member of the set
        x such that, letting y denote it, F is true.
        (E x, y)F is false in i just in case for no member of the set x is F
        true if y is interpreted as that member. Otherwise the
        whole formula is third valued (or undefined).

In the case of the Existential operator then y is constrained to be interpreted
as some member of the set x if the whole formula is true, but it doesn't
matter which member. y then has no independent referring properties, in
distinction to its use in Specific-Indefinite sentences where it is interpreted
as some particular object, albeit within the set x.

Clearly the Existential operator in Natural Logic has the essential
properties of the existential quantifier in standard logic, and it clearly
imposes different truth and falsehood conditions than does the Specific-
Indefinite operator. Since this distinction has been discussed at some length
in the literature it is perhaps some merit for our proposals that the RROs
can distinguish Specific-Indefinites from mere Existentials.

We consider briefly two other RROs which also restrict y to be interpreted within some designated set and then consider the merits of operators to a logic for English.

The universal operator, represented as $(A\ x, y)F$ has the following semantics (see Keenan (1972) for more discussion of its presuppositional nature, something we largely ignore here).

(29) $(A\ x, y)F$ is true in i just in case
         1. x is interpreted as a non-empty set, and
         2. interpreting y as any member of that set, F is true.
    $(A\ x, y)F$ is false in i just in case 1 above holds and for at least one member of the set x, F is false when y is interpreted as that member. In all other cases the formula is assigned the third value (or left undefined).

Finally, consider the *Only* operator as expressed in sentences like *Only conservatives voted for Smith* or *Only Fred voted for Smith*. Here we must allow that x may be either a definite or a common noun phrase, and y is restricted to refer to members of x if it is a common noun phrase and to be identical with x if it is a definite noun phrase. Assuming for simplicity of presentation that x is a common noun phrase the semantics of the *Only* operator is given (roughly) as follows (for more thorough discussion see, Geach (1962), and Keenan (1972)).

(30)   (Only $x, y)F$ is true in i just in case
         1. x is interpreted as a non-empty set,
         2. there is at least one member of the set x such that letting y denote it, F is true,
         3. for any object not in the set x, letting y denote it F is not true.
    (Only $x, y)F$ is false in i just in case
         1. conditions 1 and 2 above both hold, and
         2. there is some object not in the set x such that letting y denote it F is true.
    In all other cases the formula is third valued (or undefined).

Given (30) the reader can easily construct the truth and falsehood conditions for Only-restricted sentences when x is a definite noun phrase.

We consider now several advantages of adopting our RROs in the logical structures for English rather than merely having them as options provided by Natural Logic.

First, our treatment of *only* is logically more adequate than in standard logic since (Only x, y)F clearly presupposes that there are at least one such x such that F, this condition being required for both the truth and the falsehood conditions of (Only x, y)F. Thus our analysis predicts that both (31a) and (31b) below logically imply (31c).

(31a)   Only conservatives voted for Smith.
(31b)   Not only did conservatives vote for Smith (but so did . . .).
(31c)   At least one conservative voted for Smith.

Second, our treatment of *only* is more natural than in standard logic since the structures we propose correspond more closely to their surface expression in English. Compare, e.g., our logical structure for (31a), given as (32a) below, with that of standard logic, (32b).

(32a)   (Only conservatives, y) (y voted for Smith).
(32b)   ($\forall x$) (if x voted for Smith then x is a conservative).

(32b) for example contains an *if–then* connective conjoining two formulas and its surface realization in English contains no such connectives or conjoined sentences. Further, it is clear that (32b) corresponds more closely to either of (33a) or (33b) below than it does to (31a). Yet the sentences in (33) are not logically equivalent to (31a), hence the standard logic proposal violates the second Correspondence Constraint (which says that the logical structure for any sentence S must correspond more closely to it than to any sentence not logically equivalent to S).

(33a)   If anyone voted for Smith then he is a conservative.
(33b)   For any person, if he voted for Smith then he is a conservative.

Third, our treatment of universal quantification is logically more adequate than in standard logic since the restricting set (the domain of quantification) is presupposed non-empty. Thus we correctly predict that both (34a) and (34b) logically imply (34c).

(34a)   Every conservative voted for Smith.
(34b)   Not every conservative voted for Smith.
(34c)   There is (was) at least one conservative.

Fourth, our use of the identity RRO allows a more uniform representation of coreference than is the case in standard logic. Thus the coreference between the subject and object phrases in the sentences of (35) is felt to be the same by native speakers and is represented in exactly the same way in our system.

(35a)   John hates himself
         Natural Logic: (John, x) (x, y) (xHy)
         Standard Logic: jHj.
(35b)   Every student hates himself
         Natural Logic: (A student, x) (x, y) (xHy)
         Standard Logic: $(\forall x)$ (if x is a student then xHx).

Thus in Natural Logic coreference is always expressed in such cases by the use of a RRO. But in standard logic coreference on (35a) is effected by using the same proper name in the two positions, whereas in (35b) we need the additional requirement that the two occurrences of x are bound by the same quantifier phrase. Thus the third Correspondence Constraint, that structurally similar sentences should have structurally similar logical structures, seems better satisfied here using the logical structures we propose.

Fifth, our proposals provide more natural representations for sentences in which *only* affects a referential position constrained to corefer to some other. It is clear for example that (36) is more naturally represented by (37b), our proposal, than (37a), the usual formulation in standard logic.

(36)   He likes only himself.
(37)   (a) (xLx) & $(\forall y)$ (if xLy the $x=y$)
        (b) (Only x, y) (xLy).[6]

Note that if two *Only* operators apply in such sentences the correspondence failure in standard logic is massive, whereas in our logic we merely add one more operator.

(39a) (jLj) & $(\forall z)$ (if jLz then $j=z$) & $(\forall y)$ (if (if $(Vz)yLz$ then $y=z$) then $y=j$)
(39b)   (only John, x) (only x, y) xLy
(39c)   (only John, x) (only John, y) xLy.

Note as well that our logic provides a natural representation for *only John likes only John*, namely (39c).

Sixth, and finally, to the extent that transparent readings of noun phrases in opacity producing environments can be adequately represented by having the noun phrase occur outside the scope of the opacity creating operator, it seems to us that our logical structures present a better correspondence to surface forms than do those of standard logic. Thus the transparent reading of (40a) might be represented in standard logic by (40b), and in our logic by (40c).

(40a)   John was surprised that the man who won was Greek
(40b) $(\exists x)$ $((x = $ the man who won) & John was surprised that x was Greek)
(40c)   (the man who won, x) (John, y) (y was surprised that x was Greek)

Clearly (40b) looks unnatural since it presents an existential quantifier and an overt conjunction which do not correspond to anything in surface. (40c) does not present these operators however, and so corresponds better to (40a).

3. FORMALIZING NATURAL LOGIC

For illustrative purposes we present here a somewhat simplified semi-formalization of Natural Logic. We ignore the semantics of binary connectives like *and* and do not distinguish *sorts* of variables. We assume a basic familiarity with the model theoretic semantics for standard logic and present the formation rules for expressions of Natural Logic and their semantic interpretation simultaneously. Note that as part of the formation rules we recursively define the notion *free variable*.

An *interpretation* for Natural Logic is a four-tuple $\langle U, T, a, f \rangle$ where U is a non-empty set called the universe of discourse of the interpretation, T is a set of three truth values $\{t, f, z\}$, a is an assignment of values (in U) to the variables of Natural Logic (to designated subsets of U if we have more than one sort of variable), and f is the interpreting function which assigns truth values to formulas and denotations to noun phrases relative to the assignment a of values to the variables. An assignment of values to variables a' which differs at most on the variable y will be called a *y-variant* of a.

PRIMITIVE CATEGORIES AND THE INTERPRETATION
1. An infinite set of *variables*, assigned by a to members of U.
    $f(x) = a(x)$ for all variables x.
2. A set of *proper nouns* interpreted by f as members of U.
3. A non-empty set of *n-place predicate symbols*, each interpreted as a function from the set of *n*-tuples over U to the set of truth values T.
4. A set of *common nouns*, each interpreted as a subset of U.

5. The negation sign, $-$, interpreted as a function from T to T such that $f(-)(t) = f, f(-)(f) = t$, and $f(-)(z) = z$.

DERIVED CATEGORIES AND THEIR INTERPRETATION

1. *Atomic Formulas*: $Px_1, x_2, \ldots, x_n$ for P an n-place predicate symbol and each x_i a variable. (Note that proper nouns and other types of definite noun phrase (defined below) do not occur as arguments of predicates in Atomic Formulas.) The truth and falsehood conditions of atomic formulas are as in standard logic (see Keenan (1972) for a presuppositional representation of atomic formulas). All occurrences of variables in an atomic formula are *free occurrences*.

2. *Negative Formulas*: $-F$, where F is a formula.
   $f(-F) = f(-)(f(F))$. The free variables of $-F$ are exactly those of F.

3. *Common Noun Phrases*:
   (a) Common nouns are *common noun phrases* and have no occurrences of free variables.
   (b) $(X, y)F$ is a *common noun phrase*, where X is a common noun phrase, y is a variable occurring free in F, and F is a formula. The free variables of $(X, y)F$ are those of X plus those of F less y. $(X, y)F$ is interpreted (relative to an assignment a) as a subset of U such that b is in $f((X, y)F$ iff b is in $f(X)$ and $f(F) = t$ under the y-variant of a in which y is assigned to b.

4. *Definite Noun Phrases*:
   (a) Variables and proper nouns are *definite noun phrases* (proper nouns contain no free variables).
   (b) (the X) is a *definite noun phrase*, where X is a common noun phrase. The free variables of (the X) are those of X.
   $f(\text{the } X) = b$ iff $f(X) = \{b\}$.

5. *Formulas with Restricted Reference*:
   (a) If x is a definite noun phrase and F a formula in which y occurs free then $(I\ x, y)F$, $(N\ x, y)F$, and $(\text{Only } x, y)F$ are formulas.

   The free variables of $(I\ x, y)F$ and of $(\text{Only } x, y)F$ are those of x (including x itself if it is a variable) plus those of F less all occurrences of y.

   The free variables of $(N\ x, y)F$ are y, those of x (including x itself if it is a variable) plus those of F. Thus y remains free in $(N\ x, y)F$ and may be bound by further RROs.
   (1) $f((I\ x, y)F = t$ relative to an assignment a iff

1. $f(x)$ is a member of U and
2. $f(F)=t$ relative to the y-variant of a which assigns y to $f(x)$

$f((I\ x, y)F)=f$ relative to a iff

1. $f(x)$ is a member of U and
2. $f(F)=f$ relative to the y-variant of a which assigns y to $f(x)$.

$f((Ix, y)F)=z$ relative to a in all cases in which it does not equal t or f.

(2) $f((N\ x, y)F)=t$ relative to a iff

1. $f(x)$ is a member of U and
2. $f(x) \neq a(y)$ and
3. $f(F)=t$

$f((N\ x, y)F)=f$ relative to a iff 1. and 2. above hold and $f(F)=f$.

$f((N\ x, y)F)=z$ relative to a iff it does not equal t or f.

(3) $f((\text{Only}\ x, y)F)=t$ relative to a iff

1. $f(x)$ is a member of U and
2. $f(F)=t$ relative to the y-variant of a in which y is assigned to $f(x)$
3. $f(F) \neq t$ under any y-variant of a in which y is not assigned to $f(x)$

$f((\text{Only}\ x, y)F)=f$ relative to a iff conditions 1. and 2. above hold and there is a y-variant of a such that y is not assigned to $f(x)$ and $f(F)=t$.

$f((\text{Only}\ x, y)F)=z$ in all cases in which it is not t or f.

(b) If x is a common noun phrase and F a formula in which the variable y occurs free then $(\text{Spec}\ x, y)F, (E\ x, y)F, (A\ x, y)F$, and $(\text{Only}\ x, y)F$ are formulas.

The free variables of $(\text{Spec}\ x, y)F$ are y, those of x plus those of F. The free variables of other formulas in this category are those of x plus those of F, less y. We illustrate the semantics for this category with the Spec and E operators, the semantics for the others being easily constructable on the pattern given in the section 2.

(1) $f((\text{Spec}\ x, y)F)=t$ relative to a iff

1. $a(y)$ is a member of $f(x)$ and
2. $f(F)=t$

$f((\text{Spec}\ x, y)F)=f$ relative to a iff condition 1. above holds and $f(F)=f$.

$f((\text{Spec}\ x, y)F)=z$ in all cases in which it does not equal t or f

(2) $f((E\ x, y)F) = t$ relative to a iff for some y-variant of a y is assigned to a member of $f(x)$ and $f(F) = t$ relative to this y-variant.

$f((E\ x, y)F) = f$ relative to a iff there is no y-variant as above in which $f(F) = t$ and for some such y-variant $f(F) = f$.

$f((E\ x, y)F) = z$ in all other cases.

Note that in the interpretation of negatively restricted formulas and the Specific-Indefinite ones the restricted variable y remains free and may be bound by further RROs. Thus the truth value of such formulas depends on what y is assigned in the relevant assignment. For example, letting $F(y/z)$ denote the result of replacing all free occurrences of y in F by occurrences of a variable z which does not otherwise occur in F, it may be the case that $(N\ x, y)F$ and $(N\ x, z)F(y/z)$ have different truth values in the same interpretation.

On the other hand, in, e.g., identity restricted formulas the restricted variable y is bound, and the truth of the formula under an assignment does not depend on what the assignment to y is. In an earlier treatment of this topic (Keenan 1976b) the identity operator also left the y position unbound. Thus $(I\ x, y)F$ was true just in case x and y happened to be interpreted as the same object. The formulation given here says, in effect, that $(I\ x, y)F$ is true if setting y equal to x, F is true. The earlier formulation can easily be seen to be logically inadequate. Consider for example the truth conditions of (41a) below.

(41a)   Every student admires himself.
(41b)   (A student, x) (x, y) $(x$ Admire $y)$.

On the earlier formulation the truth conditions of (41b) would be roughly, 'Choose arbitrarily among the students, that student is identical to the referent of y and that student and y are in the *Admire* relation'. This obviously is not the meaning of (41a), it only gives the correct result when y is the only student. Under the current formulation the truth conditions of (41b) are roughly 'Choose an arbitrary student x; letting y denote that student, x *admires* y is true. And this is, basically, the correct result.

The fact that the y variable is bound by the identity operator also means that the instances of double binding illustrated in the awkward (42a) and the more natural (42b) cannot be represented by the identity operator as claimed in Keenan (1976b).

(42a)   The man$_j$ who insulted her$_i$ really loved the girl$_i$ who hit him$_j$

(42b)   (*Turkish*, Eser Erguvanli, personal communication)

vali$_i$-   si$_j$ köy$_j$-   ü-   nü$_i$ metetti

major$_i$-3sg poss$_j$ village$_j$- acc- 3sg poss$_i$ praised

'Its mayor praised his village'

(42c)   (y's mayor, x) (x's village, y) (x Praised y)

(42c), basically the logical structure we proposed for (42b) in Keenan (1976b) does constrain the object of *Praise* to be coreferential with the subject's village, but the subject of *Praise* is constrained only to be identical to the mayor of y, where y is a free variable, hence its interpretation depends solely on the assignment function and does not have to be the object of *Praise* at all. Hence (42c) is not an adequate representation of (42b).

UCLA, Los Angeles

NOTES

[1] The treatment of reference restricting operators given here differs in several respects from that of Keenan (1976b). Several of the claims made for the operators in Keenan (1976b) are no longer valid here (see Section 3 of this paper). On the other hand the naturalness criteria are much more developed here.

[2] We leave open here the question as to whether all the presuppositions (and assertions) can be expressed by (non-metalinguistic) sentences of the language. That is, we are not claiming that for any logical formula F there is another set of formulas true in exactly the models in which both F and $-F$ are untrue.

[3] In fact we doubt that RROs should be treated as sentential operators. To treat them purely as ways of restricting the reference of independently given referential expressions in formulas however would require an alternative analysis of relative scope phenomena, something we are not prepared to undertake in this paper.

[4] The notion 'free occurrence of a variable in a formula' is more formally defined in Section 3. Certain of the variables used in our RROs might well be called 'partially bound'.

[5] We should note however that Huisman (1973) reports only same and different location markers for one New Guinea language, Angaataha. That is, if the location of the action expressed in an early clause remains the same in the next clause a same-location marker occurs in the early clause, while if the locations of the two actions are different a different-location marker is used. The article is not however explicit as to whether there are other ways of restricting reference relative to main clause subjects, and so remains only a potential counterexample to this generalization.

[6] Steve Anderson, personal communication, informs me that this coreferencing system in Avar is not very productive, although historically it presumably was.

BIBLIOGRAPHY

Anderson, Steve (1975), ms. NE Caucasian: Avar.

Geach, P. (1962), *Reference and Generality*, Cornell University Press, Ithaca, New York.

Greenburg, J. (1963), 'Some Universals of Grammar with Particular Reference to the Order of Meaningful Elements', in J. Greenburg (ed.), *Universals of Language*, MIT Press, Cambridge, Mass.

Huisman, R. D. (1973), 'Angaataha Verb Morphology', in *Linguistics*, Vol. 110, pp. 43–54.

Jacobsen, W. H. (1967), 'Switch-Reference in Hokan-Coahuiltecan', in Dell Hymes (ed.), *Studies in Southwestern Ethnolinguistics*, Mouton, The Hague.

Keenan, E. L. (1972a), 'Quantifier Structures in English', in *Foundations of Language*.

Keenan, E. L. (1972b), 'On Semantically Based Grammar', *Linguistic Inquiry*, III.4 413–461.

Keenan, E. L. (1975a), 'Some Logical Problems in Translation', to appear in Guenthner and Guenthner-Reutter (eds.), *Meaning and Translation*, Duckworth, London.

Keenan, E. L. (1975b), 'The Logical Diversity of Natural Languages', in *Origins and Evolution of Language*, The Annals of the New York Academy of Sciences, New York.

Keenan, E. L. (1975c), 'Logical Expressive Power and Syntactic Variation in Natural Language', in Keenan, E. L. (ed.), *Formal Semantics of Natural Language*, Cambridge University Press.

Keenan, E. L. (1976a), 'Remarkable Subjects in Malagasy', in Charles Li (ed.), *Subject and Topic*, Academic Press, 249–301.

Keenan, E. L. (1976b), 'Reference Restricting Operators in Universal Grammar', BLS II, 227–240.

Munro, P. (1974), *Topics in Mojave Syntax*, PhD Dissertation, Univ. of California at San Diego.

Reinhart, T. (1976), *The Syntactic Domain of Anaphora*, PhD dissertation, MIT.

Scott, G. (1973), *Higher Levels of Fore Grammar*, Pacific Linguistics B, No. 23, The Australian National University.

Van Fraassen (1969), 'Presuppositions, Supervaluations, and Free Logic', in K. Lambert (ed.), *The Logical Way of Doing Things*, Yale University Press, New Haven.

Vattuone, B. (1975), ms. Notes on Genoese Syntax, Kernel 'VOS' strings and Theme-Rheme Structures.

TANYA REINHART

SYNTACTIC DOMAINS FOR SEMANTIC RULES

1. INTRODUCTION

My concern in this paper is to characterize certain systematic ways in which the semantic interpretation of English sentences is constrained by the syntactic properties of the surface forms of such sentences.

In Section 2, I define the syntactic domains which are relevant for semantic interpretation and propose two principles which restrict the rules which determine semantic properties of sentences to operate within these domains. In Sections 3–5, these principles are illustrated with specific rules which constrain the interpretation of coreference, relative scope of quantified expressions, and the function-argument structure of sentences.

The proposed principles constrain interpretive rules to mention only constituent structure (in a particular way) and not, for example, the linear order of nodes in a sentence. Coreference options and relative scope of quantifiers, in particular, have quite generally been assumed to depend, at least in part, on linear order. This assumption is shown to be inadequate for English. Although I will not argue that the principles proposed here are universals, they seem more likely candidates for being so than principles based on linear order, since linear order generally varies more across languages than does constituent structure.

2. SYNTACTIC DOMAINS

2.1. *The definition of 'domain'*

The syntactic domains which, I will argue, are relevant for the application of semantic interpretation rules are defined in (1):

(1)   *The domain of a node A* consists of all and only the nodes dominated by the (non-unary) branching node α which most immediately dominates A.[1]

It is easy to see that the domains defined by (1) will always be constituents (since they consist of all and only the nodes dominated by a given node). In effect, (1) determines for any given node the minimal branching constituent

107

F. Guenthner and S. J. Schmidt (eds.), Formal Semantics and Pragmatics for Natural Languages, 107–130. *All Rights Reserved.*
Copyright © 1978 by D. Reidel Publishing Company, Dordrecht, Holland.

which contains it. This may be illustrated with tree (2):

(2)

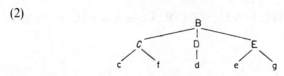

The branching node which most immediately dominates c is C, which means that the domain of c consists only of nodes dominated by C, which is the minimal branching constituent containing c. Similarly the domain of g is only the constituent dominated by E. The domain of C, on the other hand consists of all the nodes dominated by B, which is the branching node most immediately dominating C. The same is true for nodes D and E. Node d is immediately dominated by D which is a non-branching (or a unary branching) node. The first non-unary branching node which dominates d is B, which means that the domain of d, like that of D consists of all and only the nodes dominated by B, or, in other words, that B is the minimal non-unary branching constituent containing d. We note that node e, for example, is in the domain of node d, although node d is not in the domain of node e. The linear order of the nodes plays no role in determining their domain relations. C and E are equally in the domain of d, although C precedes d and E follows it.

We further define 'a head of a domain' as follows:

(3)   A node A is *a head of a domain* α if all and only the nodes in α are in the domain of A.

If we take the domain dominated by B in (2), node d (or D) is a head of this domain, since, by definition (1), all other nodes in B are in its domain. The same holds for nodes C and E. The node e, however has in its domain only g, hence it is not a head of the domain B (but it is a head of the domain E).

This use of 'head' is an extension of the common use of that term in Linguistics where a node is considered a head only if it is of the same category type as the branching node which dominates it (e.g., the NP *the boy* in the complex NP *the boy who ate the banana*). This extension enables us to speak of the subject as a head of the S domain, etc. (But note that by definition (3) there will always be more than one head per domain, e.g., the VP will also be a head of the S domain.)

Applying our notion of domain to actual sentences, consider the structure in 4 (the tree is simplified; see footnote 1):

(4)

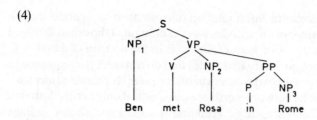

The domain of the subject, NP_1, is the whole sentence, i.e., all the nodes dominated by S, which is the branching node most immediately dominating NP_1. The domain of the object, NP_2, on the other hand consists only of the nodes in the VP, since the branching node most immediately dominating it (VP) does not dominate the subject. The domain of NP_3 consists of the nodes in the PP alone. The domains which are defined are, thus, the S, the VP, and the PP, which are all branching constituents. The resulting picture correlates, basically, with Chomsky's (1965) treatment of grammatical relations: In languages with a VP, there are structural differences between the grammatical categories. In terms of syntactic domains, the subject is a head of the S domain, the object is a head of the VP domain, and the 'object of a preposition' is a head of a PP.

2.2. *Domain restrictions on the application of semantic rules*

The fact that the domains defined by (1) are always constituents and that different grammatical categories are assigned different domains makes these domains natural candidates for linguistic rules to operate on. I suggest that the correspondence rules from surface structures to semantic representations can be stated in terms of domain relations and, further, that these rules are restricted to operate only within the domains defined in (1). The last hypothesis is more explicitely stated in (5).

(5)   Sentence-level semantic interpretation rules may operate on two given nodes A and B just in case one of these nodes is in the domain of the other (i.e., A is in the domain of B, or B is in the domain of A, or both).

If (5) is correct, it means that given a tree like (2), repeated in (6),

(6)

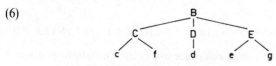

no sentence-level semantic interpretation rule can operate on nodes c and e or f and e, since neither of these nodes is in the domain of the other. But such rules operate on d and f, or E and f, since f is in the domain of d and of E.

Note that (5) does not claim that nodes that do not meet the requirement that one is in the domain of the other cannot be possibly related in any way. Various types of links between words are possible not only across domains, but also across sentences (e.g., semantic associations; sound linkage achieved by rhyme or alliteration patterns in poetry, etc.). Discourse conventions or pragmatic rules, may obviously apply across sentences (and hence, across syntactic domains). (5) restricts only the operation of strictly sentence-level semantic rules, more specifically, those rules which depend upon structural properties of the sentence (and not, say, upon its position in the discourse). Proving the hypothesis in (5), namely showing that all such rules are restricted by (5), would go beyond the scope of this paper. However, in the next sections I will exemplify three sentence-level semantic interpretation rules that meet this requirement.

A further domain restriction on the operation of semantic rules applies only to a subset of such rules, those which assign some kind of prominence or primacy to a given node. The terms 'prominence' or 'primacy' have not been rigorously defined, but it has been supposed, (for example, Langacker (1966) and Ross (1967)) that the antecedent has primacy over a (coreferential) pronoun. Following Keenan (1974), we may describe an expression α as having prominence over an expression β if the assignment of reference to α is independent of the reference of β, but the assignment of reference to β may depend on that of α. Thus, the pronoun may depend for its reference on the antecedent, but not conversely, and the choice of reference for a quantified expression may influence the choice of reference for a quantified expression within its scope, but not conversely. The hypothesis relevant to this type of case is stated in (7):

(7)   If a rule assigns node A some kind of prominence over node B, A must be a head of a domain which contains B.

Of the semantic interpretation rules discussed in the following sections I will show that the rules which restrict coreference options and assign relative scope obey restriction (7) in addition to (5).

3. THE RESTRICTION ON COREFERENCE OF DEFINITE NP's

To see how the restriction on coreference obeys the domain restrictions (5) and (7), it should be first made explicit what aspect of coreference is governed by a sentence-level semantic rule.

The question whether two nouns refer to the same object, like the question of which object a single noun refers to, is not, in the general case determined by a sentence-level semantic rule, but by conditions in the world and in the discourse of the sentence. Thus, given the discourse in (8):

(8)   A: How are Max and Rosa doing these days?
        B: Well, Rosa thinks she's coming down with the flu.

The pronoun *she* in (B) is likely to be interpreted as referring to Rosa. However, this interpretation is not necessitated by the form of the sentence. In a discourse like (9), the same pronoun in the same sentence is likely to be interpreted as referring to Sonya (since the question in *A* requires that *B* would be a statement 'about' Sonya.)

(9)   A: How is Sonya doing these days?
        B: Well, Rosa thinks she is coming down with the flu.

However, there are cases where coreference options of pronouns are restricted by the surface form of the sentence. Thus, in sentences like (10)

(10)   She thinks that Rosa is coming down with the flu,

the pronoun *she* cannot be interpreted as referring to Rosa in any possible discourse. In other words, the referential interpretation of the pronoun in this sentence is not free — it can be assigned any referential value except the one assigned to *Rosa*.

It is only the cases where the assignment of referential values to NP's is restricted by the form of the sentence, regardless of the discourse or the situation in the world, which concern us here. The resulting picture is, thus, that the assignment of coreference is not governed by a sentence-level interpretation rule, but the assignment of non-coreference is.[2] A sentence-level rule of interpretation is needed to restrict the otherwise free coreference options of NP's. If the domain hypothesis (5) is correct, it follows that this restriction applies to two given NP's only in case one is in the domain of the other. In other words, if neither NP is in the domain of the other, there is no restriction on their coreference options, and they can be assigned same (or different) referential values regardless of the question of which one of them (if any) is a pronoun. The following examples illustrate this case: (In the examples to follow, coreference will be marked by italicization of coreferential NP's).

(11a)

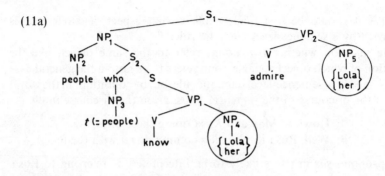

(11b)   People who know *Lola* admire *her*.
(11c)   People who know *her* admire *Lola*.
(11d)   People who know *Lola* admire *Lola*.
(11e)   People who know *her* admire *her*.

Neither of the circled NP's in (11a) is in the domain of the other: The branching node most immediately dominating NP_5 is VP_2, which does not dominate NP_4, and the branching node VP_1 which most immediately dominates NP_4 does not dominate NP_5. The sentences (11b–e) indicate that, as predicted by the domain hypothesis (5), the coreference options of these NP's are not, in fact, restricted, and coreference is possible (though, of course, not obligatory) in all possible arrangements of NP's and pronouns, including the case where the pronoun precedes a full NP, as in (11c) or the case where both NP's are full NP's, as in (11d).

The situation is different, however, in the sentences of (12) (a star in the examples of this section indicates that the sentence is ungrammatical on the coreference reading or that the coreference interpretation is impossible):

(12a)

(12b)   *Lola* admires the people who know *her*.
(12c)   *Lola admires the people who know *Lola*.
(12d)   *She admires the people who know *Lola*.
(12e)   *She* admires the people who know *her*.

Here, NP_5 is in the domain of NP_1 (though not conversely). Consequently the coreference options of these two NP's are restricted and of the four possible arrangements only two, (12b) and (12e), permit the coreference interpretation.

The restriction on coreference options that will capture the difference between (12c, d) and (12b, e) is stated in (13).[3]

(13)   Two NP's *must* be interpreted as non-coreferential if one is in the domain of the other and is not a pronoun.

Note that this same restriction is sufficient to block both (12c), where the head of the domain (NP_1) is a pronoun and (12d) where it is a full NP, since it only requires that the NP which is in the domain of the other (NP_5 in this case) be a pronoun for coreference to hold, regardless of whether the head is a pronoun or a full NP. (This aspect of the formulation of the rule follows Lasnik's (1976) rule, which is mentioned in (15) below.) In (12b) and (12e), where NP_5 is a pronoun, coreference interpretation is, correctly, not blocked by (13).

The coreference restriction (13) is also in accordance with the second domain hypothesis (7), which states that when prominence relations are involved prominence is assigned to a head of the domain. An equivalent statement of (13) which makes this clearer is that the head, NP_1 of a domain α cannot be coreferential with non pronouns in α, or, in other words, that NP's in the domain of the head must be pronouns in order to be coreferential with the head. This means that given a pair of a pronoun and a full NP (one in the domain of the other) coreference is only possible if the full NP is the head. More generally, NP's in the domain of the head may depend upon the head for their reference, but not conversely.

Restriction (13) mentions only domain relations of NP's, and, if correct, their linear order plays no role in determining coreference options. This stands in sharp contrast with the treatments of coreference restrictions in generative linguistics (e.g., Langacker (1966), Ross (1967), Jackendoff (1972), Wasow (1972) and Lasnik (1976)). It has been believed that the linear order of full NP's ('antecedents') and pronouns is a major factor in determining their coreference options and that 'forward pronominalization' is always free, i.e., that whenever a full NP precedes a pronoun the coreference interpretation is (logically) possible. To account for the possibility of coreference in cases like (11c) (*people who know her admire Lola*), where the pronoun precedes the antecedent, it was suggested that 'backward pronominalization' is also possible as long as the preceding pronoun does not command the antecedent, where 'command' is defined, following Langacker (1966) as in (14):

(14)   A node A commands a node B if neither A nor B dominates the other and the S node most immediately dominating A also dominates B.

(In (11c) the pronoun precedes, but does not command the antecedent.) Lasnik (1976) states the restriction on coreference as a semantic interpretation rule which assigns non coreference (a formulation which I followed in (13)). His restriction is roughly the one in (15)

(15) NP_1 and NP_2, must be interpreted as non coreferential if NP_1 precedes and commands NP_2 and NP_2 is not a pronoun.

This restriction is sufficient to account for the sentences in (11) and (12): Coreference is blocked in (12c) *She admires the people who know Lola* and (11d) *Lola admires the people who know Lola* since in both cases the first NP precedes and commands the second and the second is not a pronoun. Coreference is not blocked in (11c) *People who know her admire Lola* and (11d) *People who know Lola admire Lola* since the preceding NP does not command the second NP.

The precede-and-command restriction conflicts in two ways with the thesis of this paper: First, if correct, the linear order of constituents plays a role in semantic interpretation, and second, the structural unit which is relevant for semantic interpretation is the whole sentence rather than minimal branching constituents.

While it is true that the two restrictions yield the same results for the examples considered so far, there are cases where they differ in their predictions. We will see now that in these cases the precede-and-command restriction yields the wrong results, while the domain restriction (13) captures the facts. (I will only mention here a few such cases, a more detailed discussion is offered in Reinhart (1976)).

There are several counterexamples to the precede-and-command rule, many of which were noted by Lakoff (1968). First, the range of backward pronominalization is much wider than the rule predicts. In all the following cases, the pronoun precedes and commands its antecedent, but coreference is still possible.[4]

(16a) Near *him, Dan* saw a snake.

(16b) In *her* kitchen *Zelda* spent her sweetest hours.

(16c) How obnoxious to *his* friends *Ben* is.

(16d) Fond of *his* wife though *Ben* is, I like her even more.

(16e) (I predicted that Rosa would quit her job and) quit *her* job *Rosa* finally did.

(17a) The chairman hit *him* on the head before *the lecturer* had a chance to say anything.

(17b) We finally had to fire *him* since *McIntosh's* weird habits had reached an intolerable stage.

(17c) Rosa won't like *him* any more, with *Ben's* mother hanging around all the time.

(17d) We'll just have to fire *him*, whether *McIntosh* likes it or not.

Furthermore, cases like (16), with preposed constituents, provide a counterexample to the contention that coreference is always possible when the antecedent precedes the pronoun (or that forward pronominalization is free). In these cases, forward pronominalization is impossible, as can be seen in (18).[5]

(18a) *Near *Dan, he* saw a snake.

(18b) *In *Zelda's* kitchen, *she* spent her sweetest hours.

(18c) *How obnoxious to *Ben's* friends *he* is.

(18d) *Fond of *Ben's* wife though *he* is, I like her even more.

(18e) *(I predicted that Rosa would quit her job and) quit *Rosa's* job *she* finally did.

The most crucial problem for the precede-and-command rule is the asymmetry in coreference options of NP's in subject and non-subject positions: While coreference is impossible in (18) where the pronoun is the subject, it is possible in (19) where the pronoun is not the subject.

(19) Near *Dan*, I saw *his* snake.

And compare as well the following pairs:

(20a) *Ben's problems, *he* won't talk to you about.

(20b) *Ben's* problems, you can't talk to *him* about.

(21a)   *For *Ben's* car, *he's* asking 3 grand.
(21b)   For *Ben's* car, I'm willing to give *him* 2 grand.

This asymmetry shows up regardless of the linear order of the antecedent and the pronoun. In (19)–(21) the antecedent precedes the pronoun but, a comparison of the sentences in (17) and (22), in which the pronoun precedes the antecedent, reveals the same pattern: in (22), where the pronouns are subjects, coreference is impossible:

(22a)   *He* was hit on the head before *the lecturer* had a chance to say anything.
(22b)   *He* won't like Rosa any more, with *Ben's* mother hanging around all the time.
(22c)   *He'll* be fired whether *Ben* likes it or not.

The asymmetry in coreference options of subjects and nonsubjects cannot be handled by the relation of command, since this relation cannot, by definition, distinguish between subjects and nonsubjects of the same S (everything commanded by the subject is commanded by the object etc.). For the restriction in terms of syntactic domains (in (13)), on the other hand, this asymmetry is a predicted result, since subjects and non-subjects have different domains. All the cases mentioned above are captured by (13):

The counter-examples to the restriction stated in terms of precede-and-command arise typically in two types of structures:

(23a)

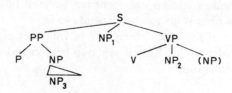

(23b)   *For *Ben's* car, *he's* asking two grand.
(23c)   For *his* car, *Ben's* asking two grand.
(23d)   For *Ben's* car, I'll give *him* two grand.
(24a)

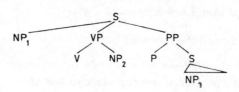

(24b)   *_He_ will be fired, whether _McIntosh_ likes it or not.

(24c)   We'll have to fire him whether McIntosh likes it or not.

Although the NP's in (23a) and (24a) differ in their linear order, they have identical domain relations: NP_3, in both trees is in the domain of the subject, NP_1. The restriction (13), therefore blocks a coreference interpretation of these two NP's when NP_3 is not a pronoun, as in (23b) and (24b). (In the same way coreference is blocked in the sentences of (18) and in (20a) and (21a), which have a structure similar to (23), and in the sentences of (22) which have the structure of (24).) The domain of the object, NP_2, on the other hand, consists, in both trees, only of nodes in the VP. Since NP_3 is not in the domain of NP_2, the restriction (13) does not apply and coreference is possible even when NP_3 is not a pronoun, as in (23d) and (24c). (The same is true for (19) and (20b) which have a structure similar to (23) and the sentences of (17) with the structure (24).) The 'backward pronominalization' in (23c) and the similar cases in (16) is permitted, since NP_3 which is in the domain of NP_1 is properly a pronoun, and NP_1 which is not a pronoun, is not in the domain of NP_3.

The comparison between (23) and (24) indicates that the linear order of NP's is not what determines their coreference options. In a right branching language like English, it is often the case that a head NP of a given domain precedes non-head NP's in its domain. (The reverse order is usually a result of the application of movement rules, as in (23).) This may help explain why the relation of 'precede' has been believed to play such a crucial role in the restrictions on coreference. Obviously in a large body of the language 'forward pronominalization' is the only grammatical option. If we consider domain relations as defined in Section 1, this fact is just a consequence of the application of restriction (13) to a right branching language. This is not true for the relation 'command', where all the nodes dominated by the same S equally command each other. A rule stated in terms of command must, therefore, introduce the relation 'precede' into the restriction on coreference.

The sharpest discrepency between the predictions of the precede-and-command restriction and the domain restrictions will show up in VOS languages (assuming that these languages have a VP), since in such languages a preceding node would often be in the domain of a following node. The following examples from Malagasy, a VOS language with some evidence for a VP (Keenan (1976)), indicate that in such languages the relation of 'precede-and-command' is indeed irrelevant. (The examples are from Ed Keenan; personal communication.)

(25a)   namono *azy* ny anadahin-d *Rakoto*
   hit/killed *him* the sister-of-*Rakoto*
   Rakoto's sister killed *him.*

(25b)   *namono   ny   anadahin-d *Rakoto izy*
   hit/killed the sister-of-*Rakoto he*
   he killed *Rakoto*'s sister.

In (25a) the pronoun precedes and commands the antecedent, hence, by the precede-and-command restriction, the sentence should have been blocked. However, since the pronoun is in the VP, and, thus, is not in the domain of the antecedent, the domain-restriction correctly permits coreference. The sentence (25b), on the other hand, does not violate the requirement of 'precede-and-command' (since the antecedent precedes the pronoun), but coreference is, nevertheless, blocked. This is precisely the prediction of the domain-restriction, since the antecedent, is in the domain of the pronoun although the antecedent precedes.

4. RELATIVE SCOPE OF QUANTIFIERS

I will now argue that the rule which assigns relative scope to quantified expressions (QE's) in surface structures operates within the hypotheses outlined in Section 2. The suggested rule is stated in (26)

(26)   A logical structure in which a quantifier binding a variable x has wide scope over a quantifier binding a (distinct) variable y is a possible interpretation for a given sentence S just in case in the surface structure of S the quantified expression (QE) corresponding to y is in the domain of the QE corresponding to x.[6,7]

This rule can be tested by checking the following claims which it implies:

(a) The linear order of QE's in surface structure plays no role in determining their relative-scope interpretation.

(b) A QE in head position will be assigned wide scope over a QE in its domain (in accordance with hypothesis (7)).

(c) If neither QE is in the domain of the other, neither of the corresponding quantifiers in the logical representation is in the scope of the other, i.e., they are not scope-related, (in accordance with hypothesis (5)), and

(d) scope ambiguity is possible if each of the QE's is in the domain of the other since, in this case, both expressions meet the condition stated in (26). Let us consider, first, examples supporting these claims.

4.1. Although it is often the case (in a right branching language) that a preceding QE is interpreted as having wider scope over a QE to its right, the sentences of (27) and (28) show that this is not always the case. In these sentences QE_1 precedes (and commands) QE_2, but QE_1 cannot, nevertheless be interpreted as having wider scope over QE_2 (the trees, particularly (27a), are again simplified, and see note 1)

(27a)

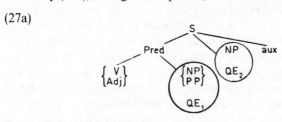

(27b)   Fond of some boy every girl is.
(27c)   (... and) break all the plates someone finally did.
(27d)   Opposed to all laws though some revolutionaries are, they all support the right of abortion.

(28a)

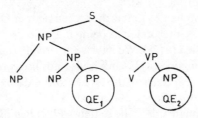

(28b)   Ben's letters to all the girls annoyed some boys.
(28c)   Ben's letters to some girls annoyed all the boys.

An intuitive way to verify that, in (27b), the quantifier corresponding to QE_1 (*some boy*) does not have wide scope over the quantifier corresponding to QE_2 (*every girl*) is to observe that if it did, the sentence would logically imply that all the girls are fond of the same boy, which it does not. In the sentences (27c, d) and (28a), where QE_1 is universally quantified, it is easier to see that the choice of reference for the existentially quantified QE_2 is independent of the choice of reference for QE_1. For example, in (27d) it must be the case that there is at least one revolutionary who is opposed to all laws, and it is not sufficient that for each law there is a revolutionary who opposes it (possibly a different one for different laws).

If we look, now, at the trees underlying these sentences, we see that in both (27a) and (28a), QE_2 is not in the domain of QE_1 (since QE_1 is dominated by a branching node which does not dominate QE_2). Rule (26), correctly, does not allow QE_1 to be assigned wide scope over QE_2. It is clear, therefore that, in these examples, the domain relations, rather than the linear order of the QE's, determine their relative-scope options.

A further examination of the structure (27a) reveals that while QE_2 is not in the domain of QE_1, QE_1 is in the domain of QE_2. Rule (26) predicts, therefore, that in (27b–d) QE_1 is interpreted as being in the scope of QE_2. This is the correct interpretation: The choice of a boy in (27b) may depend on the choice of a girl, i.e., it is sufficient that for each girl we pick, there would be at least one boy whom she likes, possibly a different boy for different girls. The same can be seen to be true for the other sentences of (27) if we reverse the order of quantifiers, e.g., in the sentence *Opposed to some law though all revolutionaries are* . . . the choice of a law may vary with the choice of a revolutionary. These facts, thus, exemplify the second claim implied by restriction (26), namely, that a QE in head position (QE_2 in this case) is assigned wide scope over QE's in its domain (and, again, regardless of the linear order of the QE's).[8]

The third claim implied by (26) is that when neither QE is in the domain of the other, neither is interpreted as being in the scope of the other. Such a situation is exemplified in (28). We have seen already that in (28), as in (27), QE_2 is not in the domain of QE_1 and is also not interpreted as being in its scope. But (27) and (28) differ with respect to the domain of QE_2. In (28), QE_2 does not have QE_1 in its domain since QE_2 is dominated by a VP which does not dominate QE_1. The sentence (28c) *Ben's letters to some girls annoyed all the boys*, shows that, in accordance with (26), the choice of reference for the variable corresponding to QE_1 (*some girls*) is independent of the choice for QE_1 (*all the boys*). The resulting picture is that neither of the quantifiers corresponding to QE_1 and QE_2 is in the scope of the other, or that they are scope independent. This may mean that such sentences require branching quantifiers analysis, but I will not elaborate on this point here.

Let us consider now some cases of scope ambiguity. The sentences in (29) have unambiguous scope interpretation $((\exists x)(\forall y) \ldots)$ is the only interpretation), while the sentences in (30) are ambiguous.[9]

(29a)

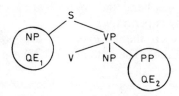

(29b)   Some reporters put tape-recorders in every room.
(29c)   Somebody found scratches in all of Ben's films.
(30a)

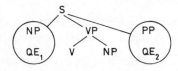

(30b)   Some reporters worship Carter in every town he visits.
(30c)   Somebody ends up stripping in all of Ben's films.

Although these sentences may appear to have identical structures, the sentences (29b, c) have the structure (29a), where the prepositional phrase (PP) is verb-phrasal, while the PP in (30b, c) is sentential. Syntactic evidence for this difference is discussed in detail in Reinhart (1976). Here I will mention briefly only one argument: As noted in Ross (1973), a possible test for whether a given constituent is attached to the VP or to S is checking its behaviour in a pseudo-cleft version of the sentence (as in (31) and (32) below): The *what*-clause of pseudo-cleft sentences can contain only non-VP material. As we see in (31b) and (32b) the PP's of (29b, c) cannot, in fact, occur in the *what*-clause of the pseudo-cleft versions of their sentences:

(31a)   What some reporters do in every town is worship Carter.
(31b)   *What some reporters did in every room was put tape-recorders.
(32a)   What somebody ends up doing in all of Ben's films is stripping.
(32b)   *What somebody did in all of Ben's films was find a scratch.

((32b) is acceptable if it means that somebody's finding scratches is what we see in Ben's film. This, however, is not the reading we consider in (29c).)

Given this structural difference between the sentences in (29) and in (30), the differences in their scope-interpretation is captured by rule (26): in (29), QE_2 is in the domain of QE_1, but not conversely, hence only one scope-interpretation is possible (the one in which QE_1 is assigned wide scope over

QE_2). In (30), on the other hand, the two QE's are in each other's domains, hence scope ambiguity is permitted.

Note, now, that when the PP's of (29) are proposed, their scope interpretation may change: The sentences of (33) are ambiguous.

(33a)

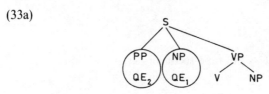

(33b)   In every room, some reporters put tape-recorders.
(33c)   In all of Ben's films, somebody found scratches.

This, again, is the predicted result of (26), since, in the surface structure of these sentences (given in (33a)), the QE's are in each other's domains.

An obvious consequence of (26) is that the famous sentence in (34a) has only one logical interpretation, namely the one with wider scope to *everybody*, since in the syntactic tree (34b) of this sentence the quantified expression NP_2 (*two languages*) is in the domain of the quantified expression NP_1 (*everybody*), but not conversely. (The disagreement among judgments here will be noted shortly.)

(34a)   Everybody speaks two languages.
(34b)

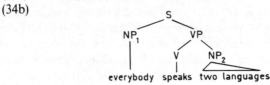

Given a sentence like (35a), on the other hand, (26) allows, correctly, two scope-interpretations, since in the syntactic tree (35b) of this sentence the quantified expressions are in each other's domain.

(35a)   Two languages, everybody speaks.
(35b)

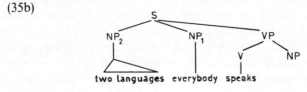

4.2. Rule (26) only restricts the set of possible logical interpretations for a given sentence. It does not require that all the possible logical interpretations it defines be acceptable in any given sentence. It has, e.g., been observed (Ioup, 1975) that lexical quantifiers differ inherently in their tendency to take wide scope. Consequently there will be cases where (26) permits in principle two scope arrangements, but, in fact, only one of them would be acceptable. Thus, while (35a) is indeed ambiguous (perhaps with intonational differences), a sentence like *some teachers, everybody likes*, which has the same structure as that of (35a), will give a strong (if not exclusive) preference to the interpretation of *some* as having wider scope since, as Ioup argues, it is both the case that *some* tends to have wider scope than *every* (when possible), and that quantified expressions in topic position have stronger preference for a wide scope interpretation than subjects. In other cases an interpretation which is permitted by (26) may be excluded on semantic grounds. Thus, in a sentence like *the policeman found a bomb in every mailbox*, the quantified expressions are in each other's domain and, therefore, (26) permits two interpretations, one of which is that there is some bomb such that the policeman found this same bomb in every box. However, since this interpretation is semantically bizarre, the sentence will not, in practice, be judged ambiguous.

The crucial question concerning (26) is, therefore, not whether it provides a sufficiently strong restriction on the set of possible interpretations of a given sentence, but whether the restriction it provides is not too strong. Many linguists have argued, for example, that sentences like (34a), *Everybody speaks two languages*, are, in fact, ambiguous, contrary to the claim I have made here. However, this is, I feel, a relatively minor problem.

In the first place, most putative examples of such ambiguities which are discussed in the literature are ones where one interpretation entails the other (e.g., the interpretation $(\exists$ two languages $x)$ $(\forall y) \ldots)$ entails the interpretation $(\forall y)$ $(\exists$ two languages $x) \ldots$. So our intuitions distinguishing ambiguity and vagueness in these cases are less clear than in cases where the two interpretations are logically independent.

And in the second place, although there may be cases where speakers' disagreement cannot be reduced to the claim that the sentence in question is vague rather than ambiguous, and we will have to assume then that these speakers permit a violation of (26), it appears that the violation is highly restricted with respect to the NP pairs which tolerate it. Thus, Ioup (1975) has observed that 'scope ambiguity' may be possible between quantified subjects and quantified objects, but judgments of such ambiguity are much harder to obtain between quantified subjects and other NP's within the VP. This may be illustrated in (36): (36b) and (36c) are unlikely to be interpreted as ambiguous even by speakers who consider (36a) and (34a) ambiguous.

(36a)   Some tourists visited all the museums.
(36b)   Some tourists spent an afternoon in all the museums.
(36c)   Some tourists were disgusted with all the museums.

A more substantial problem for (26) arises in the case of PP's within complex NP's, on which there is no disagreement in judgments. It has been observed (e.g., in Gabbay and Moravcsik (1974)) that in complex NP's like those occurring in (37) and (38) the quantified PP must have wider scope than the quantified NP.

(37a)   Santa Claus brought some gifts to every girl.
(37b)

(38)   All the gifts to some girl were wrapped in red paper.

Such examples do not yet pose a serious problem for (26). The quantified expressions in the underlying tree (roughly represented in (37b)) are in each other's domain. (26) therefore permits scope ambiguity. But as we have seen, this does not mean that other semantic considerations may not impose further restrictions on the set of interpretations permitted by (26). However, the more serious problem here is that the same order of quantifier scope holds when further PP's are embedded, e.g.,

(39a)   Santa Claus brought some gift to every girl in some country.
(39b)

(39a) has only one correct scope interpretation — the one which assigns wide scope to *some country* (i.e., there is some country such that for every girl in that country, there is a gift such that . . .). But in the corresponding tree (39b), the quantified NP_1 (*some gift*), is not in the domain of the quantified expression PP_2 (*in some country*) so (26) does not allow this scope arrangement.

It appears that this problem may be solved within our framework by restricting (26) as follows: In a complex NP of the form $NP_1 + PP$, the PP must have wider scope than NP_1. And if it happens that the PP itself contains such a complex NP, this same restriction tells us again (by transitivity) that the bottom quantified PP must have wider scope than the top NP.

To conclude, I should stress that determining quantifier scope in surface structures is known to pose many complicated problems. One simple constraint like (26) will not solve all of these problems. We may hope, however, that (26) does capture the basic restriction on the range of logical interpretations of quantified sentences, and that additional structure-specific constraints on this restriction (such as the one illustrated above for quantified PP's within complex NP's) can handle the many additional specific problems.

5. FUNCTION-ARGUMENT REPRESENTATIONS

We will see now that it is possible to define in terms of the domain relation (i.e., within the hypothesis (5)) a semantic interpretation rule which assigns function-argument representations to syntactic structures. A rough approximation of such a rule (excluding special intonation cases) is given in (40).

(40)   A function-argument formula $F(a_1, a_2, \ldots, a_n)$ is an appropriate logical translation of a phrase α iff there is a node F' in α which corresponds to F, and, for each argument expression a_i there is a corresponding node a'_i, in α, and F' has in its domain all and only the nodes $a'_1, a'_2, \ldots, a'_n$.

To illustrate the operation of (40) let us consider the interpretation of adverbs and PP's. Sentential adverbs or PP's, as in (41), are interpreted as functions from formulae to formulae, while V-phrasal adverbs or PP's, as in (42), are interpreted as restricting functions from functions to functions. This guarantees that entailments like the one in (42c) hold for sentences with V-phrasal PP's and V-phrasal adverbs but not for sentences with sentential PP's or sentential adverbs.

(41a)

(41b)   Rosa is riding a horse $\begin{Bmatrix} \text{in Ben's picture} \\ \text{probably} \end{Bmatrix}$

(42a)

(42b)   Rosa rode a horse $\begin{Bmatrix} \text{in Ben's pasture} \\ \text{gracefully} \end{Bmatrix}$

(42c)   (b) → Rosa rode a horse

The correspondence rule from syntactic structures to function-argument representations must assure, therefore, that the PP or Adv in (42) will not be interpreted as a function over the whole sentence (namely a function whose arguments are the translations of the subject NP_1 and the VP). This is precisely the type of restriction that is captured by (40). (40) permits a function corresponding to the PP or Adv in (42) to take only arguments corresponding to V and the object NP_2, since it requires that all the nodes corresponding to argument expressions would be in the domain of the node corresponding to the function expression, and the only nodes which meet this requirement are the V and NP_2.

The correspondence rule must also assure that in translating the syntactic structure in (41a) the function corresponding to the sentential adverbs will not take as an argument the translation of the VP alone (which would allow sentence (41b) to have a logical structure identical to that of (42b)). This is guaranteed by the requirement that the node corresponding to the function expression have in its domain only nodes which correspond to argument expressions. If, in tree (41a) only the VP is picked as an argument, this would mean that the PP in this tree has in its domain more than just nodes corresponding to arguments, in violation of (40).[10]

It is easy to see that in many cases rule (40) puts stronger restrictions on the interpretation of sentences than required by purely logical considerations. Thus, a sentence like (43a) permits (among several others) the two interpretations in (44), which are logically equivalent.

(43a)   Rosa kissed Dan.
(43b)

(44a)   kiss $\langle$Rosa, Dan$\rangle$
(44b)   (kiss $\langle$Dan$\rangle$) $\langle$Rosa$\rangle$.

But of these two representations only (44b) is permitted by rule (40): In the corresponding tree (43b) the node V corresponding to the function *kissed* has only the object NP_2 in its domain, hence the function *kissed* can take only the translation of NP_2 as an argument (but not the translation of NP_1, as in (44a)). The node VP, on the other hand, which corresponds to the function (*kissed* $\langle$*Dan*$\rangle$) has the subject NP_1 in its domain, hence given rule (40), (44b) is an appropriate representation for (43b). Note, on the other hand, that rule (40) does not determine which nodes in the tree would be translated as functions, and which as arguments. Thus in tree (43b) it permits a logical representation in which the subject, NP_1, corresponds to the function and the VP to the argument. This choice of functions and arguments should be determined by independent correspondence rules.

The possibility illustrated here is rather interesting: If the hypothesis (5) can be shown to hold in general for semantic rules, this would restrict the set of possible logical interpretations of sentences of natural language, forcing a choice between logically equivalent interpretations. Some independent evidence that such a choice between the equivalent representations illustrated in (44) is required by natural language is suggested by Sag's (1976) study of VP deletion. He argues that a function corresponding to the VP is needed in the logical structure to account for the full range of deletion phenomena.

6. CONCLUSION

The following hypothoses concerning the semantic interpretation of sentences of natural language are supported by my previous discussion. (a) Basic (sentence-level) semantic interpretation rules can be formulated in terms of syntactic properties of surface structures (in accordance with the assumptions of interpretative semantics). (b) The structural properties which are relevant for the rules of semantic interpretation are those of constituent structure only. Traditional — linguistics notions such as linear order and grammatical relations need not be mentioned in the formulation of such rules (grammatical relations are reducible, in the relevant cases, to domain relations). (c) The different semantic rules (at least those discussed here) apply directly and independently to uninterpreted surface structures, i.e., neither of these rules need precede or be considered more 'basic' than the others.[11]

University of Tel Aviv

NOTES

[1] The definition in (1) is simplified. In fact, in cases where the branching node α_1 most immediately dominating A is immediately dominated by a node α_2 of the same category type as α_1, the domain of A expands to the nodes dominated by α_2. This is needed to capture domain relations in cases of S over S or VP over VP, etc. The simplified definition is sufficient for the sake of this discussion, but it requires using here simplified trees, as (4) below. In a more accurate syntactic analysis, the VP in (4) should contain two VP's, as in (i)

(i)

```
                    VP
              _____/_____
            VP              PP
          /  \            /  \
         V    NP         P    NP
         |    |          |    |
        met  Rosa       in   Rome
```

[2] A similar view of the restriction on coreference is proposed in Lasnik (1976).

[3] The restriction (13) applies to NP's in a non-strict reflexive environment. When the conditions for reflexivization are met the pronoun must be, furthermore, reflexive for coreference to hold (e.g., coreference is impossible, in *Rosa hit her*, although rule (13), as stated, does not block it.) The exclusion of the strict reflexivization environment does not have to be incorporated into the restriction (13), if we assume, along the lines of Chomsky (1973) that coreference in such cases is blocked by an independent rule which applies prior to the application of the general restriction on coreference. Within this framework, (13) will apply only to NP's not already marked as noncoreferential by a previous rule.

[4] Some speakers may find the sentences of (17) (in the coreference reading) dubious out of context. This is due to discourse (rather than grammatical, or sentence-level) constraints on 'backward pronominalization'. Kuno (1972) has argued that in cases where the grammar i.e., the precede-and-command condition, in his framework, permits 'backwards pronominalization' its use is further restricted by the discourse, and is permitted only if the antecedent is a discourse topic, or 'old information'. A possible test for whether coreference is grammatically or pragmatically impossible is to place the sentence in question in a context which justifies 'backward pronominalization'. Thus, (17a) will get improved if embedded in a context like (ii).

(ii)   Since the chairman hit *him* on the head before *the lecturer* had a chance to say anything, we'll never know what the lecture was supposed to be about.

(iii)   *Since *he* was hit on the head before *the lecturer* had a chance to say anything, we'll never know what the lecture was supposed to be about.

But, as we see in (iii), sentences like (22a) below, which are grammatically impossible, are not improved when embedded in the same context.

[5] On the basis of the sentences in (16) and (18) alone, one might be tempted to attempt a solution by means of applying the coreference rule to deep structures, (namely before the application of preposing rules). However, arguments against any ordering solution to problems of coreference have been widely discussed (e.g., in Lakoff (1968), Postal (1971), Jackendoff (1972) and Wasow (1972)), and I will not repeat them here. Note, in any case, that such an account cannot capture sentences (20b) and (21b) below where coreference is possible only after the application of preposing.

[6] (26) mentions 'quantified expressions' rather than 'quantified NP's' in order to allow it to apply to quantified PP's. The expressions which are considered in determining relative scope are not the ones dominated by Q alone (namely, quantifying words like *some* and *every*). Given a quantified PP like *in all the rooms*, if we consider strictly the node Q which dominates the quantifying word (*all*), its domain under any syntactic analysis cannot extend beyond the PP. Similarly in a quantified possessive NP like *everyone's father* the domain of *everyone* is only the possessive NP itself. Still, it is obvious that these quantifiers may have wide scope over quantifiers outside the PP or the possessive NP. This means that the relevant domains in determining relative scope options of such quantifiers are those of the PP's or the possessive NP's which contain them, and which I will refer to here as 'quantified expressions'. A complete analysis of the interpretation of relative scope requires, of course, a more rigorous specification of what counts as a 'quantified expression'.

[7] Note that (26) only restricts the relative scope of two given quantifiers, i.e., their *relative* position in a logical structure. It does not state where they will go, nor does it restrict the position of a quantifier relative to anything which is not a quantified expression.

[8] Lakoff (1971) has argued on the basis of examples like (27b) that preposing rules do not affect the scope-interpretation of sentences, which, if true, would mean that the relative scope of this sentence could be determined by the linear order of the QE's in deep-structure (or before preposing). Note, however that this is not true for all types of preposing. In (iv), where only the NP *some boy* is preposed the relative scope does change (and the sentence is ambiguous).

(iv)   Some boy, every girl is fond of.

The same will be exemplified below with other sentences. Rule (26) captures the difference between (27b) and (iv): Since in (iv), unlike (27c) the second QE is in the domain of the first, the first may be interpreted as having wide scope over the second.

[9] Other semantic differences between pairs like (29c) and (30c) are discussed in Jackendoff (1975).

[10] The actual function-argument representations that rule (40) will assign to the sentences in (41) and to the VP's in (42) are those in (va) and (via) respectively.

(va) $\left\{ \begin{matrix} \text{Probably} \\ \text{In Ben's picture} \end{matrix} \right\}$ $\langle \text{Rosa, Ride a horse} \rangle$

(vb) $\left\{ \begin{matrix} \text{Probably} \\ \text{In Ben's picture} \end{matrix} \right\}$ $\langle \text{Ride a horse } \langle \text{Rosa} \rangle \rangle$

(via) $\begin{cases} \text{Gracefully} \\ \text{In Ben's pasture} \end{cases} \langle \text{Ride, A horse} \rangle$

(vib) $\begin{cases} \text{Gracefully} \\ \text{in Ben's pasture} \end{cases} \langle \text{Ride} \langle \text{a horse} \rangle \rangle$

These representations are logically equivalent to the more familiar representations in (ib) and (iib).

[11] E.g., we need not assume that the interpretations of coreference or of quantifier scope apply to logical (function-argument) representations rather than directly to syntactic trees, as was suggested in Keenan (1974).

BIBLIOGRAPHY

Chomsky, N. (1965), *Aspects of the Theory of Syntax*, M.I.T. Press.

Chomsky, N. (1973, 'Conditions on Transformations', in Anderson and Kiparsky (eds.), *A Festschrift for Morris Halle*, Holt, Reinhart and Winston.

Gabbay, D. M. and Moravcsik, J. M. (1974), 'Branching Quantifiers, English, and Montague Grammar', *Theoretical Linguistics*, Vol. 1, No. 1/2.

Ioup, G. (1975), *The Treatment of Quantifier Scope in Transformational Grammar*, (Unpublished Ph.D. Dissertation), Cuny, New York.

Jackendoff, R. (1972), *Semantics in Generative Grammar*, M.I.T. Press.

Jackendoff, R. (1975), 'On Belief-Contexts', *Linguistic Inquiry*, Vol. 6, No. 1.

Keenan, E. (1974), 'The Functional Principle: Generalizing the Notion of "subject of" ', in M. LaGaly, R. Fox and A. Bruck (eds.), *Papers from the Tenth Regional Meeting of the Chicago Linguistic Society*.

Keenan, E. (1976), 'Remarkable Subjects in Malagasy', in C. N. Li (ed.), *Subject and Topic*, Academic Press.

Kuno, S. (1972, 'Functional Sentence Perspective: A Case Study from Japanese and English', *Linguistic Inquiry*, Vol. 3, No. 3.

Lakoff, G. (1968), 'Pronouns and Reference', Indiana Club Mimeograph.

Lakoff, G. (1971), 'On Generative Semantics', in D. A. Steinberg & L. A. Jakobovits (eds.), *Semantics*, Cambridge, The University Press.

Langacker, R. (1966), 'On Pronominalization and the Chain of Command" in Reibel and Schane (eds.), *Modern Studies in English*, Prentice Hall, Englewood Cliffs, New Jersey.

Lasnik, H. (1976), 'Remarks on Coreference', *Linguistic Analysis*, Vol. 2, No. 1.

Postal, P. (1971), *Cross over Phenomena*, Holt, Reinhart and Winston.

Reinhart, T. (1976), *The Syntactic Domain of Anaphora*, Unpublished Ph.D. dissertation, M.I.T.

Ross, J. R. (1967), *Constraints on Variables in Syntax*, Unpublished Ph.D. dissertation, M.I.T.

Ross, J. R. (1973), 'Nearer to Vee', mimeographed handout, M.I.T.

Sag, Ivan (1976), *Deletion and Logical Form*, Unpublished Ph.D. dissertation, M.I.T.

Wasow, T. (1972), *Anaphoric Relations in English*, Unpublished Ph.D. dissertation, M.I.T.

ROBIN COOPER

VARIABLE BINDING AND
RELATIVE CLAUSES

0. INTRODUCTION

Rodman (1976) makes the extremely interesting and attractive proposal that quantifier scope relationships are governed by the constraints that Ross (1967) proposed for certain movement and other syntactic transformations. Similar proposals have been made by Postal (1974) and Fauconnier (1975). Such claims are of great interest to linguists since potentially they not only identify semantic properties of natural languages which distinguish them from formal languages (thereby helping to characterize that subset of all possible languages which is the set of possible natural languages) but they also point the way towards a unified account of certain characteristics of both the syntax and semantics of natural languages. In this paper I shall examine Rodman's proposal in the light of a Montague approach to the interpretation of transformational syntaxes. I shall restrict my attention mainly to the complex NP constraint with respect to relative clauses, but I believe that my remarks will generalize to other types of complex NP and also to cases involving the sentential subject constraint. I shall suggest that some rather obvious apparent counterexamples can, in fact, be explained away and I shall point out some examples where it seems extremely difficult to tell whether there is a reading associated with the sentence which would provide a counterexample. While there may be clear counterexamples I have not thought of, I hope to show, at least, that the construction of counterexamples is not as obvious as one might suspect when first viewing the data. Finally, I shall indicate two ways of incorporating the complex NP constraint on quantifier scope into a grammar of English. In the Appendix I shall exhibit a definition of a fragment of English which contains some of the key examples of the text.

Rodman (1976) presents the following data.

(1a)   John dates every woman who loves a fish.

(1b)   John has dated a woman who loves every man.

The normal treatment of such sentences within the framework of Montague grammar would predict that these sentences are ambiguous depending on

F. Guenthner and S. J. Schmidt (eds.), Formal Semantics and Pragmatics for Natural Languages, 131–169. All Rights Reserved.

which of the two quantified noun-phrases in each sentence has wider scope. We can illustrate the ambiguity by considering the different deep structures these sentences might be related to in a system where quantifier scope is represented syntactically at the deep structure level. By using this sort of system for ease of illustration I in no way wish to suggest that quantifier scope ambiguities must be represented syntactically. (See Cooper and Parsons (1976) and Cooper (1975) for discussion of system where this is not the case.) (1a) might be associated with the deep structures sketched in (2).[1]

(2a)[2]

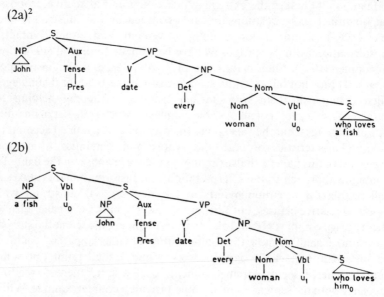

(2b)

(2b) continued in image below.

Similarly, (1b) might be associated with the two structures represented in (3).

(3a)

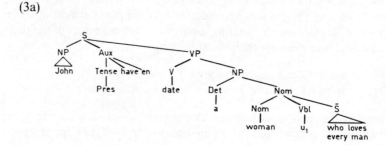

(3b)

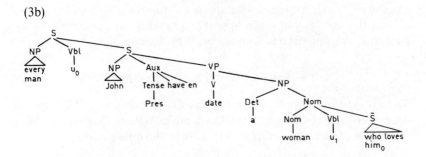

(2b) and (3b) represent readings where the NP inside the relative clause is quantified into the matrix sentence to give it wider scope. In the transformational derivation of the surface structures corresponding to these deep structures the NP which is quantified in would have to be lowered into a complex NP.[3] The sentences (1a) and (1b), however, do not appear to have readings corresponding to these structures. Thus they cannot be paraphrased as (4a) and (4b) respectively.

(4a)   A fish is such that John dates every woman who loves it.

(4b)   Every man is such that John has dated a woman who loves him.

A more startling example presented by Rodman is (5).

(5)   Guinevere has a bone that is in every corner of the house.

(5), in order to be sensible, would require that *every corner of the house* have wider scope than the existential associated with *a bone* since a single bone cannot be in every corner of the house at the same time. However, giving *every corner of the house* wider scope in this way would involve lowering it into a complex NP and (5) does, in fact, only have a nonsense reading.

The claim is, then, that an NP which in surface structure appears inside a complex NP cannot have wider scope than that complex NP. In terms of the syntactic representation of scope which we are using for expository purposes it is equivalent to the claim that a surface structure cannot be associated with a deep structure if the derivation would involve lowering an NP into a complex NP. This, then, would be a prohibition of insertion into a complex NP which would involve a slight extension of Ross' original constraint which prevented extraction from a complex NP (although he did see it also as a constraint on certain kinds of deletion and feature changing rules).[4]

In the following sections I shall discuss a number of types of examples
with relative clauses that might appear to provide counterexamples to the
claim that quantifier scope is constrained by the complex NP constraint.

1. EXAMPLES WITH PROPER NAMES

The first type of example appears to involve quantification by a proper
name where the proper name is inside a complex NP and the corresponding
pronoun is outside the complex NP. This is illustrated in (6).

(6)   A girl who John kissed bit him.

It would normally be assumed on a Montague-type analysis that *John* must
be quantified in in order to bind the variable corresponding to *him*. But this
would be a violation of the complex NP constraint as we can see from (7).

(7)

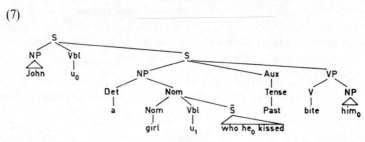

Clearly the lowering rule would violate the complex NP constraint. The
pronoun in (6), however, seems to be just the sort of pronoun that Geach
(1962) would term a pronoun of laziness.[5] Thus it would seem quite
reasonable to propose that a possible deep structure for (6) would be (8).

(8)

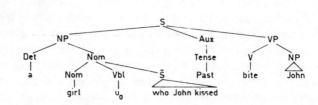

This structure would then undergo a rule of pronominalization similar to
the one which was proposed in early transformational grammar which

would change the second *John* to *him* because of its formal identity with the first *John*. Even this small adjustment is not necessary, however, in order to show that we do not have to lower into the complex NP to get the appropriate reading. We could equally well have taken the structure (9) as the basis for semantic interpretation where him_0 does not get bound.[6]

(9)

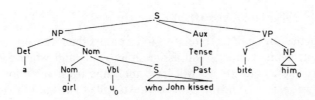

In formal language theory free variables and open sentences have mostly been regarded as a useful means to an end, namely the closed sentence without free variables. It is for the closed sentences that the general definition of truth and logical consequence is given. In Montague's work on pragmatics, however, a slightly different light is cast on the free variable. Montague interprets his formal languages with respect not only to possible worlds but also to contexts of use. The context of use "is introduced in order to permit a treatment ... of such indexical locutions as demonstratives, first- and second-person singular pronouns, and free variables (which are treated ... as a kind of demonstrative)". (Montague (1974), p. 228). To take a simple example, let us imagine that we have a formal language in which *walk'* represents a function from individuals to truth-values and u_0 is a variable over individuals. $walk'(u_0)$ will be a formula of this language (though not a closed formula). This formula is interpreted not only with respect to a possible world but also with respect to a context of use which in this case we can take to be the assignment to variables since nothing else is relevant to the present point. The context of use will be, then, a function which takes variables as arguments and assigns appropriate values to them. In the case of variables over entities the value assigned to the variable by the context of use will be an entity. Thus the semantics will be designed to require that the formula $walk'(u_0)$ gets the truth-value 1 with respect to some possible world i and some context of use j just in case the entity $j(u_0)$ walks in i.

However, there is still a general definition of truth (for example see Montague (1974), p. 259) which holds basically for closed sentences. While it is indubitably true that a useful general definition of truth for a formal language is one that makes the context of use irrelevant it is to be expected that natural languages should make greater use of a notion of truth relative to a context.

If we induce interpretation by translation into Montague's intensional logic in the manner made precise in the Appendix, the translation of (9) would have a free variable in it and in reduced form it would be (10).

(10) $\exists u[\text{girl}'(u) \wedge \text{kiss}'*(j, u) \wedge \text{bite}'*(u, u_0)]$.

If we take the notion of truth relative to a context then we will get just the right result. Some contexts will assign John to u_0 and when evaluating relative to these contexts we will have the same truth-value for a given world as we get for (7) and (8). Other contexts will not assign John to u_0 and this will get readings where *him* and *John* do not correspond to the same person. Thus there appears to be no cause to have quantification violate the complex NP constraint in order to get the appropriate readings for (6) as long as we either allow for pronouns of laziness or we take seriously the notion of truth relative to a context as Montague envisaged.[7]

2. EXAMPLES WITH DEFINITE DESCRIPTIONS

The second type of example appears to involve quantification by a definite description where the definite description is inside a relative clause and the corresponding pronoun is outside the complex NP. An example is given in (11).

(11)   A girl who the man kissed bit him.

In order to bind *him* by *the man* in (11) we would need to quantify *the man* into the top sentence and it would have to be lowered into the complex NP. But this too is the sort of sentence which one might regard as containing a pronoun of laziness. The sentence would be shown by the semantics to be equivalent if we derived it from a deep structure corresponding to (12) where the second occurrence of *the man* would become *him* by a transformational rule of pronominalization.

(12)   A girl who the man kissed bit the man.

Alternatively, we could allow *him* to represent a free variable. In this way we could have the deep structure (13a) which would translate to an expression equivalent to (13b).

(13a)

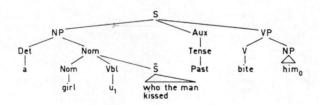

(13b) $\exists u[\text{girl}'(u) \wedge \exists x[\forall y[\text{man}'(y) \equiv x = y] \wedge \text{kiss}'*(x, u)]$
          $\wedge \text{bite}'*(u, u_0)]$.

For this sentence to be true there has to be exactly one man (in the Universe of discourse, one may assume). Some contexts of use will assign the man to u_0 and some will not.

There are, of course, cases similar to (11) where it has been argued independently, for example by Parsons (1972), that the pronoun should not represent a bound variable. Consider (14), constructed on the model of an example of Parsons'.

(14)   Every girl who kissed the man who loved her hugged him.

If we wish to bind *her* by the universal associated with *every* we cannot quantify in the NP *the man who loved her* in order to make this bind *him*. The dilemma is illustrated by the two deep structures in (15), both of which leave one or other of the two variables unbound.

(15a)

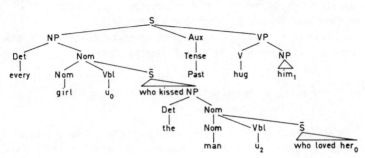

(15b)

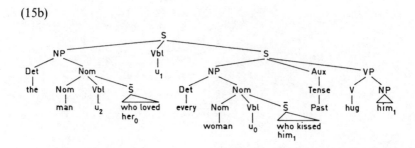

In (15a) her_0 gets bound when *girl* and *who kissed the man who loved her_0* are put together but him_1 does not. In (15b) him_1 gets bound but her_0 does not. This led Parsons (1972) to propose that pronouns like *him* in (14) should be given a pronoun of laziness type treatment and in this case the *him* would have to be paraphrased something like 'the man she kissed who loved her'. In order to make this work we might propose a deep structure such as (16).

(16)

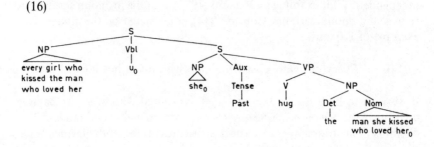

Here, in order to bind her_0 in the NP underlying the pronoun of laziness, we have had to quantify in the complex NP *every girl who kissed the man who loved her*. However, we have not had to quantify *into* the complex NP and thus we have not violated the complex NP constraint.

It is not possible to parallel the earlier examples and take (15a) as a deep structure, simply leaving him_1 unbound. The translation of (15a) would be (17).

(17) $\forall u[\text{girl}'(u) \land \exists v[\forall w[\text{man}'(w) \land \text{love}'*(w, u) \equiv w = v]$
         $\land \text{kiss}'*(u, v)] \supset \text{hug}'*(u, u_1)]$.

Any context of use, however, will give a unique value for u_1. It is clear that the sentence (14) allows there to be a different man for each girl and thus any reading that says that exactly one got hugged will be inaccurate. I believe, however, that there is a way to avoid the syntactic pronoun of laziness here if we allow pronouns to translate as definite descriptions with free variables inside them. The exact details of the proposal need not concern us here (though they can be gleaned from the Appendix and are discussed in Cooper (forth coming)). In order to treat this sentence we would have a deep structure something like (18).

(18)

Here him^0 would have the translation given in (19).

(19) $\lambda K \exists x [\forall y [[^{\vee} S(u_0)](y) \equiv y = x] \wedge K(x)]$.

x and y are variables over entities and S is a variable over functions from entities to properties. K is a variable over functions from entities to truth, which we might term characteristics. (19) may be approximately paraphrased as the set of characteristics of the unique entity which stands in the relation S to u_0.[8] The translation of the complete lower sentence after some reductions is (20).

(20) $\exists x [\forall y [[^{\vee} S(u_0)](y) \equiv y = x] \wedge \text{hug}'*(u_0, x)]$.

This may be paraphrased approximately as 'there is some unique individual which bears the relation S to u_0 such that u_0 hugs that individual'. We can now quantify in the translation of the NP *every girl who kissed the man who loved her* and we get (21a) which reduces by lambda-conversion to (21b).

(21a) $\lambda K \forall u [\text{girl}'(u) \wedge \exists v [\forall w [\text{man}'(w) \wedge \text{love}'*(w, u) \equiv w = v]$
$\wedge \text{kiss}'*(u, v)] \supset K(u)](\lambda u_0 [\exists x [\forall y [[^{\vee} S(u_0)](y) \equiv y = x]$
$\wedge \text{hug}'*(u_0, x)]])$

(21b) $\forall u [\text{girl}'(u) \wedge \exists v [\forall w [\text{man}'(w) \wedge \text{love}'*(w, u) \equiv w = v]$
$\wedge \text{kiss}'*(u, v)] \supset \exists x [\forall y [[^{\vee} S(u)](y) \equiv y = x] \wedge \text{hug}'*(u, x)]]$.

(21b) might be paraphrased approximately as 'for any individual, if it's a girl and there's a unique man who loves her and she kisses him, then there's a unique individual that bears relation S to her and she hugs that individual'. Whatever the relation S is, of course, will be determined by the context of use. According to some contexts of use $S(u)$ will represent the property of being the man who loves u and thus will correspond to the anaphoric reading of him^0. According to other contexts of use it will represent something different and this will correspond to non-anaphoric readings of him^0.

I believe that, once we introduce either a pronoun of laziness treatment or some treatment along the lines I have sketched, we should be able to explain away all examples where it seems that a definite description has to be quantified into a relative clause in order to bind a pronoun that is not within the relative clause and thus such examples would not represent counterexamples to the claim that quantifier scope obeys the complex NP constraint. As we seem to need a pronoun of laziness or similar treatment independently in order to assign reasonable meanings to English sentences, we cannot be accused of introducing extra mechanisms merely to make quantifier scope ambiguities agree with the complex NP constraint.

I will discuss other examples involving definite descriptions in Sections 4, 5 and 6 below.

3. EXAMPLES WITH INDEFINITE DESCRIPTIONS

The third type of example appears to involve quantification by an indefinite description where the indefinite description is inside a relative clause and the corresponding pronoun is outside the complex NP. Examples are given in (22).

(22a)   The girl who ate a steak enjoyed it.
(22b)   A girl who dated some guy in the English department said that he was a good conversationalist.

These examples, again, are similar to those that have led people to propose a pronoun of laziness treatment. Thus, for instance, if we change (22) to (23) we have a strictly analogous problem to that presented by (14).

(23)   Every girl who ate a steak enjoyed it.

If we give the NP *a steak* wide enough scope to bind the pronoun *it*, then the sentence will require that there is some one steak which was eaten by every girl. If, on the other hand, we allow the universal to have wider scope than the existential in order to obtain a more likely reading for this sentence then we cannot quantify in *a steak* with wide enough scope to bind the *it*. This example again suggests a pronoun of laziness treatment where we paraphrase *it* as something like 'the steak that she ate'. Or we could allow *it* to receive the sort of complex translation that I suggested earlier for pronouns. A reduced version of a translation of the appropriate structure for (23) would be (24).

(24) $\forall u[\text{girl}'(u) \wedge \exists v[\text{steak}'(v) \wedge \text{eat}'*(u, v)]$
        $\supset \exists x[\forall y[[{}^{\vee}S(u)](y) \equiv x = y] \wedge \text{enjoy}'*(u, x)]]$.

This may be paraphrased approximately as 'for anything, if it's a girl and there's a steak which she eats, then there is a unique individual which bears the relation S to her and she enjoys it'. According to some contexts of use $S(u)$ will represent the property of being the steak which u eats and this will get us a possible anaphoric reading for the pronoun. According to other contexts of use it will be an entirely different property which will get us a non-anaphoric reading.[9]

I believe that, once we introduce some treatment along these lines, we should be able to explain away all examples where it seems that an indefinite description has to be quantified into a relative clause in order to bind a pronoun that is not within the relative clause and thus such examples would not represent counterexamples to the claim that quantifier scope is constrained by the complex NP constraint.

However, there are other apparent counterexamples such as those given in (25) which were mentioned in Cooper (1975, p. 320, n. 6).

(25a)   Ford recalled all the '75 models which were put out by *a factory of theirs in Detroit.*
(25b)   John wants to date every girl who goes out with *a professor who flunked him out of Linguistics 101.*
(25c)   Mary dates every man who knows *a producer I know.*[10]

It seems that the underlined NP in each of these can be given wider scope than *every* and thus would have to lowered into a complex NP. These sentences, however, are not really counterexamples. Certainly they appear to be consistent with a world where Ford only has one factory in Detroit, John was only flunked out of Linguistics 101 by one professor or there is only one producer I know for whom it is true that Mary dates every man who knows him. But then the narrow scope reading is also consistent with such a world. For example, (25c) would translate approximately as (26) where *a producer I know* is given narrow scope.

(26) $\forall u[\text{man}'(u) \land \exists v[\text{producer I know}'(v) \land \text{know}'*(u, v)]$
          $\supset \text{date}'*(m, u)].$

(26) is consistent with a world where there is just one producer who has the required properties, although it does, of course, also allow for the possibility that there is a different producer for each man. But then so does the English sentence. There seems to be no reason *a priori* for us to suppose that the English sentences are ambiguous between a wide-scope and a narrow scope reading since the narrow scope reading will always give truth in those worlds where the wide scope reading gives truth. The narrow scope reading will cover all the cases we require. It may well be that (25a) and (25b) seem to make more sense if there is just one factory or just one professor with the appropriate properties but this is just because it seems unlikely that Ford would have more than one factory in Detroit or that John would flunk out of Linguistics 101 more than once. Thus what appears to be a preferred wide scope reading we may take to be a narrow scope reading which is restricted by our knowledge of the world. (I believe that remarks along these lines could be made about similar sentences containing *a certain* but I am not sure.)

4. EXAMPLES WITH DEFINITE AND INDEFINITE DESCRIPTIONS IN INTENSIONAL CONTEXTS

In this section we shall consider potential counterexamples which involve complex NP's in intensional contexts where it might appear that the head noun can be interpreted *de dicto* while at the same time an NP embedded in the relative clause can be interpreted *de re*. Such an example is mentioned by Hausser (1976) and is given here as (27).

(27)   John is looking for a man who stole a green pick-up truck.

It appears that, as Hausser claims, there is a reading for this sentence which would correspond to the deep structure (28).

(28)[11]

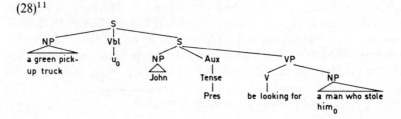

It might be thought that the sentence should be true on this reading if John has a particular green pick-up truck in mind and his search would come to an end if he found any man who stole it. However, it is not clear that this reading should be represented by the tree in (28) rather than the one in (29) where the whole complex NP is treated as *de re*

(29)

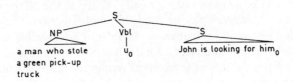

(29) differs from (28) in that it does entail that there is a man who is the thief. However, if it should be the case that John knows nothing about the thief other than that he is a man and that he stole the green pick-up truck in question, then it seems quite reasonable to suppose that even on this reading John is engaged in a search which at least in his view would come to an end if he found any man who stole the truck since the phrase *man who stole the truck* represents for John the sole identifying characteristic of the man in question. Thus in such a situation the *de re* reading represented by (29) appears intuitively to have some things in common with the *de dicto* reading represented by (28).[12]

The difference between (28) and (29) thus turns out to be rather subtle and it is difficult to tell whether the English sentence has both readings or not. Fortunately, the issue can be clarified by considering the different kinds of anaphora associated with *de re* and *de dicto* NP's. The two readings of the simple sentence (30a) can be distinguished by continuing as in (30b) or as in (30c).

(30a)   John is looking for a unicorn
(30b)   ... but he won't find one
(30c)   ... but he won't find it

Assuming that the NP's *one* and *it* are anaphorically related to a unicorn, the continuation (30b) allows the *de dicto* reading and (30c) forces the *de re* reading.[13] In fact, while it is possible to have the NP *one* anaphorically related to an NP in an extensional context, as in (31), it seems that in the case of (30a) the continuation (30b) makes the *de dicto* or intensional reading strongly preferred.

(31)   John found a unicorn but Bill didn't find one.

In the light of the examples (30) a theory of quantifying-in will make precise predictions about the acceptability of certain English sentences, at least on strongly preferred readings. If quantifying-in is not constrained by the complex NP constraint we should be able to continue the sentence *John is looking for a man who stole a green pick-up truck* in ways that will freely allow either *one* or *he* to be anaphorically related to the NP *a man* ... and either *one* or *it* to *a green pick-up truck*. If quantifying-in is constrained by the complex NP constraint then it should not be possible to have *one* anaphorically related to *a man* ... and *it* anaphorically related to *a green pick-up truck* (on the strongly preferred reading) since this would involve interpreting *a man* ... as *de dicto* and *a green pick-up truck de re*. The facts, illustrated by (32), support the view that quantifying-in is constrained by the complex NP constraint.

(32)   John is looking for a man who stole a green pick-up truck but he

can't find $\begin{Bmatrix} him \\ one \end{Bmatrix}$ because it wasn't licensed or insured last year.

It seems that the use of *one* is incompatible with the use of *it* as anaphorically related to *a green pick-up truck*. Notice that substituting *him* for *one* creates a much happier sentence since this allows that the whole complex NP has been quantified in. Notice also that the use of *one* is fine if the *because*-clause is removed since then there is nothing about the sentence which forces *a green pick-up truck* to be interpreted *de re*.[14]

Similar examples with definite descriptions cannot be explained in the same way. Cresswell (in discussion following the presentation of an earlier version of this paper) pointed out the example given as (33).

(33)   John is looking for a girl who will look after his cat.

Intuitively, there is a reading for this sentence which entails that John has a cat but not that there is a girl who will look after it. In addition we find that the NP *a girl* ... may be anaphorically related to *one* at the same time as *his cat* is anaphorically related to *it*. Thus the continuation (34) for (33) does not produce the strangeness we noted in connection with (32).

(34)   ... but he won't find one because it's such a fussy old thing.

On the present Russellian analysis of definite descriptions such examples are clear counterexamples to the claim that quantifier scope is constrained by the complex NP constraint. However, there is a good deal of discussion in the literature suggesting that definite descriptions should be treated as introducing a presupposition of existence. While I do not present such an analysis here it is possible that the difficult reading for (33) could be explained in this way without requiring that *his cat* be quantified into the NP *a girl* . . . . Such an analysis would, however, have to account for the fact that definite descriptions do not always introduce this presupposition in intensional contexts. Thus, for example, the sentences (35) do not entail the existence of a cat. (This fact was pointed out to me by Cresswell.)

(35)   John is looking for $\left\{ \begin{array}{l} \text{his} \\ \text{the} \end{array} \right\}$ cat.

These sentences could be used to describe a situation where John had been promised a cat as a Christmas present and is now looking for a suitably shaped parcel under the Christmas tree. They would be true in this situation even if nobody had managed to buy John a cat and even if cats had become extinct. A more usual example is given in (36).

(36)   John is looking for his piece of cake (but he won't find it because we didn't leave him one).

Yet another kind of potential counterexample involving intensional contexts was mentioned by Cresswell in connection with examples (25) discussed in Section 3. The examples are repeated here for convenience.

(25a)   Ford recalled all the '75 models which were put out by *a factory of theirs in Detroit.*

(25b)   John wants to date every girl who goes out with *a professor who flunked him out of Linguistics 101.*

(25c)   Mary dates every man who knows *a producer I know.*

In Section 3 we argued that these are not necessarily counterexamples to the claim that quantifier scope obeys the complex NP constraint because the apparent wide scope readings which would violate it are in fact consistent with the narrow scope readings and thus it is not necessary to posit an ambiguity. Cresswell pointed out that if such sentences are embedded as complements to verbs of propositional attitude it does nevertheless appear that the underlined NP can be interpreted *de re*. An example is given in (37).

(37)   Sue was surprised that Mary dates every man who knows *a producer I know.*

This sentence does indeed entail that the speaker knows a producer and furthermore can be interpreted in such a way as to suggest that the speaker has a specific producer-acquaintance in mind. This intuition is supported by the fact that (37) can be continued as indicated in (38).

(38)   ... because he knows lots of people.

Thus it appears that the underlined NP is outside the scope of *surprise*. The complex NP constraint would require, then, that it is not just the underlined NP but the NP *every man who knows a producer I know* which is outside the scope of *surprise*. However, this is clearly not the case, even with the continuation (38), since the sentence obviously has a reading where Sue's surprise results from the fact that Mary dates every such man. If the whole NP were outside the scope of *surprise* then the sentence would have to mean that for each individual man known by the producer, Sue was surprised that Mary dated him. On such a reading Mary may not even know that every such man is involved. Thus it seems that it should be possible to analyse (37) as in (39) and that it therefore represents a counterexample to the claim that quantifier scope obeys the complex NP constraint.

(39a)

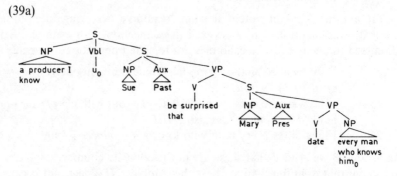

(39b) $\exists u[\text{producer I know}'\ (u) \wedge \text{be surprised}'\ (s, {}^\wedge \forall v[\text{man}'\ (v) \wedge$
         $\text{know}'{*}(v, u) \supset \text{date}'{*}(m, v)])]$

However, there is an aspect of (39) which does not, I believe, correspond to our intuitions about the sentence. This is that if the sentence were uttered on this reading then the speaker would be claiming that there is some appropriate producer such that Sue stands in the be-surprised-relation to the proposition that Mary dates every man who knows him. The fact that the man in question is a producer known by the speaker need not play any role in determining the proposition which is the object of Sue's surprise. In fact, such a reading is consistent with Sue not knowing that the man is a producer. It is difficult, however, to read sentence (37) in this way. For example, it seems at best confusing to continue (37) with (40).

(40)   ... but she was absolutely flabbergasted when she found out that he was a producer (because she figured he must have lots of friends).

This should be contrasted with (41) where a *de re* reading can be obtained without quantifying into a complex NP.[15]

(41)   Sue thinks that Mary dates a producer I know (but when she finds out that he's a producer she'll realize that she's wrong).

This evidence suggests that (37) should not in fact be analyzed as having the reading represented by (39). If quantification were to obey the complex NP constraint, this would be the case. But how then are we to explain Cresswell's original observation that (37) entails that the speaker knows a producer without requiring a *de re* reading for the underlined NP? The reason for this is that (37) entails the truth of its complement sentence *Mary dates every man who knows a producer I know* and that this in turn entails that the speaker knows a producer and may of course be used in a situation where the speaker has a particular producer in mind. *Be surprised that* is one of a class of English verbs which also includes *regret that, recognize that, know that* and *be upset that* which were first discussed in the linguistic literature by Kiparsky and Kiparsky (1970), and whose occurrence in a sentence requires the truth of the complement sentence which is embedded to them. Thus the meaning postulate (42) holds true.

(42) $\forall u \forall p \,\square\, [\delta(u, p) \supset \check{\ }p]$

where δ translates *be surprised that*, etc. This says that for any entity u and any proposition p it is necessarily the case that if u stands in the δ-relation to p then p is true.[16]

It seems that using verbs of this class produce sentences which behave like (37). Thus all the sentences in (43) seem reasonable.

(43a)   Sue $\begin{Bmatrix} \text{regrets} \\ \text{is upset} \end{Bmatrix}$ that Mary dates every man who knows a

producer I know because he has such nice friends.

(43b)   Sue $\begin{Bmatrix} \text{recognizes} \\ \text{knows} \end{Bmatrix}$ that Mary dates every man who knows a

producer I know because he told her himself.

This analysis allows for the required entailment without requiring that the NP *a producer I know* be quantified into a complex NP. In fact it does not allow a reading of (37) which does not entail that the speaker knows a producer. This is in contrast to the *de re/de dicto* analysis which would posit an ambiguity in this respect; it would allow also for a reading which did not entail that there be an appropriate producer. That there is no reading for (37) like this can be seen by adding to it the continuation (44), which creates a contradiction.

(44)   ... but I don't know a producer.

This can be contrasted with the sentence (45) where one would expect both a *de re* and a *de dicto* reading and where the meaning postulate (42) does not play a role.

(45)   Sue thinks that Mary dates a producer I know.

This sentence can be continued with (44) without creating a contradiction.

Finally, consider sentences such as those in (46) which contain verbs of propositional attitude for which the meaning postulate (42) does not hold and have an indefinite NP embedded in a complex NP.

(46)   Sue $\begin{Bmatrix} \text{claimed} \\ \text{argued} \\ \text{thinks} \\ \text{believes} \end{Bmatrix}$ that Mary dates every man who knows a

producer I know.

In these examples, where it is not entailed that the complement sentence is true, it seems more difficult, though perhaps not totally impossible, to continue the discourse with a sentence containing *he* anaphorically related to *a producer I know*. Thus (47) sounds a little peculiar after (46), except on the reading where the whole complex NP is interpreted *de re*.

(47)   He, of course, denies that Mary has even seen his friends.

More convincing evidence that *a producer I know* cannot be interpreted *de re* in (46) without the whole complex NP being so interpreted is that it is very difficult to read (46) in a way that would be consistent with Sue having claimed, argued or held the following belief: 'Mary dates every man who knows Tom' where the speaker knows that Tom is the producer but Sue does not. If Bill, Harry and John are Tom's male acquaintances then I believe that the sentence can be read in a way that would be consistent with Sue having claimed, argued or held the following beliefs: 'Mary dates Bill', 'Mary dates Harry' and 'Mary dates John'. This would be the reading where the whole complex NP was interpreted *de re*.

While the judgements for these sentences are somewhat subtle I believe that there is enough evidence to cast serious suspicion on them as counterexamples to the claim that quantification obeys the complex NP constraint.

5. SOME DUBIOUS EXAMPLES INVOLVING DEFINITE AND INDEFINITE DESCRIPTIONS AND NEGATION

In this section we shall consider potential counterexamples that would involve giving an indefinite or definite description wider scope than negation in the matrix clause and thereby requiring the description to be lowered into a relative clause. Consider the sentence (48).

(48)   John didn't see a man who kissed a girl I know.

The two possible readings that we shall consider might be represented by the deep structures in (49).

(49a)

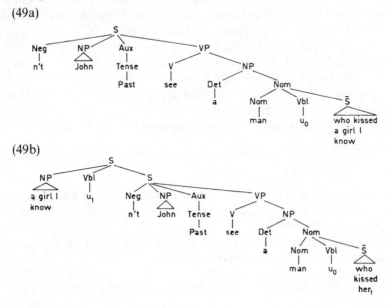

(49b)

The claim would be that (49b) does not represent a possible reading for (48) since it involves lowering into a complex NP. These deep structures will get translations equivalent to (50a) and (50b) respectively.[17]

(50a) $\sim \exists u[\text{man}'(u) \wedge \exists v[\text{girl I know}'(v) \wedge \text{kiss}'*(u, v)]$
         $\wedge \text{see}'*(j, u)]$.
(50b) $\exists v[\text{girl I know}'(v) \wedge \sim \exists u[\text{man}'(u) \wedge \text{kiss}'*(u, v)]$
         $\wedge \text{see}'*(j, u)]$.

Unlike the sentences in (25), the narrow scope reading, (50a), is not consistent with the wide scope reading, (50b). (50b) allows for the possibility of there being some girl I know such that John saw a man who kissed her. It only requires that there be at least one girl I know such that John didn't see a man who kissed her. (50a), on the other hand, does not allow for the possibility of there being any girl I know such that John saw a man who kissed her. Thus we cannot say, as we did for the sentences in (25), that the reading represented by (50a) is sufficient for all cases. Now, however, we must ask the question whether (48) can in fact have the reading represented by (50b). It seems easy to get a reading where the whole NP *a man who kissed a girl I know* is inside the scope of negation, (50a), or a reading where the whole NP is outside the scope of negation. However, the reading which violates the complex NP constraint, (50b), seems unlikely. Even if we choose an example and a context where the reading would be the most natural one it is extremely difficult to interpret the sentence in the required way. Imagine the following situation: the Dean has heard that I am a rather hopeless teacher and has been interviewing students in order to put a critical report together. There were, however, just two courses that I taught which were good but he did not interview any of the students who took one of them although he did interview some of the students who took the other one. It seems unlikely that I would voice a complaint with the sentence (51).

(51)   The Dean didn't interview a single student who took a course I taught that was very good.[18]

Intuitions are certainly not clear but it does appear that at least it is a lot more difficult to process such sentences on readings which would violate the complex NP constraint.

Things are not so complicated if we substitute a definite description inside the relative clause of (48) as in (52).

(52)   John didn't see a man who kissed the girl I know.

Here, the two relevant readings are those represented in (53).

(53a) $\sim \exists u[\text{man}'(u) \wedge \exists v[\forall w[\text{girl I know}'(w) \equiv w = v]$
$\wedge \text{ kiss}'*(u, v)] \wedge \text{see}'*(j, u)]$.

(53b) $\exists v[\forall w[\text{girl I know}'(w) \equiv w = v] \wedge \sim \exists u[\text{man}'(u)$
$\wedge \text{ kiss}'*(u, v) \wedge \text{see}'*(j, u)]]$.

The difference between these two is that (53b) requires that there be some unique girl that I know whereas (53a) does not. However, I think (53a) is consistent with (53b) and so there is no need for us to posit the offending reading.

Hausser (1976) mentions examples involving the relative scope of negation and *any*. (54) is his example.

(54)   John didn't find a farmer who rents any horses.

It seems that people who find this sentence acceptable (for me it is unacceptable with normal stress) assign it the reading represented in (55) which presents a counterexample to the claim that quantifier scope is restricted by the complex NP constraint.

(55a)

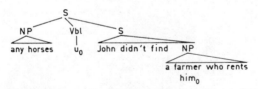

(55b) $\forall u[\text{horse}'(u) \supset \sim \exists v[\text{farmer}'(v) \wedge \text{rent}'*(v, u)$

$\wedge \text{ find}'*(j, v)]]$.

While the unacceptability of this sentence in my dialect might be explained by the fact that *any* would normally be required to have wider scope than the negation but cannot here because of the complex NP constraint; the other dialect where (54) is acceptable on the relevant reading provides a counterexample which I cannot explain.

6. SOME MORE DUBIOUS EXAMPLES INVOLVING DEFINITE AND INDEFINITE DESCRIPTIONS AND TENSE

In this section we shall consider potential counterexamples that would involve giving an indefinite or definite description wider scope than a tense operator represented in the matrix clause and thereby requiring the description to be lowered into a relative clause. Consider the sentences in (56).

(56a)   Every congressman who remembers the President will be at the party.

(56b)   Every girl who knew the President (when he was a congressman) was at the party.

It seems that (56a) could be said now about Gerald Ford and a party which is to be held when he is out of office for every congressman at the time of the party who remembers him, e.g., it might be a reunion for those congressmen still in office who remember the days when Gerald Ford was still president. In order to get this reading, it seems, *every* and *congressman* would have to be in the scope of the future operator while *the President* would have to be outside its scope. In order to achieve this we would have to have a deep structure like (57).

(57)

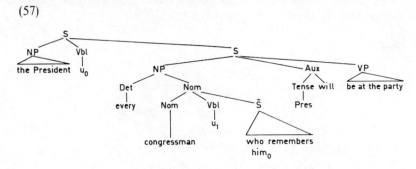

In order to derive the surface structure, of course, we will have to lower *the President* into a complex NP. Similarly we may think of (56b) as being said now about Gerald Ford and a party which was held before he became president at which every girl who knew him then was present. Thus *every* should be within the scope of the past tense operator but *the President* should be outside the scope of the past tense operator. On this reading (56b) would have to have a deep structure which is essentially similar to (57). It seems, then, that we have some clear counterexamples here to the claim that quantifier scope obeys the complex NP constraint. However, the examples are suspect. Consider the sentence (58), which is like (56a) except that we have an indefinite description inside the relative clause.

(58)   Every congressman who remembers a President will be at the party.

I believe that this sentence could be said now about a time in the future after the presidency has been abolished. The sentence might indicate plans for a future reunion of elderly congressmen who remember the days when there were presidents. Thus we want *every* to be in the scope of the future operator since it is not every present congressman remembering a president who will be at the party. However, at that future time, we are assuming, there will not be any presidents. Thus we would want *a president* to be outside the scope of the future operator. However, this would require that *a president* has wider scope than *every* and it does not seem that the English sentence requires that there be one particular president that every congressman remembers, even in the situation we have described. The two readings we have to choose from are represented by the translations in (59).

(59a) $W[\forall u[\text{congressman}'(u) \wedge \exists v[\text{president}'(v) \wedge \text{remember}'*(u, v)]$
          $\supset$ be at the party$'(u)]$.
(59b) $\exists v[\text{president}'(v) \wedge W[\forall u[[\text{congressman}'(u) \wedge \text{remember}'*(u, v)]$
          $\supset$ be at the party$'(u)]]]$.

I do not understand what is going on here but it seems that in order to get *a president* within the scope of *every* as it seems we should, then we must allow *president* to denote, relative to a given time, a superset of the set of entities which are presidents in office at that time, i.e., at least some presidents who are in office at different times. If this is the case then the motivation for giving *the president* wider scope in the earlier examples disappears, though we still have to explain the use of the definite description.

7. EXAMPLES WITH EVERY, ANY, NO, EACH

Having cast suspicion on a number of potential counterexamples I should like to examine some examples which support the claim that quantifier scope obeys the complex NP constraint. Such examples are provided by the quantifiers *every, any, no, each*. It is impossible to obtain an anaphoric reading for the pronoun in the following sentences.

(60a)   The man who dates every woman loves her.[19]
(60b)   The man who doesn't date any woman loves her.

(60c)   The man who dates *any* woman loves her.

(60d)   The man who dates no woman loves her.

(60e)   The man who dates each woman loves her.[20]

Clearly the facts represented in (60) will be explained if we do not allow quantifying into relative clauses. Here our pronoun of laziness or free variable treatment will not help us by interpreting the pronoun in any way that would make it seem anaphoric to the NP inside the relative clause and there will be no way of binding a variable underlying the pronoun in these sentences.

There are other examples not involving pronouns, constructed on the model of Rodman's original examples, which show that NP's containing these quantifiers cannot take wide scope outside of a relative clause. Thus, for example, the sentences in (61).

(61a)   Guinevere has a bone which is in every corner of the house.

(61b)   Guinevere doesn't have a bone which is in any corner of the house.

(61c)   Guinevere has a bone which is in *any* corner of the house.

(61d)   Guinevere has a bone which is in no corner of the house.

(61e)   Guinevere has a bone which is in each corner of the house.

Unlike the sentences with an indefinite inside the relative the narrow scope reading here is not consistent with the wide scope reading. The fact that the quantifier is inside a complex NP in each of these sentences seems to force unlikely readings on nearly all of these sentences since the NP inside the relative cannot have wider scope than *a bone*. As Rodman points out about the first sentence, if the relevant NP is not inside a complex NP then the wide scope reading is perfectly natural. Thus compare the sentences in (62) with those in (61).

(62a)   Guinevere has a bone in every corner of the house.

(62b)   Guinevere doesn't have a bone in any corner of the house.

(62c)   Guinevere has a bone in *any* corner of the house.

(62d)   Guinevere has a bone in no corner of the house.

(62e)   Guinevere has a bone in each corner of the house.

(I am assuming that these sentences do not represent reduced versions of relative clauses but that the prepositional phrase is directly dominated by VP. Thus the deep structure for (62a), representing the fact that the NP is quantified into the prepositional phrase, would look something like (63).)

(63)

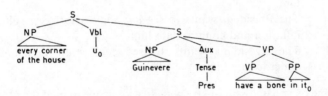

The facts represented by examples (60)–(62) would be accounted for by allowing the quantifying in mechanism to obey the complex NP constraint.

8. WHERE TO LOOK FOR AN EXPLANATION

Although I have talked only about relative clauses, I believe that similar remarks could be made about sentences involving other complex NP's and also sentential subjects. Thus we cannot have an anaphoric reading for the pronoun in the sentences (64) since this would involve quantifying into a complex NP.

(64a)   The claim that every man was sick bothered him.
(64b)   The claim that Mary didn't love any man bothered him.
(64c)   The claim that Mary loved *any* man bothered him.
(64d)   The claim that no man was sick bothered him.
(64e)   The claim that each man was sick bothered him.

Similar examples with sentential subjects suggest that quantifying in obeys the sentential subject constraint.

(65a)   That every man was sick bothered him.
(65b)   That Mary didn't love any man bothered him.
(65c)   That Mary loved *any* man bothered him.
(65d)   That no man was sick bothered him.
(65e)   That each man was sick bothered him.[21]

It seems, however, that the coordinate structure constraint is not completely obeyed by the quantifying in mechanism. Thus, for instance, it seems that NP's with quantifiers like *every* can be quantified into conjoined VP's as is illustrated by the examples in (66).

(66a)   The President wants to see every man personally and congratulate him.

(66b)   The President doesn't want to see anybody and congratulate him.

(66c)   The President wants to see *any*body who has a solution for inflation and congratulate him.

(66d)   The President wants to see each man personally and congratulate him.

For some reason one cannot give *nobody* wide scope to bind the pronoun in (67).

(67)   The President wants to see nobody and congratulate him.

If it should turn out that the quantifying in mechanism does in fact obey both the complex NP constraint and sentential subject constraints there are at least two ways we might consider to represent this in a grammar of English. One way involves using the sort of syntactic representation of scope ambiguities that I have used to illustrate the examples in this paper. Such a treatment involves a syntactic rule of lowering which would automatically obey the complex NP constraint if it applied to insertion rules as well as extraction rules. This, as has been suggested by Postal (1974), would give an interesting general account of syntactic and semantic facts in English. However, it would not necessarily explain why any of these rules should obey such a constraint.[22] I would like to speculate that there is a different account, at least of the semantic facts, which might explain why the quantifying in mechanism obeys the complex NP constraint and the sentential subject constraint but not the coordinate structure constraint. The idea draws on a reanalysis of the Ross constraints proposed by Horn (1974). Horn proposes that the complex NP and sentential subject constraints should be unified into a single constraint which prevents extraction from an NP.[23] Apparent counterexamples to this simple constraint are explained by a pruning convention which removes NP nodes under certain conditions, thus allowing extraction at a later stage in the derivation from what had been an NP in underlying structure. If the facts of the complex NP constraint are viewed entirely in terms of whether it is possible to quantify into or extract out of an NP then I think there might well be a motivated explanation for the semantic facts.

The account would be given in terms of the treatment of quantifier scope given in Cooper (1975, Chapter 4) where ambiguous structures of English were mapped directly into sets of expressions of intensional logic. Quantifier scope ambiguities are not represented in the syntax under that treatment but instead a storage mechanism was introduced which would allow the translation of an NP to be stored and have its place held in the translation by a variable. At a later stage in the processing of the tree the NP translation could be taken out of storage and quantified in. Thus, for example, the deep structure of *John seeks a unicorn* would be something like (68).

(68)

This deep structure would yield both the *de dicto* and *de re* readings. The *de dicto* reading would be obtained by translating the tree in the normal way. The *de re* reading would be obtained by allowing the NP *a unicorn* to translate as a sequence rather than a single expression of intensional logic. Thus it might translate as (69), where him'_0 represents the usual translation of him_0 and *a unicorn'* is the usual translation of *a unicorn*.

(69) $\langle him'_0, \langle$ a unicorn'$, u_0 \rangle \rangle$.

The first member of this sequence is a variable translation which will act as a place-holder and will eventually get quantified by the stored translation *a unicorn'*. The second member is itself a sequence which acts as the store for the usual translation of the NP. It consists of the translation of *a unicorn* together with a variable encoding over which variable it will be subsequently quantified in. The translation of the remainder of the tree now proceeds as usual except that the translation of *seek* and *John*, etc. will combine with the first member of the sequence in (69), i.e., the variable translation. When the complete sentence structure has been translated, the translation of *a unicorn* can be taken out of storage and quantified into the first member of the translation sequence in the usual way.

In this sort of system the NP constraint would say that although a complete NP translation can be stored, an NP cannot be translated with a constituent NP stored. Thus, for example, the deep structure of *A girl who every man kissed bit him* would be something like (70).

(70)

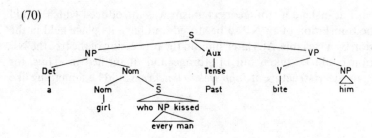

In translating *every man* we would have the option of storing the NP and giving it a translation like (71).

(71) $\langle he'_0, \langle every\ man', u_0 \rangle \rangle$.

If, by the time we got to translate the larger NP we had not quantified in *every man'* we would get the result (72) which would not be allowed by the constraint.

(72) $\langle a\ girl\ who\ he_0\ kissed', \langle every\ man', u_0 \rangle \rangle$.

If we did in fact allow (72) as a translation it would be possible to store the translation of an NP, part of which is already stored, since every time we hit an NP we have the option of storing it to quantify it in later. Thus the constraint would prevent the possibility of an NP, part of which is already stored, being stored again. Allowing double storage of this type would in fact have disastrous consequences in the system proposed in Cooper (1975). Thus in terms of the semantics, the constraint would turn out to be something akin to a prevention of self-embedding. This way of viewing the constraint, although the details of it are anything but clear at present, is appealing in that it might offer an account which could be related to the difficulty for the human mind of interpreting self-embedded structures.

APPENDIX: A FRAGMENT CONTAINING
SOME OF THE EXAMPLE SENTENCES
OF THE TEXT

The following definition of a fragment of English containing a number of examples in the text is presented merely to make the claims made about the semantics of those examples precise in some measure. No attempt is made to incorporate the complex NP constraint.

For the sake of clarity I have followed the style and conventions of Cooper (1975), Chapter II, and Cooper and Parsons (1976), Sections 1–3. The reader is referred to those works for explanation. This style employs a syntactic representation of scope and variables. I believe, however, that the fragment could also be defined employing the conventions of Cooper (1975), Chapter IV, where this is not the case and that some formulation along those lines would ultimately accommodate constraints on quantification in a more adequate fashion than the present formulation.

The treatment of gender in this fragment is purely syntactic and no account is given of gender of unbound pronouns. For a suggestion for how this might be improved see Cooper (1975), Chapter III.

A.1. *Syntax*

Phrase structure rules

1. S → $\begin{cases} \text{NP} & \text{Vbl} & \text{S} \\ \text{NP} & \text{Aux} & \text{VP} \\ \text{Neg} & \text{NP} & \text{Aux} & \text{VP} \end{cases}$ (a) (b) (c)

2. Aux → Tense

3. VP → $\begin{cases} \text{VP} & \text{PP} \\ \text{V}_t & \text{NP} \\ \text{V}_S & \text{S} \\ \text{V}_{PP} & \text{PP} \end{cases}$ (a) (b) (c) (d)

4. NP → $\begin{cases} \text{Det} & \text{Nom} \\ \text{N}_{prop} \end{cases}$ (a) (b)

5. Nom → $\begin{cases} \text{Nom} & \text{Vbl} & \bar{\text{S}} \\ \text{Adj} & \text{Nom} \\ \text{Nom} & \text{PP} \\ \text{N}_{com} \end{cases}$ (a) (b) (c) (d)

6. $\bar{\text{S}}$ → COMP   S

7. PP → P   NP

8. Vbl → $u_0, u_1, \ldots$

9. V_t → kiss, bite, love, hug, eat, enjoy, date, know, seek, look after, see, rent, remember, have

10. Det → a, the, every, any, no, each, his_0, his_1, ...

11. N_{com} → congressman [+masc.], president [+masc.], party [+neut.], woman [+fem.], bone [+neut.], house [+neut.], girl [+fem.], man [+masc.], steak [+neut.], producer [+masc.], pick-up truck [+neut.], unicorn [+neut.], farmer [+masc.], horse [+neut.], fish [+neut.]

12. N_{prop} $\rightarrow$ John [+ masc.], WH, Mary [+ fem.], I, Guinevere [+ fem.],
    he_0, he_1, ..., $he_{[i_0, \tau_0], ..., [i_{n-1}, \tau_{n-1}]}$ for any $n \geqslant 1$ where if $0 \leqslant j < n$, i_j is a natural number and $\tau_j \in Type$

13. COMP $\rightarrow \Delta$
14. Tense $\rightarrow$ Past, will
15. Adj $\rightarrow$ green
16. V_S $\rightarrow$ be surprised that, think that
17. Neg $\rightarrow$ n't
18. V_{PP} $\rightarrow$ be
19. P $\rightarrow$ at, in, of

A.2. *Transformations* (S-cyclic)

Pruning-convention

(i) Any node which exhaustively dominates a single element is itself deleted if that element is deleted.

(ii) any node which immediately and exhaustively dominates a node with the same label is removed.

Transformations apply as many times as their structural description is met.

20. *Pronominalization* (obligatory)

NP	u_i	X	he_i	Y	$\begin{cases} he_i \\ his_i \end{cases}$	
1	2	3	4	5	6	$\Rightarrow$
1	2	3	4	5	(a) he	
					(b) his	
					(c) she	
					(d) her	
					(e) it	
					(f) its	
					(g) he_j	
					(h) his_j	
					(k) I	
					(l) my	

i, j are natural numbers.

The choice of pronoun is:

(a) if and only if 6 is he_i and the leftmost N_{prop} or N_{com} in 1 directly dominates an item with the feature + masc.

(b) if and only if 6 is his_i and 1 is as for (a).

Similarly for (c) through (f).

If 6 is he_i then the choice is (g) or (k) if and only if the N_{prop} in 1 directly dominates he_j, I respectively.

The choice is similarly (h) or (l) if 6 is his_i,

21. *NP-lowering* (obligatory)

NP u_i X $[he_i]_{NP}$
1   2   3   4 $\Rightarrow$
θ θ 3   1

22. *Neg-placement* (obligatory)

n't   NP $\begin{Bmatrix} Past \\ will \end{Bmatrix}$
1   2   3 $\Rightarrow$
θ 2   3+1

23. *Do-suppletion* (obligatory)

Past   n't
1   2 $\Rightarrow$
1+do   2

24. *Affix-hopping* (obligatory)

Past   X
1   2 $\Rightarrow$
θ 2+1

X is a single terminal element (word)

25. *Case marking* (obligatory)

$\begin{Bmatrix} V_t \\ P \end{Bmatrix}$ $\begin{Bmatrix} he_\alpha \\ I \end{Bmatrix}$
1   2 $\Rightarrow$
1   2
           [+accusative]

α is a natural number or a subscript as specified in rule 12.

26. *wh-movement* (obligatory)

Nom   Vbl $[\Delta]_{COMP}$ $[X$ WH $Y]_S$
1   2   3   4   5   6 $\Rightarrow$
1   θ (a) which   4 θ 6
              (b) who

The choice of relative pronoun is (a) if the leftmost N_{com} in 1 directly dominates an item with the feature [+Neut.] and (b) otherwise.

27. *Relative clause reduction* (optional)

$$\left\{ \begin{array}{l} \text{who} \\ \text{which} \end{array} \right\} \quad \text{NP}$$

$$\begin{array}{ccc} 1 & 2 & \Rightarrow \\ \theta & 2 & \end{array}$$

We define the set of *sentences of the fragment* as the set of terminal strings of the surface structures generated by rules 1–27 (according to the usual conventions of transformational grammars) excepting those surface structures which contain Vbl, WH or Δ.

A.3. *Translation*

Notations of the logic which differ from those in PTQ

Let u, v, w, x, y, z represent $v_{1,e}, v_{3,e}, v_{5,e}, v_{7,e}, v_{9,e}, v_{11,e}$ respectively. (We let z be distinguished, i.e., it cannot be used for relettering or in any translation unless explicitly required.)

Let u_i represent $v_{2i,e}$ where i is a natural number.

Let K, J represent $v_{1,\langle e,t \rangle}, v_{3,\langle e,t \rangle}$ respectively.

Let $\mathcal{K}$ represent $v_{1,\langle\langle e,t\rangle,t\rangle}$.

Let P_i represent $v_{2i,\langle s,\langle e,t\rangle\rangle}$ where i is a natural number.

Let $\mathfrak{K}$ represent $v_{1,\langle s,\langle\langle e,t\rangle,t\rangle\rangle}$.

Let P represent $v_{1,\langle s,\langle e,t\rangle\rangle}$.

Let R represent $v_{1,\langle e,\langle e,t\rangle\rangle}$.

Let S represent $v_{1,\langle e,\langle s,\langle e,t\rangle\rangle\rangle}$.

Let A represent $v_{1,\langle\langle s,\langle e,t\rangle\rangle,\langle e,t\rangle\rangle}$.

We let i, g be constants of type e.

Adjustments to the semantics of the logic in PTQ

In addition to the $\mathfrak{A}$-assignments to variables we introduce $\mathfrak{A}$-assignments to the constant i. This necessitates the following revisions to the semantics of the logic as defined in PTQ. We define an $\mathfrak{A}$-assignment to the constant i as a function c with domain $\{i\}$ such that $c(i) \in D_{e,\mathrm{A, I, J}}$. ($c(i)$ is to be regarded as the speaker of the utterance.) We now define notions of intension relative to $\mathfrak{A}, g, c$ and extension relative to $\mathfrak{A}, i, j, g, c$ adding c into the definitions whenever g appears. In particular we change clause 1 of Montague's recursive definition of these notions to:

> If α is a constant and $\alpha = i$, then $\alpha^{\mathfrak{A}, g, c}$ is that function f with domain $I \times J$ such that for any $\langle i, j \rangle \in I \times J, f(i, j) = c(\alpha)$. If α is a constant other than i, then $\alpha^{\mathfrak{A}, g, c}$ is $F(\alpha)$.

Translation of terminal elements of deep structures

be	— $\lambda A[\lambda x[\exists P[A(P)(x)]]]$
n't	— $\lambda p[\sim[^{\vee}p]]$
Past	— $\lambda p[H[^{\vee}p]]$
will	— $\lambda p[W[^{\vee}p]]$
Δ	— z
John	— $\lambda K K(j)$
WH	— $\lambda K K(z)$
Mary	— $\lambda K K(m)$
Guinevere	— $\lambda K K(g)$
I	— $\lambda K K(i)$
he_i	— $\lambda K K(u_i)$ for any natural number i

$he_{[i_0, \tau_0], \ldots, [i_{n-1}, \tau_{n-1}]}$

$\quad\quad$ — $\lambda K \exists x[\forall y[[^{\vee}f(v_{i_0, \tau_0}, \ldots, v_{i_{n-1}, n-1})](y) \equiv y = x] \wedge K(x)]$

$\quad\quad\quad$ where:

$\quad\quad\quad\quad$ if $n > 1$, f is that n-place composition of the syntactic operation of functional application which obtains a meaningful expression of type $\langle e, \langle s, \langle e, t \rangle\rangle\rangle$ consisting of $v_{i_0, \tau_0}, \ldots, i_{n-1}, \tau_{n-1}$ (in that order) and parentheses (v_{i_k, τ_k} is the i_kth variable of type τ_k),

$\quad\quad\quad\quad$ *or* if there is no such composition, f is the n-place constant function whose value is P_0,

$\quad\quad\quad\quad$ if $n = 1$, f is the identity function.[24]

a	— $\lambda J \lambda K \exists u[J(u) \wedge K(u)]$
the	— $\lambda J \lambda K \exists u[\forall v[J(v) \equiv v = u] \wedge K(u)]$
every, any, each	
	— $\lambda J \lambda K \forall u[J(u) \supset K(u)]$
his_i	— $\lambda J \lambda K \exists u[\forall v[J(v) \wedge [^{\vee}S(v)](u_i) \equiv v = u] \wedge K(u)]$
no	— $\lambda J \lambda K \sim \exists u[J(u) \wedge K(u)]$
u_i	— u_i

Otherwise any terminal element α translates into a constant represented by α', which is of type:

$\langle\langle s, \langle\langle e, t \rangle, t\rangle\rangle, \langle\langle s, \langle e, t \rangle\rangle, \langle e, t \rangle\rangle\rangle$ if α is generated from P

$\langle\langle s, t \rangle, \langle e, t \rangle\rangle$ if α is generated from V_s

$\langle\langle s, \langle e, t \rangle\rangle, \langle e, t \rangle\rangle$ if α is generated from Adj

$\langle e, t \rangle$ if α is generated from N_{com}

$\langle\langle s, \langle\langle e, t \rangle, t \rangle\rangle, \langle e, t \rangle\rangle$ if α is generated from V_t.

Translation of branching structures

19′–8′, 5d′, 4b′, 2′   If α is a tree of the form

$$A$$
$$|$$
$$\beta$$

then α′ (the translation of α) is the translation of β.

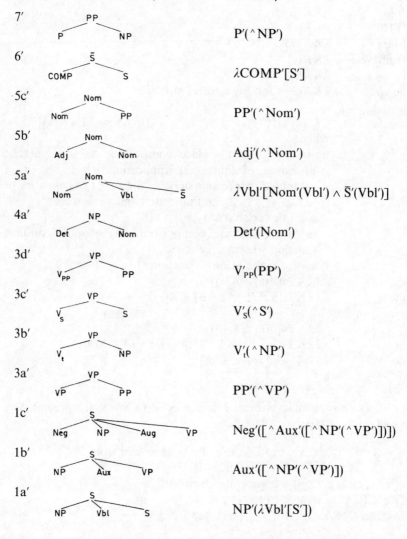

7'   P'(^NP')

6'   λCOMP'[S']

5c'   PP'(^Nom')

5b'   Adj'(^Nom')

5a'   λVbl'[Nom'(Vbl') ∧ S̄'(Vbl')]

4a'   Det'(Nom')

3d'   V'_PP(PP')

3c'   V'_s(^S')

3b'   V'_t(^NP')

3a'   PP'(^VP')

1c'   Neg'([^Aux'([^NP'(^VP')])])

1b'   Aux'([^NP'(^VP')])

1a'   NP'(λVbl'[S'])

We restrict our attention at least to those interpretations of the logic for which the following meaning postulate holds.

$$\exists R \forall u \forall \mathfrak{R} \,\Box\, [\delta(\mathfrak{R})(u) \equiv [\,{}^{\vee}\mathfrak{R}](\lambda w[R(w)(u)])]$$

where δ translates *kiss, bite, love, hug, eat, enjoy, date, know, look after, see, rent, remember, have.*

University of Wisconsin, Madison

NOTES

* I am extremely grateful to Lauri Karttunen and Sue Schmerling for helpful discussion of matters concerning this paper and particularly to Stanley Peters for his invaluable help in straightening out my ideas. Barbara Partee made valuable comments on an earlier version. These people are not responsible for shortcomings of this paper.

[1] I shall abbreviate structures in order not to obscure the argument with unnecessary detail. Exact versions can be found for many of the sentences by working through the rules in the definition of the fragment in the Appendix.

[2] It may seem that the Vbl in the relative clause structure here is gratuitous but it is not as will be seen by working through the rules of the Appendix. The $\bar{S}$ *who loves a fish* translates as (reduced):

$$\lambda z[\exists u[\mathrm{fish}'(u) \wedge \mathrm{love}'*(z, u)]].$$

The larger Nom translates as:

$$\lambda u_0[\mathrm{woman}'(u_0) \wedge \lambda z[\exists u[\mathrm{fish}'(u) \wedge \mathrm{love}'*(z, u)]](u_0)].$$

[3] For the purposes of this paper we may consider a complex NP to be any NP of the form

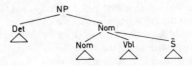

[4] Note that the claim is not that no variable inside a complex NP may get bound by a quantifier which is outside the complex NP whether the quantifying NP gets lowered into the complex NP or not. This claim would be too strong since there are clear examples where the quantifying NP remains outside the complex NP in surface structure but binds a variable inside it as in (i).

(i)   Every man kissed the girl who loved him.

[5] See Partee (1972, 1975) and Parsons (1972) for recent discussion of the usefulness of this notion in the analysis of natural language.

[6] If we allow for variables to be in the syntax, which I do not think is necessary (see Cooper and Parsons (1976) and Cooper (1975)), we may assume that they are pronounced without their subscripts and that besides he_i there is also she_i and it_i for any natural number. See Cooper (1975, Chapter 3) for a specific proposal. I shall ignore problems of gender entirely in this paper.

[7] As I am assuming that individual denoting constants are rigid designators (as Montague did) it is impossible to tell whether a proper name in a relative clause should take wider scope than an operator having scope over the higher sentence.

[8] I am using the term *relation* here imprecisely.

[9] An advantge of this analysis is that there might be other possible anaphoric readings which do not require that every girl ate one steak but discussion of this here would take us too far afield. See Cooper (forthcoming) for discussion.

[10] This example is due to Elan Dresher.

[11] *Is-looking-for* is treated as an unanalyzed verb merely for the sake of simplicity of exposition here.

[12] The fact that John does not have what Kaplan (1969) would call a vivid name for the thief does not, on the present theory, prevent the sentence from being true on the reading represented by (29).

[13] This can be explained by letting *one* correspond to a set of translations of the form $\lambda K[\exists u[^{\vee} P_i(u) \wedge K(u)]]$. (This could be achieved by letting the common noun *one* correspond to variables over properties and the noun-phrase *one* be derived from underlying *a one*). A possible translation of *he won't find one* would be equivalent to the expression given in (i).

(i) $\sim [W[\text{find}'(^{\wedge} \lambda K[\exists u[^{\vee} P_0(u) \wedge K(u)]])(u_0)]]$.

(i) can now be compared with (ii) which is equivalent to the translation of (30a).

(ii) $\text{look-for}'(^{\wedge} \lambda K[\exists u[\text{unicorn}'(u) \wedge K(u)]])(j)$.

If we interpret (i) relative to a context of use which assigns John to u_0 and the property of being a unicorn to P_0 then (i) says that John will not stand in the find relation to exactly the same property of characteristics that is represented in (ii) which says that John stands in the look for relation to it. The fact that the NP's *a unicorn* and *one* correspond to the same property of characteristics is what causes the effect of anaphora on the *de dicto* reading of (30a). This, of course, would not be the case with any of the translations of *it* and thus we would not expect anaphora with *it* on the *de dicto* reading although we would on the *de re* reading. (See Cooper (forthcoming), for discussion of relevant examples.)

[14] It may be thought that the oddity of (32) with *one* results from certain aspects of the meaning of the verb *steal*, namely that if there is more than one thief involved then none of the accomplices can be said to have separately stolen the truck on the given occasion. Thus it might be argued that the use of the NP *a man who stole a green pick-up truck* suggests that there was in fact only one thief and hence the use of *one* is inappropriate. I am not sure whether this is in fact a property of the meaning of *steal* but it seems that this problem can be avoided by substituting *was involved in the theft of* for *stole* in (32) and that the intuitions remain the same.

[15] I have changed the verb from *be surprised that* to *think that* because it seems that an NP in a complement sentence embedded to the former cannot be interpreted *de re*. Thus (i) is again at best confusing.

(i)   Sue is surprised that Mary dates a producer I know (but when she finds out that he's a producer, she'll be flabbergasted).

I believe that an explanation of this might lie in an adaptation of Horn's (1974, 1975) NP constraint (see Section 9 of the present paper). If the complements of factives such as *be surprised*, *regret* etc. are dominated by NP at all stages of the derivation then requiring that quantification obeys the NP constraint would explain why (i) is peculiar. Non-factives like *think* could be strictly-subcategorized to be followed by S. (Those like *believe* could be strictly subcategorized for either NP or S, thus eliminating, I believe, the need for Horn's pruning convention.) Note that on this kind of analysis the NP constraint also explains facts such as those in (ii).

(iia)   Who does Sue think that Mary dates?
(iib)   *Who is Sue surprised that Mary dates?

[16] For these particular verbs the relation is usually considered to be presupposition rather than entailment but it is not necessary to build in the required apparatus for the present discussion.

[17] There is a third possible reading where the whole NP *a man who kissed a girl I know* would be quantified in with wider scope than negation.

[18] This example and context were supplied by Stanley Peters.

[19] Similar examples, such as (i), which were first noted by Geach (1962), I believe, provide apparent counterexamples to the claim.

(i)   The woman who every Englishman admires is his mother.

Here it seems that the reading represented by (ii) is possible.

(ii)

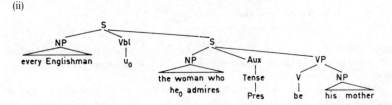

However, it has been pointed out by Higgins (1976) that such sentences are really pseudo-cleft sentences with noun antecedents. That is, they should have the same kind of structure as (iii).

(iii)   The one who every Englishman admires is his mother.

That such sentences differ in a systematic way from normal relative clause constructions can be shown by substituting a non-copula verb in the main sentence as in (iv).

(iv)   The $\left\{ \begin{matrix} \text{woman} \\ \text{one} \end{matrix} \right\}$ who every Englishman admires hates his mother.

As these sentences do not have the copula verb in the main sentence they must be treated as containing normal relative clauses and not as pseudo-clefts. They do not have a reading where *every Englishman* binds *his*. This is predicted by the complex NP constraint. Pseudo-clefts in general exhibit the characteristic that what appears to the right of the copula may be 'connected' with what appears in the *wh*-clause, e.g., it may contain an NP which would normally be required to be within the same sentence as material in the *wh*-clause. (See Higgins (1976) and the references cited there for detailed discussion.) Thus, for example, the pseudo-cleft (va) is acceptable although normally *own* has to occur in the same clause as its antecedent. (vb), on the other hand, which contains a normal relative clause is unacceptable on the expected reading.

(va) $\begin{Bmatrix} \text{The animal} \\ \text{What} \end{Bmatrix}$ every Englishman cherishes is his own dog.

(vb) $\begin{Bmatrix} \text{The animal} \\ \text{What} \end{Bmatrix}$ every Englishman cherishes hates his own dog.

Similar examples can be constructed with reflexives.

(via) $\begin{Bmatrix} \text{The thing} \\ \text{What} \end{Bmatrix}$ every Englishman insists on is shaving himself.

(vib) $*\begin{Bmatrix} \text{The thing} \\ \text{What} \end{Bmatrix}$ every Englishman insists on prevents shaving himself.

These characteristics are shared by cleft sentences like (vii).

(vii)   It is his (own) mother who every Englishman admires.

The semantics of cleft sentences has been studied in the present framework by Halvorsen (1976a, b) who points out that sentences like (viiia) and (viiib) have a *de dicto* reading for an NP which is normally permitted only when the NP is in the object position of the intensional verb.

(viiia)   It is a banana that Mary wants.
(viiib)   What Mary wants is a banana.

While I am not in a position to present an analysis of either clefts or pseudo-cleft I feel that there should be some systematic account of such characteristics and that such an account may not involve violations of the complex NP constraint.

[20] Stanley Peters has pointed out to me the following example which shows that it is possible at least for some speakers to construct sentences where *each* does appear to take wider scope and bind the pronoun:

(i)   The man who builds each television set also repairs it.

Although it is clear that the usual pronunciation of this sentence involves a different intonation pattern than the usual pronunciation of (60e) I really have no idea why this sentence should sound so much better with an anaphoric reading for the pronoun.

[21] This sentence seems marginally good with an anaphoric reading for the pronoun, inviting comparison with the sentence mentioned in footnote 20.

[22] It is interesting to note that if it were incorporated into the fragment in the Appendix as a syntactic constraint on variables in transformations (e.g., along the lines of Cooper, 1975, Chapter VI) it would produce incorrect results since it would incorrectly constrain pronominalization. This disadvantage would not arise in the kind of system discussed in Cooper (1975), Chapter IV where there is no syntactic rule of pronominalization.

[23] His constraint actually accounts for more data than those handled by the complex NP and sentential subject constraints.

[24] It should be noted that the inelegant nature of this definition is an artifact of the requirement that we specify a translation for each member of the set of syntactic variables. See Cooper (forthcoming) for an indication of how this would be improved by interpreting pronouns in the manner of Cooper (1975), Chapter IV.

BIBLIOGRAPHY

Cooper, Robin (1975), *Montague's Semantic Theory and Transformational Syntax*, Unpublished Ph.D. dissertation, University of Massachusetts at Amherst.

Cooper, Robin (forthcoming), The Interpretation of Pronouns, in Frank Heny and Helmut Schuelle (eds.), *Proceedings of the Third Groningen Round Table*.

Cooper, Robin and Parsons, Terence (1976), 'Montague Grammar, Generative Semantics, and Interpretive Semantics', in Barbara Partee (ed.), *Montague Grammar*, Academic Press, New York.

Fauconnier, Gilles (1975), 'Pragmatic Scales and Logical Structure', *Linguistic Inquiry*, VI.3, 353–376.

Geach, Peter (1962), *Reference and Generality: An Examination of Some Medieval and Modern Theories*, Cornell University Press, Ithaca, Emended Edition, 1968.

Halvorsen, Per-Kristian (1976a), 'Syntax and Semantics of Cleft-Sentences', Papers from the 12th Regional Meeting of the Chicago Linguistic Society (Edited by S. Mufwene, C. Walker and S. Steever).

Halvorsen, Per-Kristian (1976b), 'Transformational Syntax and Modeltheoretic Semantics for Pseudo-clefts', Paper delivered at the Winter LSA meetings, Philadelphia.

Hausser, Roland (1976), 'Scope Ambiguity and Scope Restrictions in Montague Grammar', in J. Groenendijk and M. Stokhof (eds.) *Amsterdam Papers in Formal Grammar*, Vol. I, Centrale Interfaculteit, Universiteit van Amsterdam.

Higgins, F. Roger (1976), *The Pseudo-cleft Construction in English*, Indiana University Linguistics Club.

Horn, George (1974), *The Noun Phrase Constraint*, unpublished Ph.D. dissertation, University of Massachusetts at Amherst.

Horn, George (1975), 'On the Nonsentential Nature of the POSS-ING Construction', *Linguistic Analysis*, 1.4, 333–387.

Kaplan, David (1969), 'Quantifying in', in D. Davidson and J. Hintikka (eds.), *Words and Objections: Essays on the Work of W. V. Quine*, Dordrecht, Reidel.

Kiparsky, Paul and Kiparsky, Carol (1970), 'Fact', in Manfred Bierwisch and Karl Heidolph (eds.), *Progress in Linguistics*, Mouton, The Hague.

Montague, Richard (1974), *Formal Philosophy: Selected Papers of Richard Montague*, Edited and with an introduction by Richmond H. Thomason. Yale University Press, New Haven.

Parsons, Terence (1972), *A portion of a draft of a projected work entitled "A Semantics for English"*, Ditto, University of Massachusetts at Amherst.

Partee, Barbara (1972), 'Opacity, Coreference, and Pronouns', in Donald Davidson and Gilbert Harman (eds.), *Semantics of Natural Language*, Reidel, Dordrecht.

Partee, Barbara (1975), 'Deletion and Variable Binding', in E. Keenan (ed.), *Formal Semantics of Natural Language*, Cambridge, Cambridge University Press.

Postal, Paul (1974), 'On Certain Ambiguities', *Linguistic Inquiry*, Vol. 3, pp. 367–424.

Rodman, Robert (1976), 'Scope Phenomena, "Movement Transformations", and Relative Clauses', in Barbara Partee (ed.), *Montague Grammar*, Academic Press, New York.

Ross, John (1967), *Constraints on Variables in Syntax*, Indiana University Linguistics Club.

M. J. CRESSWELL

ADVERBS OF SPACE AND TIME

This paper is part of a larger project concerned with the formal semantics, considered along model-theoretic and truth-conditional lines, of adverbial and prepositional modification. It very soon became apparent to me that the role of space and time in adverbial modification was far greater than I, in company with most logicians, had ever assumed. It also became clear that a great many general puzzles about modification could be looked at using spatio-temporal modifiers as illustrations. In the end it turned out that the whole paper is centred on a single adverb, *viz* **quickly**, and I am very conscious of having barely begun to touch the surface of even this restricted area, but it has seemed to me for some time now that logicians can no longer be content with merely proposing general frameworks and discussing the so-called 'logical words' of a natural language but must actually dirty their hands and try to support the framework by showing, in as much detail as they can, how particular words behave within it. It is in this endeavour that I hope to have made a start.

One further word of warning. This analysis is not concerned with the mathematical or physical structure of space and time. It is concerned solely with how our language talks about space and time. For this reason a very simple view of space and time is frequently supposed. In general I have made use of only those structural features of space and time which seemed needed to express the semantics of the words being analysed.

1. POSSIBLE-WORLDS SEMANTICS

Adverbial modification is of course the stumbling block for semantic theories based on standard logic. In the first place adverbs are not, on the surface at least, either predicates or individual symbols. In order to preserve a treatment in first-order logic one must therefore do as Donald Davidson has done and resort to rather complex paraphrases which give sentences containing adverbs an underlying form very different from their surface form.[1] All I want to say about this at the moment is that paraphrase into first-order logic conflicts with a prejudice of mine which I have dignified by describing as the *proximity principle* ([11, p. 460]), *viz* that one important

171

F. Guenthner and S. J. Schmidt (eds.), Formal Semantics and Pragmatics for Natural Languages, 171–199. All Rights Reserved.

task of a truth-conditionally-based formal semantics is to produce a formal analysis which is as close as possible to the surface. I have myself used to this end things I have called λ-categorial languages.[2] I have now been convinced that it is possible to get even closer to the surface if we abandon the requirement that the formal base language be a categorial one; in fact Richard Montague's work is a clear example of this.[3] Nevertheless, λ-categorial languages can get pretty close and they have the advantage of coming equipped with almost all of their syntactical and semantical framework, once the category and value of each particular symbol is specified.

In a categorial language a verb seems naturally represented by a predicate, a one-place predicate for an intransitive verb, and a two-place predicate for a transitive verb.[4] A one-place predicate (*vide* the Appendix) is a functor which makes a sentence out of a name, thus **runs** makes the sentence **John runs** out of the name **John**. If we use 1 to designate the category of name and 0 to designate the category of sentence then a one-place predicate will be in category $\langle 0, 1 \rangle$ and a two-place predicate will be in category $\langle 0, 1, 1 \rangle$. If an intransitive verb like **dances** is represented by a one-place predicate then an adverb like **beautifully** seems best represented as a *predicate modifier* which makes the complex (one-place) predicate **dances beautifully** out of **dances**.[5] In a categorial language predicate modifiers are in category $\langle\langle 0, 1 \rangle, \langle 0, 1 \rangle\rangle$ and sentence modifiers, like **not**, are in category $\langle 0, 0 \rangle$.

There is however a problem here if we want to keep close to first-order logic. That is that first-order logic is extensional. Let us suppose an interpretation in which **dances** is equivalent to **sings**, i.e., that those and only those are dancing who are singing. If predicate modifiers are added to an extensional predicate calculus then it would follow, in this interpretation, that those who dance beautifully are precisely those who sing beautifully. And of course it does not follow from the fact that the dancers are precisely the singers that those who dance beautifully are those who sing beautifully. This means that if we want to retain adverbs as predicate modifiers we will have to move beyond an extensional predicate logic. Obviously those who want to retain an extensional predicate logic will choose this point to abandon the predicate-modifier view of adverbs.[6] Some of us however are quite happy to abandon extensionality, and welcome the ready-made device, available to us from modal logic, of possible-worlds semantics. In possible-worlds semantics the meaning of a sentence is identified with the set of worlds in which it is true.[7]

Using possible-worlds semantics the meaning of *dance* can be distinguished from the meaning of *sing* provided that in at least one possible world (not necessarily the actual one) there is at least one person who satisfies one predicate but not the other. So even if the actual dancers are the actual singers it does not follow that, even in the actual world, those who dance beautifully are precisely those who sing beautifully. In exactly the same way as from the fact that p and q have the same truth value in the actual world, it does not follow that Lp and Lq[8] have the same truth value in the actual world.

In fact the parallel between adverbs and modal operators goes even further, for it is possible to read L as *necessarily* and it can be plausibly argued that many adverbs must be regarded as sentential modifiers rather than predicate modifiers. This fact is less *ad hoc* than appears at first sight since it is quite natural to regard sentences simply as 0-place predicates. The reason why some adverbs seem best regarded as sentential modifiers can be illustrated by the adverb *necessarily*. If we consider the sentence

(1)   *someone wins necessarily*

we find that there is an ambiguity between[9]

(2) $\langle$*someone*, $\langle \lambda, x, \langle\langle$*wins*, $x\rangle$, *necessarily*$\rangle\rangle\rangle$

and

(3) $\langle\langle$*someone*, $\langle \lambda, x, \langle$*wins*, $x\rangle\rangle\rangle$, *necessarily*$\rangle$

necessarily, being a sentence modifier, is in category $\langle 0, 0\rangle$, *someone* is in category $\langle 0, \langle 0, 1\rangle\rangle$ and *wins* is in category $\langle 0, 1\rangle$. Where x is a variable in category 1 the formation rules described in the Appendix (using the convention that a functor may sometimes follow its arguments) will ensure that both (2) and (3) are well-formed sentences of a λ-categorial language.

If we suppose that the kind of necessity involved in (1) is captured by the rules of a game then it may be that (3) is true (for the rules may specify that there be at least one winner), yet (2) may be false. It is difficult to see how to solve this, at least to solve it neatly, if *necessarily* is a predicate modifier, but not at all difficult when it is treated as a sentential modifier. (This fact has been noted by a number of logicians and linguists; it is more complicated than I have made out but it seems to be a distinction which is there.[10])

Another class of sentential adverbs are some which involve temporal reference. Examples are *yesterday* (a simple adverb) or *at midnight on Christmas day* (a complex adverbial phrase).

Yesterday can be seen to be a sentential adverb by an argument similar to that used for *necessarily*, though we shall have to take liberties with the tense of *wins* for the moment. Instead of the quantifier *someone*, I shall use the complex quantifier *a widow*. We distinguish between[11]

(4) $\langle$ *a widow*, $\langle \lambda, x, \langle\langle$ *wins*, $x \rangle$, *yesterday* $\rangle\rangle\rangle$

and

(5) $\langle\langle$ *a widow*, $\langle \lambda, x, \langle$ *wins*, $x \rangle\rangle\rangle$, *yesterday* $\rangle$

(4) means that someone who is now a widow won yesterday, while (5) means that yesterday someone who was a widow won. Obviously (4) and (5) can have different truth values.

2. TEMPORAL INDICES

Let us then see what kind of a semantics *yesterday* requires. Our earlier strategy was to move into possible-worlds semantics and say that a sentence is assigned as its value the set of worlds in which it is true. It is not hard to see that this is not sensitive enough for the semantics of *yesterday*. Consider the following two sentences

(6)   **The last week of 1974 began.**
(7)   **The last week of 1974 ended.**

It seems to me plausible to suggest that (6) and (7) are true in precisely the same set of worlds. I can imagine a world in which neither makes much sense, or a world in which some catastrophic event makes the week shorter than normal, but not a world in which one is true and the other false.
    Clearly

(8)   **The last week of 1974 began yesterday.**

and

(9)   **The last week of 1974 ended yesterday.**

need not have the same truth value. Even if *yesterday* could be regarded as referring to a particular context-determined moment of time,[12] it would still not permit (6) and (7) to be assigned merely sets of possible worlds. For if they are assigned the same set of worlds then (8) and (9) would likewise have to have the same truth value. And they do not.

The 'traditional' answer in this case has been that a sentence like (6) does not express merely a set of possible worlds, but rather it expresses a function from moments of time to sets of possible worlds.[13] Or, to put it in a slightly different way, we can say that (6), e.g., is true with respect to the pair $\langle w, t \rangle$ iff in world w the last week of 1974 begins at time t. Looked at in this way (6) and (7) do not have the same value, for the time at which the week begins in any given world will be different from the time at which it ends in that world.

The semantics for *yesterday* then becomes quite simple

(10) $\langle yesterday, \alpha \rangle$

is true with respect to $\langle w, t \rangle$ iff α is true with respect to $\langle w, t' \rangle$ where t' is a time which occurs on the day preceding the day on which t occurs.

More recently it has been shown that single moments of time are not sufficiently discriminating and that the appropriate temporal indices are time intervals.[14] It is not hard to see why this is so plausible. Consider the sentence

(11)   **John polishes all the boots.**

polishes is what is known as an achievement verb.[15] (11) does not become true until John has finished his polishing. Or rather (11) is true of the whole time interval at which the polishing takes place though not of any subinterval of that interval. This view of things allows a very neat and appealing analysis of the continuous or progressive tense.

(12)   **John is polishing all the boots.**

is true at an interval t iff there is an interval t' such that t is a subinterval of t' and t' is an interval of John's polishing all the boots but t is not. I shall return to this point a little later though it is not my purpose to discuss the complexities of the analysis of tense and aspect which are involved in treating temporal indices as intervals, except to say that what has already been done is, in my opinion, impressive enough to provide independent reasons for having intervals as indices, reasons which are not connected with the use to which I am about to put time intervals in the semantics of adverbs.

A similar argument to the one used to introduce temporal indices might also suggest that spatial indices are necessary. Consider, for example, the sentences

(13)   **The desert road has an end.**
(14)   **The desert road has a middle.**

Even when a temporal index is used it would seem that if at any time (13) is true so is (14). Yet of course the two sentences

(15)   *The desert road has an end at Waiouru.*
(16)   *The desert road has a middle at Waiouru.*

may (indeed do) differ in truth value. As with the temporal case there may be ways out by modifying the syntax, but our present object is to retain the predicate-modifier view of adverbs. The solution is obvious, we add a spatial index.[16] The spatial index could be thought of as a point of space but is perhaps better thought of as a spatial region. The argument for spatial regions rather than merely points lies in the semantics of phrases like *in Wellington* where

(17)   *It is raining in Wellington.*

does not mean that rain is occurring in all points in the Wellington area but in an acceptable set of them.[17]

In fact we would need an even more complicated characterization. For, in order to investigate adverbs of motion such as *quickly*, we are going to have to consider the path an object might trace over a period of time. Suppose we have a point on the edge of a gramophone turntable going round and round. If we let p merely be the circle described by this point there is no way of telling, over an interval of time, whether the point went round many times or few; and such information will obviously be crucial in deciding whether it went round quickly or not. p must in fact be a function which associates with each moment of time a set of points of space. We could loosely describe it as a spatial *path*.

I do not wish to dispute the force of these arguments, and indeed it is quite likely that spatial indices will eventually be needed. However in this paper I am going to consider predicate modification when applied to objects considered as wholes rather than as parts. The introduction of the desert road and the gramophone turntable can therefore serve to remind us of the need for later refinement.[18] Where an object a is considered as a whole it is not difficult to define the function p, with respect to a world w and a time interval t, as the function such that for each moment $m \in t$, $p(m)$ is the space occupied by a at m in world w.

We shall therefore speak of a sentence as true or false at a pair $\langle w, t \rangle$ where w is a world and t a time interval. We will refer to the set of all $\langle w, t \rangle$ pairs as W, and our domain D_0 of what we have previously called, and will continue to call, 'propositions' will now contain subsets of W, which are sets of pairs now, not merely sets of worlds. It might be possible to add even further indices and I shall return to this theme later in the paper but what I want to do now is to discuss the semantics of some modifiers which seem to require only spatio-temporal indices. I shall spend most of the time on *quickly*. George Lakoff[19] has protested at the detailed study of a few words and thinks that it upsets the delicately balanced mobile of language. I'm basically unrepentant about doing this though I will try to take note of some of his specific complaints.

I am going to assume that adverbial phrases of space and time can be profitably studied by looking at a very literally physical core meaning for each of them. That is, I shall assume that a sentence like

(18)   *This country changes quickly*.

is to be understood as a slightly less central use of *quickly* which is parasitic upon its use in sentences like

(19)   *This stone moves quickly*.

In (19) we shall be able, I shall claim, to understand *quickly* as making reference to a ratio between time taken and distance travelled. In (18) it cannot be so taken. My claim that (18) is parasitic on (19) is that in (18) we, as it were, pretend that there is something analogous to distance in measuring an amount of change.[20] This means that although the semantics of (18) will not be directly produced, the semantics that will be produced can be regarded as a prelude to the more sophisticated treatment required for (18).

This point is a very important general point regarding the whole approach of formal semantics. It embodies the principle that natural language grows by analogy. What begins as a metaphor ends up looking like a new sense of a word. It is of course ultimately part of the task of semantics to explain this process decently and we are alas far from doing so. In the meantime the best we can do is look at certain first and crude approximations to various words in the hope that we are at least making a correct beginning. All this must be borne in mind in what follows.

3. SEMANTICS OF *QUICKLY*

We must first establish that *quickly* is a predicate modifier rather than a sentence modifier, i.e., we must establish that in a categorial language it is in category $\langle\langle 0, 1\rangle, \langle 0, 1\rangle\rangle$ rather than in category $\langle 0, 0\rangle$ as was erroneously stated in [10, p. 141]. Consider the two sentences

(20)   ***Arabella precedes Bill.***
(21)   ***Bill follows Arabella.***

These sentences seem true at any given time in exactly the same set of possible worlds and so, if ***quickly*** operated on (20) and (21) as whole sentences, it would make (22) and (23) also have the same truth conditions

(22)   ***Arabella precedes Bill quickly.***

and

(23)   ***Bill follows Arabella quickly.***

But of course (22) and (23) can easily differ in truth value. And of course this is because in (22) the predicate being modified is ***precedes Bill*** and in (23) the predicate being modified is ***follows Arabella***, and since these are not equivalent predicates it is not surprising that they are still different when modified by ***quickly***.

Since ***quickly*** is in category $\langle\langle 0, 1\rangle, \langle 0, 1\rangle\rangle$ then where $\langle D, V\rangle$ is an interpretation[21] for a λ-categorial language containing ***quickly***, V(***quickly***), the semantic value of ***quickly*** under $\langle D, V\rangle$, will be a function from $D_{\langle 0, 1\rangle}$ into $D_{\langle 0, 1\rangle}$. Not all members of $D_{\langle 0, 1\rangle}$ will be fit arguments for V(***quickly***), only those which involve motion. Sentences involving other predicates will be semantically undefined when modified by ***quickly***. I shall not try to specify exactly what counts as a predicate of motion, and for this reason the domain of V(***quickly***) will be left a little vague. (I shall sometimes speak of 'appropriate' arguments for various functions, or give the false impression that the functions are total.) Nevertheless, it is possible to give illustrations of the kind of predicates which ***quickly*** typically modifies. I shall give a semantics for ***moves*** and ***walks***.

move(s) and ***walk***(s) are both in category $\langle 0, 1\rangle$ and therefore their semantic values in an interpretation $\langle D, V\rangle$ are functions from the domain of things D_1 to the domain of propositions D_0. For present purposes D_0 contains sets of $\langle w, t\rangle$ pairs. The formal semantics we shall give for ***move*** and ***walk*** are, as always, to be understood as crude first approximations. ***move*** is one of the most neutral of verbs which admit ***quickly*** and can be given the following semantics.[22]

V(***move***) is the function ω in $D_{\langle 0, 1\rangle}$ whose domain consists of all physical objects and is such that for any $a \in D_1$ in the domain of ω and any $\langle w, t\rangle \in W$; $\langle w, t\rangle \in \omega(a)$ iff for at least one pair of moments m_1 and m_2 in t

the space occupied by a at m_1 is different from the space occupied by a at m_2.

It is obvious that this is about the simplest account of moving that could possibly be given. V(*move*) simply says that an object can be said to move over an interval if it is in one place at one moment in that interval and at another place at another moment at that interval. Certain refinements suggest themselves immediately. For instance, the turning gramophone will not count as moving on this account although its parts will. Nevertheless I would like to stick with what I consider to be a core sense of moving.

In giving V(*walk*) I shall not try to define what counts as walking. In my opinion walking is an activity which we learn to recognize by observation, i.e., whether or not we know the meaning of the word 'walk' or its equivalent in any language, we can still recognize walking when we see it. Given that we can, then we can define V(*walk*) as follows:

V(*walk*) is the function ω in $D_{\langle 0, 1 \rangle}$ such that for any $a \in D_1$ and any $\langle w, t \rangle \in W$; $\langle w, t \rangle \in \omega(a)$ iff t is an interval and a is walking throughout t.

There is probably a difference between *move* and *walk* in terms of minimal periods. That is, if a is moving during an interval t then a can probably be said to be moving throughout any subinterval of t. But it is not clear that what takes place during any subinterval of a walking can itself be said to be a walking.[23]

The semantics of *quickly* is concerned with the ratio of spatial distance covered to time taken to cover it. What we have to do is to set the length of a time interval against the length of a line which represents the distance traversed by an object as it satisfies a predicate. Since the object will not in general be a point, this line will have to be determined in a slightly vague way.

Given a spatial object a and a time interval t and a world w, we let $p(a, t, w)$ be a function from moments in the interval t such that for any $m \in t$, $(p(a, t, w))(m)$ is the centre point of the space occupied by a at m. For the intuitively reasonable choices of a, t, and w this function will determine a line which marks out the path traced by the centre point of a as it proceeds through the interval t. (The notion of the centre of an object is best left unspecific. It could be made precise in a variety of ways and it is not clear which way ordinary language chooses.)

We now let d be what is called a metric. Where t is a time interval then $d(t)$ is to be a real number which represents the distance between its beginning and its end[24] according to some unit of measurement which need not be specified provided it is assumed to be constant. Similarly $d(p(a, t, w))$ is to represent the distance of the line $p(a, t, w)$.

The simplest semantics for **quickly** would be one where the ratio of distance to time of a particular walking is compared with the average ratio for all walkings. However Franz Guenthner has convinced me that it is better to take as basic a slightly different sense. When we say that a man walks quickly we more probably mean that he walks in a quick manner. The case is different, as we shall see, when he walks quickly to the station. In that case there is a sense, perhaps the normal sense, in which we do talk about the distance covered by the whole walk during the interval. It will be one of the merits of taking the manner sense as basic that we can use scope distinctions to disambiguate the two senses and do not need to suppose a lexical ambiguity in **quickly**.

The manner sense of **quickly** involves, I claim, not taking the distance of the whole walk and comparing it with the time taken, but rather taking the minimal subintervals of that interval which are intervals of walking and saying that the ratio of distance to time in most of them is above average for walkings occurring during intervals of that length.

$V(\textbf{\textit{quickly}})$ is the function $\zeta \in D_{\langle\langle 0, 1\rangle, \langle 0, 1\rangle\rangle}$ such that for any appropriate $\omega \in D_{\langle 0, 1\rangle}$, any $a \in D_1$ (in the domain of ω) and any $\langle w, t\rangle \in W$:

$\langle w, t\rangle \in \zeta(\omega)(a)$ if $f\langle w, t\rangle \in \omega(a)$ and for most subintervals t_1 of t which are minimal (in the sense that $\langle w, t_1\rangle \in \omega(a)$ but there is no proper subinterval t_2 of t_1 such that $\langle w, t_2\rangle \in \omega(a)$). $d(p(a, t_1, w))/d(t_1)$ is considerably greater than the average of $\{d(p(b, t', w')/d(t'): w' = w$ and $d(t') = d(t_1)$ and $\langle w', t'\rangle \in \omega(b)\}$.

The notion of the average of an infinite number of ratios is another notion which can be made mathematically precise in a number of ways. Intuitively what $V(\textbf{\textit{quickly}})$ says is that where α is any predicate, any object a satisfies $\langle \textbf{\textit{quickly}}, \alpha\rangle$ at $\langle w, t\rangle$ iff the ratio of the path it covers during most minimal intervals t_1 of t to the interval t is greater than average ratio for α. In addition of course a must actually satisfy ω at $\langle w, t\rangle$. It should be obvious how the essential reference to a in the definition shows how Arabella can precede Bill quickly without Bill following Arabella quickly. In the former case we look at Arabella's speed, in the latter case at Bill's.

It is worth noting that $\{d(p(b, t', w'))/d(t'): w = w'$ and $d(t') = d(t)$ and $\langle w', t'\rangle \in \omega(b)\}$ is the average of the class of all walkings at all times provided only that they are in the same world at which the predicate is being evaluated. This is because we want to compare a's movings with all movings. a may be moving quickly by comparison with *his* usual speed though slowly by comparison with others.[25] We shall later examine the use of the preposition *for* in restricting comparison classes so that

(24)   ***Bill moves quickly for him.***

can be true. While

(25)   ***Bill moves quickly.***

may be false. Actually of course the comparison class is frequently heavily context-dependent, and it may be that a contextually dependent *for* phrase should be understood to be present although not there on the surface.[26]

The other feature of the comparison class is that a is said to be walking quickly in a given world if he walks quicker than the average for that world.[27] I am not entirely sure whether this is always the appropriate comparison class since one may sometimes want to claim that there are some activities that no-one ever does quickly, and here one is comparing what people actually do with what they might do in worlds very like but not the same as the real one. Having raised this point however I shall leave it dangling.

We can now cut our teeth on a simple sentence:

(26) $\langle$ ***John***, $\langle$ ***walks, quickly*** $\rangle\rangle$.

I'll treat ***John*** as in category 1 [28] and I am still treating ***walks*** as a semantically simple present tense. Using V(***quickly***) and V(***walks***), (26) will be true at $\langle w, t \rangle$ iff for most minimal subintervals t^* of t which are intervals of John's walking in w $d(p(\text{John}, t^*, w))/d(t^*)$ is greater than the average $\{d(p(b, t', w'))/d(t'): w' = w$ and t' is an interval during which b is walking$\}$.

This last class is the class of all walkings and we can see at once why a quick walking does not have to be a quick moving, even if the walking is a moving.

4. SOME SCOPE DISTINCTIONS

Even at this stage we can produce one or two useful disambiguations.

The first is the difference between two senses of

(27)   ***John walked quickly to the station.***

one where he walked quickly, and his walking was to the station, and the other in which it was a quick walking to the station. To illustrate this ambiguity we shall need to give the semantics for the phrase ***to the station***. Like all prepositions ***to*** has many senses and we shall be illustrating one only. ***the station*** is a nominal made up from ***the*** and ***station*** in the way indicated in [10, pp. 135–138]. The semantics of **station** is obvious but the semantics of **to** needs providing: **to**, being a preposition, is in category $\langle\langle\langle 0, 1\rangle, \langle 0, 1\rangle\rangle, 1\rangle$. That is to say it makes an adverbial expression out of a name.

$V(to)$ is the function ζ of category $\langle\langle\langle 0, 1\rangle, \langle 0, 1\rangle\rangle, 1\rangle$ such that where $a \in D_1$, and $\omega \in D_{\langle 0, 1\rangle}$, and $\langle w, t\rangle \in W$ and $b \in D_1$: $\langle w, t\rangle \in ((\zeta(a))(\omega))(b)$ iff $\langle w, t\rangle \in \omega(b)$ and there is no interval t' of which t is a subinterval such that $\langle w, t'\rangle \in \omega(b)$ and t has a last moment m and there is a spatial point which is part of both the region occupied by a at m and the region occupied by b at m.

The idea of course is that something is proceeding *to* something else over a given interval if the position reached at the end of the interval overlaps with where that other thing is at the end of the interval. (*from* would have the same semantics except that the overlapping would have to be at the beginning of the interval.) The importance of requiring that a walk to the station be a maximal period of walking will emerge in a moment.

It might be objected that this account entails that John can be said to be walking *to* the station only if he actually reaches it. It is worth noting therefore that some recent work by David Dowty on the progressive aspect shows how we can say that John is walking to the station without having to say that John walks to the station. Roughly, Dowty's solution is that we can say that John *is walking* to the station at t iff in some possible world which is like the real one up to t but may diverge thereafter, John performs a walking to the station; and in that other world he does reach the station though not in the real world. There is of course a word in English which does not entail that the action reaches the point in question, *viz* **towards**. (28) and (29) can clearly have distinct truth values:

(28)   **John walked to the station.**
(29)   **John walked towards the station.**

We are now able to disambiguate a simple present version of (27):

(30) $\langle\langle \lambda, x, \langle \textbf{\textit{John}}, \langle\langle \textbf{\textit{quickly, walks}}\rangle, \langle \textbf{\textit{to}}, x\rangle\rangle\rangle\rangle, \langle \lambda, y, \langle \textbf{\textit{the, station}},$ $y\rangle\rangle\rangle$.

(31) $\langle \textbf{\textit{John}}, \langle \textbf{\textit{quickly}}, \langle \lambda, z, \langle\langle \lambda, x, \langle\langle \textbf{\textit{walks}}, \langle \textbf{\textit{to}}, x\rangle\rangle, z\rangle\rangle, \langle \lambda, y, \langle \textbf{\textit{the}},$ $\textbf{\textit{station}}\rangle\rangle\rangle\rangle\rangle\rangle$.

Those unfamiliar with λ-categorial languages may find (30) and (31) a bit forbidding. The idea is simply that in (30) **quickly** operates first on **walks** to form the complex predicate **quickly walks** and then the prepositional phrase **to the station** operates on this complex predicate to form **quickly walks to** *the station.* In (31) *to the station* operates on *walks* to form *walks to the station* and *quickly* operates on this whole thing.

One can think of it as the difference between

(32)   *John [[quickly walks] to the station].*

and

(33)   *John [quickly [walks to the station]].*

The difference is a difference of scope, but the crucial feature is not in the mere fact that we can use (30) and (31) to classify and exhibit the difference but that the semantics of categorial languages in conjunction with the meanings of the symbols in (30) and (31) actually enable us to provide different meanings. This point is worth stressing because at least one discussion of the role of scope differences in formal representations of natural language[29] has not realized that scope is only important as a precise instruction for semantic evaluation. In the present case the meanings given earlier to the symbols in (30) and (31) mean that (30) is true if John in walking to the station performs an action most minimal portions of which which are walkings are quicker than the average walking. (31) is true if most minimal periods of his walkings which are walkings to the station walking is quicker than the average walking to the station. Since the semantics of *to* requires that an interval of walking to the station be maximal there can be no minimal walkings to the station apart from the whole walking. These are obviously different classes and so (30) and (31) are not synonymous. (I spare the reader the details of getting these two meanings. A reader who does not accept my assurance that these are the two meanings is very welcome to work through (30) and (31) on his own.)

There is a possible sense of (27) which we have not captured. On the semantics given, the speed with which John walks to the station is obtained by using the route he actually took. Sometimes I believe (27) can be used to suggest that John took a quick route, i.e., to say that John walked quickly to the station suggests that the time he took was short for the most reasonable route. If he took a roundabout route he may indeed have covered that route quickly yet not, it is alleged, have walked quickly to the station. I must admit that I am not really convinced by this example. It seems to me that although (27) may *suggest* that John took a direct route, it does not entail it. On pragmatic grounds it is reasonable to assume that one who does something quickly does it because he is in a hurry and therefore is likely, though not certain, to do it in the shortest way possible.

There is a use of *quickly* which at first sight looks very different from the one we have so far considered [30, p. 334]. This is the *quickly* of

(34)   *Someone quickly entered.*

or

(35)   *All the guests left quickly.*

In (34) it is not implied that the entering was a quick action but rather that it took place after a relatively short interval of time. In (35) it is not implied that each particular guest left quickly but rather that the whole departure didn't take long. This use of *quickly* is often synonymous with *soon* but it turns out that it has a rather pretty analysis which reveals that it belongs in the same family as the *quickly* that we have already been discussing.

The first thing we notice though about this use of *quickly* is that it does not seem to bear the literal and physical meaning which we have so far been studying. For this reason I will do no more here than offer a few suggestions. The key idea, I would suggest, is that studied by Lennart Åqvist and Franz Guenthner in an interesting paper on tense and aspect. Their idea is that every proposition has associated with it an ordering of the set of moments of time which represent increasing closeness to the proposition's truth. A proposition can therefore be said to be *becoming* true over an interval if, during that interval, the moments are getting closer to its truth and at the last moment the proposition actually is true. We could then say that the proposition becomes true *quickly* if the interval during which it becomes true is short relative to some appropriate comparison class. This makes the semantics of quick becoming much closer to that offered above in V(*quickly*), though as I remarked it is not the physical sense with which this paper is concerned.

A final comment is perhaps in order about the connection between *to* and the manner sense of *quickly*. By insisting that a walking can only be a walking *to* the station if it is a maximal period of walking which ends at the station we have enabled an adverbial (in this case prepositional) phrase to prohibit an adverb from applying to minimal parts of the activity (by saying of course that an activity of that kind has no proper parts which also count as the activity). Thus walking to the station is an activity of a different logical kind from walking and the manner sense of *quickly* arises when *quickly* applies not to *walks to the station* taken as a whole, but only to *walks*.

Quick walking of this kind may well be like Lakoff's running on the spot [30, p. 332] and need not suggest that John is going anywhere, let alone taking the shortest route to the station. This idea that an adverb can sometimes apply piecewise to the parts of an action as well as to the action as a whole may be what is involved in such distinctions as

(36)   ***Deliberately he ate the soup.***

and

(37)   ***He deliberately ate the soup.***

In the former case the deliberation refers to the act considered as a whole, in the latter case to the parts of it, each of which was done deliberately. Since I have no semantics at present to offer for such a psychologically oriented adverb as ***deliberately*** I am not in a position to say any more about manner adverbials in general and so we shall return to the discussion of ***quickly***.

Although I am reasonably happy with the general outline of the analysis, I cannot pretend that it is entirely plain sailing. One difficulty is this. In saying that a man is running in a quick manner it may be that we are claiming that all the little submovements which go to make up the running *but which are not themselves runnings* are all quick. The semantics given does not of course reflect this and the problem is to know what other things and what kind of movements are relevant to establishing the quickness of the running. At this stage all I feel able to do is to suggest it as a line for further research.

5. COMPARISON CLASSES

We mentioned earlier a problem about knowing what comparison class is involved. Sometimes this is made explicit.

One way is to use a *for* phrase. With all analyses of prepositions there seem a great many senses for each one.[30] This particular *for* seems to introduce a phrase which modifies adverbs. Thus we have:

(39)   ***John walks quickly for a policeman.***

(39) implies that John is a policeman, that policemen do not walk as quickly on the whole as others and that John walks quickly in comparison with the class of all policemen. The first question is the category of the *for a* phrase, and indeed whether the *a* goes with ***policeman*** or whether *for a* is a single symbol. I incline to the former view because of sentences like

(40)   *He was defeated ignominiously for Alexander.*

(Another man might not have been degraded by the defeat.)

(41)   *They were tall for girls.*

(42)   *Louis XII always arrived early for the king of France.*

Nevertheless, it does not seem that all determiners can occur with *for* phrases, *viz.*

(43)   **He is tall for every king of France.*

I shall adopt the view that a phrase like *a policeman* is a nominal and therefore in category $\langle 0, \langle 0, 1 \rangle \rangle$. The *for* at issue here seems to operate directly on the nominal to make an adverb-modifying functor. Its semantic category therefore looks quite monstrous, *viz.* $\langle\langle\langle\langle 0, 1 \rangle, \langle 0, 1 \rangle\rangle, \langle\langle 0, 1 \rangle, \langle 0, 1 \rangle\rangle\rangle, \langle 0, \langle 0, 1 \rangle\rangle\rangle$. This can be made more comprehensible if we replace $\langle\langle 0, 1 \rangle, \langle 0, 1 \rangle\rangle$ by *adv* and $\langle 0, \langle 0, 1 \rangle\rangle$ by *nom* to get $\langle\langle adv, adv \rangle, nom \rangle$. If *a policeman* is a nom then *for* makes out of it the adverb modifier *for a policeman*, which in turn makes out of the adverb *quickly* the adverbial phrase *quickly for a policeman*.

The semantics of *for* is a little complicated but we can make it easier by looking at how it ought to work for (39). The idea is that *for* must use *a policeman* to extract from it the property of being a policeman. It must then make *quickly* when applied to *walks* act as if it were applying to the conjunctive property of being a walking policeman. It must in addition entail that the entity in question is a policeman, and further that most policeman do not satisfy the predicate *walks* when modified by *quickly* (cf. [30, p. 340]).

We first show how in general to obtain from a function ζ in $D_{\langle 0, \langle 0, 1 \rangle\rangle}$ a property ω_ζ which stands to ζ the way the property of being a policeman stands to the semantic value of *a policeman*. Not all nominals will generate such a property. ω_ζ is the property (if such exists in $D_{\langle 0, 1 \rangle}$) such that for any $\omega \in D_{\langle 0, 1 \rangle}$ and $\langle w, t \rangle \in W$, $\langle w, t \rangle \in \zeta(\omega)$ iff there is some $a \in D_1$ such that $\langle w, t \rangle \in \omega_\zeta(a) \cap \omega(a)$.

We can show that this is the correct definition by looking at *a policeman*. Let us suppose that the property of being a policeman is ω^*, i.e., $\langle w, t \rangle \in \omega^*(a)$ iff a is a policeman in w at t. We show that where $V(a\ policeman)$ is ζ then $\omega_\zeta = \omega^*$.

Now for any $\omega \in D_{\langle 0, 1 \rangle}$, $\langle w, t \rangle \in \zeta(\omega)$ iff there is some a such that a is a policeman in w at t and $\langle w, t \rangle \in \omega(a)$, i.e., $\langle w, t \rangle \in \zeta(\omega)$ iff there is some a

such that $\langle w, t \rangle \in \omega^*(a)$ and $\langle w, t \rangle \in \omega(a)$, i.e., $\langle w, t \rangle \in \zeta(\omega)$ iff there is some $a \in D_1$ such that $\langle w, t \rangle \in \omega^*(a) \cap \omega(a)$.

Let ω_a denote the property possessed, in any world and time, by a alone, i.e., $\langle w, t \rangle \in \omega_a(b)$ iff $a = b$. Now for any $a \in D_1$, $\langle w, t \rangle \in \zeta(\omega_a)$ iff there is some b such that $\langle w, t \rangle \in \omega^*(b)$ and $\langle w, t \rangle \in \omega_a(b)$, i.e., iff there is some b such that $a = b$ and $\langle w, t \rangle \in \omega^*(b)$, i.e., iff $\langle w, t \rangle \in \omega^*(a)$. Similarly, $\langle w, t \rangle \in \zeta(\omega_a)$ iff $\langle w, t \rangle \in \omega_\zeta(a)$. Thus $\omega^*(a) = \omega_\zeta(a)$ for any $a \in D_1$. (This argument depends on the assumption that each ω_a is in $D_{\langle 0, 1 \rangle}$, but that assumption is not an unreasonable one I think.)

We are now ready to give $V(for)$. $V(for)$ is the function $\eta \in D_{\langle\langle\langle 0, 1 \rangle, \langle 0, 1 \rangle\rangle, \langle\langle 0, 1 \rangle, \langle 0, 1 \rangle\rangle\rangle, \langle 0, \langle 0, 1 \rangle\rangle\rangle}$ such that where $\zeta \in D_{\langle 0, \langle 0, 1 \rangle\rangle}$, $\theta \in D_{\langle\langle 0, 1 \rangle, \langle 0, 1 \rangle\rangle}$, $\omega \in D_{\langle 0, 1 \rangle}$, $a \in D_1$ and $\langle w, t \rangle \in W$; $\langle w, t \rangle \in (((\eta(\zeta))(\theta))(\omega))(a)$ iff

(i) $\langle w, t \rangle \in \omega_\zeta(a)$.

(ii)   For most b's such that $\langle w, t \rangle \in \omega_\zeta(b)$ it is not the case that $\langle w, t \rangle \in (\theta(\omega))(b)$.

(iii) $\langle w, t \rangle \in \theta(\omega \cap \omega_\zeta)(a)$ (where $\omega \cap \omega_\zeta$ is the function such that for any $b \in D_1$ and $\langle w, t \rangle \in W$, $\langle w, t \rangle \in (\omega \cap \omega_\zeta)(b)$ iff $\langle w, t \rangle \in \omega(b)$ and $\langle w, t \rangle \in \omega_\zeta(b)$.

We can loosely read $(((\eta(\zeta))(\theta))(\omega)(a)$

      'a ω's θ'ly for a ζ'.

6. REMAINING PROBLEMS

The beginning of this paper contained a warning about the unfinished state of this research. No doubt there are many more problems than are alluded to here but in this section I would like to indicate some ways in which I see the most pressing problems as being dealt with.

The first problem is connected with the comparison of adverbs. We can say that someone ran more quickly than another, or too quickly for comfort, and so on. The semantics of comparison is not undisputed[31] but I will briefly indicate how my own analysis of adjectives within a λ-categorial framework may be applied to adverbs.

The crucial idea of [16] is to make adjectives (and therefore adverbs) two-place rather than one-place modifiers. Thus **quickly** would mean something like

      'x ω's y-much quickly'.

Formally, *quickly* would be in category $\langle\langle 0, 1, 1\rangle, \langle 0, 1\rangle\rangle$ and its meaning would involve the notion of a *degree of quickness*. A *degree*, in the terminology of [16, p. 172], is a point on a scale. The scale is a relation $>$ and formally the degree is a pair $\langle u, > \rangle$ consisting of one of the terms of the relation and the relation itself. In the case of quickness it would seem best to let the terms of the relation be themselves pairs, and in fact u would be a pair $\langle d_1, d_2 \rangle$ where d_1 is an equivalence class of all paths of the same distance, and d_2 the equivalence class of all time intervals of the same length and $\langle d_1, d_2 \rangle > \langle d_3, d_4 \rangle$ iff the ratio of the distance of d_1 to the length of d_2 is higher than the ratio of the distance of d_3 to the length of d_4.

When the basic semantic unit is 'x ω's y-much quickly' the problems concerning a comparison class arise when *quickly* is used in the absence of any more specific degree indicator. It is therefore very natural to think of them as being supplied by the context.[32]

I should like now to say something about the relation between adverbs and adjectives. In particular we need to consider the semantic relations between

(44)   *John runs quickly.*
(45)   *John is a quick runner.*
(46)   *John's quick running took place.*

It is obvious that if not synonymous these sentences are at least closely related (as Lakoff has demonstrated with some syllogisms).[33] (44) and (45) are not too difficult to relate, at least if we suppose that a runner is someone who runs from time to time and that a quick runner is one who runs quickly from time to time.

(46) however causes more difficult problems, for here the *quick* modifies the predicate 'is a running' and while this is indeed a one-place predicate its argument does not denote the one who runs but rather the running. The proper analysis of (46) is therefore considerably obscure, because it is not at all easy to see at present how a truth-conditional semantics should best link 'is running' with 'is a running'.[34]

Finally a comment on other kinds of adverbs. This paper has been deliberately restricted to spatio-temporal modification. The arguments of the first two sections of this paper suggested that the reason we require possible worlds is because we have to analyse modal adverbs; the reason we require temporal indices is because we have to analyse temporal adverbs and the reason we require spatial indices is because we have to analyse spatial adverbs.

How then are we to deal with an adverb like **loudly**? Are we to suppose that x ω's loudly at a degree of loudness l iff l is greater than the average degree of loudness at which x ω's? It sounds a bit absurd to have to suppose such an index though it is not clear to me that we may not find ourselves forced to do so. Obviously the ontological purists will object to degrees of loudness. But then the ontological purists have no business dabbling in possible-worlds semantics in the first-place. In [16] I showed how things like degrees of loudness could easily be manufactured, using the method of equivalence class, out of entities already available to a possible-worlds theorist; provided that loudness comparisons are legitimate.

The real problem that I see with the loudness index solution is that there does not seem any way of saying in advance just how many indices are required. Yet it seems that we need to say it in advance, because of the fact that adverbial modification has to be predictable on the basis of the words we already know. I mean that our ability to understand a new sentence involving an adverbial phrase requires that we can piece together its meaning from what we already know; so that we would already have to know the value of the embedded sentence at the index required by the adverb, in order to understand the meaning of the new sentence thus formed.

The number of possible adverbial phrases is infinite, yet one feels that the number of distinct indices should be finite. There will of course be many more adverbs than there are indices. For instance, **yesterday**, **at midnight** and **quickly** are all temporal adverbs, or adverbial phrases, and the semantics of all of them can be accommodated by means of an index in terms of time intervals. It may prove that a loudness index can be expressed in terms of something more basic, e.g., the spatial and temporal properties of soundwaves.[35] All this suggests a connection with theories of semantic features, which may well deserve following up.

Nevertheless it would be pleasing if one could avoid the need for having this apparently open-ended sequence of possible indices which may be required. In *Logics and Languages* I tried to deal with this indeterminateness of contextual indices by suggesting that indices be regarded as properties of utterances. Thus, instead of saying that α is true at $\langle w, t \rangle$ we say that w is one of the worlds that the meaning of α associates with the property of being uttered at t. The current problem is to see whether the introduction of properties like that of having a certain degree of loudness can help to avoid any of the difficulties I have just mentioned, or whether they do not reappear in some other form. For the purposes of this paper however we can leave problems such as this alone, having found more than enough to occupy us in dealing with adverbs whose index *is* spatio-temporal.

7. APPENDIX ON λ-CATEGORIAL LANGUAGES

In this Appendix I shall set out briefly, for those who have not met it before, the syntax and semantics of λ-categorial languages. This appendix in the main summarizes the account presented in [10]. The principal divergence is in the analysis of context. In Chapter 8 of [10] an elaborate framework was set up in which contexts of use were construed as properties of utterances. For the issues discussed in the present paper the only contextual index needed is a temporal one and it is the only one given here. A minor difference is that we will not be concerned to discuss the nature of possible worlds and their contents, nor shall we be concerned with the problem of propositional attitudes which led, [10, pp. 39–44], me to take an approach to propositions which some have found a little too high flying for their taste.[36]

A categorial language is based on the notion of a *syntactic category*. There are two basic categories, 0 the category of *sentence* and 1 the category of *name*. Given any categories $\tau, \sigma_1, \ldots, \sigma_n$ then $\langle \tau, \sigma_1, \ldots, \sigma_n \rangle$ is also a category. (It is understood as the category of a *functor* which makes an expression of category τ out of expressions of categories $\sigma_1, \ldots, \sigma_n$ respectively.)

A λ-categorial language L is specified by assigning to finitely many syntactic categories a finite set of *symbols*. These can be thought of as the words of the language. This is done formally by letting F be a function from syntactic categories such that for any category σ, F_σ is the (finite) set of symbols of category σ. All variable-binding is done by an *abstraction operator* which we denote by λ. To deal with variable-binding we require, for each category σ, a denumerably infinite set, X_σ of *variables of category σ*. Given F, X, and λ we can define the set E_σ of (well-formed) expressions of category σ as the smallest set such that:

(i)　　　$F_\sigma \subseteq E_\sigma$

(ii)　　　If $\alpha_1, \ldots, \alpha_n$ are in $E_{\sigma_1}, \ldots, E_{\sigma_n}$ respectively and $\delta \in E_{\langle \tau, \sigma_1, \ldots, \sigma_n \rangle}$ then $\langle \delta, \alpha_1, \ldots, \alpha_n \rangle \in E_\tau$

(iii)　　　If $x \in X_\sigma$ and $\alpha \in E_\tau$ then $\langle \lambda, x, \alpha \rangle \in E_{\langle \tau, \sigma \rangle}$.

(i) says that every symbol of category σ is also an expression of category σ.

(ii) says that when a functor expression in category $\langle \tau, \sigma_1, \ldots, \sigma_n \rangle$ is placed before expressions in category $\sigma_1, \ldots, \sigma_n$ then it forms an expression in category τ.[37] The best way of understanding $\langle \lambda, x, \alpha \rangle$ is to read it as 'is an x such that α'. (iii) makes this in category $\langle \tau, \sigma \rangle$ where σ is the category of x and τ the category of α. $\langle \lambda, x, \alpha \rangle$ is called an *abstract*.

We can associate with a λ-categorial language L an *interpretation*. It is of course possible to associate many different interpretations with the same language. The model-theoretic approach to semantics is based on the idea of specifying things which are understood as the meanings of symbols of L and providing rules for showing how the values of complex expressions of L are determined by the values assigned to the symbols of L. More specifically we want the interpretation to be set-theoretical and truth-conditional.

Each syntactic category σ has associated with it a domain D_σ which is understood as the set of things which are appropriate values for expressions in E_σ. D_0, the values of sentences, is a set of subsets of the set W of all pairs $\langle w, t \rangle$ where w is a possible world and t a moment of time.[38] D_1 is the set of all 'things' where this includes both possible and actual things. $D_{\langle \tau, \sigma_1, \ldots, \sigma_n \rangle}$ is a set of total or partial functions from $D_{\sigma_1} \times \ldots \times D_{\sigma_n}$ into D_τ. Given such a system D of domains, we interpret a language by means of an assignment function V which assigns a value in D_σ to each symbol in F_σ. Where α is in F_σ we refer to its value under V as $V(\alpha)$. Thus we speak of $\langle D, V \rangle$ as an interpretation for L.

In order to interpret all the expressions of the language we have made assignments to the variables as well. We distinguish between an assignment to the variables and an assignment to the constants because the expressions we shall be finally interested in will contain no free variables. Although the assignment function to the variables is important in obtaining the semantic value of an expression without free variables, it turns out that the value of such an expression is invariant under different assignments to the variables. We let v be an assignment to the variables. Where $x \in X_\sigma$ then $v(x) \in D_\sigma$. Further, where $a \in D_\sigma$ then $(v, a/x)$ is the function exactly like v except that $v(x) = a$.

We are now ready to show how V and v together induce a uniquely determined assignment V_v to all the expressions of L.

(i)   If $\alpha \in F_\sigma$ then $V_v(\alpha) = V(\alpha)$.

(ii)   If $x \in X_\sigma$ then $V_v(x) = v(x)$.

(iii)   If $\delta \in D_{\langle \tau, \sigma_1, \ldots, \sigma_n \rangle}, \alpha_1, \ldots, \alpha_n \in E_{\sigma_1}, \ldots, E_{\sigma_n}$ respectively then $V_v(\langle \delta, \alpha_1, \ldots, \alpha_n \rangle) = (V_v(\delta)(V_v(\alpha_1), \ldots, V_v(\alpha_n))$.

(iv)   If $x \in X_\sigma$ and $\alpha \in E_\tau$ then $V_\nu(\langle \lambda, x, \alpha \rangle)$ is the function ω such that for any $a \in D_\sigma$, $\omega(a) = V_{(\nu, a/x)}(\alpha)$.

These rules are all understood of course under the proviso that the appropriate expressions are defined for their arguments. By allowing partial function in D it frequently happens that an expression is not defined. It is then said to be semantically anomalous in this interpretation. (iii) means that the value of a functorial expression is obtained by taking its value, which is a function, and letting it apply to the values of the expressions which follow it. (iv) says that $\langle \lambda, x, \alpha \rangle$ defines a function whose value, for any a is (loosely) what you get from α by putting a in where x goes.

Given an expression α in category 0 and an interpretation $\langle D, V \rangle$ of L we say that α is *true* under $\langle D, V \rangle$ in world w at time t iff $\langle w, t \rangle \in V(\alpha)$. This is why we speak of the semantics as truth-conditional.

In applying a λ-categorial language to a natural language, the idea is to get formulae which look as much like English sentences as possible. One test is to see whether representing the sentences as English words (I use boldface italic type when I can get it) produces a formula which becomes an English sentence when the brackets, the λ's and the variables are omitted. Of course there is still a place for transformational syntax in obtaining the surface structure but the transformations look to be a great deal simpler than many of those who advocate a base in logic seem to require. At any rate the material in this appendix is presented at much greater length in [10].

Victoria University of Wellington and Universität Stuttgart

NOTES

Certain substantial improvements to this paper were suggested to me by Franz Guenthner and Lennart Åqvist while I was associated with the research project at Stuttgart on the formal semantics of tense and aspect supported by the German Science Foundation. In addition students of Christian Rohrer's seminar in Stuttgart made other suggestions for improvement.
[1] Davidson's suggestion was first made in Davidson [19]. Other work along these lines has been done by Wheeler [50] and others. In Cresswell [11] I attempted to incorporate some aspects of Davidson's analysis in an intensional framework. Although I still feel that it may be interesting to see why and how this could be done, I am less convinced that it is the most desirable way, and the present paper represents a return to the view of adverbs as modifiers.
[2] An account of the syntax and semantics of categorial languages is presented in the appendix. It is basically a summary of the framework presented in [10] except that the more

complex analysis of context dependence presented there is here replaced by an indexical approach which will give a favoured place to worlds and times.

[3] Montague [33], in particular Chapters 6–8. A similar treatment for German is given in von Stechow [44] and [45]. A discussion of the relative merits of Categorial versus more direct formal syntax and semantics occurs in Cresswell [18].

[4] It is true that Montague [33, p. 250] offered a different analysis of transitive verbs, an analysis which enabled him to solve certain paradoxes. Nothing I have to say in this paper however will be affected by this.

[5] The predicate-modifier view of adverbs is now well entrenched in the literature although it is by no means universally accepted. This paper is not intended as a survey of work done so far but some important papers are [36], [35], [9], [33], [48] and [37]. The view is criticized by, among others, Heny [25] and Taylor [47]. Some of their criticisms are discussed below since they apply to some of the points made in the text.

[6] As of course those who follow Davidson (*vide* Note 1) have done. One of the difficulties of any work in this area is that arguments which appear conclusive often depend on the framework in which they are set. In the present case the argument that adverbial modification shows that natural language is not extensional only works if adverbs are analysed as predicate modifiers. It therefore will not convince a confirmed extensionalist. Many of the arguments in the remainder of the paper will be unconvincing to those determined to resist their conclusions. My only answer is that this paper is not polemical in intent but represents a genuine desire to probe the structure of adverbs of space and time.

An interesting example of how different aims can dictate quite different value scales occurs in Harman [24]. Harman sets up five requirements for a semantic theory. One of these requirements is that the analysis be as close to first-order logic as possible (a similar desire is crucial in Taylor [47]). This requirement is incompatible with the analysis adopted in the present paper, but all that that shows is that Harman and I are looking for different things; for instance, I place a much higher value than he does on the proximity principle.

[7] Some philosophical motivation for this view is provided in my [17] and Stalnaker's [43].

[8] L is one of the basic sentential operators of modal logic (Hughes and Cresswell [26]). Its intended interpretation is 'it is necessary that'.

[9] I have written these examples in the terminology of [10], which I shall be using later. If we write **necessarily** as L and replace **someone** by a more standard-looking quantifier and **wins** by ϕ we get the more familiar formulae $(\exists x)L\phi x$ and $L(\exists x)\phi x$ which are well known to modal logicians as different in meaning [26, p. 144]. $\langle \lambda, x, \langle \textbf{wins}, x \rangle \rangle$ is of course equivalent to the plain **wins** [10, p. 84], but is kept here to preserve the parallel. In a λ-categorial language, where the variable-binding is done separately, **everyone** emerges as a symbol in category $\langle 0, \langle 0, 1 \rangle \rangle$. In [10, p. 130] I called expressions in this category *nominals* and argued that it is the category of most expressions which linguists call noun phrases.

[10] There is a fuller discussion in Thomason and Stalnaker [48, pp. 200–206].

[11] For the present we treat *a widow* as a simple expression in category $\langle 0, \langle 0, 1 \rangle \rangle$. In [10, p. 137f] it is shown how to manufacture it from *a* and *widow*.

[12] Each utterance of the sentence would have to be construed as using a different name. Some ingenious ways in which this might be done are studied in Bigelow [5]. Although it does not seem to work for tense, it may be that Bigelow's analysis is the best way to deal with most pronouns, both personal and demonstrative, and possibly also with the definite article. This would enable us to dispense with an utterer index.

[13] This approach has been called by Montague [33, p. 96f] 'pragmatics'. Alternatively, it is sometimes called indexical semantics. *Vide* Scott [40, p. 148f] and Lewis [31, p. 175f].

[14] This seems to have been first realised by Bennett and Partee [4]. It is also used by Taylor [47] and Dowty [21]. My summary of their analyses is oversimplified and the interested reader is advised to consult the original articles. My purpose here is merely to present evidence for evaluating formulae with respect to intervals rather than moments. An alternative approach to the analysis of the progressive aspect is presented in Åqvist and Guenthner [1]. They make use of a phenomenon known sometimes as *double indexing* and sometimes as *two dimensional modal logic*. A key paper is Kamp's [27]. Kamp observes that the adverb *now* always refers to the moment of utterance however far it is embedded. Thus he requires all formulae to be evaluated at two temporal indices, one representing the moment of evaluation and one the moment of utterance. Åqvist and Guenthner use these two moments to determine an interval and thus can achieve many of the purposes for which intervals are needed. (There are of course some independent reasons for double indexing and a full account of temporal modification would have to take account of them.) A more general account of two dimensional modal logic is given in Segerberg [41]. Some interesting questions connecting action and opportunity are raised by Walton [49] who asks whether there is a moment during the interval over which an action is being performed when it becomes (logically) impossible for the agent to stop it.

[15] For this distinction and its importance *vide*, in addition to Taylor, *op. cit*, Kenny [29, p. 172], Dowty [20] and Chafe [7].

[16] Propositional logics based on this general idea have been studied under the slightly inappropriate name 'topological logic' in [39] and [23].

[17] There is probably in fact a minimal spatial region which could count as a region at which it is raining.

[18] An ingenious example is raised by Taylor [47, p. 208f] who imagines a stone which is falling downwards quickly but sideways slowly. What seems to be happening here is that the adverb *downwards* acts as an instruction to measure not the actual path of the object over the time interval but a vertical projection of that path, while *sideways* is an instruction to measure the horizontal projection. Obviously at the very least spatial co-ordinates would be needed to deal with this kind of case within the framework of this paper.

[19] Lakoff [30]. Although I find Lakoff's comparisons between the farsightedness of linguists and the shortsightedness of logicians a little unconvincing, I nevertheless do try in what follows to take account of at least some of the problems he brings up which face a semantic analysis of adverbs. In particular I try to show how a great many things which Lakoff supposes cannot be analysed within a Montague framework (e.g., rates of change, p. 331) in fact can be.

[20] Lakoff [30, p. 329] assumes rates as the primitive entities in some places. He does not however seem to realise that a time index is essentially tied to the notion of a rate for he observes on p. 331 that a semantics involving rates makes no mention of times. One useful observation which Lakoff does make however is on p. 332 where he seems to be suggesting that it is the meaning of the predicate being modified which provides the appropriate unit for measuring the amount of change. He says "To understand how *slowly* modifies *walks* one must realise that slowly indicates a change of something with respect to time, and in the case of walking that something is location". The suggestion is intriguing and worth following up. I suspect it may have links with the discussion of mass terms in [16, pp. 180–183] and that some such predicate as 'x performs y-much walking' might be needed. For the present though I shall rest content with looking at predicates in which the amount is a clearly spatial one.

[21] This is set out explicitly in the Appendix.

[22] V is of course a value assignment in an interpretation to the λ-categorial language in which *move* is a symbol. (*Vide* the Appendix.) I have always preferred to give a direct specification of functions like V(*move*) rather than do as Montague does and give a rule for translating it into the language of intensional logic. It is after all the function itself which is the important thing, not the way we choose to express it.

[23] *Vide* Taylor [47, pp. 166–181] for a fairly detailed discussion of problems of this kind.

[24] The notion of a metric can be formally defined, *vide*, e.g., Chapter Seven of [32] but an intuitive grasp is all that is required for understanding this paper. In addition, the present paper contains no discussion of the difference between open and closed intervals, though some authors, e.g., Taylor [47] and Åqvist and Guenthner [1] have considered the difference important.

[25] The comparison class also seems to depend on the kind of thing which is moving. A quickly-moving pencil may indeed be moving far more slowly than a slowly moving car. Some of the problems might be illuminated if the question of the comparison class were studied in conjunction with the analysis of the comparative form of adverbs. Some hints about this are given in section eight. (Some discussion occurs in Lakoff [30, p. 330] citing Harman [24, p. 48].) One feature which may be important is that, according to Clark [8], a great deal of our spatio-temporal language is grounded in the framework determined by an average size human observer standing in an upright position. It may be that there is a principled way of deriving the appropriate comparison classes from such a source.

[26] Some ways in which this might be done are discussed in Bigelow [5]. It is however undesirable to postulate such 'invisible' phrases unless very strongly motivated. The context-dependence of comparison classes has lead Kamp [28] to suggest that adjectives are not modifiers but are, after all, predicates. Even if this view could be supported for adjectives, it is hard to see it working for adverbs. (It is perhaps interesting that Bach [2] derives those adjectives which do not look like predicates, but seem genuine modifiers, from adverbs.)

[27] This makes *quickly* an extensional adverb. And this in turn means that it will not distinguish between co-referential definite descriptions. In particular it will have the consequence that an 'opaque' and a 'transparent' reading of many formulae will be equivalent. Taylor [47, pp. 102–109] puts forward several arguments against the predicate modifier analysis of adverbs. One defect he claims for it is that the transformational base must be allowed to generate only the 'transparent' formulae. What he fails to realise is that the base can be allowed to generate both the transparent and the opaque formulae but that in the case of *quickly* the two readings will be logically equivalent in the sense of being true in the same set of world-time pairs. There is no more reason to argue for a syntactic difference between predicates which do and predicates which do not admit replacement of co-referential definite descriptions than there is to argue that $\sim$ and L are in different syntactic categories because the former does, while the latter does not, admit replacement of co-referential definite descriptions. It may be that Taylor wants to make the distinction because Thomason and Stalnaker use the 'referential opacity' test to distinguish between predicate and sentence adverbs. I have argued in [13] that the puzzles surrounding opaque contexts arise from failure to realise that definite descriptions behave as nominals rather than as names.

Taylor's other reason for distinguishing between what he calls verb phrase adverbs and predicate adverbs is that only the former admit negation. Thus we can say

(i)   *John deliberately did not eat his soup.*

but we cannot so happily say

(ii)   *John quickly did not eat his soup.*

In the semantics given in the present paper it should be fairly clear that nonsense will result if we try to compare the speed at which John does not eat his soup on a particular occasion with the speed of all occasions on which he is not eating soup.

[28] In [10, p. 131] it was argued that even names should be treated as nominals, and be in category $\langle 0, \langle 0, 1 \rangle \rangle$. However, in the case of names, economies are obtained, for illustrative purposes, by pretending names are in category 1 and have, as their semantic value, the thing of which they are the name.

[29] Heny [25, p. 224]. To be fair to Heny however he is discussing the views of Thomason and Stalnaker (an ancestor of [45]). These authors in fact postpone, for what they no doubt consider sound pedagogical reasons, mention of the formal semantics of their categorial language to a separate section where its connection with the rest of the paper is perhaps understressed; and they perhaps unwittingly give the impression that scope distinctions are nothing more than taxonomy. Heny [25, p. 232f] produces an argument purporting to show that opacity is not a matter of scope. The argument may be valid but I am unfortunately unable to follow it although I have tried very hard. (As far as I can tell, the argument could only be conclusive if the sentences on which it is based were given a formal analysis which it is not clear that they have to be given.)

[30] Obviously a great deal of work must be done on the formal semantics of prepositions. Perhaps a start might be made by looking at certain core spatial uses of some of them. (The spatial basis for many of our prepositions is strongly argued by Clark in [8].) In addition there is the question of whether there is a distinction between 'genuine' prepositions and those which mark deep structure cases, if such things exist [22] and [46, p. 35f].

[31] At least four quite different treatments are known within a 'logical' base. As well as my own in [16] there is the extended study by Bartsch and Vennemann [3], a paper by Seuren [42] and Kamp [28].

[32] In [16, p. 178] the comparison class entered via the semantics of a morpheme called *pos* which appeared, without surface realization, in the absence of any more specific degree indicator. *pos tall* was suggested to mean 'tall enough to make it sensible to distinguish it from other things of the same kind'. It might well be that *pos* would be one of Bigelow's 'invisible quotation' operators [5, Section 4] which picks something out of the context as the comparison class and adds it for the time being to the language.

[33] A reminder might be worthwhile at this point that in possible-worlds semantics the correct entailments (and therefore the validity of syllogisms like Lakoff's) are automatically taken care of once we get the truth-conditions of all sentences right [11, p. 469f]. This is one reason for the privileged position of the possible world index. A fairly full account of the logical relations between tensed sentences within the framework of the kind presented in this paper is developed in Cresswell [12].

[34] Displaying the connection between these two predicates is obviously one of the strengths in Davidson's analysis [19] whose basic predicate is 'x is a running by y'. 'y is running' then becomes $(\exists x)(x$ is a running by $y)$ and 'x is a running' becomes $(\exists y)(x$ is a running by $y)$. If it could be shown that there is no appealing solution in the predicate-modifier framework then Davidson's solution would emerge as a very strong rival. Taylor brings up as an objection to Davidson's analysis the diagonally-moving ball mentioned in footnote [18]. Unfortunately

the analysis presented in this paper does not, as it stands, solve Taylor's problem so that his argument cannot be used in our favour.

[35] The uncertainty of the question of whether space–time and world co-ordinates are sufficient for all modification was the problem which led me in [11, p. 465–468] to opt for a Davidsonian solution. By restricting itself to spatio-temporal modification, the present paper has not had to face it. It is clear to me that the predicate modifier theory is *syntactically* much nicer than the Davidsonian theory and that is why, despite my flirtation with Davidson in [11], I would like to see it work.

[36] [38], [34]. A different approach to the problem of hyperintensional contexts is taken in Cresswell [15] and Bigelow [6] following Lewis' [31, pp. 182–186] insight that meanings are entities which possess a similar structure to the sentence which expresses them.

[37] Since it is easy to tell which is the functor in an expression of this kind, we do not have to insist that the functor be placed before its arguments. It can go between them or after them [10, p. 78]. This liberalization is used in many of the examples in this paper.

[38] In [10] I made an attempt in Chapter Three to say what kinds of things possible worlds are. While such attempts may be laudable, it is not necessary for present purposes to have anything more than an intuitive conception of a 'way the world might have been'. I also tried to say something about the domain of things in Chapter Seven.

BIBLIOGRAPHY

[1]   Åqvist, L. E. G. and Guenthner, F. (1977), 'Fundamentals of a Theory of Verb Aspect and Events Within the Setting of an Improved Tense-logic', F. Guenthner and C. Rohrer (eds.), *Studies in Formal Semantics*, Amsterdam, North Holland, 1977.

[2]   Bach, E. (1968), 'Nouns and Noun Phrases', in E. Bach and R. T. Harms (eds.), *Universals in Linguistic Theory*, Holt, Rinehart and Winston, New York.

[3]   Bartsch, Renate and Vennemann, T. (1972), *Semantic Structures*, Athenaum Verlag, Frankfurt/Main.

[4]   Bennett, M. R. and Partee, Barbara H. *Toward the Logic of Tense and Aspect in English* (unpublished).

[5]   Bigelow, J. C., 'Context and Quotation I and II', *Linguistische Berichte*, No. 38 (1975), pp. 1–21, No. 39 (1975), pp. 1–21.

[6]   Bigelow, J. C., 'Semantics of thinking, saying, and translation', in M. Guenthner-Reutter and F. Guenthner (eds.), *Meaning and Translation: Philosophical and Linguistic Approaches*, Duckworth, London 1978.

[7]   Chafe, W. L. (1970), *Meaning and the Structure of Language*, University of Chicago Press, Chicago.

[8]   Clark, H. H. (1973), Space, Time, Semantics and the Child', in J. T. Moore (ed.), *Cognitive Development. The Acquisition of Language*, Academic Press, New York.

[9]   Clark, R. L. (1970), Concerning the Logic of Predicate Modifiers, *Noûs*, Vol. 4, pp. 311–335.

[10] Cresswell, M. J. (1973), *Logics and Languages*, London, Methuen.

[11] Cresswell, M. J. (1974), 'Adverbs and Events', *Synthese*, Vol. 28, pp. 455–481.

[12] Cresswell, M. J. (1975), 'Hamblin on Time', *Noûs*, Vol. 9, pp. 193–204.

[13] Cresswell, M. J. (1975), 'Identity and Intensional Objects', *Philosophia*, Vol. 5, pp. 47–68.

[14]   Cresswell, M. J. (1975), 'Semantic Deviance', *Linguistische Berichte*, No. 35, pp. 1–9.

[15]   Cresswell, M. J. (1975), 'Hyperintensional Logic', *Studia Logica*, Vol. 34, pp. 25–38.

[16]   Cresswell, M. J. (1976), 'The Semantics of Degree', in Barbara H. Partee (ed.), *Montague Grammar*, Academic Press, New York, pp. 261–292.

[17]   Cresswell, M. J. 'Semantic Competence', in Monica Guenthner-Reutter and F. Guenthner (eds.), *Meaning and Translation: Philosophical and Linguistic Approaches*, Duckworth, London 1978.

[18]   Cresswell, M. J. 'Categorial Languages', (Indiana University Linguistics club and forthcoming in *Studia Logica*).

[19]   Davidson, D. (1967), 'The Logical of Action Sentences', in N. Rescher (ed.), *The Logic of Decision and Action*, University of Pittsburgh Press, Pittsburgh, pp. 81–95.

[20]   Dowty, D. R. (1972, *Studies in the Logic of Verb Aspect and Time Reference in English*, Ph.D. dissertation, University of Texas.

[21]   Dowty, D. R. (1977), 'Toward a Semantic Analysis of Verb Aspect and the English "Imperfective" Progressive', *Linguistics and Philosophy* Vol. 1, pp. 45–77.

[22]   Fillmore, C. J. (1968), 'The Case for Case', in E. Bach and R. T. Harms (eds.), *Universals in Linguistic Theory*, Holt, Rinehart and Winston, New York, pp. 1–88.

[23]   Garson, J. W. (1973), 'Indefinite Topological Logic', *Journal of Philosophical Logic*, Vol. 2, pp. 102–118.

[24]   Harman, G. H. (1972), 'Logical form', *Foundations of Language*, Vol. 9, pp. 38–65.

[25]   Heny, F. W. (1973), 'Sentence and Predicate Modifiers in English', J. P. Kimball (ed.), *Syntax and Semantics*, Vol. 1, Seminar Press, New York, Vol. 1, pp. 217–245.

[26]   Hughes, G. E. and Cresswell, M. J. (1968), *An Introduction to Modal Logic*, Methuen, London.

[27]   Kamp, J. A. W. (1971), 'Formal Properties of "Now" ', *Theoria*, Vol. 37, pp. 227–273.

[28]   Kamp, J. A. W. (1975), 'Two Theories about Adjectives', in E. L. Keenan (eds.), *Formal Semantics of Natural Language*, Cambridge University Press, Cambridge, pp. 123–155.

[29]   Kenny, A. J. P. (1963), *Action, Emotion and Will*, Routledge and Kegan Paul, London.

[30]   Lakoff, G. P. (1973), 'Notes on what it would take to understand how one adverb works', *The Monist*, Vol. 57, pp. 328–343.

[31]   Lewis, D. K. (1972), 'General Semantics', in D. Davidson and G. H. Harman (eds.), *Semantics of Natural Language*, Reidel, Dordrecht, pp. 169–218.

[32]   Mansfield, M. J. (1963), *Introduction to Topology*, Van Nostrand, Princeton.

[33]   Montague, R. M. (1974), *Formal Philosophy*, R. H. Thomason (ed.), Yale University Press, New Haven.

[34]   Over, D. E. (1975), 'Review of Logics and Languages', *Mind*, Vol. 84, pp. 623–625.

[35]   Parsons, T. (1972), 'Some Problems Concerning the Logic of Grammatical Modifiers', in D. Davidson and G. H. Harman (eds.), *Semantics of Natural Language*, Reidel, Dordrecht, pp. 127–141.

[36]   Reichenbach, H. (1947), *Elements of Symbolic Logic*, McMillan, New York.

[37]   Rennie, M. K. (1974), *Some Uses of Type Theory in the Analysis of Language*, Canberra: Department of Philosophy A.N.U. Monograph series No. 1.

[38]   Rennie, M. K. (1974), 'Review of Logics and Languages', *Australasian Journal of Philosophy*, Vol. 52, pp. 277–282.

[39]   Rescher, N. and Garson, J. (1968), 'Topological Logic', *The Journal of Symbolic Logic*, Vol. 33, pp. 537–548.

[40]   Scott, D. S. (1970), 'Advice on Modal Logic', in K. Lambert (ed.), *Philosophical Problems in Logic*, Reidel, Dordrecht, pp. 143–173.

[41]   Segerberg, K. (1973), 'Two Dimensional Modal Logic', *Journal of Philosophical Logic*, Vol. 2, pp. 77–96.

[42]   Seuren, P. A. M. (1973), 'The Comparative', in F. Kiefer and N. Ruwet (eds.), *Generative Grammar in Europe*, Reidel, Dordrecht, pp. 528–564.

[43]   Stalnaker, R. C. (1972), 'Pragmatics', in D. Davidson and G. H. Harman (eds.), *Semantics of Natural Language*, Reidel, Dordrecht, pp. 380–397.

[44]   von Stechow, A. (1974), ε–λ-kontextfreie Sprachen, Ein Beitrag zu einer natürlich formalen Semantik, *Linguistische Berichte*, No. 34, pp. 1–33.

[45]   von Stechow, A. (1975), *Zur formalen Syntax und Semantik des Deutschen*, Sonderforschungsbereich 99 Universitat Konstanz.

[46]   Stockwell, R. P., Schachter, P. S., Partee, Barbara H. (1973), *The Major Syntactic Structures of English*, Holt Rinehart, New York.

[47]   Taylor, B. (1974), *The Semantics of Adverbs*, D.Phil. thesis, University of Oxford.

[48]   Thomason, R. H. and Stalnaker R. C. (1975), 'A Semantic Theory of Adverbs', *Linguistic Inquiry*, Vol. 4, pp. 195–220.

[49]   Walton, D. N. (1976), 'Time and Modality in the "Can" of Opportunity', in M. Brand and D. N. Walton (eds.), *Action Theory*, D. Reidel, Dordrecht, pp. 271–287.

[50]   Wheeler, S. C. (1972), 'Attributives and Their Modifiers', *Noûs*, Vol. 6, pp. 310–334.

FRANZ GUENTHNER

TIME SCHEMES, TENSE LOGIC
AND THE
ANALYSIS OF ENGLISH TENSES

Only recently have linguists and philosophers of language begun to apply other logical systems than ordinary predicate logic in the area of formal semantics for natural language. One of these 'non-standard' branches of logic — which deals with notions just as central as predication or quantification — is *tense logic*. The major motivation for developing tense logics was certainly to accommodate the temporal factor in everyday discourse within languages of propositional and predicate logic. In this paper I would like to examine to what extent existing systems of tense logic have been useful in describing and explaining tensed constructions in ordinary language, in particular, in English.

I will not be primarily interested in the syntax of English tenses, or more specifically, in establishing — *à la manière* de Montague (1974) — a systematic relation between the syntax of English and a language of tense logic. This will be the subject of a forthcoming paper. It should, however, be fairly clear how such a translation relation could be defined for the language of tense logic described in Section 4.

1

In languages of classical propositional or predicate logic one can only express *omnitemporal* propositions. For instance, a standard translation of *Socrates thinks* in predicate logic is Ts, where T is a 1-place predicate of individuals and s is a name. Such sentences contain no special marking for *tenses*. There are several ways tenses can be added to an ordinary language of predicate logic. The two most well-known consist (a) in the addition of sortal variables $t_1 \ldots t_n \ldots$ which range over moments of time, and (b) in the addition of temporal operators. E.g., *Socrates thought* could be represented as $\exists t(t < n \land T(s,t))$, where n is a special constant for the present moment (the moment of utterance) and *think* is represented by a 2-place predicate of individuals and times. According to the other proposal, we could translate the English sentence into PTs where P is an intensional operator, whose meaning can be roughly described as 'it has been the case that'. Since English sentences (e.g., *John runs* (present), *John will be running* (future

201

F. Guenthner and S. J. Schmidt (eds.), Formal Semantics and Pragmatics for Natural Languages, 201–222. *All Rights Reserved.*
Copyright © 1978 *by D. Reidel Publishing Company, Dordrecht, Holland.*

progressive), etc.) always contain an indication of tense, it is necessary to translate them into a formal language in which temporal references can be expressed. For reasons which will not be discussed here (cf. Guenthner, forthcoming) we opt for the latter — Priorian — approach to the analysis of tense.

Quite a few proposals concerning the systematic generation of all possible tense forms in English are available at present, but none of these is accompanied by an equally systematic semantic account. Perhaps the most well-known description of the verb phrase is the transformational one, originally due to Chomsky (1957), where all tense forms are generated by a rule, roughly like (1):

(1) $\text{Aux} \rightarrow T(\text{Have} + \text{en}) (\text{Be} + \text{ing}) V$.

Unfortunately, it is not obvious what the corresponding semantic rules for (1) would be. Later on in this paper we shall make a suggestion as far as a semantics for such rules is concerned.

An approach which tries to indicate (admittedly in a programmatic fashion) what kind of semantics might be postulated for tensed constructions in English is contained in Montague (1974). The basic idea in that paper is this: first, English sentences are generated according to a set of syntactic rules S, whose proper nature need not concern us here; independently of this syntax for the natural language, there is a formal language IL which contains tense operators in addition to other things. To each syntactic rule in S a translation rule — which associates expressions in L to structures generated by S — is assigned. One such rule is the following:

(2) $F_{\text{fut}}(\alpha, \beta) = \alpha \hat{\ } \beta'$ where β' is the result of replacing the first verb in β by its third person singular future form (where α is a noun phrase and β a verb phrase).

This rule, which combines both syntactic and morphological operations, applies for instance to expressions like *every student* and *dance* and yields as a result *every student will dance*.

The corresponding translation rule looks like this:

(3)   If α translates into α' and β into β', then $F_{\text{fut}}(\alpha, \beta)$ translates into $F\alpha'(\beta')$.

According to Montague's translation rules for quantified noun phrases and intransitive verbs, *every student* translates into $\lambda P \forall x(Sx \rightarrow Px)$ and *dance* into the 1-place predicate D; if we then apply (3) as well as lambda-conversion, the translation of the entire sentence is $F\forall x(Sx \to Dx)$. According to Montague's rules the English sentence turns out to be ambiguous depending on the order of application of the tense rule and the rule of quantification. The two analyses are:

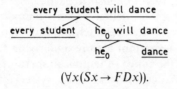

$$(F\forall x(Sx \to Dx)$$

and

every student will dance

every student he_0 will dance

he_0 dance

$$(\forall x(Sx \to FDx)).$$

The first tree assigns wide scope to the future tense and means something like 'in the future everyone who is a student then dances'; the second analysis places only the predicate within the scope of the future tense and means something like 'everyone who is a student now will dance (at some time in the future)'. Notice that this translation does not entail that they will dance at the same (future) time.

The expression 'F' ('it will be the case that') is a tense operator; it forms sentences out of sentences. We shall discuss in some detail below a system of tense logic — due essentially to Arthur Prior — which contains in addition to 'F' an analogous operator 'P' corresponding to the paraphrase 'it has been (was) the case that'. In what follows I will try to point out some inadaquacies of pure Priorian tense logic; but instead of arguing that tense logical semantics for natural language tenses should be abandoned altogether, I will rather propose some modifications which make the underlying semantics more adequate as far as English tenses are concerned.

For the moment it is already quite interesting to point out several important differences between the operators of tense logic and the forms of English tenses. First, if one were to try and interpret structures like those generated by (1) directly, the elements responsible for the tenses would not be *sentential* modifiers, whereas of course 'P' and 'F' apply only to sentences. Second, there seems to be no real *iteration* of tenses in natural language, at least not in English, whereas iteration of tense operators is an essential property of tense logic. Third, tense in ordinary language is rarely just a relation between points of time; e.g., there is an important difference between the simple past and the present perfect which involves more than simple temporal relations. Fourth, tense, aspect, temporal conjunctions and the semantic properties of verbs are so intricately connected in natural language that it seems quite a hopeless task to aim for an analysis of just the 'tenses' alone. And, fifth, simple moments of time will not suffice as either evaluation or reference points. Priorian tense logic (with 'P' and 'F' alone) cannot handle *intervals* in any way.

In the next section, we present several approaches to the structure of time as it relates to the tenses of English; in particular, we show how systems of tense logic can be used to 'define' various temporal notions used by grammarians like Jespersen, Reichenbach and Bull. In the following section we shall argue that an important feature underlying tenses in English — namely, restrictions of the range of temporal operators — is absent from ordinary tense logic. We go on to sketch a system of tense logic which contains a new approach to time adverbials and their relation to tenses.

2

In the analysis of tenses, be it in natural language or in systems of tense logic, frequent use is made of 'schematisations' of time, i.e., of the way what Reichenbach called 'points of speech', 'points of event' and 'points of reference' can be temporally located with respect to each other. The aim of this section is to examine several proposals for such representations of time and to attempt a uniform representation of them within the setting of the framework outlined in Åqvist and Guenthner (1977).

The most intuitive and simplest approach to the possible relations between these 'points' is given by beginning with a representation of time as (at least) a dense linearly ordered series of moments:

(4)

(T)

Let T be the set of points of time and $<$ a strict linear ordering of them. Let us pick an arbitrary point t_0 in T and call it the *speech point*:

(5)

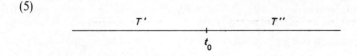

This point separates T in two distinct segments T' and T'' and allows the following observation:

(6)   For any point $t' \in T$, either $t' \in T'$ or $t' \in T''$ or $t' = t_0$.

If we now pick a point t' ($t' \neq t_0$), this point will either be 'to the left of' (or *before*) t_0 or 'to the right of' (or *after*) t_0,

(7)

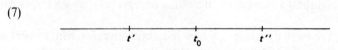

In (7), $t' < t_0$ and $t_0 < t''$. We can now specify further segments of T, among which

(8)

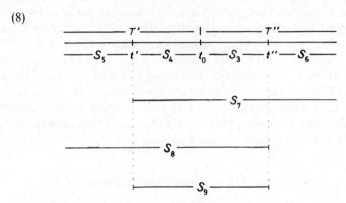

These segments are defined as follows:

(9) $S_1 = T' = \{t: t < t_0\}$
$S_2 = T'' = \{t: t_0 < t\}$
$S_3 = \{t: t_0 < t < t''\}$
$S_4 = \{t: t' < t < t_0\}$
$S_5 = T' \backslash S_4$
$S_6 = T'' \backslash S_3$
$S_7 = T \backslash S_5$
$S_8 = T \backslash S_6$
$S_9 = S_3 \bigcup S_4 \bigcup \{t_0\}.$

With respect to the elements t of T, we shall say that *sentences* are either true or false at a given t, or equivalently, that *events* occur at a given t or do not occur at t. Tensed sentences serve to locate events with respect to a time structure $\mathcal{T}$ ($= \langle T, < \rangle$) and with respect to the moment of speech t_0 in T, and in more complex cases with respect to other moments as well. If an event e occurs at a moment t in T' (T''), it is in the *past* of t_0 (the *future* of t_0). When an event occurs at t, we shall say that t is an *event point* for that event. In (7) we have designated three possible event points, one of which is identical to the speech point. On the basis of such a scheme (essentially Jespersen's diagram) a number of interesting observations about tenses can be made.

In order to show in a precise way how temporal reference with respect to Jespersen's diagram functions, we introduce the following simple language for a tense logic L_t: the language L of L_t is to have *atomic sentences* P_1, $P_2, \ldots$ and two tense operators 'P' (read 'it has been the case that') and 'F' (read 'it will be the case that'), as well as the truth-functional operators '$\neg$' and '$\&$'. A model for a language of L_t with respect to a time structure $\mathcal{T}$ is a function f which assigns to each atomic sentence a set of points in T, intuitively, those points t at which the sentence is true (or at which the event which the sentence expresses occurs). The set of sentences (well-formed formulas) is built up recursively in a very simple way: if ϕ is an atomic sentence of L, then ϕ is a well-formed formula; if ϕ and ψ are well-formed formulas of L, then $\neg \phi$, $(\phi \wedge \psi)$, $P\phi$ and $F\phi$ are well-formed formulas of L.

The truth conditions for L are the following:

(i) $\models_t \phi$ iff $t \in f(\phi)$, if ϕ is an atomic sentence of L

(ii) $\models_t \phi$ iff it is not the case that $\models_t \phi$

(iii) $\models_t (\phi \ \& \ \psi)$ iff both $\models_t \phi$ and $\models_t \psi$

(iv) $\models_t P\phi$ iff $\models_{t'} \phi$ for some $t' \in T$ such that $t' < t$

(v) $\models_t F\phi$ iff $\models_{t'} \phi$ for some $t' \in T$ such that $t < t'$.

(We have written $\models_t \phi$ instead of the more explicit $\models_t^{M} \phi$, which we read 'ϕ is true at t in the model M'.)

We also introduce the following abbreviations:

(i) $\quad H\phi =_{df} \neg P \neg \phi$
(ii) $\quad G\phi =_{df} \neg F \neg \phi$

A number of different ways a sentence of L expressing an event can be true with respect to Jespersen's diagram and the designated points and intervals can now be expressed in L; let t_0, t' and t'' be as in (7) and S_i as in (9) above:

(i) $\qquad \phi$ is true$_{T'} \rightarrow \overline{\underset{t_0}{\big|\!\!=\!\!=}} H\phi$

(ii) $\qquad \phi$ is true$_{T''} \rightarrow \overline{\underset{t_0}{\big|\!\!=\!\!=}} G\phi$

(iii) $\qquad \phi$ is true$_{t_0} \rightarrow \overline{\underset{t_0}{\big|\!\!=\!\!=}} \phi$

(iv) $\qquad \phi$ is true$_{t'} \rightarrow \overline{\underset{t_0}{\big|\!\!=\!\!=}} P\phi$

(v) $\qquad \phi$ is true$_{t''} \rightarrow \overline{\underset{t_0}{\big|\!\!=\!\!=}} F\phi$

(vi) $\qquad \phi$ is true$_{S_5} \rightarrow \overline{\underset{t_0}{\big|\!\!=\!\!=}} PH\phi$

(vii) $\qquad \phi$ is true$_{S_6} \rightarrow \overline{\underset{t_0}{\big|\!\!=\!\!=}} FG\phi$

(viii) $\qquad \phi$ is true$_{S_7} \rightarrow \overline{\underset{t_0}{\big|\!\!=\!\!=}} PG\phi$

(ix) $\qquad \phi$ is true$_{S_8} \rightarrow \overline{\underset{t_0}{\big|\!\!=\!\!=}} FH\phi.$

Notice that there is no sentence of L whose truth conditions correspond to

(x) $\qquad \phi$ is true$_{S_9}$ or to
(xi) $\qquad \phi$ is true$_{S_4}.$

In fact, many other conditions do not correspond to sentences of L (cf. below for a stronger language of tense logic which does accomodate these and other cases).

Reichenbach's analysis of English tenses is based on the interrelation between three points: the points of speech, event and reference respectively.

What are the analogues of these points in the semantic system outlined above? We can say the following: if ϕ is a formula of L which is not contained in any larger formula, then any point of evaluation for ϕ is the speech point for ϕ. (If we assume further, as we will do below, that for a given model there is always to be a point t_0 — the *actual* speech point of M — then t_0 is the speech point for all sentences of L with respect to M.) In the course of evaluation of a formula ϕ each occurence of P and F will introduce a *reference point* for the formula ϕ' in its immediate scope. If ϕ' is a subformula of ϕ and contains no occurences of P and F, then the *event point* for ϕ' is identical to the last reference point introduced in the course of the evaluation of ϕ. For instance, let ϕ be $FP\phi'$, then we have

$$\underset{t}{\vdash\!\!=\!\!=} FP\phi' \text{ iff } \underset{t'}{\vdash\!\!=\!\!=} P\phi' \text{ for some } t' \text{ such that } t < t' \text{ and}$$

$$\underset{t'}{\vdash\!\!=\!\!=} P\phi' \ (t < t') \text{ iff } \underset{t''}{\vdash\!\!=\!\!=} \phi' \text{ for some } t'' < t'.$$

Here, t is the speech point for $FP\phi$, t' is a reference point for $P\phi'$, and t'' is the event point for ϕ' (as well as the last reference point).

Notice that if we assume with Reichenbach the following correspondence between English tenses and possible combinations of speech, event and reference points, we are not able to come up with corresponding distinct L_t sentences which are to express these tenses:

Past Perfect	$E — R — S$
Simple Past	$(E, R) — S$
Past Posterior	$R — E — S$
Present Perfect	$E — (S, R)$
Present	(S, E, R)
Simple Future	$(S, R) — E$
Future Perfect	$S — E — R$
Posterior	$S — R — E$
Simple Future	$S — (E, R)$.

where $A — B — C$ means A is before B and B is before C and (A, B) means A and B are the same point.

One of the problems in L is to account for instance for the difference between the present perfect and the simple past forms. If we write '$P\phi$' we seem to get a representation of the former, but how are we to indicate the latter? In his formalization of Reichenbach's system, L. Åqvist makes use of a complex operator, which we shall denote by 'R' (for 'reference point') whose function it is to mark a point arrived at by evaluating P or F as the new reference point. Informally this means that in the representation of the simple past tense, we are sent by the operator P to a point in the past of the speech point, and application of R converts this point into a new reference point, i.e., makes out of this point a new actual speech point. The semantic clause for the operator R refers to both the actual speech point of the model as well as to the point of evaluation:

$$\left.\frac{M_{t_0}}{t}\right|\!\!=\!\!= R\phi \text{ iff } \left.\frac{M_t}{t}\right|\!\!=\!\!= \phi.$$

'$R\phi$' is true at t in a model whose actual speech point is t_0 iff ϕ is true at t in a model whose actual speech point is t. This yields the following representations of the present perfect and simple past:

Present perfect:	$P\phi$
Simple past:	$PR\phi.$

In the former, the designated point in M (i.e., t_0) remains the same, only the point of event for ϕ is specified to lie in the past of t_0; in the latter, we first come to a point in the past of t_0 and then we make that point the actual speech point.

Before presenting precise semantics for such 'doubly-indexed' constructions, it is useful to illustrate in more detail what the relation between speech points and reference points amounts to.

Consider the extension of Jespersen's as well as Reichenbach's time schemes presented in Bull's detailed work (1968) on tenses. Instead of working with just one series of moments of time (as discussed in 2 above), Bull suggests the following representation:

(10)

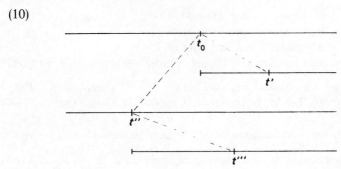

t_0 is the actual speech point and time extends infinitively in both directions from t_0. Let us call t_0 the *primary perspective*, and the first line in (10) the *primary dimension*. t'' is a primary perspective which is in the past (relative to t_0); from t'' as well, time extends infinitively in both directions. Intuitively, t'' is a point in the past *conceived* as the primary point. t' is a point in the future of t_0 conceived as the primary point. t''' is a future point with respect to t''; in other words, t''' is a point in the future of a point in the past of t_0. Let us call all the points mentioned so far, with the exception of t_0, *secondary* perspectives, or secondary reference points. It is important to note that if only one line (of time) were to be considered, i.e., if we projected the four-dimensional representation onto a one-dimensional one, the relativity of the various reference points would be lost:

(11)
$$\overline{\hspace{2cm} \underset{t''}{|} \hspace{1.5cm} \underset{t'''}{|} \hspace{1.5cm} \underset{t_0}{|} \hspace{1.5cm} \underset{t'}{|} \hspace{2cm}}$$

Once the reference points are located on a dimension like (11) above, they would all be directly relatable to t_0, whereas in (10) there is no direct way of relating for instance t''' and t_0.

We have now seen that the introduction of new dimensions amounts to treating certain points as new reference points in their own right. Let us now see how this can be represented in a tensed formal language.

Let L now be a language for a tense logic TL which is an extension of the language of L_t containing in addition to the atomic formulas, the operators 'P' and 'F' and the sentential connectives, the following sentential operators:

$$\boxed{d}, \boxed{x}, \boxed{X}, \boxed{s}, N, \boxed{w}, \boxminus \!\!\!\!\! \to \text{ and } \Longleftrightarrow$$

and let the set of well-formed formulas of L be built up in the usual way. M is a model for L iff $M = \langle T, \langle t_0, t_0 \rangle, < , f \rangle$, where

(i) T is the set of times ($T \neq \phi$)
(ii) t_0 is the actual speech point of M
(iii) $<$ is a strict linear ordering of T
(iv) f is a function from the set of atomic formulas of L into $\mathcal{P}(T)$.

Let M^t/t' be the model just like $M (= M^{t_0}/t_0)$ except that M^t/t' is $\langle T, \langle t, t' \rangle, <, f \rangle$. Let M_T be the set of all models M^t/t' such that $\langle t, t' \rangle \in T \times T$.

The truth value of formulas of L will now be defined with respect to arbitrary members of M_T at a moment of time t'' in T; i.e. $\left. \dfrac{M^t/t'}{t''} \right| \phi$ is to be read 'ϕ is true at t'' in the model M^t/t''. Before we explain the role of the various indices, we give the truth conditions for each type of formulas:

(i) $\overset{M^t/t'}{\underset{t''}{\models}} \phi$ iff $t'' \in f(\phi)$, if ϕ is an atomic formula

(ii) $\overset{M^t/t'}{\underset{t''}{\models}} \phi$ iff it is not the case that $\overset{M^t/t'}{\underset{t''}{\models}} \phi$

(iii) $\overset{M^t/t'}{\underset{t''}{\models}} (\phi \,\&\, \psi)$ iff both $\overset{M^t/t'}{\underset{t''}{\models}} \phi$ and $\overset{M^t/t'}{\underset{t''}{\models}}$

(iv) $\overset{M^t/t'}{\underset{t''}{\models}} P\phi$ iff $\overset{M^t/t'}{\underset{t'''}{\models}} \phi$ for some $t''' \in T$, $t''' < t''$

(v) $\overset{M^t/t'}{\underset{t''}{\models}} F\phi$ iff $\overset{M^t/t'}{\underset{t''}{\models}} \phi$ for some $t''' \in T$, $t'' < t'''$

(vi) $\overset{M^t/t'}{\underset{t''}{\models}} \boxed{s}\,\phi$ iff $\overset{M^t/t'}{\underset{t_0}{\models}} \phi$

(vii) $\overset{M^t/t'}{\underset{t''}{\models}} \boxed{d}\,\phi$ iff $\overset{M^t/t'}{\underset{t}{\models}} \phi$

(viii) $\overset{M^t/t'}{\underset{t''}{\models}} N\phi$ iff $\overset{M^{t_0}/t_0}{\underset{t_0}{\models}} \phi$

(ix) $\overset{M^t/t'}{\underset{t''}{\models}} \boxed{x}\,\phi$ iff $\overset{M^{t''}/t'}{\underset{t}{\models}} \phi$

(x) $\overset{M^t/t'}{\underset{t''}{\models}} \boxed{X}\,\phi$ iff $\overset{M^t/t''}{\underset{t'}{\models}} \phi$

(xi) $\overset{M^t/t'}{\underset{t''}{\models}} \boxed{w}\,\phi$ iff $\overset{M^t/t'}{\underset{t'}{\models}} \phi$

(xii) $\overset{M^t/t'}{\underset{t''}{\models}} \boxminus\,\phi$ iff $\overset{M^t/t'}{\underset{t'''}{\models}} \phi$ for every $t''' \in \,]t'', t'[$, i.e., in the open interval $]t'', t'[$ which is defined by:

$$]t'', t'[\,= \begin{cases} \{t \in T : t'' < t < t'\}, & \text{if } t'' < t' \\ \{t \in T : t' < t < t''\}, & \text{if } t' < t'' \\ \{t'\}, & \text{if } t' = t'' \end{cases}$$

(xiii) $\overset{M^t/t'}{\underset{t''}{\models}} \diamondsuit\,\phi$ iff $\overset{M^t/t'}{\underset{t'''}{\models}} \phi$ for some $t''' \in \,]t'', t'[$, where $]t'', t'[$ is defined as above.

We can express the change of a dimension (or 'axis' in Bull's terminology) in the following way with respect to TL: points of time on the primary dimension are directly relatable to t_0; i.e., the model which the primary dimension represents is simply M^{t_0}/t_0. Points of time on the dimension of t'', on the other hand, are points relative to the model $M^{t''}/t_0$; for t'' is now the new primary reference point on the dimension obtained from the primary dimension (i.e., from t_0). The same thing applies to the future point t'. Consider now the case of a point t on the dimension of t'''. Truth now amounts to truth in a model whose primary reference point is t''' but which was obtained from a model whose primary reference is t''; i.e., we have truth at the moment t with respect to the model $M^{t'''}/t''$.

Let us now see how we can express in TL that a formula ϕ is true at different points or during different intervals. For this, we single out (as does Bull) in addition to the points in (7) the following intervals:

(12)

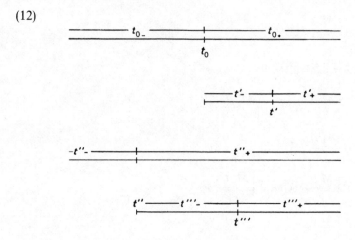

Let ϕ be an atomic formula (expressing an event) and suppose we are in the model M^{t_0}/t_0, then:

(i) ϕ is $\text{true}_{t_0-} \rightarrow \left| \dfrac{M^{t_0}/t_0}{t_0} \right. H\phi$

(where $H\phi$ is defined as $\neg P \neg \phi$)

(ii) ϕ is $\text{true}_{t_0+} \rightarrow \left| \dfrac{M^{t_0}/t_0}{t_0} \right. G\phi$

where $G\phi$ is defined as $\neg F \neg \phi$)

(iii) ϕ is true$_{t'-}$ $\rightarrow$ $\dfrac{M^{t_0}/t_0}{t_0}\, F\; \boxed{x}\; \boxed{d}\; \boxdot\; \phi$

(iv) ϕ is true$_{t'+}$ $\rightarrow$ $\dfrac{M^{t_0}/t_0}{t_0}\, F\; \boxed{x}\; \boxed{d}\; G\phi$

(v) ϕ is true$_{t''-}$ $\rightarrow$ $\dfrac{M^{t_0}/t_0}{t_0}\, P\; \boxed{x}\; \boxed{d}\; H\phi$

(vi) ϕ is true$_{t''+}$ $\rightarrow$ $\dfrac{M^{t_0}/t_0}{t_0}\, P\; \boxed{x}\; \boxed{d}\; G\phi$

(vii) ϕ is true$_{t'''-}$ $\rightarrow$ $\dfrac{M^{t_0}/t_0}{t_0}\, P\; \boxed{x}\; \boxed{d}\; \boxed{X}\; \boxed{w}\; F\; \boxed{x}\; \boxed{d}\; \boxdot\; \phi$

(viii) ϕ is true$_{t'''+}$ $\rightarrow$ $\dfrac{M^{t_0}/t_0}{t_0}\, P\; \boxed{x}\; \boxed{d}\; \boxed{X}\; \boxed{w}\; F\; \boxed{x}\; \boxed{d}\; G\phi.$

Besides these many other ways of specifying how an event can be temporally located are of course possible in TL.

Bull's time scheme, which we shall not discuss here as far as its generality or adequacy for systematizing the possible tenses in natural languages are concerned, foresees twelve tense forms "representing all possible order relations between all possible events and four axes of orientation":

(i) $E(t_{0-})$ — the event E takes place in the past of t_0
$P\phi$ (where ϕ expresses the event E)

ii) $E(t_0)$ — the event takes place at t_0
ϕ

(iii) $E(t_{0+})$ — the event E takes place after t_0
$F\phi$

(iv) $E(t'-)$ — the event E takes place in the past of t'
$F\; \boxed{x}\; \boxed{d}\; \diamondminus\; \phi$

(v) $E(t')$ — the event E takes place at t'
$F\; \boxed{x}\; \boxed{d}\; \phi$

(vi) $E(t'+)$ — the event E takes place in the future of t'
$F\; \boxed{x}\; \boxed{d}\; F\phi$

(vii) $E(t''-)$ — the event E takes place in the past of t''
$P\; \boxed{x}\; \boxed{d}\; P\phi$

(viii) $E(t'')$ — the event E takes place at t''
$P\; \boxed{x}\; \boxed{d}\; \phi$

(ix)　　$E(t''+)$ — the event E takes place in the future of t''
$P \boxed{x} \boxed{d} F\phi$

(x)　　$E(t'''-)$ — the event E takes place in the past of t'''
$P \boxed{x} \boxed{d} \boxed{X} \boxed{w} F \boxed{x} \boxed{d} \diamondsuit \phi$

(xi)　　$E(t''')$ — the event E takes place at t'''
$P \boxed{x} \boxed{d} F \boxed{x} \boxed{d} \phi$

(xii)　　$E(t'''+)$ — the event E takes place in the future of t'''
$P \boxed{x} \boxed{d} F \boxed{x} \boxed{d} F\phi$

The tenses exemplified in English according to Bull (cf. his diagram 5, p. 31) can thus be represented in a straightforward way in TL (taking into account the propositional structure of sentences only; a more adequate treatment would have to be based on a predicate logic extension of TL). Bull's nine tenses for English correspond in the following way to formulas of TL (cf. the translations (i) to (xii) above):

> *has* ϕ*'d* = (i)
> ϕ*'s* = (ii)
> *will* ϕ = (iii)
> *will have* ϕ*'d* = (iv)
> *had* ϕ*'d* = (vii)
> ϕ*'d* = (viii)
> *would* ϕ = (ix)
> *would have* ϕ*'d* = (x)

As can be easily seen, the combination of the operators $\boxed{x} \boxed{d}$ amounts to the operator R mentioned above which introduces new primary reference points; the combination $\boxed{X} \boxed{w}$ amounts to keeping track of the previous primary reference points as the points *from where* the new reference points are obtained.

3. RESTRICTING THE RANGE OF TEMPORAL OPERATORS

It is a common assumption in model-theoretic semantics for natural languages that a model (structure, interpretation) represents a state of the world (a situation, context). In addition, it is commonly assumed that among the class of all models for a given language there is one which 'represents' the actual state of the world. Even though *this* model cannot be specified it is this intuition which underlies more or less all applications of intensional semantics to natural languages. A good case in point is, for instance, the status of the domain of objects in models for ordinary predicate logic. Such models can vary in essentially two respects: they can have domains of different sizes or they can have different interpretations of the non-logical constants. For instance, two models M_1 and M_2 can be based upon the same domain D but assign different denotations to the constants of the language. Or, they can have different (but non-disjoint) domains but assign nevertheless the same extensions to the constants. In such a case, the two models will assign the same truth values to the atomic sentences, but not necessarily to the complex sentences. Thus, let us say that M_1 and M_2 interpret the predicate *Run* as a subset of $D_1 \cap D_2$. An object in this intersection runs iff the assertion that it runs is true in both models. But a sentence like *Everyone runs* might be true in one of the two models but not in the other. For this to be the case, it suffices that the set of runners is co-extensive with the domain of one of the two models but only with a subset of the domain of the other model.

One way to say that a certain set of objects runs in the model where everyone fails to be true is to *restrict* the range of the universal quantifier. In a language like English this can be done in a variety of ways; the most direct way of restricting the range is to use common nouns or restrictive relative clauses. Instead of everyone runs we can have *every student runs* or a combination of these *Every student who attends a physics course runs*. The semantic analysis of the role of common nouns (e.g., as sortal variables) and of relative clauses has been extensively discussed in many places and need not concern us further here.

We would like to argue that the above observation about the role of domains in predicate logic is equally valid in other domains as well, in particular, in the area of tenses.

A model for predicate tense logic is based on a set T of moments of time as well as on a domain of objects. How are we to regard the set T? It is well-known that different systems of tense logic make different assumptions about the structure of T; e.g., T can be assumed to be finite, infinite, discrete, dense, etc. In what follows we will not deal with these structural properties of T; we shall rather consider the question of temporal references and their specification. As we remarked above, the ordinary semantics for the operators 'P' and 'F' seems to be inadequate for the representation of the simple past and the simple future in English. First of all, the use of the simple past (and perhaps also of the simple future) is quite similar to the use of indefinite noun phrases. E.g., *a man runs* is usually translated into predicate logic as $\exists x(Mx \wedge Rx)$. This kind of translation can however be contested, for (at least if no specific pragmatic rules accompany such translations) it does not incorporate the idea of a definite reference.

4. A TENSE LOGIC WITH RESTRICTING OPERATORS

In this section I would like to sketch a language L of tense logic which differs from those discussed in Section 2 in essential ways: first, it contains operators of a new kind which restrict the range of the ordinary tense operators; second, it contains predicate modifiers which correspond roughly to the use of the perfect and the progressive in English. (For a more extensive treatment of English tenses along these lines in the framework of a Montague Grammar, cf. F. Guenthner & C. Rohrer [forthcoming] this paper will also contain a discussion of the interplay of verbal categories (*'Aktionsarten'*) and tenses and aspect.

4.1. *Syntax of L*

The non-logical vocabulary of a language L for L consists of elements in the following disjoint sets:

(1)   a set of *basic* 1-place predicates: $P_1, \ldots, P_n$
(2)   a set of *basic* 2-place predicates: $R_1, \ldots, R_n$
(3)   a set of individual constants: $C_1, \ldots, C_n$.

The following symbols make up the logical vocabulary:

(1)   quantifiers: $\forall, \exists$
(2)   sentential connectives: $\neg, \&, \vee$
(3)   individual variables: $v_1, \ldots, v_n \ldots$ (for every natural number n)
(4)   tense operators: P, F, PR (the first two could be read 'it was the case that', 'it will be the case')
(5)   indexical adverbials: N, T, Y, TO (read 'now', 'tomorrow', 'yesterday', 'today')
(6)   temporal relators: $\mapsto, \leftarrow\!]$ (read 'after', 'before')
(7)   predicate modifiers: Being, Have.

Several sets of well-formed expressions of L are specified by the following recursive rules:

(1)   *Predicates*:
        (a) if A is a 1-place or basic 2-place predicate, then A and Being A are a 1-place or 2-place *predicate* respectively
        (b) if A is a 1-place or 2-place predicate, then Have A is a 1-place or 2-place *perfective predicate*.

(2)   *Formulas*
        If A is a 1-place or 2-place predicate or perfective predicate, and

t_1, t_2 either individual variables or constants, then At_1 and At_1t_2 are *atomic formulas* of L.

(3)   Every Boolean combination of atomic formulas is a formula.

(4)   If A is a formula, then PRA, PA and FA are *time-dependent formulas* (TDF).

(5)   Every Boolean-combination of time-dependent formulas is a time-dependent formula.

(6)   If A is a formula (or atomic formula), or a time-dependent formula and v a variable, then $\forall vA$ and $\exists vA$ are formulas or time-dependent formulas respectively.

(7)   If A is a time-dependent formula then $Y A$, $T A$, $TO A$, and $N A$ are (indexically) restricted time-dependent formulas.

(8)   If A is a formula and B a time-dependent formula then $\vdash\!\!\to AB$ and $\dashv\!\!\vdash AB$ are restricted time-dependent formulas.

(9)   Only formulas constructed according to the above rules are *well-formed formulas* of L.

4.2. Semantics for L

A *model* for L is a 6-tuple $M = (T, <, t_0, I-, I+, D, f)$ where

(i) $T \neq \phi$ (the set of times).

(ii) $<$ is a strict ordering of T.

(iii) $t_0 \in T$ (the speech point of M).

(iv) $I-$ is an interval in T prior to t_0.

(v) $I+$ is an interval in T after t_0.

(vi) $D \neq \phi$ (the domain of individuals).

(vii) f is an interpretation function defined on the nonlogical constants of L such that:

(a) $f(c) \in D^T$,   *if* c is an individual constant of L,

(b) $f(P) \in (2^D)^T$,   if P is a 1-place basic predicate of L.

(c) $f(R) \in (2^{D \times D})^T$, if R is a 2-place basic predicate of L.

Before we can give the truth conditions for the well-formed formulas of L, we must specify certain denotations conditions for complex expressions of L which are not of the formula type. We write $V(A)(t)$ for 'the denotation of A at t in M'.

An assignment of values to the variables relative to M is a function g from the set of variables to the domain D. g^d/v is the assignment just like g except that it assigns the object d to the variable v.

4.3. *Denotation clauses*

1. $V(A)(t) = f(A)(t)$, if A is a 1-place basic predicate.
2. $V(A)(t) = f(A)(t)$, if A is a 2-place basic predicate.
3. $V(A)(t) = f(A)(t)$, if A is an individual constant.
4. $V(v)(t) = g(v)$,   if v is an individual variable.
5. $V(\text{Being }A)(t)$ is $\{d \in D : \exists I(t \in I, \ \& \ \forall t'(t' \in I \to d \in V(A)(t')),$
         if A is a *basic* predicate
6. $V(\text{Have }A)(t)$ is $\{d \in D : \exists t'(t' < t \ \& \ d \in V(A)(t'))\},$
         if A is a basic predicate or a 1-place predicate.
         Similarly for A a 2-place predicate.

4.4. *Truth clauses*

We read $[\phi]_{t,g}^{M,I} = 1$ as 'ϕ is true in M at the moment t with respect to the assignment g and the reference interval I'. (We shall drop the reference to M from now on.)

1. $[At_1]_{t,g}^{I} = 1$ iff $V(t_1)(t) \in V(A)(t)$, if A is a 1-place predicate.
2. $[At_1t_2]_{t,g}^{I} = 1$ iff $\langle V(t_1)(t), V(t_2)(t) \rangle \in V(A)(t)$, if A is a 2-place predicate.
3.   The usual clauses for the Boolean connectives.
4. $[\forall v \phi]_{t,g}^{I} = 1$ iff $[\phi]_{t,g^{u/v}}^{I} = 1$ for all u in D.
      Similarly for the existential quantifier.
5. $[P\phi]_{t,g}^{I} = 1$ iff $[\phi]_{t',g}^{I} = 1$ for some $t' \in I$ and $t' < t$.
6. $[F\phi]_{t,g}^{I} = 1$ iff $[\phi]_{t',g}^{I} = 1$ for some $t' \in I$ and $t < t'$.
7. $[PR\phi]_{t,g}^{I} = 1$ iff $[\phi]_{t',g}^{I} = 1$ for all $t' \in R(|\varphi|, t)$,
      where R is a function from $P(T) \times T$ into $P(T)$,
      and $|\varphi| = \{t \in T : [\varphi]_{t,g} = 1\}$.
8. $[Y\phi]_{t,g}^{I} = 1$ iff $[\phi]_{t,g}^{yes} = 1$ ⎫   where $y(t_0)$, $to(t_0)$ and $t(t_0)$ are
9. $[TO\phi]_{t,g}^{I} = 1$ iff $[\phi]_{t}^{tom} = 1$ ⎬   the appriate intervals
10. $[T\phi]_{t,g}^{I} = 1$ iff $[\phi]_{t,g}^{tod} = 1$ ⎭
11. $[N\phi]_{t,g}^{I} = 1$ iff $[\phi]_{t,g}^{\{to\}} = 1$.
12. $[\leftarrow\! A\phi]_{t,g}^{I} = 1$ iff $[\phi]_{t,g}^{I'} = 1$ where $I' = {}^{I}[A$.
13. $[[\to A\phi]_{t,g}^{I} = 1$ iff $[\phi]_{t,g}^{I'} = 1$ where $I' = A]^{I}$.

${}^{I}[A$ is defined only when A is a unique subinterval of I. In that case ${}^{I}[A$ is $\{t \in I : \forall t'(t' \in |A| \to t < t'\}$.

$A]^{I}$ is defined only when A is a unique subinterval of I. In that case $A]^{I}$ is $\{t \in I : \forall t'(t' \in |A| \to t > t')\}$.

We shall say that a well-formed formula of L is true in M iff ϕ is true at t_0

with respect to its proper reference interval in M. If ϕ is a P-formula then its proper reference interval in M is $I-$, if ϕ is a PR-formula then its proper reference interval in M is T, if ϕ is an F-formula then its proper reference interval in M is $I+$.

5. COMMENTS

Let us begin with some examples: (T stands for 'translates into')

(1)   John is running T (Being R)j.
(2)   John has run T (Have R)j.
(3)   John came today T $TOPCj$.
(4)   Before Mary arrived, John left T $\dashv AmPLj$.
(5)   Yesterday John left before Mary arrived T $Y \dashv AmPLj$.
(6)   John sleeps in this bed T $PRSj$.

Contrary to most treatments of the progressive we chose to represent this form as a predicate modifier; a predicate like Being A holds of an individual at a moment of time t, if that individual has the property expressed by A during some interval around t. (It might be more realistic however to demand only that there be an interval which finishes with t, since we have sentences like *John was talking to Mary, when he was shot.*) Similarly, we treat the present perfect basically as a form of the present and not as a past operator, even though semantically there are of course some similarities. What is important here is that the speech point functions as the point of reference. It might also be necessary to change the denotation clause of perfective verbs in such a way as to specify that the individuals in the extension of Have A at a time t are to be a subset of those individuals existing (or 'relevant') at t, but we shall not enter upon this problem here.

It is easily seen from the translation of sentence (5) what we take the function of expressions like *today, yesterday* to be be. They restrict the range of the temporal operators which follow them. A past operator alone will have as its range the entire interval $I-$, i.e., the relevant past of the model. However, if an event occurs several times in $I-$, we can restrict $I-$ to a smaller interval. This is what we intend the semantics of these words to do; basically they are intersecting operations. We should add that there are some problems with negation in such contexts. For instance, a sentence like *Yesterday John didn't play tennis* cannot be translated into $YP-Tj$ — which might be true even if John did play at some but not at all times — but into $Y-PTj$. The latter is perfectly compatible with John's having played tennis before yesterday.

The analysis of temporal subordinate phrases like *Before Mary left, after John arrived*, (or others which we have not included for lack of space, e.g., *when Mary arrived, before lunch*, etc.) is roughly like that of the indexical temporal adverbs. They also restrict the range of temporal operators. Not with respect to some segment of time obtainable from the speech point alone, but rather with respect to the interval of reference to which temporal adverbs have already led us or with respect to the primary reference intervals $I-$ or $I+$. Thus *after John arrived* is to be evaluated with respect to the reference interval in such a way as to yield a new reference interval which consists of all those points of time in I which are after John's arrival. If John arrived more than once or not at all during the first reference interval, I' will not be defined and the entire sentence is to have the truth value false. This is obviously a semantic treatment of a phenomenon which might better be treated in pragmatic terms. We shall not develop such an account here however.

It is also interesting to consider the iteration of temporal adverbials as in sentence (5). It has often been suggested that there can only be one temporal modifier per matrix phrase in English. On this view, one might be tempted to treat the adverbial prefixes in *Yesterday after John left and before Mary arrived, Bill played tennis* as a single block. On our analysis this is not necessary since we can get an equivalent result by letting the adverbials apply recursively on each other. All we need to do is pay heed to the kinds of syntactic combinations which we are to allow. For instance, we would not like to have an adverb like *yesterday* in the scope of a past operator, or allow the iteration of indexical time restriction operators as in **Yesterday John came the day before yesterday.* We have provided for certain restrictions of this kind in the syntax of *RTL*. Others will certainly still have to be added.

Certain uses of the present tense pose one of the most complicated problems in the formal semantics of English verb tenses. Thus, one almost never uses a simple present form in the 'reportive' sense where one asserts that the event described takes place at the moment of utterance. For these cases, it is almost always the present progressive. Of the many uses of the present we have chosen to represent something like the generic present, i.e., in a sentence like *Bill sleeps here* we do not intend to mean that Bill is sleeping (at the moment of utterance) in the place referred to with *here*, but rather something like 'at all relevant times in the model Bill does in fact sleep here', for instance at night. We obtain this effect by specifying a function which picks out for each proposition p and for each t in T expressed by a non-tensed sentence a set of relevant times T_p. The present then simple asserts that during those times the sentence is true. We thus have two forms which correspond in different ways to the present — the untensed form which as in most versions of tense logic corresponds to the 'reportive' sense and which does not seem to correspond to any form (except the present progressive) in English, and the 'generic' (or perhaps 'habitual') present.

6. EXTENDING THE LANGUAGE AND SEMANTICS OF RTL

There are quite a few constructions which we have not been able to include in the present sketch of the formal language with which English temporal constructions might be described. We shall indicate a few of these now and leave a more detailed presentation for another occasion.

(1) *Temporal* adverbs involving names of times and events. It is easy to see how we could extend the language to include constructions like *John left after lunch*. We should have to introduce a set of temporal names which could be combined with operators like ←] and [→, to form temporal restricting adverbs. The semantics for such constructions would pick out relative to reference intervals, those points of subintervals which satisfy the temporal names, e.g., *after lunch* would take us to that subinterval of some reference interval I which consists of all those points in I after the lunch in I.

(2) Similarly we could extend the treatment of *before* and *after* to other subordinating conjunctions, in particular to those treated in Åqvist, Guenthner and Rohrer (1977); e.g., *when, while, as long as, since, until*, etc.

(3) *Aspectual verbs.* In connection with the above it will be necessary to distinguish at least two senses of some subordinating conjunctions, namely, with respect to the beginning and ending of events. Thus, we should also provide an analysis of *begin to, finish, resume, continue to*, etc. For some discussion of these 'aspects', cf. Åqvist and Guenthner (1977).

(4) Finally, the most important extension of the present framework will be a formal reconstruction of what some have called '*Aktionsarten*', i.e., of certain verb classes (cf. Vendler (1967) which interact in quite complicated ways with tenses on the one hand and temporal conjunctions on the other). For a beginning of a precise account of certain types of verbs, cf. Åqvist (1977) or Hoepelman (1977).

Universität Tübingen

BIBLIOGRAPHY

Åqvist, L. (1976), 'Formal Semantics for Verb Tenses as Analyzed by Reichenbach', in T. A. van Dijk (ed.), *Pragmatics of Language and Literature*, North Holland, Amsterdam.

Åqvist, L., 'A System of Chronologic Tense Logic' (this volume).

Åqvist, L. (1977), 'On the Analysis of Some Accomplishment Verbs', in C. Rohrer (ed.), *The Logic of Tense and Aspect*, Niemeyer, Tübingen.

Åqvist, L. and Guenthner, F. (1977), 'Fundamentals of a Theory of Aspect and Events Within the Setting of an Improved Tense-Logic', to appear in F. Guenthner and C. Rohrer (eds.), *Studies in Formal Semantics*, North Holland, Amsterdam.

Åqvist, L., Guenthner, F., and Rohrer, C. (1977), 'Definability in ITL of Some Temporal Conjunctions in English', in F. Guenthner and C. Rohrer (eds.), *Studies in Formal Semantics*, North Holland , Amsterdam.

Bull, W. (1968), *Time, Tense and the Verb*, Los Angeles.

Chomsky, N. (1957), *Syntactic Structures*, Mouton, La Haye.

Gabbay, D., 'Tense Logic with Split Truth Tables' (to appear).

Jesperson, O. (1958), *The Philosophy of Grammar*, London.

Hoepelman, J. (1977), 'The Analysis of Activity Verbs in Montague Grammar', in F. Guenthner and C. Rohrer (eds.), *Studies in Formal Semantics*, North Holland, Amsterdam.

Kamp, H. (1971), 'Formal Properties of "Now"', *Theoria*.

Keenan, L. (1972), 'On Semantically Based Grammar', *Linguistic Inquiry*.

Montague, R. (1974), 'The Proper Treatment of Quantification in Ordinary English', in R. H. Thomason (ed.), *Formal Philosophy*, Yale UP, New Haven.

Needham, P. (1976), 'On the Speaker's Point of View', *Synthese*.

Prior, A. (1967), *Past, Present, Future*, Oxford UP, Oxford.

Reichenbach, H. (1947), *Elements of Symbolic Logic*, New York.

Vendler, Z. (1967), *Linguistics in Philosophy*, Cornell UP, Ithaca.

Vlach, H. (1973), '"Now" and "Then"', Diss., UCLA.

LENNART ÅQVIST*

A SYSTEM OF CHRONOLOGICAL TENSE LOGIC

1. INTRODUCTION

The present study is an exercise in what may be called *metric* or *chronological* tense logic, according to the terminology of, e.g., Prior (1967) and Rescher and Urquhart (1971). Our purpose, however, is more in the direction of Wunderlich (1970), viz., to give a logically and linguistically acceptable analysis of such current locutions in ordinary speech as *date indications* and *Uhrzeitangaben* (Sections 5 and 9 below), such as specify *week days*, *months* and *days of the month* (Sections 6, 7, 8 and 9), constructions relating to those just mentioned which involve *tense* and certain *temporal conjunctions* and *prepositions* (Section 10) as well as, finally, of some *speech point related* locutions involving time adverbs like 'today', 'tomorrow', 'yesterday', 'next month', 'last Monday', etc. and temporal prepositions such as, e.g., 'ago' and 'in' (Section 11).

Methodologically, we proceed as follows. We take as our starting point the system ITL of 'improved tense logic' which was first presented by Åqvist and Guenthner (1976) and further developed and refined by Åqvist, Guenthner and Rohrer (1976, 1977). On the semantical or model-theoretic level we enrich the frames of ITL-models with more structure of an algebraic and measure-theoretic kind; the resulting structures are called *chronological frames* and are obtained *via* the conceptions of an *integral temporal frame* (developed in Section 2 below) and of an *integral temporal frame together with a measurement of duration* (developed in Section 3 below). Relatively to chronological frames we are then able (in Section 4) to define a number of familiar measures of time-length. On the syntactical level we enrich our formal languages of ITL with various constructions which are to match those mentioned in the initial paragraph above and try to give a treatment of them within our chronological extension of the system ITL by laying down appropriate *truth conditions* for them relatively to ITL-models with chronological frames. This program is realized in Sections 5–11 below.

A comment on our proposed treatment of *dates*. The first account (given in Section 5) is based on the *measure-theoretic* machinery developed in the

223

F. Guenthner and S. J. Schmidt (eds.), Formal Semantics and Pragmatics for Natural Languages, 223–254. All Rights Reserved.

four initial sections which is largely inspired by the set-theoretical analysis of music and musical form given by Åqvist (1973) which, in turn, profited a good deal from Wedberg's work on additive measures (Wedberg (1963)). The second, alternative account of dates (given in Section 9) employs different *enumerations* of items like days, months, years and days-of-the-month. We feel that, from an intuitive viewpoint, this second account is likely to be more 'natural' than the first one. On the other hand it should be possible to prove the equivalence of the two accounts, but that task is not dealt with in the paper. We should also point out here that the second account requires a little bit of elementary *modular* arithmetic in order to be properly understood.

Finally, we must emphasize that the reader is taken to possess some preknowledge of the aforementioned contributions by Åqvist and Guenthner (1976) and Åqvist, Guenthner and Rohrer (1976, 1977). At any rate, this is the case as far as the technical machinery of the system ITL is concerned.

2. INTEGRAL TEMPORAL FRAMES

By an *integral temporal frame* we shall understand a structure $F = \langle T, <, \tau, Z, s, g \rangle$ where:

(i) $T \neq \varnothing$ (a non-empty set of *times* or *moments*);

(ii) $< \subseteq T \times T$ is a *strict linear* and *dense* ordering of T, in the sense of a binary relation of temporal *precedence*, which is at least irreflexive, transitive, connected and dense in T;

(iii) $\tau \in Z \subset T$ and s, g are functions from T into Z, such that the following axioms are fulfilled:

A1. $Z =$ the smallest set $S \subseteq T$ such that (a) $\tau \in S$, and (b) if $t \in S$, then so are $s(t)$ and $g(t)$.

A2.   For all t, u in Z: if $s(t) = s(u)$, then $t = u$.

A2.1.   For all t, u in Z: if $g(t) = g(u)$, then $t = u$.

A3.   For all t in T: $g(t) < t < s(t)$.

A4.   For all t in T: $t \in Z$ iff $g(s(t)) = t = s(g(t))$.

A5.   For all t in T: $t \notin Z$ iff $g(s(t)) = g(t)$.

A5.1.   For all t in T: $t \notin Z$ iff $s(g(t)) = s(t)$.

A6.   For all t, u in T: if $t, u \notin Z$, then $g(t) = g(u)$ iff $s(t) = s(u)$.

A7.   For all t, u in T: if $t \notin Z$ and $g(t) < u < s(t)$, then $u \notin Z$, $g(u) = g(t)$, and $s(u) = s(t)$.

A8.   For all t, u in T: if $t \in Z$ and $g(t) < u < t$, then $u \notin Z$, $g(u) = g(t)$, and $s(u) = t$.

A8.1.   For all t, u in T: if $t \in Z$ and $t < u < s(t)$, then $u \notin Z$, $s(u) = s(t)$, and $g(u) = t$.

Remark. Given an integral temporal frame $F = \langle T, <, \tau, Z, s, g \rangle$, we can think of its initial segment $\langle T, < \rangle$ as being isomorphic to the series of rational numbers, which is admittedly densely ordered by the $<$-relation. The remainder $\langle \tau, Z, s, g \rangle$ then introduces the series of integers into the frame *via* the following 'translation':

$\tau = 0$;
Z = the set of integers (positive, negative, as well as zero);
s = the operation of taking, for any member of T, the *smallest integer greater than* it; and
g = the operation of taking, for any member of T, the *greatest integer smaller than* it.

Our set of axioms A1–A8.1 purports, of course, to give a characterization of this procedure; however, a *caveat* should be made both as to the completeness of the axiom-set and as to its irredundancy. Fortunately, those matters are not terribly important for our purposes in the present paper.

3. INTEGRAL TEMPORAL FRAMES WITH MEASURES OF DURATION

We begin by introducing some preliminary conceptions. Given a frame F as above, we define the set $\text{Int}(T)$ of all (bounded) *intervals* of T as follows:

$\text{Int}(T) = \{x \in \mathscr{P}T \text{ (the power-set of } T\text{)}$: there are t, t' in T such that

either   (i) $x = [t, t']$
or   (ii) $x = [t, t'[$
or   (iii) $x =]t, t']$
or   (iv) $x =]t, t'[\}$.

Here, the respective notions of the *closed* interval determined by t and t', the *half-open* interval *closed to the left*, the *half-open* interval *closed to the right*, and the *open* interval determined by t and t' are defined as in Åqvist and Guenthner (1976, Section 9, Definition 3).

Again, let $F = \langle T, <, \tau, Z, s, g \rangle$ be an integral temporal frame: by a *measurement of duration* or *time-length on F* we shall understand, as in Åqvist (1973), an ordered quadruple $\langle E, L, E^+, m \rangle$ where:

(i) E and L are the binary relations *is of the same length as* and *is shorter than*, respectively, on the set Int(T);

(ii) E^+ is the ternary relation on Int(T) such that for any x, y, z in that set: $\langle x, y, z \rangle \in E^+$ iff x *is of the same length as y and z put together*;

(iii) m is an *additive measure for* the structure $\langle$Int(T), E, L, $E^+ \rangle$ in the sense of a function from Int(T) into the set of non-negative real numbers such that for all x, y, z in Int(T):

(1) $m(x) = m(y)$ iff $\langle x, y \rangle \in E$.

(2) $m(x) < m(y)$ iff $\langle x, y \rangle \in L$.

(3) $m(x) = m(y) + m(z)$ iff $\langle x, y, z \rangle \in E^+$.

Remark. In order for our notion of a measurement of duration on a frame to be a useful one, various additional assumptions have to be made, e.g., to the effect that E, L, and E^+ be non-empty relations in Int(T), that E be an equivalence-relation in Int(T), and so forth. See in particular Wedberg (1963, p. 277f.), conditions I–V. At present, we wish to draw attention to, and to make, the following special assumptions concerning E and m:

(a)   For all t in Z: $\langle [g(t), t], [t, s(t)] \rangle \in E$.

(b)   For all t, t' in T: $m([t, t']) = m([t, t'[) = m(]t, t']) = m(]t, t'[)$.

(c)   For all t, t' in T: if $t = t'$, then $m([t, t']) = 0$.

Here, condition (b) asserts, roughly, that the exact character of the interval (closed, open etc.) does not affect its length according to m. (a) then asserts that all intervals, both determining coordinates of which are 'adjacent integers' in Z, are of equal length. And (c), finally, claims that all intervals with identical coordinates in T ('singleton' intervals, unit sets of singular points in time) are of length $= 0$.

We can now tell what is to be meant by a *chronological frame*, viz., any structure $C = \langle F, \langle E, L, E^+, m \rangle\rangle$ with $F = \langle T, <, \tau, Z, s, g \rangle$ such that:

(i) F is an integral temporal frame,   and

(ii) $\langle E, L, E^+, m \rangle$ is a measurement of duration on F.

4. SOME FAMILIAR MEASURES OF TIME-LENGTH

We are all acquainted with units of time like these: *second, minute, hour, day, week, month, year, decade, century*, etc. Inasmuch as those terms are used to indicate time-length, we can explicate their meaning on the basis of the framework so far developed as follows.

Let C be a chronological frame (in the sense just defined); relatively to C, we then introduce the following series of equations, applicable to all $x \in \text{Int}(T)$:

$$(0) \qquad m_{\text{sec}}(x) = m(x)$$

$$(1) \qquad m_{\text{min}}(x) = \frac{m_{\text{sec}}(x)}{60}$$

$$(2) \qquad m_{\text{hour}}(x) = \frac{m_{\text{min}}(x)}{60}$$

$$(3) \qquad m_{\text{day}}(x) = \frac{m_{\text{hour}}(x)}{24}$$

$$(4) \qquad m_{\text{week}}(x) = \frac{m_{\text{day}}(x)}{7}$$

$$(5) \qquad m_{\text{month-January}}(x) = \frac{m_{\text{day}}(x)}{31}$$

$$(5a) \qquad m_{\text{month-February ('normal')}}(x) = \frac{m_{\text{day}}(x)}{28}$$

$$(5b) \qquad m_{\text{month-February ('bissextile')}}(x) = \frac{m_{\text{day}}(x)}{29}$$

$$(5c) \qquad m_{\text{month-April}}(x) = \frac{m_{\text{day}}(x)}{30}$$

$$(6) \qquad m_{\text{year ('normal')}}(x) = \frac{m_{\text{day}}(x)}{365}$$

$$(6a) \qquad m_{\text{year ('bissextile')}}(x) = \frac{m_{\text{day}}(x)}{366}$$

Remarks. (i) The measures just introduced are to be understood in accordance with the following reading-paradigms:

$m_{\text{sec}}(x)$: the *length-in-seconds of* the interval x
$m_{\text{month-January}}(x)$: the *length-in-months-like-January of* x
$m_{\text{year ('normal')}}(x)$: the *length-in-normal-years of* x.

(ii) As pointed out, e.g., in Wunderlich (1970, Section 4.6, p. 239), it is by no means necessary to take seconds as our basic unit of time. We might as well choose days as such, for instance. From a formal point of view, this procedure amounts to the following: first, we replace the 'basic' equation (0) with

$$(0') \qquad m_{\text{day}}(x) = m(x)$$

on the basis of which we obtain the measures m_{hour}, m_{min}, and m_{sec} *via* the equations:

(3') $\quad m_{hour}(x) = 24 \cdot m_{day}(x) \quad$ (*cf.* (3)).

(2') $\quad m_{min}(x) = 60 \cdot m_{hour}(x) \quad$ (*cf.* (2)).

(1') $\quad m_{sec}(x) = 60 \cdot m_{min}(x) \quad$ (*cf.* (1)).

On the other hand, equations (4), (5), (5a), (5b), (5c), (6), and (6a) can still be used to derive the corresponding measures, when (0') is taken as basic. And so on.

(iii) The reasons why we need four measures to express length-in-months and two for length-in-years are obvious, of course, and reflect well known features of our Gregorian calendar.

5. INDICATION OF DATES AND OTHER TIMES: A MEASURE-THEORETIC ACCOUNT

Suppose a formal language L of tense logic to be at our disposal. How are we reasonably to introduce into L counterparts to the following locutions of ordinary discourse:

(I) $\quad$ It is March 11 1975.

(II) $\quad$ It is 5 minutes past/to 3 (o'clock).

Clearly, (I) gives an indication of a definite *day* or *date*; similarly, (II) provides what the Germans pertinently call an *Uhrzeitangabe*. In order to deal with (I), we suggest first to paraphrase it as follows, in the manner which is nowadays favored, e.g., by Swedish bureaucracy:

(Ia) $\quad$ It is 1975–3–11

or, more generally:

(Ib) $\quad$ It is i–j–k

where i is a natural number ≥ 0, where $1 \leq j \leq 12$, and where $1 \leq k \leq 31$ (disregarding, for simplicity, further refinements). Let us now ask what may reasonably be an adequate condition for the truth of (Ib) at the *speech point* t_0 in an *original* ITL-*model* in the sense of Åqvist, Guenthner and Rohrer (1976, 1977), whose frame is expanded into a *chronological* one (as explained above). Letting M^{t_0}/t_0 be such a model, we want to fill the blank in the following condition:

$$\left|\frac{M^{t_0}/t_0}{t_0}\right. \text{It is } i\text{–}j\text{–}k \text{ iff } \underline{\qquad\qquad} .$$

Well, in accomplishment of this task, we suggest the following statement:

$$(365 \cdot i + a) + (31 \cdot (j-1) - b) + (k-1) \leq m_{\text{day}}([\tau, t_0[) < (365 \cdot i + a)$$
$$+ (31 \cdot (j-1) - b) + k;$$

where:

(i) τ is the origin of our calendar, i.e., τ is assumed to be the first moment of the first day in the year 0 in which Christ is supposed to be born;

(ii) $m_{\text{day}}([\tau, s(\tau)[) = m([\tau, s(\tau)[) = 1$, so that days are taken as our basic unit of time-measurement, and the length of any day is assumed to be $= 1$; furthermore,

(iii) 365 is the number of days of a normal year, and a is the appropriate number of bissextile days that have to be added;

(iv) 31 is the number of days in months like January, so b will be a suitable number to be subtracted from the product $31 \cdot (j-1)$, depending on what exactly the latter factor is; again, (v) $k-1$ is the number of whole-day intervals in the j-th month that have elapsed up to the point t_0; clearly, *at least $k-1$* and *no more than $k-1$* whole-day intervals must have elapsed in the j-th month in order for the considered statement (Ib) to be true. Analogously, exactly $j-1$ 'whole-month' intervals must have elapsed in the $(i+1)$st year when (Ib) is true. Note, finally, that the year $i =$ the $(i+1)$st year according to our chronology, since we start counting from 0 in the case of years (so that the year $0 =$ the 1st year), whereas we start from 1 in the case of months-of-the-year and in that of days-of-the-month.

With these explanations, the above formula should be easy to understand, and we suggest that it be used to obtain the truth-condition for statements of the form 'It is i–j–k'. Let us add that the proposed analysis does not just apply to the speech point t_0 in an original ITL-model, but is readily generalized to any $t \in T$ taken as the point of evaluation in any ITL-model with arbitrary indices t' and t''.

We now pass to consideration of the locution (II) above, which we take to instantiate the more general sentential forms:

(IIa)   It is n minutes past p (o'clock).
(IIb)   It is n minutes to p (o'clock).

where n, p are non-negative integers such that, in the case of (IIa), $0 \leq n < 60$ and $0 \leq p < 24$, and, in the case of (IIb), $0 \leq n < 60$ and $0 < p \leq 24$. Beginning with the latter form, we suggest that (IIb) is true at t_0 in an original ITL-model M^{t_0}/t_0 just in case the following condition is satisfied:

$$m_{hour}([g(t_0), t_0[) = p - \frac{n}{60}.$$

Using this truth-condition, a sentence such as

It is 0 minutes to 24

will be true at t_0 just in case the length-in-hours $(=m_{hour})$ of the interval $[g(t_0), t_0[= 24 - (0/60) = 24$. Since this is equivalent to saying that the length-in-days $(=m_{day}=m)$ of that interval $=1$, it obviously follows that $t_0 \in Z$ in the present case with $n=0$ and $p=24$. For all other admissible combinations of values of n, p, we will instead have the result that $t_0 \notin Z$, as far as (IIb) is concerned.

Turning next to the analysis of (IIa), we distinguish two cases, viz. (i) where it is not the case that both $n=0$ and $p=0$, and (ii) where both $n=0$ and $p=0$. In case (i), then, we suggest that (IIa) is true at t_0 in M^{t_0}/t_0 iff

$$m_{hour}([g(t_0), t_0[) = p + \frac{n}{60}$$

so that, for instance,

It is 15 minutes past 14

is true at t_0 just in case the length-in-hours of $[g(t_0), t_0[= 14 + \frac{15}{60} = 14\frac{1}{4}$.

It remains to deal with case (ii): we suggest that

It is 0 minutes past 0

is to mean exactly the same as

It is 0 minutes to 24

the truth-condition of which was given a moment ago. Note then that the case where both n and p are $=0$ requires a separate treatment, if we want to avoid the absurd requirement that the length-in-hours of $[g(t_0), t_0[=0$; the correct requirement, to the effect that that length should be $=24$, is then guaranteed by our adopted method of handling case (ii).

Again, our proposed analysis of (IIa) and (IIb) does not just apply to the speech point t_0 in an original ITL-model, but is readily generalized to any $t \in T$ in *any* ITL-*model* $M^{t'}/t''$ with arbitrary t', $t'' \in T$. See Åqvist, Guenthner and Rohrer (1976, 1977).

Let us now deal with the locution

(III)   It is p o'clock sharp

where p is any integer such that $0 \le p \le 24$. To that purpose we lay down the conditional definition:

D1.   It is p o'clock sharp $= df$ $\begin{cases} \text{It is 0 minutes past } p, \text{ if } p = 0 \\ \text{It is 0 minutes to } p, \text{ otherwise.} \end{cases}$

Finally, we can introduce *combined dates*-with-*Uhrzeitangaben*, like

(IV)   It is n minutes past/to p on the i–j–k

as equivalent by definition to the *conjunction* of

(Ib)   It is i–j–k

and

(IIa)   It is n minutes past p

or

(IIb)   It is n minutes to p

as the case may be.

As an exercise to the reader we suggest that he/she calculate, on the basis of the above analyses, the truth-condition in an ITL-model of, say, the statement:

It is 9 minutes past 20 on October 19 1904.

Remark. In connection with our treatment of (IIa) and (IIb) we ought to observe that we have assumed them to be understood in the following 'exactly' sense:

(IIa-exactly)
        It is *exactly* n minutes past p (o'clock).
(IIb-exactly)
        It is *exactly* n minutes to p (o'clock).

We must not, however, forget about the existence in ordinary language of idioms like these:

(IIa,b-at least)
        It is *at least* n minutes past/to p
and
(IIa,b-at most)
        It is *at most* n minutes past/to p.

Treatments of these variant idioms are easily obtained as follows: as for the first one, we simply replace '=' by '⩾' in the matching truth-condition for the 'exactly' version; in the second case, we substitue '⩽' for '='. Thus, for example,

It is at most 21 minutes to 9

will be true at t_0 in an ITL-model just in case

$$m_{\text{hour}}([g(t_0), t_0[) \le 9 - \tfrac{21}{60} = 8\tfrac{39}{60}.$$

The 'degenerate' case when $t_0 \in Z$ will again call for some special treatment: 'it is *at least* 0 minutes past 0' will be taken to be true just in case $m_{\text{hour}}([g(t_0), t_0[) > 0$ or $= 24$, for instance.

6. NAMES OF WEEK-DAYS AND MONTHS INTERPRETED

Let $ZInt(T)$ ($\subseteq Int(T)$) be the following set of intervals on the set T of any chronological frame C: $\{\ldots, [g(g(\tau)), g(\tau)[, [g(\tau), \tau[, [\tau, s(\tau)[, [s(\tau), s(s(\tau))[, \ldots\}$. Any interval in $ZInt(T)$ is then such that both its determining co-ordinates are adjacent members of the 'integer-like' set Z. We then take $\#$ to be the one-to-one correspondence between the set Z of 'ordinary' arithmetical integers and $ZInt(T)$ defined by the following series of equations:

$$\#(1) = [\tau, s(\tau)[\qquad\qquad \#(0) \;\; = [g(\tau), \tau[$$
$$\#(2) = [s(\tau), s(s(\tau))[\qquad \#(-1) = [g(g(\tau)), g(\tau)[$$
$$\#(3) = [s(s(\tau)), s(s(s(\tau)))[\qquad \#(-2) = [g(g(g(\tau))), g(g(\tau))[$$
$$\text{etc.} \qquad\qquad\qquad\qquad \text{etc.}$$

We now assume that each member of $ZInt(T)$ represents precisely one *day*. Formally speaking, this amounts to requiring that, for each $x \in ZInt(T)$, $m_{\text{day}}(x) = m(x) = 1$. Moreover, we shall assume that the day $[\tau, s(\tau)[$ was indeed a Sunday. We then define the following subsets of $ZInt(T)$, where $i \equiv j \pmod{k}$ means that i and j are congruent modulo k (see, e.g., Birkhoff and MacLane (1948, p. 23f.):

$$\begin{aligned}
\text{SUNDAY} &= \{\#(i): i \equiv 1 \ (\mathrm{mod}\ 7)\} \\
\text{MONDAY} &= \{\#(i): i \equiv 2 \ (\mathrm{mod}\ 7)\} \\
\text{TUESDAY} &= \{\#(i): i \equiv 3 \ (\mathrm{mod}\ 7)\} \\
\text{WEDNESDAY} &= \{\#(i): i \equiv 4 \ (\mathrm{mod}\ 7)\} \\
\text{THURSDAY} &= \{\#(i): i \equiv 5 \ (\mathrm{mod}\ 7)\} \\
\text{FRIDAY} &= \{\#(i): i \equiv 6 \ (\mathrm{mod}\ 7)\} \\
\text{SATURDAY} &= \{\#(i): i \equiv 7 \ (\mathrm{mod}\ 7)\}.
\end{aligned}$$

To illustrate a bit, WEDNESDAY will be the following subset of $ZInt(T)$:

$$\{\dots \dots \#(-10),\ \#(-3),\ \#(4),\ \#(11),\ \#(18),\ \#(25),\dots \dots\}.$$

Consider the set {SUNDAY, MONDAY, ..., SATURDAY}. We note that it is a *partition* of $ZInt(T)$ in the familiar sense that (i) the intersection of any two of its members is empty, and (ii) the union of all its members exhausts, i.e., equals, the full set $ZInt(T)$. We may also note here, *en passant*, that $ZInt(T)$ is a partition of T in the very same sense.

We now propose a treatment of the *months* in our model-theoretic metalanguage. Define $MInt(T)\ (\subseteq Int(T))$ as the following set of intervals on the T-set of a chronological frame C:

$$\{\dots,\ [g^{30+31}(\tau),\ g^{31}(\tau)[,\ [g^{31}(\tau),\ \tau[,\ [\tau,\ s^{31}(\tau)[,\ [s^{31}(\tau),$$
$$s^{31+28}(\tau)[,\ [s^{31+28}(\tau),\ s^{31+28+31}(\tau)[,\dots\}.$$

Here, for any positive integer k, the functions g^k and s^k are defined as follows:

$$g^k(\tau)=\overbrace{gg\dots g}^{k\ \text{times}}(\tau)$$
$$s^k(\tau)=\overbrace{ss\dots s}^{k\ \text{times}}(\tau)$$

where, of course, unnecessary parantheses have been dropped.

We then take ♮ to be the one-to-one correspondence between the set Z of ordinary integers and $MInt(T)$ which is defined by the following series of equations:

$$♮(1)\ \ =[\tau, s^{31}(\tau)[$$
$$♮(2)\ \ =[s^{31}(\tau), s^{31+28}(\tau)[$$
$$♮(3)\ \ =[s^{31+28}(\tau), s^{31+28+31}(\tau)[$$
$$♮(4)\ \ =[s^{31+28+31}(\tau), s^{31+28+31+30}(\tau)[$$

etc.

$$♮(0)\ \ =[g^{31}(\tau), \tau[$$
$$♮(-1)=[g^{30+31}(\tau), g^{31}(\tau)[$$
$$♮(-2)=[g^{31+30+31}(\tau), g^{30+31}(\tau)[$$

etc.

Clearly, we want the members of $MInt(T)$ to represent months, the length of which is supposed to vary in the following familiar way:

$m_{\text{day}}(\natural(1)) = 31$, so that $m_{\text{month-January}}(\natural(1)) = 1$;

$m_{\text{day}}(\natural 2)) = 28$, so that $m_{\text{month-February ('normal')}}(\natural(2)) = 1$;

$m_{\text{day}}(\natural(3)) = 31$, so that $m_{\text{month-January}}(\natural(3)) = 1$;

$m_{\text{day}}(\natural(4)) = 30$, so that $m_{\text{month-April}}(\natural(4)) = 1$;

$m_{\text{day}}(\natural(-1)) = 30$, so that $m_{\text{month-April}}(\natural(-1)) = 1$.

And so on. For the measures that are relevant here, see Section 4 above. Given our enumeration function $\natural$, we now define the following subsets of the set $MInt(T)$:

$$
\begin{aligned}
\text{JANUARY} \quad &= \{\natural(i): i \equiv 1 \ (\text{mod } 12)\} \\
\text{FEBRUARY} \quad &= \{\natural(i): i \equiv 2 \ (\text{mod } 12)\} \\
\text{MARCH} \quad &= \{\natural(i): i \equiv 3 \ (\text{mod } 12)\} \\
\text{APRIL} \quad &= \{\natural(i): i \equiv 4 \ (\text{mod } 12)\} \\
\text{MAY} \quad &= \{\natural(i): i \equiv 5 \ (\text{mod } 12)\} \\
\text{JUNE} \quad &= \{\natural(i): i \equiv 6 \ (\text{mod } 12)\} \\
\text{JULY} \quad &= \{\natural(i): i \equiv 7 \ (\text{mod } 12)\} \\
\text{AUGUST} \quad &= \{\natural(i): i \equiv 8 \ (\text{mod } 12)\} \\
\text{SEPTEMBER} &= \{\natural(i): i \equiv 9 \ (\text{mod } 12)\} \\
\text{OCTOBER} \quad &= \{\natural(i): i \equiv 10 \ (\text{mod } 12)\} \\
\text{NOVEMBER} &= \{\natural(i): i \equiv 11 \ (\text{mod } 12)\} \\
\text{DECEMBER} &= \{\natural(i): i \equiv 12 \ (\text{mod } 12)\}.
\end{aligned}
$$

In order to illustrate a little, MAY will be the following subset of $MInt(T)$:

$$\{\ldots \ \ldots \ \natural(-19), \ \natural(-7), \ \natural(5), \ \natural(17), \ \natural(29), \ \ldots \ \ldots\}.$$

Consider the set {JANUARY, FEBRUARY, ..., DECEMBER}. We observe that it is a partition of $MInt(T)$, because (i) the intersection of any two of its members is empty, and (ii) the union of all its members exhausts the full set $MInt(T)$. In like manner, $MInt(T)$ is a partition of T, of course.

7. SOME LOCUTIONS CONTAINING WEEK-DAY SPECIFICATIONS

Consider the sentence

(V)   It is Monday.

The problem is to find the adequate condition of truth for (V) relatively to t_0 in an original ITL-model with chronological frame, and, in general, relatively to any $t \in T$ in any ITL-model with such a frame. We then suggest the following:

$$\left|\frac{M^{t_0}/t_0}{t_0}\right.$$ It is Monday, iff $[g(t_0), s(t_0)[\in$ MONDAY, provided that $t_0 \notin Z$; and iff $[t_0, s(t_0)[\in$ MONDAY, otherwise (i.e., if $t_0 \in Z$).

Here, $\left.'\middle|\frac{M^{t_0}/t_0}{t_0}\right.$ It is Monday' means, as usual, that the sentence 'It is Monday' is *true at* t_0 *in* M^{t_0}/t_0. The proposed condition can then be generalized by substitution of t for t_0 throughout, and by replacing the original model M^{t_0}/t_0 with any model $M^{t'}/t''$ ($t, t', t'' \in T$). Note (i) that the half-open intervals $[g(t_0), s(t_0)[$ and $[t_0, s(t_0)[$ are always members of $Z\mathrm{Int}(T)$ according as the provisos $t_0 \notin Z$, $t_0 \in Z$ are respectively satisfied, and (ii) the *conditional* character of the present truth-condition, due to the fact that we must take two different possibilities into account.

Our present analysis of (V) can obviously be generalized in another direction as well: if we replace 'MONDAY' by any other week-day name and replace 'MONDAY' by the set-theoretical capitalized designation matching that week-day name, we obtain a full treatment of all sentences having the form of (V), i.e. 'It is _____', where the blank is filled by a week-day name.

On the basis of our present truth-conditions, we can now extend our treatment in Section 5 above of date-indications and *Uhrzeitangaben* as follows: Consider

(VI)   It is Sunday, October 17, 1976.

We take (VI) to be equivalent by definition to the following *conjunction*:

(VIa)   It is Sunday & It is 1976–10–17

the truth-condition of which is already known to us. Again,

(VII)   It is Tuesday, 3 p.m. sharp

which we take to be definitionally equivalent to

(VIIa)   It is Tuesday & It is 0 minutes to 15

whose truth-condition is again familiar to us in the light of previous considerations. A final example,

(VIII)   It is 11 minutes past 11 on Saturday, October 16, 1976

is equated to the conjunction

(VIIIa) It is 11 minutes past 11 & It is Saturday & It is 1976–10–16.

Remark. (VII) contains the symbol 'p.m.', which we take to designate a one-place function from the integers q such that $0 < q < 12$ into the integers, and definable by:

$$q \text{ p.m.} = q + 12.$$

The function a.m., with the same domain of definition, is simply the identity function: $q \text{ a.m.} = q$.

8. INDICATION OF MONTHS

Consider the set $M\text{Int}(T)$ of month intervals which was introduced in the next to last section above. Corresponding to $M\text{Int}(T)$ we form the set $M (\subset Z \subset T)$ of determining coordinates of elements in $M\text{Int}(T)$:

$$M = \{\ldots, g^{30+31}(\tau), g^{31}(\tau), \tau, s^{31}(\tau), s^{31+28}(\tau), \ldots\}.$$

Here, the members of M are listed in their 'natural' order according to the $<$-relation. Again, we may define two functions s and g from T into M by putting, to start with:

$$s(\tau) = s^{31}(\tau) \qquad g(\tau) = g^{31}(\tau)$$
$$s(s(\tau)) = s^{31+28}(\tau) \qquad g(g(\tau)) = g^{30+31}(\tau)$$
$$\text{etc.} \qquad\qquad\qquad \text{etc.}$$

In general, we assume τ, M, s and g to satisfy analogues of our axioms A1–A8.1 which are obtained by uniformly replacing reference to Z, s, and g by reference to M, s and g, respectively. For example, the resulting analogue of A1 will assert that M is the smallest set $S \subseteq T$ such that (a) S contains τ as a member, and (b) S is closed under the operations s and g. And so on for other analogues of our original axioms.

Let us now consider the problem of laying down conditions of truth at t_0 in an original ITL-model with chronological frame for the following sentences of ordinary English:

(IXa)   It is January
(IXb)   It is February

and so forth. We then suggest the following truth-condition:

$$\left| \frac{M^{t_0}/t_0}{t_0} \right. \text{ It is January, iff } [g(t_0), s(t_0)[\in \text{JANUARY, provided}$$

that $t_0 \notin M$; and iff $[t_0, s(t_0)[\in$ JANUARY, otherwise (i.e. if $t_0 \in M$).

With respect to this condition we should pay attention (i) to its conditional character, and (ii) to the fact that the half-open intervals $[g(t_0), s(t_0)[$ and $[t_0, s(t_0)[$ are always members of $M\mathrm{Int}(T)$ according as the provisos $t_0 \notin M$ and $t_0 \in M$ are fulfilled, respectively.

Again, replacing 'January' in this truth-condition by any other name of a month and 'JANUARY' by the matching capitalized set-theoretical designation, we obtain a treatment of all sentences having the form 'It is . . .', where the dots are filled with a name of a month. Also, the proposed condition can be generalized by uniform substitution of t for t_0 and by replacement of the original model M^{t_0}/t_0 with any model $M^{t'}/t''$ $(t, t', t'' \in T)$.

A *combined week day*-with-*month* specification, such as

(X)   It is a Sunday in August

can be treated as being definitionally equivalent to the *conjunction*

(Xa)   It is Sunday & It is August

the truth condition of which is now known to us. Note that in our semantics, if $t_0 \notin Z$, the day interval $[g(t_0), s(t_0)[$ which is claimed by (Xa) to be a member of the set SUNDAY will be a *proper* subset of the month interval $[g(t_0), s(t_0)[$, which is claimed by (Xa) to be an element of the set AUGUST.

9. AN ALTERNATIVE ACCOUNT OF DATES

Given a chronological frame C we define the set $Y\mathrm{Int}(T)$ of *year intervals* (over T) as follows:

$$Y\mathrm{Int}(T) = \{\ldots, [g^{2 \cdot 365}(\tau), g^{365}(\tau)[, [g^{365}(\tau), \tau[, [\tau, s^{365}(\tau)[, [s^{365}(\tau), s^{2 \cdot 365}(\tau)[, \ldots\}.$$

We then define the following enumeration function $\flat$ from Z onto $Y\mathrm{Int}(T)$:

$$
\begin{aligned}
\flat(0) &= [\tau, s^{365}(\tau)[\\
\flat(1) &= [s^{365}(\tau), s^{2 \cdot 365}(\tau)[\\
\flat(2) &= [s^{2 \cdot 365}(\tau), s^{3 \cdot 365}(\tau)[\quad \text{etc.} \\
\flat(-1) &= [g^{365}(\tau), \tau[\\
\flat(-2) &= [g^{2 \cdot 365}(\tau), g^{365}(\tau)[\quad \text{etc.}
\end{aligned}
$$

For any k in Z, the locution $\flat(k)$ may be read: *the year no. k*. We also presuppose that allowance has been made for bissextile or leap years in such a way that, e.g.,

$$\flat(4) = [s^{4 \cdot 365}(\tau), s^{5 \cdot 365 + 1}(\tau)[.$$

As for the length of the members of $Y\mathrm{Int}(T)$, we assume that

$$m_{\mathrm{day}}(\flat(k)) = \begin{cases} 365, & \text{if } k \text{ is not divisible by 4} \\ 366, & \text{otherwise.} \end{cases}$$

Remark. If we do not want $\flat(1700)$, for instance, to be a leap year, the above assumption has to be slightly modified and refined.

Corresponding to the set $Y\mathrm{Int}(T)$ we now form the set Y ($\subset M \subset Z \subset T$) of determining coordinates of elements in $Y\mathrm{Int}(T)$, listed in their natural order:

$$Y = \{\ldots, g^{2 \cdot 365}(\tau), g^{365}(\tau), \tau, s^{365}(\tau), s^{2 \cdot 365}(\tau), \ldots\}.$$

Again, we define two functions S and G from T into Y by putting, to begin with:

$$S(\tau) = s^{365}(\tau) \qquad\qquad G(\tau) = g^{365}(\tau)$$
$$S(S(\tau)) = s^{2 \cdot 365}(\tau) \qquad G(G(\tau)) = g^{2 \cdot 365}(\tau)$$
$$\text{etc.} \qquad\qquad\qquad \text{etc.}$$

And, in general, τ, Y, S and G are assumed to satisfy analogues of the axioms A1–A8.1, obtained by uniformly replacing reference to Z, s and g by reference to Y, S and G, respectively. Cf. our construction in the case of M, s and g, Section 8 above.

We now want to find the condition of truth at t_0 in an original model with chronological frame for sentences of the following form:

(XI)   It is /in the year/ 1789

We then propose the condition:

$$\left|\begin{array}{l} M^{t_0}/t_0 \\ \hline \\ t_0 \end{array}\right.$$ It is /in the year/ 1789, iff, $[G(t_0), S(t_0)[= \flat(1789)$, if t_0

$\notin Y$; and iff $[t_0, S(t_0)[= \flat(1789)$, otherwise.

Here, we can obviously generalize to any integer $i \in Z$, so that we obtain a treatment of any sentence 'It is /in the year/ i', where $i \in Z$. Again, we note that our present condition is *conditional* in character; it can be replaced, however, by the following simpler, *unconditional* requirement:

$$t_0 \in \flat(1789)$$

and, in general, for $i \in \mathbf{Z}$,

$$t_0 \in \flat(i).$$

The equivalence of this alternative analysis to the first one can be left as an exercise to the reader. As usual, our proposed treatments can also be generalized to any ITL models M'/t'' and to any $t \in T$.

We are now in a position to give the alternative account of dates which is promised in the title of the present section. Consider, for example, the sentence

(XII)   It is July 4, 1776.

Clearly, (XII) should be true at t_0 in a model with chronological frame only if the following statements are so true at t_0:

(XIIa)   It is /in the year/ 1776
(XIIb)   It is July

which means that $t_0 \in \flat(1776)$ and, assuming $t_0 \notin Z$ and $t_0 \notin M$, that the month interval $[g(t_0), s(t_0)[\in$ JULY. So the only thing that remains to be dealt with is the day specification 4; according to (XII) the day is to be the *fourth* of July in the year 1776. In order to understand this day specification, we first consider the result of intersecting the *closed* interval $[g(t_0), s(t_0)]$ with the integer-like set Z, i.e.,

$$[g(t_0), s(t_0)] \cap Z$$

Now, obviously, this intersection is equal to the set

$$\{s^k(\tau), s^{k+1}(\tau), s^{k+2}(\tau), \ldots, s^{k+31}(\tau)\}$$

where k is some positive integer, and where $s^k(\tau) = g(t_0)$ and $s^{k+31}(\tau) = s(t_0)$ in the case at issue. Again, by *the sequence of day intervals contained in the month interval* $[g(t_0), s(t_0)[$ we then mean the set

$$\{[s^k(\tau), s^{k+1}(\tau)[, [s^{k+1}(\tau), s^{k+2}(\tau)[, \ldots, [s^{k+30}(\tau), s^{k+31}(\tau)[\}$$

which we shall refer to as $D([g(t_0), s(t_0)[)$.

Relatively to this set we now define an enumeration § by requiring that, for any integer i such that $1 \leq i \leq 31$,

$$\S(i) = |[s^{k+i-1}(\tau), s^{k+i}(\tau)[.$$

As the condition of the truth at t_0 of the sentence form

(XIIc)   It is the i-th of the month ($1 \leq i \leq 31$)

we then suggest, provided that $t_0 \notin Z$:

$$[g(t_0), s(t_0)[= \S(i).$$

Going back to the problem of analyzing

(XIId)   It is July 4, 1776

we then propose that it be treated as definitionally equivalent to

It is /in the year/ 1776 & It is July & It is the 4th of the month

i.e., the conjunction of the statements (XIIa), (XIIb), and (XIIc) with $i = 4$.

The above analysis of 'It is the i-th of the month' should be extended so as to cover the possibility that $t_0 \in Z$; similarly, the case where $t_0 \in M$ should be taken into account and $\S(i)$ be defined relatively to the set $D([t_0, s(t_0)[)$. Thirdly, provision should be made for the well known dependency of the maximal value of i on the month at issue. These, as well as other obvious generalizations are all left to the reader.

A somewhat informal summing up of the analysis of (XII) that we have just given is the following. Given that $t_0 \notin Z$, for simplicity, the year specification says something about the year interval $[G(t_0), S(t_0)[$ to which t_0 belongs, viz. that it has such and such a number according to the ♭ enumeration. Then the month indication in (XII) locates the month interval $[g(t_0), s(t_0)[$ to which t_0 belongs in exactly one of the twelve possible classes JANUARY, ..., DECEMBER, which were defined by appealing to the ♮ enumeration. Finally, the day-of-the-month specification says something about the day interval $[g(t_0), s(t_0)[$ to which t_0 belongs, viz., that it has such and such a number according to the $\S$ enumeration defined relatively to the month interval $[g(t_0), s(t_0)[$ by way of the D function.

In the case of a *complete* date specification such as (XII), we eventually arrive at a *definite* location of the day interval $[g(t_0), s(t_0)[$ of which t_0 is a member in the set $Z\text{Int}(T)$ of day intervals. If, by way of contrast, we consider such *incomplete* date specifications as

(XIII)   It is November 15
(XIIIa)   It is November 1973
(XIIIb)   It is the 28th of the month in the year 1973

or, for that matter, (XIIa) and (XIIb) above, the specification does not result in any definite location of the day interval $[g(t_0), s(t_0)[$ in the set $Z\mathrm{Int}(T)$. Note that the present complete *vs.* incomplete distinction is thus drawn on the basis of *days* being our fundamental units of time length.

10. SOME CONSTRUCTIONS INVOLVING TENSE AND TEMPORAL CONJUNCTIONS

In Section 9 above we gave an analysis of the meaning of the sentence

(XII)   It is July 4 1776

appealing to the enumerations ♭, ♮, and §. Let us now consider some possible syntactical constructions into which (XII) may enter as an analytic component, viz. the following:

(1)   It *had been* the case that A
(2)   It *was* the case that A
(3)   It *was going to* be the case that A
(4)   It *has been* the case that A
(5)   It *is* (*now*) the case that A } *on* July 4 1776.
(6)   It *is going to* be the case that A
(7)   It *will have been* the case that A
(8)   It *will* be the case that A
(9)   It *will be going to* be the case that A

What we are considering here is, of course, nothing but Reichenbach's nine *fundamental forms* of verb tense, presented towards the end of Section 51 in his book (1947), and *combined with* the date specification at issue in the way just indicated. Following the reconstruction of Reichenbachian tenses given in Åqvist (1976), we now propose a series of definitions in our present chronological version of the system ITL:

D1.   HadBeen A On July 4 1776 $=df$ $\langle\hat{P}\rangle$ $\boxed{x|d}$ $\langle\hat{P}\rangle$ ((It is July 4 1776) & A)

D2.   Was A On July 4 1776 $=df$ $\langle\hat{P}\rangle$ $\boxed{x|d}$ ((It is July 4 1776) & A)

D3.   WasGoingTo A On July 4 1776 $=df$ $\langle\hat{P}\rangle$ $\boxed{x|d}$ $\langle\hat{F}\rangle$ ((It is July 4 1776) & A)

D4.   HasBeen A On July 4 1776 $=df$ $\langle\hat{P}\rangle$ ((It is July 4 1776) & A)

D5.   Is/Now/ A On July 4 1776 $=df$ $\boxed{d}$ ((It is July 4 1776) & A)

D6.   IsGoingTo A On July 4 1776 $=df$ $\langle\hat{F}\rangle$ ((It is July 4 1776) & A)

D7.   WillHaveBeen A On July 4 1776 $= df$ $\langle F \rangle$ $\boxed{x|d}$ $\langle P \rangle$ ((It is July 4 1776) & A)

D8.   Will A On July 4 1776 $= df$ $\langle F \rangle$ $\boxed{x|d}$ ((It is July 4 1776) & A)

D9.   WillBeGoingTo A On July 4 1776 $= df$ $\langle F \rangle$ $\boxed{x|d}$ $\langle F \rangle$ ((It is July 4 1776) & A).

Comments. (i) An operator such as 'HadBeen . . . On July 4 1776' is to be thought of as a one-place sentential one, which forms a new sentence of L when applied to any L-sentence A. The readings of the *definienda* in the series D1–D9 are provided by the members of the series (1)–(9) in the obvious way.

(ii) Let us ask with respect, e.g., to the *definiendum* of D1 under what condition it is true at t_0 in an original ITL-model with chronological frame. We then obtain the result:

$$\frac{M^{t_0}/t_0}{t_0} \text{ HadBeen } A \text{ On July 4 1776 iff}$$

$$\frac{M^{t_0}/t_0}{t_0} \langle P \rangle \boxed{x|d} \langle P \rangle \text{ ((It is July 4 1776) \& } A)) \text{ iff}$$

there are $t, u \in T$ with $u < t < t_0$ such that

(a) $\dfrac{M^t/t_0}{u}$ It is July 4 1776, *and* (b) $\dfrac{M^t/t_0}{u}$ A; where, provided that $u \notin Z$, the first conjunct holds iff, first, $u \in b(1776)$, second, $[g(u), s(u)[\in$ JULY and, third, $[g(u), s(u)[= \S(4)$. See Section 9 above.

Another example:

$$\frac{M^{t_0}/t_0}{t_0} \text{ IsGoingTo } A \text{ On July 4 1776 iff there is } u \in T \text{ with } t_0 < u$$

such that (a) $u \in b(1776)$, $[g(u), s(u)[\in$ JULY, and $[g(u), s(u)[= \S(4)$, and (b) $\dfrac{M^{t_0}/t_0}{u}$ A. (Again, we assume $u \notin Z$.)

Some obvious conclusions can be drawn on the basis of the two illustrations just given. (I) A necessary condition for the truth at t_0 of the *definiendum* of D1 (in fact, of the *definienda* of D1, D2 and D4 is that the event point u, which is claimed to satisfy the conjuncts (a) and (b), is *earlier* in time than the speech point t_0. (II) A necessary condition for the truth at t_0

of the *definiendum* of D6 (and of D8 and D9) is that the event point u is *later* in time than the speech point t_0. We take the latter circumstance to explain why it seems absurd to assert any sentence of the form IsGoingTo A On July 4 1776 at any date *later* than July 4 1776. Similarly, we take the former fact to explain the absurdity of asserting a sentence of the form HadBeen A On July 4 1776 at any date *prior* to July 4 1776.

(iii) From the ordinary language point of view we may question the adequacy of definitions D1, D3, D7 and D9, which combine a date specification with *composite* tenses such as the *past perfect*, the *posterior past* (in Reichenbach's 'new' terminology), the *future perfect*, and the *posterior future* (in Reichenbach's 'new' terminology), respectively. Our reason is this. Obviously, according to those definitions, conjuncts like (a) and (b) above are both claimed to be true of an *event point u* in the sense of Reichenbach (1947, Section 51), a point, then, which may be related to his so called *point of reference* and to the speech point t_0 in different ways in different cases. Now, as appears from the quotations that he gives on pp. 288ff., one may feel that, in the case of the composite tenses at issue, the date specification should qualify and determine the point of reference rather than the point of the event, contrary to what is the case according to our definitions. In order to realize this purpose we then propose the following fresh alternative definitions:

D1′. On July 4 1776 HadBeen $A =df$ ⟨P⟩ ⌐x|d⌐ ((It is July 4 1776) & ⟨P⟩ A)

D3′. On July 4 1776 WasGoingTo $A =df$ ⟨P⟩ ⌐x|d⌐ ((It is July 4 1776) & ⟨F⟩ A)

D7′. On July 4 1776 WillHaveBeen $A =df$ ⟨F⟩ ⌐x|d⌐ ((It is July 4 1776) & ⟨P⟩ A)

D9′. On July 4 1776 WillBeGoingTo $A =df$ ⟨F⟩ ⌐x|d⌐ ((It is July 4 1776) & ⟨F⟩ A)

Again raising the question as to the condition of truth at t_0 in the past perfect case, according to D1′, we find that

$$\underset{t_0}{\models} \frac{M^{t_0}/t_0}{} \; ⟨P⟩ \; ⌐x|d⌐ \;((\text{It is July 4 1776}) \;\&\; ⟨P⟩ \; A) \text{ iff there are } t, u \in T$$

with $u < t < t_0$ such that (a) $\underset{t}{\models} \dfrac{M^t/t_0}{}$ It is July 4 1776, *and*

(b) $\underset{u}{\models} \dfrac{M^t/t_0}{} A$. Here, t is the point of reference (determined by the date specification), and u is the point of the event expressed by A; hence, the requirement made above is satisfied by D1'.

(iv) Our analysis of the locutions (1)–(9) can obviously be generalized in at least two directions, viz., (a) by substituting *any* date specification for 'July 4 1776', and (b) by replacing the adverbial '*on* July 4 1776' with phrases like the following:

> *In* 1789
> *At n* minutes past/to *p* (o'clock)
> *On* a Sunday in August

Appealing to our semantical analysis of the sentences (XI), (IIa)–(IIb) and (X), we can use the technique illustrated by D1–D9, D1', D3', D7' and D9' to handle the locutions that result from the three substitutions just mentioned, respectively. For the time being, we leave further details and extensions of our analysis to the reader.

Finally, we wish to show how one can combine the results of the present paper with some of those obtained in Åqvist, Guenthner and Rohrer (1976), where certain subordinate temporal conjunctions in English are at issue. Consider the following list of sentences:

(10)   Since 2 o'clock sharp I have been playing the *Waldstein* sonata.

(11)   Until a quarter to 9 p.m. I will be playing *Les Adieux*.

(12)   I became aware of the *Appassionata* on a Sunday in August.

(13)   On November 25 1976 I worked all day long on this paper.

(14)   Max arrived in Stuttgart before May 15 1976.

(15)   Pierre arrived in Stuttgart after the 1st of September.

Note that in these examples the occurrences of 'since', 'until', 'before' and 'after' should be grammatically classified as *prepositions* rather than, of course, as conjunctions. We claim, however, that the prepositional use of these words in (10)–(15) can be analyzed in terms of their use as conjunctions, or, in the logician's jargon, *two-place sentential connectives*. We then propose to translate (10)–(15) into the following sentences (10a)–(15a), respectively:

(10a)   SinceWas–HasAlwaysBeen (It is 2 o'clock sharp, I am playing the *Waldstein* sonata); cf. D3.1.0 of Section 3.1 in Åqvist, Guenthner and Rohrer (1976).

(11a)   UntilWillBe–IsAlwaysGoingTo (It is 15 minutes to 21, I am playing *Les Adieux*); cf. D3.1.4 of Section 3.1 in Åqvist, Guenthner and Rohrer (1976).

(12a)   Was–$\overline{\text{when}}_4$Was (I become aware of the *Appassionata*, It is a Sunday in August); cf. D4.2.4$\tilde{}_{smpst}$ of Section 4.2 in Åqvist, Guenthner and Rohrer (1976).

(13a)   Was–AtLeastAsLongAsWas (I work on this paper, It is November 25 1976); cf. D4.1.6$_{smpst}$ of Section 4.2 in Åqvist, Guenthner and Rohrer (1976).

(14a)   Was–BeforeWas (Max arrives in Stuttgart, It is May 15 1976); cf. D5.2.4 of Section 5.2 in Åqvist, Guenthner and Rohrer (1976).

(15a)   Was–AfterWas (Pierre arrives in Stuttgart, It is September & It is the 1st of the month); cf. D5.2.5 of Section 5.2 in Åqvist, Guenthner and Rohrer (1976).

Note that, in the context of (12) and (13), the meaning of the preposition 'on' is analyzed in terms of such temporal conjunctions as 'when' (in one sense) and 'at least as long as' (which is but another 'when').

11. ON THE ANALYSIS OF SOME SPEECH POINT RELATED LOCUTIONS

Consider any ITL model $M^{t'}/t''$ with chronological frame $\langle\langle T, <, \tau, Z, s, g\rangle, \langle E, L, E^+, m\rangle\rangle$ as well as any $t \in T$. Let L be a language of the system ITL of 'improved' tense logic as presented in Åqvist and Guenthner (1976), and in Åqvist, Guenthner and Rohrer (1976); assume L to be supplemented with two one-place sentential operators γ and σ, which are to obey the following truth conditions, respectively:

(1) $\left|\frac{M^{t'}/t''}{t}\right. \gamma A$ iff $\left|\frac{M^{t'}/t''}{g(t)}\right. A$

(2) $\left|\frac{M^{t'}/t''}{t}\right. \sigma A$ iff $\left|\frac{M^{t'}/t''}{s(t)}\right. A$

Furthermore, we call attention to the presence in L of the *speech point modality* $\boxed{s}$, read as 'it is now the case that', which obeys the following truth condition:

(3) $\left|\frac{M^{t'}/t''}{t}\right. \boxed{s}A$ iff $\left|\frac{M^{t'}/t''}{t_0}\right. A$

where, for any ITL model $M^{t'}/t''$, t_0 is the designated member of T in the *original* ITL model M ($= M^{t_0}/t_0$) from which $M^{t'}/t''$ is generated. See again the two papers mentioned above. Finally, a vitally important role is played by our two *interval-restricted* operators $\boxminus$ ('in the open interval determined by ... and _____ it is always the case that') and $\Diamond\!\!\!\!\rightarrow$ ('in the open interval determined by ... and _____ it is at least once the case that'), which were first presented and characterized in Åqvist and Guenthner (1976, Section 4).

We now lay down a series of explicit definitions in *L*, all of which involve one or other of the time adverbs 'today', 'tomorrow', and 'yesterday':

D1.0   TodayHasOnceBeen $A =_{df} \boxed{s}\ \boxed{X|w}\ \gamma \Diamond\!\!\!\!\rightarrow A$

D1.1   TodayOnceWas $A =_{df} \boxed{s}\ \boxed{X|w}\ \gamma \Diamond\!\!\!\!\rightarrow \boxed{x|d}\ A$

D1.2   TodayIsOnceGoingTo $A =_{df} \boxed{s}\ \boxed{X|w}\ \sigma \Diamond\!\!\!\!\rightarrow A$

D1.3   TodayWillOnceBe $A =_{df} \boxed{s}\boxed{X|w}\ \sigma \Diamond\!\!\!\!\rightarrow \boxed{x|d}\ A$

D1.4   TodayHasAllDayLongBeen $A =_{df} \boxed{s}\ \boxed{X|w}\ \gamma \boxminus A$

D1.5   TodayWasAllDayLong $A =_{df} \boxed{s}\ \boxed{X|w}\ \gamma \boxminus \boxed{x|d}\ A$

D1.6   TodayIsAllDayLongGoingTo $A =_{df} \boxed{s}\ \boxed{X|w}\ \sigma \boxminus A$

D1.7   TodayWillAllDayLongBe $A =_{df} \boxed{s}\ \boxed{X|w}\ \sigma \boxminus \boxed{x|d}\ A$

D2.0   TomorrowIsOnceGoingTo $A =_{df} \boxed{s}\ \sigma \boxed{X|w}\ \sigma \Diamond\!\!\!\!\rightarrow A$

D2.1   TomorrowWillOnceBe $A =_{df} \boxed{s}\ \sigma \boxed{X|w}\ \sigma \Diamond\!\!\!\!\rightarrow \boxed{x|d}\ A$

D2.2   TomorrowIsAllDayLongGoingTo $A =_{df} \boxed{s}\ \sigma \boxed{X|w}\ \sigma \boxminus A$

D2.3   TomorrowWillAllDayLongBe $A =_{df} \boxed{s}\ \sigma \boxed{X|w}\ \sigma \boxminus \boxed{x|d}\ A$

D3.0   YesterdayHasOnceBeen $A =_{df} \boxed{s}\ \gamma \boxed{X|w}\ \gamma \Diamond\!\!\!\!\rightarrow A$

D3.1   YesterdayOnceWas $A =_{df} \boxed{s}\ \gamma \boxed{X|w}\ \gamma \Diamond\!\!\!\!\rightarrow \boxed{x|d}\ A$

D3.2   YesterdayHasAllDayLongBeen $A =_{df} \boxed{s}\ \gamma \boxed{X|w}\ \gamma \boxminus A$

D3.3   YesterdayWasAllDayLong $A =_{df} \boxed{s}\ \gamma \boxed{X|w}\ \gamma \boxminus \boxed{x|d}\ A$

D1.8   TodayOnceIs $A =_{df}$ TodayHasOnceBeen $A \vee \boxed{s}\ \boxed{X|w}\ A \vee$ TodayIsOnceGoingTo A

D1.9   TodayIsAllDayLong $A =_{df}$ TodayHasAllDayLongBeen $A\ \&$ $\boxed{s}\ \boxed{X|w}\ A\ \&$ TodayIsAllDayLongGoingTo A

Comments. (i) The above *definienda* are to be more fully read in accordance with the following patterns: 'Today it has at least once been the case that *A*', 'Today it was at least once the case that *A*', 'Tomorrow it will all day long be the case that *A*', and so on. We do not claim that all the *definienda* introduced are quite idiomatic in ordinary English; those of D3.0 and D3.2 probably fail to be entirely grammatical, for one thing.

(ii) The force of 'today', 'tomorrow', and 'yesterday' in the above definitions is essentially rendered by the operators $\boxed{s}$, $\boxed{s}\,\sigma$, and $\boxed{s}\,\gamma$, respectively. Note that 'today' combines with (a) past tenses (D1.*i*, *i* = 0, 1, 4, 5), (b) the present tense (D1.*i*, *i* = 8, 9), as well as with (c) future tenses (D1.*i*, *i* = 2, 3, 6, 7). By way of contrast, 'tomorrow' only combines with future tenses (D2.*i*, *i* = 0, 1, 2, 3), _____ at least, this is so in our explicative or reconstructive definitions. Similarly, 'yesterday' only combines with past tenses (D3.i, $i = 0, 1, 2, 3$) on our present analysis.

(iii) The above *definienda* involve a contrast between '/at least/ once' and 'all day long'. As is readily seen, this contrast is matched, or reflected, by the shift from the 'possibility' interval operator $\Leftrightarrow$ to the 'necessity' one $\boxminus$ in the *definientia*. As usual, the compound operator $\boxed{X\lceil w}$ is needed in order for these interval operators to do their appropriate job. See Åqvist and Guenthner (1976, e.g., Section 8).

(iv) As was explained in, e.g., Åqvist, Guenthner and Rohrer (1976, Section 3.1), the presence or absence of the compound operator $\boxed{x\rceil d}$ in our *definientia* is intended to capture distinctions between the *simple past* ('was') and the *present perfect* ('has been') and between the *simple future* ('will be') and the *posterior present* ('is going to'), according to the reconstruction of Reichenbachian verb tenses given in Åqvist (1976) and based on the analysis presented in Reichenbach (1947, Section 51).

(v) As for the conditions of truth at t in an ITL model $M^{t'}/t''$ with chronological frame of the defined constructions, we have, e.g., the following results:

Ad D1.4: $\left|\dfrac{M^{t'}/t''}{t}\right.$ TodayHasAllDayLongBeen A iff

$\left|\dfrac{M^{t'}/t''}{t}\right.$ $\boxed{s}$ $\boxed{X\lceil w}$ γ $\boxminus$ A iff for all u in the open interval

$]g(t_0), t_0[$: $\left|\dfrac{M^{t'}/t_0}{u}\right.$ A.

Ad D3.1: $\left|\dfrac{M^{t'}/t''}{t}\right.$ YesterdayOnceWas A iff $\left|\dfrac{M^{t'}/t''}{t}\right.$ $\boxed{s}$ γ $\boxed{X\lceil w}$ γ

$\Leftrightarrow$ $\boxed{x\rceil d}$ A iff for some u in the open interval $]g(g(t_0)), g(t_0)[$:

$\left|\dfrac{M^u/g(t_0)}{u}\right.$ A.

(vi) A final remark: as to the adequacy of the definitions in our series, we should like to point out that, from a semantical or model theoretic viewpoint, they appear to be plausible enough *as long as*, that is to say, the speech point t_0 is *not* a member of the 'integer-like' set Z. When $t_0 \in Z$, however, some uncertainty may arise as to exactly what interval is denoted by 'today', for instance: Is it $[g(t_0), s(t_0)[$? Or is it $[g(t_0), t_0[$? Or is it $[t_0, s(t_0)[$? If the first possibility were accepted, it would make for a neat and uniform treatment of the locutions at issue; however, the length-in-days of that interval $=2$, and thus is not $=1$. On the remaining two alternatives, that length is correctly $=1$, but problems remain concerning (a) which alternative are we to choose? (b) how is our choice to be justified once it is made? Moreover, (c) counterintuitive results may be obtained on either of those latter alternatives, when $t_0 \in Z$. Similar doubts may arise in this case as to adequacy of our definitions of locutions involving 'tomorrow' and 'yesterday'.

We do not propose any solution to these difficulties pertaining to the (perhaps 'degenerate') case when $t_0 \in Z$. It would be nice if one along the lines of the first possibility could be defended, however. For the time being we content ourselves with having pointed out that the case under discussion indeed raises the problems mentioned.

Let $\sigma^k = \overbrace{\sigma\sigma\ldots\sigma}^{k\text{ times}}$ and $\gamma^k = \overbrace{\gamma\gamma\ldots\gamma}^{k\text{ times}}$ for any positive integer $k > 0$, i.e., σ^k and γ^k are to be k-termed sequences of consecutive occurrences of the operators σ and γ, respectively. If in the definition series D2.i ($i = 0, 1, 2, 3$) we replace the *first* occurrence of σ in the *definiens* by σ^k, we obtain definitions of the following locutions:

> In/Exactly/ k Days/FromNow/IsOnceGoingTo A
> In/Exactly/ k Days/FromNow/WillOnceBe A
> In/Exactly/ k Days/FromNow/IsAllDayLongGoingTo A
> In/Exactly/ k Days/FromNow/WillAllDayLongBe A

Similarly, if in the series D3.i ($i = 0, 1, 2, 3$) we replace the *first* occurrence of γ in the *definiens* by γ^k, the resulting *definienda* will be:

> /Exactly/ k DaysAgoHasOnceBeen A
> /Exactly/ k DaysAgoOnceWas A
> /Exactly/ k DaysAgoHasAllDayLongBeen A
> /Exactly/ k DaysAgoWasAllDayLong A

where the first one and the third one are really bad in English (as well as in Swedish, for that matter), whereas they are certainly acceptable, e.g., in German and French.

Thus, the indicated substitutions of σ^k for σ and of γ^k for γ yield a treatment of the time adverbials '*in* (exactly) k days . . .' and '(exactly) k days *ago* . . .'. Comments analogous to (i)–(vi) apply to our new definitions, too. Note also that, in the case where $k = 1$, the eight locutions introduced above will be equivalent to the *definienda* of D2.0, . . . , D2.3, D3.0, . . . , D3.3, respectively, because $\sigma^1 = \sigma$ and $\gamma^1 = \gamma$.

We go on to propose a treatment of some locutions involving such time adverbials as (i) 'this month', 'next month' and 'last month', as well as (ii) 'this year', 'next year' and 'last year'. To that purpose, we enrich L with four one-place sentential operators Γ, Σ, $\mathscr{G}$ and $\mathscr{S}$, obeying the following truth conditions, respectively:

$$(4) \qquad \frac{\left| M^{t'}/t'' \right.}{t} \models \Gamma A \text{ iff } \frac{\left| M^{t'}/t'' \right.}{g(t)}$$

$$(5) \qquad \frac{\left| M^{t'}/t'' \right.}{t} \models \Sigma A \text{ iff } \left\| \frac{\left| M^{t'}/t'' \right.}{s(t)} \right. A$$

$$(6) \qquad \frac{\left| M^{t'}/t'' \right.}{t} \models \mathscr{G} A \text{ iff } \frac{\left| M^{t'}/t'' \right.}{G(t)}$$

$$(7) \qquad \frac{\left| M^{t'}/t'' \right.}{t} \models \mathscr{S} A \text{ iff } \frac{\left| M^{t'}/t'' \right.}{S(t)} A.$$

In these conditions, of course, $g(t)$ and $s(t)$ will always be members of the set M of 'month interval determining coordinates' and $G(t)$, $S(t)$ will be members of the set Y of 'year interval determining coordinates'. See Sections 8 and 9 above.

Now, if in the series of definitions D1.i ($i = 0, 1, \ldots, 7$) we replace the occurrence of γ in the *definiens* by Γ and that of σ by Σ, we obtain definitions of the following locutions:

$$\text{ThisMonth}\begin{cases} \text{HasOnceBeen } A \\ \text{OnceWas } A \end{cases}$$

$$\text{ThisMonth}\begin{cases} \text{IsOnceGoingTo } A \\ \text{WillOnceBe } A \end{cases}$$

$$\text{ThisMonth}\begin{cases} \text{HasAllMonthLongBeen } A \\ \text{WasAllMonthLong } A \end{cases}$$

$$\text{ThisMonth}\begin{cases} \text{IsAllMonthLongGoingTo } A \\ \text{WillAllMonthLongBe } A. \end{cases}$$

Similarly, if in D1.i ($i = 0, 1, \ldots, 7$) we replace γ by $\mathscr{G}$ and σ by $\mathscr{S}$ in the relevant *definientia*, we obtain definitions of locutions which are like those above except for having 'Year' in the place of 'Month'.

Again, we may substitute Σ for both occurrences of σ in the *definientia* of the series D2.i ($i = 0, 1, 2, 3$) and obtain the following resulting *definienda*:

NextMonthIsOnceGoingTo A
NextMonthWillOnceBe A
NextMonthIsAllMonthLongGoingTo A
NextMonthWillAllMonthLongBe A

Substitution of $\mathscr{S}$ for σ here would then yield locutions with 'Year' in the place of 'Month'.

Again, we substitute Γ for the two occurrences of γ in the *definientia* of D3.i ($i = 0, 1, 2, 3$) and obtain definitions of

$$\text{LastMonth} \begin{cases} \text{HasOnceBeen} & A \\ \text{OnceWas} & A \end{cases}$$

$$\text{LastMonth} \begin{cases} \text{HasAllMonthLongBeen} & A \\ \text{WasAllMonthLong} & A \end{cases}$$

Finally, we can substitute $\mathscr{G}$ for γ in the *definientia* of D3.i and obtain locutions which are like those above except for having 'Year' in the place of 'Month'.

Furthermore, if we replace the first occurrence of Γ, Σ, $\mathscr{G}$ and $\mathscr{S}$ by Γ^k, Σ^k, $\mathscr{G}^k$ and $\mathscr{S}^k$, respectively, in the relevant *definientia*, we obtain a treatment of such time adverbials as '*in* (exactly) k months/years ...' and '(exactly) k months/years *ago* ...'. Here, as usual, an operator with numerical superscript k (>0) denotes the k-termed sequence of consecutive occurrences of the operator at issue.

So far we have dealt with speech point related locutions involving reference to days, months and years. As a reader's exercise we suggest that he extends our present treatment to the analogous locutions referring to weeks, centuries, etc. The methodology required for that purpose should by now be quite obvious.

Finally, we address ourselves to the problem of accounting for locutions involving such phrases as 'next Monday', 'last Thursday', 'next January', 'last October', etc. Let us first consider as our paradigm the set
MONDAY $= \{ \#(i): i \equiv 2 \pmod 7 \} = \{ \ldots \ldots \#(-5), \#(2), \#(9), \ldots \ldots \}$
$= \{ \ldots \ldots [g^6(\tau), g^5(\tau)[, [s^1(\tau), s^2(\tau)[, [s^8(\tau), s^9(\tau)[, \ldots \ldots \}$. (See Section 6 above.) Corresponding to this set we form the set MON of determining coordinates of elements in MONDAY, listed in their natural order:

$$\text{MON} = \{ \ldots, g^6(\tau), g^5(\tau), s^1(\tau), s^2(\tau), s^8(\tau), s^9(\tau), \ldots \}.$$

We then define two functions g_{MON} and s_{MON} from T into MON by putting, to start with:

$$g_{MON}(\tau) = g^5(\tau) = g_{MON}(s^1(\tau)) \qquad s_{MON}(\tau) = s^1(\tau)$$
$$g_{MON}(g_{MON}(\tau)) = g^6(\tau) \qquad\qquad s_{MON}(s_{MON}(\tau)) = s^2(\tau)$$
$$\text{etc.} \qquad\qquad\qquad\qquad\qquad \text{etc.}$$

And, in general, we assume $s^1(\tau)$, MON, g_{MON} and s_{MON} to satisfy analogues of our axioms A1–A8.1 which are obtained by uniformly replacing reference to τ, Z, s and g by reference to $s^1(\tau)$, MON, s_{MON} and g_{MON}, respectively. Cf. our constructions in the case of M, s and g, Section 8 above, and in that of Y, S and G, Section 9 above.

Next, we supplement our formal language L with two one-place sentential operators γ_{mon} and σ_{mon}, which are to obey the truth conditions:

(8)
$$\left|\frac{\overline{M^{t'}/t''}}{t}\right. \gamma_{mon} A \text{ iff } \left|\frac{\overline{M^{t'}/t''}}{g_{MON}(t)}\right. A.$$

(9)
$$\left|\frac{\overline{M^{t'}/t''}}{t}\right. \sigma_{mon} A \text{ iff } \left|\frac{\overline{M^{t'}/t''}}{s_{MON}(t)}\right. A.$$

We now propose the following *conditional* definitions in L:

D4.0.a $\sim$ (It is Monday) $\rightarrow$ (NextMondayIsOnceGoingTo A
$\leftrightarrow$ $\boxed{s}$ σ_{mon} $\boxed{X}\boxed{w}$ σ_{mon} $\diamondsuit$ A).

D4.0.b   (It   is   Monday) $\rightarrow$ (NextMondayIsOnceGoingTo A
$\leftrightarrow$ $\boxed{s}$ σ^2_{mon} $\boxed{X}\boxed{w}$ σ_{mon} $\diamondsuit$ A).

Here of course, $\sigma^2_{mon} = \sigma_{mon}\sigma_{mon}$.

D4.1.a $\sim$ (It   is   Monday) $\rightarrow$ (NextMondayWillOnceBe A
$\leftrightarrow$ $\boxed{s}$ σ_{mon} $\boxed{X}\boxed{w}$ σ_{mon} $\diamondsuit$ $\boxed{x}\boxed{d}$ A).

D4.1.b   (It   is   Monday) $\rightarrow$ (NextMondayWillOnceBe A
$\leftrightarrow$ $\boxed{s}$ σ^2_{mon} $\boxed{X}\boxed{w}$ σ_{mon} $\diamondsuit$ $\boxed{x}\boxed{d}$ A).

'All day long' versions are obtained in the obvious way from the above definitions by substitution of $\boxminus$ for $\diamondsuit$. Again, if in these definitions we replace σ_{mon} by γ_{mon}, we obtain a treatment of such locutions as

LastMondayHasOnceBeen A
LastMondayOnceWas A
LastMondayHasAllDayLongBeen A
LastMondayWasAllDayLong A

We leave the following tasks to the reader:

(i)   Explain why conditional definitions are needed, as indicated.
(ii)   Extend the treatment given above to other week days.
(iii)   Indicate the constructions required for an analogous treatment of locutions involving 'next/last January', 'next/last February', etc.

12. LIST OF SENTENCES DEALT WITH

(I)   It is March 11 1975
(II)   It is 5 minutes past/to 3 (o'clock)
(Ia)   It is 1975–3–11
(Ib)   It is i–j–k
(IIa)   It is n minutes past p (o'clock)
(IIb)   It is n minutes to p (o'clock)
(III)   It is p o'clock sharp
(IV)   It is n minutes past/to p on the i–j–k
(V)   It is Monday
(VI)   It is Sunday, October 17, 1976
(VII)   It is Tuesday, 3 p.m. sharp
(VIII)   It is 11 minutes past 11 on Saturday, October 16, 1976
(IXa)   It is January
(IXb)   It is February
(X)   It is a Sunday in August
(XI)   It is /in the year/ 1789
(XII)   It is July 4, 1776
(XIIc)   It is the i-th of the month
(XIII)   It is November 15
(XIIIa)   It is November 1973
(XIIIb)   It is the 28th of the month in the year 1973

(1)   It had been the case that A on July 4 1776
(2)   It was the case that A on July 4 1776
(3)   It was going to be the case that A on July 4 1776
(4)   It has been the case that A on July 4 1776
(5)   It is (now) the case that A on July 4 1776
(6)   It is going to be the case that A on July 4 1776
(7)   It will have been the case that A on July 4 1776

(8)   It will be the case that A on July 4 1776
(9)   It will be going to be the case that A on July 4 1776
(10)   Since 2 o'clock sharp I have been playing the *Waldstein* sonata
(11)   Until a quarter to 9 p.m. I will be playing *Les Adieux*
(12)   I became aware of the *Appassionata* on a Sunday in August
(13)   On November 25 1976 I worked all day long on this paper
(14)   Max arrived in Stuttgart before May 15 1976
(15)   Pierre arrived in Stuttgart after the 1st of September.

Besides, in Section 11, one should pay attention to the *definienda* of the series D1.i $(i=0, 1, \ldots, 9)$, D2.j $(j=0, 1, 2, 3)$, D3.j $(j=0, 1, 2, 3)$, D4.0.a, D4.0.b, D4.1.a and D4.1.b, as well as to the results of making various substitutions in the *definientia* of these definitions.

Universitat Stuttgart

NOTE

* The present contribution reports research done under the auspices of the Deutsche Forschungsgemeinschaft (DFG) project "Die Beschreibung mithilfe der Zeitlogik von Zeitformen und Verbalperiphrasen im Französischen, Portugiesischen und Spanischen", led by Chr. Rohrer. In connection with the hammering out of the present results, the author is greatly indebted to his Stuttgart colleagues and friends Franz Guenthner, Monica Guenthner, Christian Rohrer, J. Ph. Hoepelman and Pierre Yves Racca.

BIBLIOGRAPHY

Åqvist, L. (1973), 'Music from a Set-Theoretical Point of View', *INTERFACE-Journal of New Music Research 2*, pp. 1–22.
Åqvist, L. (1976), 'Formal Semantics for Verb Tenses as Analyzed by Reichenbach', in Teun A. van Dijk (ed.), *Pragmatics of Language and Literature*, pp. 229–236, North-Holland Publishing Co., Amsterdam.
Åqvist, L. and Guenthner, F. (1976), 'Fundamentals of a Theory of Verb Aspect and Events within the Setting of an Improved Tense Logic', forthcoming in F. Guenthner and C. Rohrer (eds.), *Studies in Formal Semantics*, North-Holland, Amsterdam.
Åqvist, L., Guenthner, F., and Rohrer, C. (1976), 'Definability in ITL of Some Subordinate Temporal Conjunctions in English, forthcoming in F. Guenthner and C. Rohrer (eds.), *Studies in Formal Semantics*, North-Holland, Amsterdam.
Åqvist, L., Guenthner, F. and Rohrer, C. (1977), 'Soon and Recently', forthcoming.
Birkhoff, G. and MacLane, S. (1948), *A Survey of Modern Algebra*, Macmillan, New York.
Prior, A. (1967), *Past, Present and Future*, Clarendon Press, Oxford.

Reichenbach, H. (1947), *Elements of Symbolic Logic*. Collier-Macmillan, London.
Rescher, N. and Urquhart, A. (1971), *Temporal Logic* (= Library of Exact Philosophy No. 3),
  Springer Verlag, Wien and New York.
Wedberg, A. (1963), 'Additive Measures', *Philosophical Essays Dedicated to Gunnar Aspelin*,
  pp. 272–294, Gleerup, Lund.
Wunderlich, D. (1970), *Tempus und Zeitreferenz im Deutschen*, , (= Linguistische Reihe no. 5),
  Hueber, München.

HANS KAMP

SEMANTICS VERSUS PRAGMATICS [1]

I.

Consider the sentences

(1)   You may take an apple,
(2)   You may take a pear,   and
(3)   You may take an apple or take a pear.

In one sense of 'may' these convey permissions and thus would seem to fall within the province of deontic logic.[2] According to deontic logic the logical forms of (1) and (2) must be

(1')   It is permitted that (x take an apple),   and
(2')   It is permitted that (x take a pear)

while that of (3) would have to be either

(3')   It is permitted that (x take an apple or x take a pear)

or alternatively

(3")   It is permitted that (x take an apple) or it is permitted that (x take a pear)

Many systems of deontic logic postulate that both (3') and (3") are logical consequences of either of (1') and (2'), while no deontic system countenances (1') and (2') as consequences of either (3') or (3"). This appears to be in conflict with the common intuition that it is (3) which 'entails' (1) and (2), rather than the other way round.

Some years ago I sketched a solution to this problem in [6]. The ideas on which that solution is based are closely related to an unpublished paper by David Lewis [10], which gives a model-theoretic analysis of the illocutionary force of permissions and commands. Lewis observes that the pragmatic effect of a command is to restrict the options of the addressee. Similarly a permission statement tends to effect a broadening of his options. The question which Lewis asks, and partly answers, is: By how much do particular permissions and commands extend or restrict the addressee's options for action?

255

F. Guenthner and S. J. Schmidt (eds.), Formal Semantics and Pragmatics for Natural Languages, 255–287. All Rights Reserved.

Lewis's explicatory model is simple and persuasive. Consider a community of language users consisting, we shall here assume for simplicity, of two persons, A and B, and in which A has authority over B. We study the development in time of the options for action open to B, and in particular the ways in which these options are affected by permissions and commands that are issued from time to time by A.

The effect of a command is easily stated. Suppose that A gives B at time t the command; 'Polish my shoes!' In so doing he limits the options of B to those futures in which, at some time after t, B polishes A's shoes.

By the *options* of an agent, at time t, we shall understand here, as the preceding sentence may already have indicated, those possible continuations of the world after t in which the agent fulfills all his obligations and forbears doing the things from which he is prohibited. I shall represent these possible continuations in a manner which I have found convenient in another study [7], where I adopted the convention that each possible continuation of world w at time t is a possible world which spans the full course of time — from the most distant past to the most distant future — but which, in as much as it is a possible continuation of w after t, coincides with w in all respects throughout the period which precedes t. Among the possible continuations of w after t will of course be in particular w itself; w will be the only such continuation just in case w is completely deterministic from t onwards.

We shall denote the set of possible continuations of w after t as $\text{Pos}(w,t)$. Those continuations in which B honors his obligations and does not transgress any prohibitions by which he is constrained form a subset of $\text{Pos}(w,t)$, which we shall refer to as $\text{Per}(w,t,B)$. Pos and Per change with time. One source of change is the occurrence of events which are not fully determined by what went before: If such an event e occurs in the world w at t then the worlds w' in which e does not occur or in which it has different features from those it has in w, and which belongs to $\text{Pos}(w,t')$ for times t' preceding t no longer belong to $\text{Pos}(w,t')$ for t' later than t. Indeed, for all we know, at all times something is going on that is not completely determined by the past, in which case Pos is shrinking continuously. These changes in Pos will in general produce corresponding changes in Per.

Besides this probably continuous change in Per there are the modifications effected by A's permissions and commands. We will assume that the performance of these speechacts is instantaneous and that the effect they have on Per manifests itself first at the hypothetical instant of performance. Thus if A tells B in w at t: "Polish my shoes!" then the effect of this shows up in $Per(w,t,B)$, but not in $Per(w,t',B)$ for any t' before t. To state what the effect of the command on Per is we must refer to what $Per(w,t,B)$ would have been had the command been absent. This set we may identify with the limit of the sets $Per(w,t',B)$ for t' approaching t from the past. Now it seems reasonable to assume that there must be some open interval (t_0,t), with t as end-point, during which no commands or permissions are issued. Then the limit of $Per(w,t',B)$ will be equal to $\cap_{t' \in (t_0,t)} Per(w,t',B)$. We shall denote this set as $Per^-(w,t,B)$.

The effect of A's command to B at t now comes to this: Let S be the set of all worlds in $Pos(w,t)$ in which B polishes A's shoes at some time later than t. Then

(4) $Per(w,t,B) = Per(w,t,B) \cap S.$[3]

A command has thus the effect of modifying the set Per into a new set which results from intersecting the old set with a set determined by the content of the sentence used. A permission on the other hand tends to enlarge the set Per. The question is: by how much? This is Lewis's Problem about Permission. The solution to this problem is by no means simple. [6] contains an elementary suggestion, which appears to be correct for at least some cases. Suppose that B's options at time t are restricted only by a number of standing prohibitions $P_1, \ldots P_k$ and that each prohibition P_i is represented as an intransitive verb phrase φ_i, which P_i prohibits B from satisfying at any time after t. Suppose moreover that A gives B at t the permission 'You may φ_i,' where φ_i is the verb phrase that represents P_i. According to the proposal of [6] the effect of A's utterance is to lift the prohibition P_i while the remaining prohibitions are all upheld. In other words, the set that is added to $Per(w,t,B)$ consists of those worlds in which B satisfies, at some future time, the verb phrase φ_i, but satisfies none of the verb phrases representing the other prohibitions at any time later than t.[4]

Of course this solution is adequate only in those cases where the permission sentence used corresponds unambiguously to one particular standing prohibition, and where moreover it is possible to violate that prohibition without violating any of the others. These conditions are by no means always fulfilled.

Robert Stalnaker, in a comment on Lewis's paper [14], suggested a more general analysis of the effect of permissions. His proposal assumes that the members of $Pos(w,t)$ can be compared with respect to the extent to which B departs in them from the standard of irreproachable conduct. Formally this comparability can be represented (as it is also done in Lewis's theory of the counterfactual conditional; see [9]) as a nest of sets whose union is $Pos(w,t)$; whose smallest number is $Per(w,t,B)$; and which moreover is such, that if w_1 belongs to a member of the nest to which w_2 does not belong then w_2 is a world in which B behaves on the whole more reprehensibly than he does in w_1. The effect of a permission of the form 'You may φ' is to add to the set Per all those worlds in which B satisfies φ at some time after t and which belong to the smallest member of the nest in which there are any such worlds. I shall refer to the nest of subsets of $Pos(w,t)$ as $Pos(w,t,B)$.

The proposal of [6] becomes a special case of Stalnaker's theory on the reasonable assumption that $Pos(w,t,B)$ contains a set in which there are worlds in which B violates the prohibition that the permission he has been given cancels, but no such worlds in which he violates some of the remaining prohibitions as well. But, as I already intimated, there are many cases to which the theory of [6] cannot be applied, at least not the simple version of it which I have presented so far here. Suppose e.g. that the standing prohibitions include the prohibition against taking an apple and the prohibition against taking a pear, and that A gives B a permission by uttering (3). There is then no obvious correspondence between the permission sentence[5] used and any one particular member of the set of standing prohibitions (the two prohibitions which I just mentioned being equally good, and thus equally bad, candidates). Stalnaker's theory on the other hand applies to this case as well. And it might seem at first that it handles it correctly.

In particular if we assume that the prohibition against taking an apple and the prohibition against taking a pear are equally strong then the theory makes exactly the right prediction. For in this case any set in $Pos(w,t,B)$ that contains a world in which B satisfies the verb phrase 'take an apple' should also contain worlds in which B satisfies the verb phrase 'take a pear', and conversely. So the set Per will be extended with worlds in which B takes an apple and also with worlds in which he takes a pear. And this is just as it should be.

Not in all cases does the theory give us the correct answer, however. Consider for example a situation in which there are again separate prohibitions against, respectively, taking an apple and taking a pear, but in which the prohibition against taking an apple is much stronger than that against taking a pear (e.g. because the apples have to be bought, while the pears come from the garden). Stalnaker's theory predicts that the set of worlds added to $Per(w,t,B)$ by a performative utterance of (3) in this situation consists exclusively of worlds in which B takes a pear. Yet even here, it would seem intuitively, (3) conveys that taking an apple is all right too.

This appears to refute the theory. But we should not be too hasty to reject it. In particular we should first consider whether we could not apply the theory of conversation to the counterintuitive prediction it makes for the effect of (3) in this last situation. We might expect this to be possible, as Stalnaker's proposal claims that in a situation of this kind the effect of (3) is identical with that of the simpler sentence (2). Thus something like the maxim of brevity would require the use of (2) rather than (3) if this were indeed the effect intended. We might hope to find additional conversational principles which justify the further inference that if A does use the sentence (3) his intention must have been to permit not only worlds in which B takes a pear but also some in which he takes an apple.

We will explore this possibility later, in section III. Before that I wish to reexamine, in the next section, the account of (3) which I sketched in [6] and which does give the correct prediction for the effect of (3) in either of the two situations we have considered above.

To conclude this section let me reiterate the observation, already made at some length in [6], that the analysis of permission sentences we have discussed in this section offers a way to explain the apparent puzzle about the logical relations between (1), (2) and (3): (3) is 'stronger' than e.g. (1) in as much as the set of worlds which a performative utterance of (3) adds to the options of the addressee includes, but is not necessarily included in, the set added through a performative use of (1). Indeed it is tempting to introduce, as was proposed in [6], a relation of 'entailment' specific to permission sentences by putting:

Permission sentence φ (*permission*) — *entails* permission sentence ψ iff in every situation the set of worlds added to the options of the addressee through the use of φ includes the set of worlds added to the set of options through the use of ψ.

We have just seen that as it stands (3) does not permission entail (1) according to Stalnaker's theory. (3) does entail (1) according to the proposal which we shall investigate in the next section. That investigation will lead us, however, to questions of a much more general and theoretical nature. The entailment relation defined above will not be of any further concern.

I I.

It will be convenient to generalize somewhat the framework which I sketched when expounding the Lewis-Stalnaker account. Henceforth I shall always assume that with each utterance is associated a situation, or *context, of use*. Moreover we shall also consider contexts of use in which no utterance actually takes place, e.g. to contemplate what the effect of uttering a certain sentence *would* have been in that context *if* it had been made. For simplicity I shall continue to consider only contexts in which there is one speaker, A, and one addressee, B; A will always be assumed to have the authority over B which is necessary to make his permission statements to B effective. Each context c determines a world w_c, the world in which that context is situated, and a time t_c, the time at which the utterances we consider in connection with B are, or would have been, made. We retain the functions Pos and Per, writing 'Pos(c)' for 'Pos(w_c, t_c)', 'Per(c, B) for 'Per(w_c, t_c, B)', etc.

We denote as $[\![\varphi]\!]_c^{\text{Per}}$ the set of those worlds which are added to the options of the addressee through the permission granting utterance of the permission sentence φ in the context c. In cases where such an utterance actually takes place in c this set can be expressed as Per(c, B) $\diagdown$ Per$^-$(c, B). It is reasonable to assume, however, that this set is fully determined by (i) the sentence φ; and (ii) contextual features whose presence in the context c is independent of whether the utterance is actually made. (Both proposals for the computation of Per(c, B) from Per$^-$(c, B) which we considered in Section I. exemplify this principle). On this assumption it is meaningful to speak about the set $[\![\varphi]\!]_c$ also when it is not uttered in c.

In Section I. we considered two situations in which A utters (3). In each of these, I maintained, the 'net effect' of this speech act, $[\![(3)]\!]_c^{\text{Per}}$, is equal to the union of the net effects produced by utterances of, respectively, (1) and (2):

$$(5) \qquad [\![(3)]\!]_c^{\text{Per}} = [\![(1)]\!]_c^{\text{Per}} \cup [\![(2)]\!]_c^{\text{Per}}.$$

In [6] I claimed that this equation must always hold, i.e.

$$(6) \qquad [\![\text{you may } \varphi \text{ or } \psi]\!]_c^{\text{Per}} = [\![\text{you may } \varphi]\!]_c^{\text{Per}} \cup [\![\text{you may } \psi]\!]_c^{\text{Per}},$$

for any intransitive verb phrases φ and ψ; and I formulated a general hypothesis about the uniform character of logical operators such as 'or' and about their function in sentences that are typically used in performative utterances, which was intended to explain why equation (6) holds. I shall briefly restate that hypothesis and retrace the line of thought that led up to it.

One of the central assumptions of modern semantics is that a theory of truth conditions for a language must include a component which has the form of a recursive definition (usually a definition of truth or of satisfaction). There is in general no fully fixed format for this component. Even the truth definition for so simple a language as the classical propositional calculus can be written down in a number of different though essentially equivalent ways. Among these there is one which makes that aspect of the sentential operator 'or' that is here crucial explicit. I shall give the essentials of this particular form of the truth definition for propositional logic first.

I assume that the assertoric use of a sentence φ of propositional calculus in the context c determines — in ways which we need not analyse right now — the *propositions* expressed in c by the atomic components of φ. For each atomic component q_i of φ we identify the proposition expressed by q_i in c, $[\![q_i]\!]_c$, with the set of all those worlds w' in which q_i is true at t_c. The propositions expressed in c by arbitrary compounds built up from these components by means of the sentential connectives are then given by a recursive definition with such clauses as:

(7) $\quad [\![\neg\varphi]\!]_c \ | = W \setminus [\![\varphi]\!]_c$ (where W is the set of all possible worlds);

(8) $\quad [\![\varphi \& \psi]\!]_c = [\![\varphi]\!]_c \cap [\![\psi]\!]_c;$

(9) $\quad [\![\varphi \lor \psi]\!]_c = [\![\varphi]\!]_c \cup [\![\psi]\!]_c.$

Such definitions invite the view that the meanings of the sentential connectives are given by the corresponding clauses of the definition.

Now observe the similarity between (5) and (9). It was this similarity which led me to the following three-part hypothesis:

(10)   (i) logical particles, such as 'not', 'and', and 'or', represent semantic operations of a simple set-theoretic nature (operations such as complementation, intersection, and union);
(ii) they represent these operations *uniformly*, i.e. for all occasions of use; and
(iii) the role played by the sets on which these operations are performed, as well as the sets they produce, depends on the type of speech act that is performed by uttering the sentence in which the operator occurs.

According to this hypothesis 'or', in particular, has the same semantic function in (3) as it has in (11)

(11)   Jones has taken an apple or has taken a pear.

The difference between (3) and (11) is that the sets $[\![(1)]\!]_c^{\text{Per}}$, $[\![(2)]\!]_c^{\text{Per}}$ and $[\![(3)]\!]_c^{\text{Per}}$ represent new options for the addressee, while the sets $[\![$ Jones has taken an apple $]\!]_c$, $[\![$ Jones has taken a pear $]\!]_c$, and $[\![(11)]\!]_c$ are *truth sets* – sets of which the corresponding assertoric utterances claim that the actual world is among them.

It is an appealing feature of this hypothesis that it avoids the need to postulate for such occurrences of 'or' as we find in (3) a different meaning or function from the one it is supposed to have in the linguistic environments which have traditionally been the primary concern of formal logic. To postulate such a separate function for occurrences of 'or' without further explanation of how they are connected with the function of 'or' in sentences such as (11) is particularly unsatisfactory in view of the fact that precisely the same puzzle about disjunctive permission arises in many languages other than English. This is evidently a systematic phenomenon that cannot be dismissed as an idiomatic curiosity of one particular vernacular. Note however that the Lewis-Stalnaker theory avoids such *ad hoc* assumptions too. The choice between that theory and the analysis we are now considering must therefore be made on different grounds.

According to (5) the set $[\![(3)]\!]_c^{\text{Per}}$ is determined as the union of the sets $[\![(1)]\!]_c^{\text{Per}}$ and $[\![(2)]\!]_c^{\text{Per}}$. If the operation that forms $[\![(3)]\!]_c^{\text{Per}}$ out of $[\![(1)]\!]_c^{\text{Per}}$ and $[\![(2)]\!]_c^{\text{Per}}$ is indeed the last step of the computation of the effect of A's permission granting utterance, what are the other steps of this computation like?

One of the factors which determine the set $[\![$ You may $\varphi]\!]_c^{\text{Per}}$ is the sentence 'You may φ' itself. It should be clear, moreover — and the specific proposals for the computation of the sets $\text{Per}(w,t,B)$ which we considered in the previous section bear this out — that it is more specifically the satisfaction conditions for the verb phrase[6] which are needed for this computation. In particular the computations of $[\![(1)]\!]_c^{\text{Per}}$ and $[\![(2)]\!]_c^{\text{Per}}$ require the truth conditions in c of the verb phrases

(12)   take an apple,   and
(13)   take a pear.

I will take it for granted that the theory must specify the satisfaction conditions of complex verb phrases via the type of recursion on the syntactic complexity of these expressions which is by now familiar from the work of, in particular, Montague and his school. If we assume for example — the exact details are insignificant for the present discussion — that (12) is constructed by first forming the singular term 'an apple' by combining the noun 'apple' with the indefinite article, and then forming the verb phrase by combining this term with the verb 'take'; and if we assume moreover — as is usual in Montague Grammar — that the computation of the satisfaction conditions of (12) follows this grammatical construction process step by step, then the computation of (12) (and similarly that of (13)) will involve at least two recursion steps.

The picture which emerges from these considerations is the following. To compute the set $[\![(3)]\!]_c^{\text{Per}}$, we first have to perform a number of steps of the kind familiar from extant work in formal semantics to obtain the satisfaction conditions for (12) and (13); from these we compute by what would appear to be typically pragmatic considerations the sets $[\![(1)]\!]_c^{\text{Per}}$ and $[\![(2)]\!]_c^{\text{Per}}$: and from these we then finally obtain $[\![(3)]\!]_c^{\text{Per}}$, by a step which according to our hypothesis (9) constitutes an application of the very same recursive clause that enables us to compute e.g. the truth conditions of (11) in c from the truth conditions in c of 'Jones has taken an apple' and 'Jones has taken a pear'.

Permission sentences are used not only for the purpose of granting permissions but also for making assertions. Suppose e.g. that A has decided to give B the permission to draw from his, i.e. A's, bank account, and that he has already made the formal arrangements which this entails (such as depositing a statement to this effect with the bank). B then visits the bank and the teller says to him: 'You may draw from A's account.' Clearly this utterance must be taken as a report that a certain permission has been given; it is not a performative which creates a permission.

There are moreover many cases where it is difficult to say whether the utterance is a performative or an assertion. Suppose e.g. that A himself says to B: 'You may draw from my account' after having made the arrangement. Is this utterance to be taken as an act of granting the permission or of communicating that it has been granted? Another problematic case is that where A wants to give B a certain permission; say, the permission to take an apple, and instructs C to tell B this in case B turns up at a time when he himself is absent. If then B does turn up in A's absence and C says to B: 'You may take an apple', has C given a permission to B or only *reported* A's permission?[7]

It is worth noting that it is not only difficult to decide for some such cases whether the utterance was an assertion of a performative; from the point of view of the addressee it is usually also quite unnecessary. For as long as he has good reason to believe that the utterance is *appropriate*, then, whether he interprets it as a performative or as an assertion the practical consequences will be precisely the same. For either the utterance is a performative and as such creates a certain number of new options, or else it is an assertion; but then if it really is appropriate it must be true; and its truth then guarantees that these very same options already exist.

I am making this observation because it brings out a general principle that correlates the assertoric and the performative uses of permission sentences. This principle can be roughly stated as:

(14)   An assertoric utterance of a permission sentence φ in the context c is true iff all those worlds already belong to the options of the addressee that a performative use of φ would have added to the set of his options if they had not already belonged to it.

(This formulation leaves something to be desired as there are obvious problems with the interpretation of the counterfactual construction; it is unnecessary in the present context to eliminate this element of vagueness.)

It is important for us to realize that this principle holds not only for simple sentences such as (1) but also for more complicated permission sentences. Assertoric utterances of (3) for example often have the force of reports that both taking an apple and taking a pear are permissible acts. Notice that this is in conflict with what one is led to expect by the familiar semantic accounts of disjunctive declarative sentences. This discrepancy requires an explanation no less than the problem relating to performative uses of (3) with which we set out. One possible explanation is the following: The performative use is the *primary* use of permission sentences; it is primary in the sense that the truth conditions governing the assertoric use of these sentences reflect in the manner indicated by (14) the pragmatic effects produced by the corresponding performative uses.[8] Given what we have said about permission sentences earlier such an account seems natural enough, and we will pursue it a little further.

Its formal implementation requires that we add to the recursive component a further clause which determines the truth conditions of a permission sentence φ in the context c in terms of $[\![\varphi]\!]_c^{\text{Per}}$; for example:

(15) $[\![\varphi]\!]_c = \{\langle w,t \rangle : (\exists c')(w = w_{c'} \ \& \ t = t_{c'} \ \& \ [\![\varphi]\!]_{c'}^{\mathrm{Per}} \subseteq \mathrm{Per}(c', B_c))\}$

(where B_c is the addressee of c)[9] [10]

The recursive definition will then determine the set $[\![(3)]\!]_c$ via a computation in which the last computation step of $[\![(3)]\!]_c^{\mathrm{Per}}$ is followed by a step which leads us back to another value of the same function $(\lambda\varphi)[\![\varphi]\!]_c$ with which the first steps of the computation are also concerned.

I stress the order in which these various computation steps follow each other because it seems to me to conflict with a widespread, though not often articulated, view about the general form that a comprehensive theory of language should take. In much of the recent formally oriented thinking about language there has been, I believe, the implicit assumption that the semantic and pragmatic components of such a theory are *separable*, in a sense which I shall try to explain presently.

I have already referred to the generally recognized view that any language theory which is to account for, at least, the truth conditions of declarative sentences of unbounded complexity must incorporate a component which has the form of a recursive definition. If we accept this view, the implicit assumption to which I just alluded can be formulated as consisting of the following two parts:

(SSP)   (i) The concept, or concepts, characterized by the recursive component of the theory belong(s) to semantics.
(ii) Moreover no notion to which this component refers belongs to pragmatics.

The distinction between semantic and pragmatic notions which this principle presupposes goes back at least to the work of C. S. Morris [ ], who introduced the tripartite division of the theory of language into syntax, semantics and pragmatics.[11]

Although the literature which discusses the relations between semantics and pragmatics is voluminous what is supposed to distinguish the two categories is only rarely made explicit; consequently the terms are often applied with less consistency than one might wish. It may well be impossible to give a coherent account of the distinction that does justice to the entire spectrum of intuitions associated with it, even were one to take into account only what has been said about semantics and pragmatics during the last decade. What I have to say about the subject should not be taken as an attempt to do this, although I will repeatedly appeal to certain intuitions about the nature of pragmatics and semantics which I believe to be quite general and deeply entrenched.

Morris's original distinction, according to which semantics is concerned with the relations between signs and the objects to which they refer, while pragmatics has for its subject the interaction between signs and their users, still leaves considerable room for manoeuvre to the theorist who wants to convert this characterization into a formally precise definition. By way of a first step in the direction of a precise distinction we shall consider the following principle, which seems to accord well with Morris's intentions:

(DSP) Semantic (as well as syntactic) concepts can be applied to linguistic expressions irrespective of how and when they are used; pragmatic concepts on the other hand can be properly applied only to individual utterances of expressions, as the question whether such a concept applies depends essentially on features of the context in which, and on the purpose for which, the expression is used.

It should be pointed out at once that DSP has certain implications which may at first seem counterintuitive. For example the truth value of a statement

(16)   The sun is shining

is according to DSP a pragmatic concept. For what the truth value is depends on when and where the statement is made. Notice however that on the other hand the truth *conditions* of (16), i.e. the conditions which specify in what circumstances an assertoric utterance of (16) would be true, are classified by DSP as semantic. Similarly the truth value of an assertion of

(17)   I am thirsty

is a property which can be ascribed to the utterance, but not to (17) in isolation; but again, if by the truth conditions of (17) we are prepared to understand conditions that specify in what circumstances, including information about the time of utterance and the identity of the speaker, an assertion of (17) is true, then these truth conditions are part of semantics. As these two examples indicate the properties of truth and falsehood are, at least with respect to a language as rich as English, to be regarded as pragmatic properties. Yet there remains a sense — viz. that of truth conditions — in which the 'concept of truth' may still be said to be part of semantics. This last observation should render the conclusion that the properties of truth and falsehood belong to pragmatics less unpalatable.

The examples we have just considered illustrate at the same time something else: To the property of truth, which is, as we have seen, a property of utterances, there corresponds a semantic functional concept which assigns to a sentence a function that determines for each context of use whether an assertoric utterance of the sentence in that context is true or false. This correspondence is evidently of a general nature. Indeed, suppose that P is any property of utterances such that the question whether an utterance of sentence φ in context c has P is fully determined by (i) the syntactic form of φ and (ii) certain contextual features which c has independently of whether φ is asserted in c (i.e. if c has, respectively lacks, any of these features then it would have done so equally if φ had not been asserted). Then it is always possible to introduce a concept P' which assigns to each sentence φ that function $P'(\varphi)$ from contexts to truth values such that for any context c $P'(\varphi)(c) = 1$ iff an assertoric utterance of φ in c would have P. P' is a sentence concept and thus qualifies according to DSP as a semantic notion.

This possibility of converting pragmatic concepts into corresponding semantic notions might make us wonder if the distinction which DSP draws is a genuine distinction. For it might seem that many of the sentence concepts which result from these conversions are classified as semantic and yet incorporate essentially pragmatic information.

Before we dismiss DSP on these grounds, however, it is worthwhile to devote a few remarks to a recent paper by David Kaplan [ ], in which he draws a distinction quite similar to that marked by DSP. To explain the here relevant aspects of Kaplan's paper it is best to summarize what he has to say about simple indexicals such as e.g. the word 'I'. On the one hand the reference of 'I' varies with the context of use so that we cannot associate any particular referent with the word as such. On the other hand there is a simple *rule* which tells us for any context of use c what the referent is of 'I' in c (viz. the speaker of c). This rule defines a function from contexts to individuals, which Kaplan calls the *character* of the word 'I'. Kaplan argues persuasively that it is natural to identify this character with the meaning of 'I'. For it is this function, or alternatively the rule of which it is the crystallization, which a speaker may be supposed to have assimilated when he can be said to have mastered the use of the word.

Generalizing from examples such as this Kaplan argues for a theory in which each meaningful expression has a character, i.e. a function which associates with each context of use c a representation of what might be roughly described as the 'semantic content' of the expression in that context.[12] The argument that characters can be regarded as meanings also generalizes naturally.

If we accept this identification of characters with meanings then it becomes almost imperative that we regard the *character concept*, i.e. the concept which assigns to each expression its character, as a semantic concept. For what could semantics be if it is not the theory of meaning?

The preceding paragraphs indicate that it is reasonable to classify certain sentence concepts as semantic even though they may be felt to incorporate pragmatic aspects. There is however an important distinction that this observation threatens to obscure. Compare e.g. the sentences (17) and

(18)   The Ohio is a tributary of the Mississippi.

(17) contains an indexical element while (18) does not. This difference is reflected by the characters of the two sentences: the character of (18) is a constant function on contexts; the character of (17) is not. This difference between the two characters arises because the computation of $[\![(17)]\!]_c$ involves a step which imports into it information specific to c (the identity of the speaker of c) while the computation of $[\![(18)]\!]_c$ involves no such step. Indeed we might want to say that the pragmatic nature of $[\![(17)]\!]_c$ is a consequence of the fact that some step of its computation is an application of a clause which refers to pragmatic notions. This however won't help us in drawing the line between pragmatic and semantic concepts. For how are we to decide which of the notions referred to by the clauses of the definition are pragmatic notions? As long as we confine our attention to characters it may appear that we can circumvent this circularity by capitalizing on the difference between constant and non-constant context-functions. Let us try this and call a character concept for a language *purely semantic* if it assigns to each expression of the language a constant character.

The recursive definition which we have just been discussing thus characterizes a concept which is not purely semantic in this sense. It should be noticed however that the theory of indexicals and demonstratives can be reformulated in such a manner that its recursive component does define a purely semantic character concept. All one needs to do is to first associate with each expression that contains indexical or demonstrative elements an abstract representation in which the indexicals and demonstratives are replaced by variables. The satisfaction conditions for these representations will then be independent of context; and so all representations will have constant character. The pragmatic component of the theory can evidently extract all the required information from these satisfaction conditions. It will specify, e.g. that an assertoric utterance of the sentence φ in c is true iff the representation associated with φ is satisfied in w_c at t_c by any sequence which assigns to the variables those objects which the context c provides as references for the indexicals and demonstratives corresponding to these variables.[13] I mention the possibility of this reformulation to make it clear that at least as far as indexicals are concerned we can design the theory in a fashion that insures that the recursive component generates a purely semantic character concept.

Let us now return to the computation of $[\![(3)]\!]_c$, and the recursive definition which yields that computation. It is my intuition — but I think it is one I share with many others — that the steps which compute the sets $[\![(1)]\!]_c^{Per}$ and $[\![(2)]\!]_c^{Per}$ out of $[\![(12)]\!]_c$ and $[\![(13)]\!]_c$ introduce a pragmatic element into the computation, and that by the same token the clause[14] of which they are applications introduces a pragmatic aspect into the recursive definition.

The formal considerations of the preceding pages confirm this intuition. For, of the two concepts $(\lambda\varphi)(\lambda c)[\![\varphi]\!]_c$ and $(\lambda\varphi)(\lambda c)[\![\varphi]\!]_c^{Per}$[15] that the recursive definition which I have sketched simultaneously defines, the second assigns context functions that are not constant and so is not purely semantic. As a matter of fact the concept $(\lambda\varphi)(\lambda c)[\![\varphi]\!]_c$ also assigns non-constant functions to certain expressions; e.g. $(\lambda c)[\![(3)]\!]_c$ depends on c because the right hand side of (15) asks for the addressee of c. We have seen however that the context dependencies created by such simple indexicals as 'I' and 'You' can be eliminated from the recursive component of the theory if we associate with each expression that contains such terms a representation in which they are replaced by variables.[16] When thus modified the definition will assign to each meaningful expression φ a constant function $(\lambda c)[\![\varphi]\!]_c$, *even* when the computation of this function involves intermediate steps which compute values of $(\lambda\varphi)(\lambda c)[\![\varphi]\!]_c^{Per}$.

However the definition which results from this modification is still in violation of SSP, for one of the concepts it defines viz. $(\lambda\varphi)(\lambda c)[\![\varphi]\!]_c^{Per}$, will assign non-constant context functions no less than it did according to the unmodified definition.

One might want to look upon the recursive component in a somewhat different perspective, and take it as a definition of just the concept $(\lambda\varphi)(\lambda c)[\![\varphi]\!]_c$. The pragmatic component of the theory will then account for the effect of performative utterances of permission sentences on the basis of the satisfaction conditions for the representations of the sentences used. This would presumably involve an appeal to (14) in the 'opposite direction' (more about this in the next section). One could then consider the concept $(\lambda\varphi)(\lambda c)[\![\varphi]\!]_c^{Per}$ as no more than a side product of the recursive definition, needed as an auxiliary in the characterization of $(\lambda\varphi)(\lambda c)[\![\varphi]\!]_c$, but not among the concepts that the first part of SSP refers to. However, even when conceived in this way the new definition remains in conflict with SSP, in virtue of SSP.ii; for some clauses, such as e.g. (15′)[16] will refer in their right hand sides to a concept that is not purely semantic.

It must be asked at this point whether this really matters. Does SSP express a conception about the form of linguistic explanation that should be taken at all seriously? In order to speak to this question I must say a little more about the considerations that motivated me to state SSP in the form I gave here, within the context of our discussion of permission sentences. The conception of which I tried to capture the relevant consequences in SSP goes back at least to Frege. Frege assumed[17] that the content of an expression is the same no matter in what type of speech act it is used. This speech act neutral content is determined from the contents of the smallest constituents of the expression by a recursive process the successive steps of which are dictated by the syntactic structure of the expression. The contribution which the expression makes to the speech act in which it is used is completely accounted for by its content.

Linked with this picture is the notion that the part of the theory which deals with the contents of expressions is its semantic component, while the parts which deal with the properties of utterances are to count as pragmatic. This accords well with what has been said earlier about the difference between semantics and pragmatics. For on the one hand we have already mentioned that the analysis of the properties of speech acts belongs to the province of pragmatics. I might add to this that those parts which are specifically concerned with the illocutionary effects of performative utterances seem to have a further claim to being pragmatic in as much as these effects are instances of the interaction between signs and their users which is the proper subject of pragmatics according to Morris's original definition. On the other hand there is good reason to believe that the systematic analysis of content is the one and only possible form for a theory of meaning.[18] So in as much as semantics is the theory of meaning it is natural to identify the component of the theory which deals with content as its semantic component.

I must confess that I can see no good reason why semantics and pragmatics should be separate in the sense that SSP tries to articulate. In particular, if we think of the recursive component of the theory as representing, in some way, the means of processing expressions that are available to the speakers, there are no a priori grounds, it seems to me, that would favor a theory which agrees with SSP over one that violates it: computation processes that SSP prohibits appear no less accessible than those which it allows. This is an extremely delicate matter however, to which we shall briefly return in the last section.

I must now mention some other objections to the theory which we have considered in this section, and which are more specifically concerned with the details of the analysis of disjunctive permission sentences it proposes.

First, it must be conceded that assertoric utterances of (3) need not be interpreted as saying that both taking an apple and taking a pear are permitted actions. There is nothing wrong, say, with C's responding to B's inquiry about what permission A has given, by saying:

(20)   You may take an an apple or take a pear; but I don't know which.

It appears, moreover, that in certain fairly infrequent situations even performative utterances of disjunctive permission sentences can be taken in this weaker sense. Suppose e.g. that we have just arrived in the town where we shall spend our holiday, and that in the immediate environment of this town there are two swimming areas, the first a part of Shoal Creek, the second a part of Shingle Creek. We have heard that one of these areas is dangerous and that in fact only a week earlier some boy drowned there. But I don't know which of these two it is. Suppose further my son comes to me and asks if he may join tomorrow some of his newly acquired friends for a swim. I can then reply: 'You may go to Shoal Creek or go to Shingle Creek. But stay away from the dangerous one.' I think it is right to hold that in this case a permission, viz. the permission to go for a swim somewhere, has been issued; but it is only the permission to realize the disjunctive verb phrase 'go to Shoal Creek or go to Shingle Creek'. Nothing has been said about the disjuncts separately.

In [6] I already gave a brief indication of how we might accommodate both interpretations of disjunctive permission sentences within the framework there advocated. I suggested that a sentence such as (3) has two distinct analyses which induce different computations. Besides the analysis we have already discussed there is another in which the union operation is applied *before* the transitions from $[\![\ ]\!]_c$ to $[\![\ ]\!]_c^{Per}$ take place: it operates on $[\![(12)]\!]_c$ and $[\![(13)]\!]_c$ rather than on $[\![(1)]\!]_c^{Per}$ and $[\![(2)]\!]_c^{Per}$. From the union so obtained we then compute the set $[\![(3)]\!]_c^{Per}$, as indicated earlier.[19] It will be helpful to represent these two analyses as trees:

(21)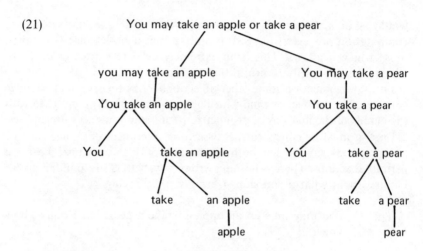

(22)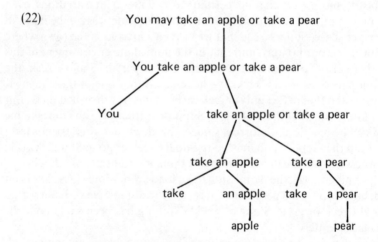

If we look at these diagrams we cannot help noticing that from a purely grammatical point of view (21) is decidely less plausible than (22). For according to (21) (3) results through combining the sentences (1) and (2) by means of 'or'. And this operation must have the syntactic effect of not only inserting 'or' between the two constituents but moreover of deleting the second occurrence of 'may'. This is certainly not the way to obtain (3) which purely syntactic considerations would suggest. Of course we could try to defend the analysis by claiming that (3) can be derived through verb phrase deletion from

(23)   You may take an apple or you may take a pear

which can be used for the very same purposes (both assertoric and performative) that are served by (3) itself. This defense is less than fully satisfactory, however. For sentence (23), though it *can* be used to license simultaneously both the act of taking an apple and the act of taking a pear, sounds somewhat strained when used in this way, whereas (3) doesn't at all. (23) is a much more natural choice of expression, it seems, when we want to report that a certain permission is in force but are unsure which it is.

A second syntactic problem for our theory already arises with (1) and (2). Our present analysis of (1) assumes that the sentence is formed from combining 'may' with the sentence 'You take an apple'. From a purely syntactic point of view it seems more natural, however, to assume that 'may' is combined with the verb phrase 'take an apple' to give 'may take an apple'. This second verb phrase is then combined with 'You' to yield (1). If we were to adopt such a syntactic analysis for (1), we could either (i) retain the semantic account given earlier but thereby give up the strict correspondence between syntactic and semantic recursion steps which we have observed so far (it is a difficult question how important this is; but I will continue to take it here that there always must be *good* grounds to justify a departure from the principle); or (ii) revise the theory in such a way that $[\![\text{take an apple}]\!]_c$ yields an appropriate interpretation for 'may take an apple', and that from this interpretation we can compute in turn $[\![(1)]\!]_c^{\text{Per}}$. This is possible but makes the theory rather more awkward. (I will spare the reader the uninteresting details of this modification).

A third source of criticism is the fact that permission sentences are, unlike imperatives, indicative sentences. The view that indicatives are primarily used for the purpose of asserting, and that in all cases where they appear in speech acts of a different type there must be a special account of why this should be possible, is as problematic as it is old. And the theory of indirect speech acts — which as far as I know is the only serious effort to make this thesis work — has only sharpened our awareness of all the difficulties that a defense of it must overcome. Nonetheless it might be maintained that the prima facie evidence for such a view is so strong that a theory which conflicts with it can be accepted only after we have tried in earnest to deal with its problems in a manner with which the view is compatible.

So let us try to account for the assertoric use of permission sentences while ignoring, for the time being, that they are also used in performatives, and to deal with their performative uses subsequently. Our primary task is now to state the truth conditions of permission sentences. We shall begin by considering this question for simple sentences such as (1) and (2).

Again we might consider a number of different syntactic analyses for these sentences which would dictate different computations; but, as the reader will see, this time there is no good reason to consider any but the intuitively most natural analysis. For (1) the analysis we adopt is given by the following tree:

(27)

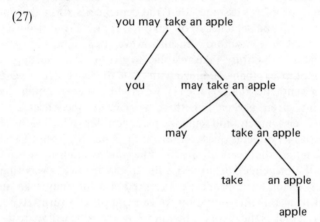

The crucial step in the computation of $[\![(1)]\!]_c$ is now the one that corresponds to the formation of

(28)   may take an apple

out of

(12)   take an apple.

As (12) and (28) are both intransitive verb phrases they ought to be assigned the same type of semantic entity. So if we stay with our earlier proposal for $[\![(12)]\!]_c$ (see p. 263), then $[\![(28)]\!]_c$ must be a function from world-time pairs to sets of individuals.

But which function? Well, the function, surely, which assigns to the pair $\langle w,t \rangle$ the set of individuals u such that taking an apple belongs to the permissible options of u in w at t. Generalizing from this particular case we may conclude that the computation of $[\![\text{may}\varphi]\!]_c$ from $[\![\varphi]\!]_c$ requires the following recursion clause:

(29) $[\![\text{may } \varphi]\!]_c(\langle w,t\rangle) = \{u: (\exists w')(w' \in \text{Per}(w,t,u)$
        $\& \ (\exists t')(t' > t \ \& \ u \in [\![\varphi]\!]_c(\langle w,t\rangle)\}$

The other steps in the computation of $[\![(1)]\!]_c$ need, after all that has been said on the subject in the previous section, no further comment.

Before we try to deal with the truth conditions of more complex permission sentences such as (3), let us first consider the question how we might account, on the basis of these truth conditions for the fact that utterances of a sentence such as (1) are so often taken to be performatives, whose function it is to grant a permission. Towards an explanation of this phenomenon we might consider the following argument. Suppose that A has authority over B and that this fact is common knowledge shared between A and B. Then B may be expected to react to A's utterance: 'You may take an apple' with the reflection: 'It is up to A whether I may take an apple or not. Therefore he knows whether what he says is true or false. It may be assumed moreover that he is not saying what he knows to be false, as this would go against established principles of conversational propriety. So I may conclude that I have the permission to take an apple.'

The effect of A's utterance is thus to make B realize that he has been given the permission.

The problem with this explanation is that it doesn't go quite far enough. For it fails to establish that there is an actual *institution* of giving permissions by uttering permission sentences.[20] Suppose A says to B 'You may take an apple', B then takes an apple, whereupon A berates him for doing so, claiming he had no permission to take an apple. In such a situation it is not just that B can excuse himself by pointing out that he was *misled* by A's utterance. No, B can justly claim that he *had* the permission, in virtue of what A said to him. There are situations where A just cannot mislead B simply because his utterance constitutes the granting of the permission. The hypothesis that the addressee of an utterance of, say, (1) tends to respond with the kind of reasoning I have just sketched can at best provide an intuitive explanation of how this institution could have developed in a language which already allows for the assertoric use of permission sentences. It does not show, however, that there *must* be such an institution. A theory which is to deal with the various aspects of language from a purely sunchronic perspective must therefore postulate the performative use of permission sentences without the possibility of justifying this claim conclusively by an appeal to conversational rules.

Of course the theory must not only imply that permission sentences can be used to give permissions; it must also specify what effects such sentences produce when they are so used. Once again the theory of conversation goes some way towards predicting these effects. For we may suppose the addressee B to continue the reflections which A's utterance of (1) provokes roughly as follows: 'If what A says is true then there must be some futures in which I take an apple and to which he does not object. For all I knew there were no such futures. However, some of the futures in which I take an apple are less objectionable than others. Now it is reasonable to assume that if future w is now permitted and w' is no more objectionable than w then w' is permitted too. So if any such futures are permitted then surely all those are which from what I knew are as unobjectionable as could be given that in each of them I will take an apple.'

The value of this argument is as limited as that of the previous appeal to conversational principles. We may feel that it articulates a valuable insight into the coherence between, and possibly the origin of, certain linguistic conventions; but I do not see how it could be so formulated that the existing conventions regarding the power of permission granting utterances becomes strictly derivable from the truth conditions of the permission sentences used in these utterances together with conversational principles which are general enough to be supported by other evidence than their power to correctly predict the effects of performative utterances of sentences such as (1).

If indeed there is no hope of actually *deriving* from the assumption that permission sentences are used for assertoric purposes and from the conditions which specify when an assertoric utterance of such a sentence is true either the fact that permission sentences are also used to give permissions or the effects that their performative uses produce; then the difference between an account of such sentences which follows the strategy we have thus far outlined in this section on the one hand and on the other the theory sketched in the preceding section is not really that big. In fact the only difference so far is that while the earlier theory derives the truth conditions of permission sentences from the effects they produce when used performatively, the present theory treats truth conditions and performative effects separately, allowing only for a partial, and thus far purely informal, explanation of how the performative use could have developed out of the assertoric use.

The crucial question however is, as before, the treatment of (3), and we must now consider how the new theory might cope with this sentence. If we analyze (3) so as to give 'or' wide scope over 'may' then there is no hope of obtaining the strong reading for (3), at least not if we are to use no more than the resources that the present theory offers. (This is something which I will not argue for. But it can easily be verified, especially after reading what follows below.) Indeed the most promising syntactic analysis is the one which meets all the objections which we mentioned at the end of the preceding section and which is given by:

(30)

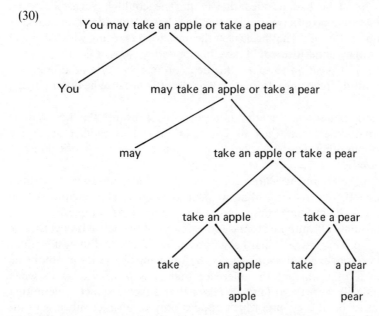

If we compute the truth conditions of (3) in accordance with (30), using the principles already mentioned — and in particular clause (29) — then we find that $\langle w,t \rangle$ belongs to $[\![(3)]\!]_c$ iff there is some permissible continuation of w after t in which the addressee of c takes either an apple or a pear; it is not required that his options include continuations in which he may take an apple as well as continuations in which he may take a pear.

How shall we explain that (3) has nevertheless so often the stronger reading, according to which continuations of either type belong to the addressee's options? Again our only hope of finding an explanation lies in the theory of conversation:

Suppose it is common knowledge between A and B that A has the relevant authority over B. Suppose further that A addresses B with (3). Then B may be expected to infer not only that he has the permission to satisfy the disjunctive verb phrase

(31)   take an apple or take a pear;

he is likely to reason moreover: 'There must be a reason why A used (3) rather than e.g. (1) or (2). His use of (3) cannot but signify that while he allows me to satisfy (31) he has left it undecided which of its disjuncts I shall satisfy; for if he had decided this matter he could have used — and conversational propriety would in that case have demanded that he use — the simpler (1) or (2). That he has left the question regarding which disjunct I shall satisfy undecided could have one of two reasons; it is either that he isn't yet in a position to make this decision (e.g. because he doesn't yet possess all the relevant information); or else it is because he doesn't really care.'

In many situations B will be in a position to dismiss the first of these two possibilities, and thus to conclude that A is indifferent to the question; in other words that he, B, may realize either the first disjunct or the second.

Again the argument is unsatisfactory as it stands, and to incorporate it into our theory requires that we articulate general principles which, together with specific assumptions about the utterance in question which can reasonably be imputed to the addressee, yield the desired conclusion by pure logic. This is a task that I shall not undertake here. But even without carrying it out explicitly we can make the following observation: Among the principles that warrant the inference that A is *indifferent* as to which disjunct will be realized (and therefore that either disjunct is permitted) there must be at least one which applies only to a small subclass of the set of all indicative sentences which contain disjunctive constructions. For in general disjunctive indicatives do not have the 'strong reading' which the principle must allow us to assign to disjunctive permission sentences.

I mention this fact as it enters into the question whether these principles introduce a pragmatic element into the recursive component of the theory. At this very point the form of the new principles must appear irrelevant to this issue, in as much as we have only contemplated the possibility of adding them to the pragmatic component of the theory, which we assume to provide no feed-back to the truth definition. But the matter with which we are trying to deal is more complicated than the examples at which we have looked so far suggest. Consider, to begin with,

(32)   You may take an apple or take a pear, but if you do not peel it you will be sick.

Just as (3) can have its 'strong reading' when used by itself, so it can also have this reading when part of the larger (32). In order for the pragmatic component of the theory to assign this strong reading to certain utterances of (32) it must evidently operate not on the truth conditions of (32) as a whole, but rather on the truth conditions of its conjunct (3).

Cases like (32) are still relatively easy to accommodate. We could for example add a new principle to the effect that an assertoric utterance of a conjunction may be reinterpreted as a succession of assertions of the respective conjuncts. In fact the need for such a principle has been implicit in the theory of conversation from the very start. For in as much as implicatures are inferred from individual sentences they are usually inferred from *parts* of continuing pieces of discourse. Often such a piece of discourse is equivalent to a single sentence which is the conjunction of the various sentences which constitute the piece; and an assertoric utterance of this conjunction must therefore carry the same implicatures as the discourse fragment. The only way in which the theory can do this is by using as imputs the truth conditions of the individual conjuncts.

There are however other ways in which (3) can occur embedded in larger sentences while yet allowing the strong reading. Take e.g. the two-sentence utterance.

(33)   Usually you may only take an apple. So if you may take an apple or take a pear, you should bloody well be pleased.

Here (3) occurs as antecedent of (33.ii). Yet it is most naturally interpreted there as having the strong reading. But how could an essentially conversational argument establish this on the basis of the truth conditions of (33.ii)? The difficulty we are facing is this. The truth conditions our theory assigns to (33.ii) are the same as those which it assigns to

(34)   You should be pleased if you may take an apple and you should be pleased if you may take a pear.

The reading which the pragmatic component must produce on the basis of these truth conditions does not *entail* these truth conditions. The effect of applying the pragmatic component must therefore be not just to *add* an implicature to given truth conditions, but rather to *undo* what the recursive component of the theory has already established. For this the theory of implicature, as traditionally conceived, has no provision; and indeed one would be hard-put to introduce such powers into it.

One who takes the conversational arguments we have presented so far at all seriously cannot escape the impression that in certain cases, such as in particular that of (3), an implicature which the sentence typically carries when used by itself, becomes conventionally attached to that sentence in such a way that it may contribute to the interpretation of compounds in which the first sentence is so embedded that it becomes inaccessible as imput to the conversational component of the theory in the usual way. We might contemplate adding to the pragmatic component of our theory a principle that makes this intuition precise — although how such a principle should be stated I am unable to say. But in any case this principle would introduce the feed-back of the pragmatic component into the truth definition which we precisely wanted to exclude.[21]

At this point it appears that the present theory must, just as the theory of section 2, run into conflict with SSP. We should not be too hasty with such a conclusion, however. For rather than introducing a principle into the theory that will somehow make it possible to use the implicatures assigned by the pragmatic component to certain sentences in the computation of the truth conditions of compounds that contain them as parts, we could add directly to the truth definition a clause which gives the strong reading of permission sentences by spelling out the effect that the interaction between 'or' and 'may' produces in them. The clause should be to the effect that:

$$(37) \qquad [\![\text{may } \varphi_1 \text{ or } \varphi_2 \text{ or } \ldots \text{ or } \varphi_n]\!]_c(\langle w,t\rangle) =$$

$$\left\{ u: \bigcup_{i=1,\ldots,n} [\![\varphi_i]\!]^{\text{Per}}_{w,t,u} \subseteq \text{Per}(w,t,u) \right\}$$

where $[\![\varphi_i]\!]^{\text{Per}}_{w,t,u}$ is short for: $\{w': w'$ is a world in which u satisfies φ_1 at some time after t and which belongs to the smallest member of the nest $\text{Pos}(w,t,u)$ which contains such worlds$\}$.

(37) allows us to compute for (3) truth conditions that accord with its strong reading. Yet the truth definition still agrees with SSP, at least according to the formal criteria developed in this paper.[22]

But this is at a price. For the theory now fails to give any account of why there should be besides the separate clauses for 'or' and 'may' the further clause (37), which formulates a joint effect of the two lexical items that no combination of applications of the separate clauses can produce. (The theory of [6] was designed precisely to explain why the effect that (37) describes is produced on the basis of the functions which 'or' and 'may' fulfill in general.)

Before we can assess how serious a defect this is I must draw attention to the fact that what we have called the strong reading is possible not only for permission sentences, but for certain other types of disjunctive sentence as well. Examples are:

(38)   We may go to France or stay put next summer (in the 'possibility sense' of 'may')

(39)   I can drop you at the next corner or drive you to the bus stop.

(40)   If John had come to the party with Alice or with Joan we might have had some fun.

If, as it seems reasonable to assume, there are only a finite number of different sentence types which allow this reading then we might accommodate them by adding for each a separate clause similar to (37), and thus preserve compliance with SSP. But our suspicion that the theory misses a significant generalization should now be even stronger. For it is hard to ignore the hypothesis that behind this multiplicity of clauses lies some unifying principle. As I have here presented the theory of [6] it does not provide such a unifying principle either. In [6] however I did make a suggestion as to what it might be. To develop that suggestion into a respectable doctrine is a major task on which I shall again default. But I will outline once more the general idea.

The sentences (38), (39) and (40) share with (3) that they are all typically used in speech acts whose function it is to bring a certain number of possibilities to the attention of the audience. What distinguishes these speech acts from each other lies only in the different purposes for which they bring these possibilities into focus. In the case of permission sentences the purpose is to convey to the hearer that these possibilities are all acceptable; in the case of sentences such as (38) or (39) it is to point out that these possibilities are to be reckoned with (e.g. in making plans for the future); an utterance of (40) offers a set of possible situations to claim of each of these that a certain condition — expressed by the consequent of (40) — holds in it. In all these cases the set of possibilities to which the hearer's attention is drawn consists of those in which the truth conditions of the relevant subsentence are fulfilled and which are among the less outlandish possible situations in which this is so.

In [6] I implied that the strong readings of disjunctions that are used in any such speech acts arise because there is the option to apply the union operation which 'or' signals to the sets which the two separate disjuncts would have placed in focus had they been used by themselves. However, we can also justify the strong readings by means of the conversational argument which we already considered in connection with (3): In each of these cases the speaker's use of the disjunction can be interpreted as testifying to his indifference whether the possibilities he wants to bring to the hearer's attention satisfy the first or the second disjunct; and so it may be inferred that he wants to bring both kinds of possibilities to his attention.

This latter argument strikes me as particularly persuasive within the present more general setting, in which we try to deal not only with permission sentences. This, together with the implausibility of the syntactic analyses which the theory of [6] requires inclines me now to the opinion that that theory should probably be rejected. There remains however the larger question to which it led us, viz. whether it is possible for a comprehensive theory of language to conform to SSP.

The preceding discussion has revealed some of the difficulties we must face if we wish to answer this question. We saw that although it is possible to draft a theory which treats the problems on which we have focussed here correctly, this theory will fail to capture certain systematic correlations between its different parts, and in particular between different parts of its recursive component. On the other hand it appears that we could also formulate the theory in such a way that it does account for these correlations; but so formulated the theory will allow its truth definition to call on the pragmatic component for imputs and therefore would have to violate SSP.

In fact it seems to me that there is still a third alternative. This is suggested by our earlier consideration of the theory of indirect speech acts. We noted that the arguments which are meant to explain the practice of using permission sentences performatively from the fact that they are used assertorically and the truth conditions which govern their assertoric uses cannot be formalized to the point where they could be incorporated into the formal theory itself. Yet it might be said that these arguments provide a modicum of insight why that theory should be the way it is. This suggests that a combination of (i) a strict formal theory, and (ii) a conglomerate of less formal explanations of various aspects of the formal theory; might be the best we can do if we want to give an account of language which is precise and yet optimally illuminating. Within the scientific methodology bequested by the great philosophers of science of the end of the last and the first half of the present century (in particular E. Mach and the Vienna Circle in its various ramifications) there appears to be no room for scientific accounts of this format. It seems to me to be a worthwhile task to see how the methodology of theories of such forms might be worked out; but it is not a task which I shall undertake now.

Let us return to the more specific question which of the proposals we have considered provides the best account of permission sentences. I want to ask this question, not because I have an answer to it, but rather because it leads to the further query whether questions of this sort can be answered at all. I said earlier that I could not see why we should prefer one theory over another just because the first satisfies SSP while the second does not, as there appears to be no reason why the computation processes which SSP rules out are any less plausible from the perspective of actual language processing than are those which it licenses. In this consideration there is an implicit acknowledgement that the ways in which speakers process the sentences of their language is relevant to the comparison of linguistic theories. It implies more specifically for the theories we have sketched in this paper that they too must ultimately compare in regard of their faithfulness to the ways in which speakers determine the truth conditions of those sentences that the theories deal with.

As soon as one makes this claim, however, he realizes how hard it is to attach a clear sense to it. What precisely should be understood by the 'ways in which speakers determine the truth conditions' of certain sentences? Remarks throughout this paper have suggested that speakers do this by going through certain computations the successive steps of which are indicated by the syntactic structure of the sentence in question.

But how are these computations to be identified? Questions of this sort are deep and immensely difficult. And at the present time it isn't even possible to make an educated guess at how long it will be before we acquire the degree of understanding of the workings of the human mind necessary to give these questions a coherent interpretation that will render them at least in principle amenable to definite answers. Yet, until then nothing much can be said about the psychological adequacy of linguistic theories.

It is my conjecture that if we ever reach this level of sophistication we will find there to be not just one computation procedure for each (un-ambiguous) expression, but in general a multiplicity of such procedures —

different computations being used by different speakers of the same language and perhaps even by the same speaker on different occasions. If this is indeed so then it might turn out that each of the theories we have considered in this paper correctly mimicks a procedure that is actually in use.

This might also be taken to imply that in as much as linguistic theory has the task to account for those aspects of language the knowledge of which is common to all competent speakers, some of the distinctions between alternative theories that came up in the course of this paper are not really relevant to linguistics. But I am not so sure that it would be right to draw this conclusion. For it could well be that once we have reached the understanding of mental processes that will allow us to speak meaningfully about individual computation procedures we shall no longer be content with theories that deal only with the output of those procedures; but demand that a comprehensive account of language deal with the diversity of computation strategies realized, or realizable in human language users, as well as with the uniformity of their outputs; and that it explain how the shared linguistic experience of those users ensures that uniformity of output without which communication would be impossible; and semantics, as it is generally conceived today, would not exist.

Bedford College

NOTES

[1] The history of this paper is long and rather unfortunate. In the summer of 1973 I produced a draft part of which I subsequently incorporated into [6]. Since then I have given several talks on the material that had remained unpublished, with increasing diffidence and a corresponding inability to persuade the audience. I should mention in particular presentations at the conference in Bad Homburg which led to these proceedings, and to the Oxford Philosophy Society in the winter of 1976. I am grateful for the many criticisms that I have received on those occasions, in particular from Richmond Thomason in Bad Homburg and from Michael Woods in Oxford; they have helped me to face up to my growing doubts about the solution to the problem of disjunctive permission sentences of which I gave a sketch in [6] and about the elaborate theory I had built upon that solution.

[2] I assume that the 'may' of permission and the 'may' of possibility are distinct lexical items. Unless the contrary is stated explicitly (which will happen only once, towards the very end of the paper) the occurrences of 'may' in the examples we shall discuss will always be instances of the first of these two 'may's.

[3] One could object to (4) on the ground that commands often require compliance within a limited time span. Sometimes the limit is given explicitly, such as when A says: 'Polish my shoes before tomorrow morning'. But just as often the command itself contains no such specific reference to time, and in these cases the limit is essentially vague in as much as there is no time t' after t such that the addressee has unambiguously obeyed if he performs the required action before t', but has failed to do so if he performs it at any time after t'. With permission we find a similar phenomenon: many permissions are to be understood as licensing a certain action only for a restricted period; if the action hasn't been performed by the end of that period then the permission lapses. As this aspect of permissions and commands is irrelevant to the main issue of this paper I have decided to ignore it.

Another, and related, problem with commands is that many are to be understood as 'standing orders'. This is typically the case when the imperative uttered contains a negation, as in 'Do not lean out of the window', or 'Do not covet thy neighbour's wife'. But there are also negation-free commands which are thus intended, e.g. the 'Keep left' signs which admonish the continental driver upon his entry into Britain. Again there is a parallel complication in the analysis of permission sentences: 'You may smoke' can be used not only to convey that the addressee may have one cigarette, but also to lift the prohibition against smoking for an extended period of time, possibly even for good. This complication will also be ignored here.

[4] Usually the intention of the permission is that the verb phrase which represents the cancelled prohibition may be satisfied only once, although this is not always so. Compare note 3. As I already said there, this type of complication we shall ignore.

[5] By a *permission sentence* I will understand in this paper any sentence of the form 'You may φ' where φ is an intransitive verb phrase, and 'may' is the 'may' of permission. As sentences of this form are by no means the only ones to be used for the purpose of granting permissions, the term 'permission sentence' could be misleading. It is intended strictly to facilitate the discussions of the present article.

[6] I am assuming that intransitive verb phrases are semantically treated as one place predicates of individuals; and I will take this to imply that the satisfaction conditions for an intransitive verb phrase φ in the context c are represented by a function which for each pair $\langle w,t \rangle$ gives the set of individuals satisfying the verb phrase in w at t. I will denote this function as $[\![\varphi]\!]_c$.

[7] Our uncertainty about such questions is reflected by the practical uncertainty we feel in situations where B has acted in a way which is acceptable only if the permission is in force, but without having been told this explicitly. Suppose e.g. that B has taken an apple before C has had the opportunity to say to him 'You may take an apple', but after A has instructed C to tell B this. Has B been guilty of a transgression?

[8] Very much more would have to be said about the general framework within which an explanation of this form would naturally fit. This would require among other things a systematic classification of utterances into speech act types, and an elaboration of the idea that certain types of speech acts are the primary speech acts associated with certain grammatically characterized types of sentences. I cannot even begin to do this here. For some ideas along these lines see Searle [13].

[9] An exact version of the recursive definition would have to make explicit that (15) applies only to those φ for which $[\![\varphi]\!]_c^{Per}$ is defined, and for which moreover the permission granting use is primary. This class should include all permission sentences as defined in note 5, whether it should include other expressions as well is a question I shall not consider here.

[10] As we have defined them here the sets $[\![\varphi]\!]_c^{Per}$ and $[\![\varphi]\!]_c$ show an asymmetry that may seem awkward: the former is a set of worlds while the latter consists of world-time pairs. It would of

course be possible to eliminate this asymmetry by redefining $[\![\varphi]\!]_c^{Per}$ as a set which also consists of pairs $\langle w,t\rangle$. I can see no real merit in doing so however.

[11] The distinction between syntax and semantics is irrelevant to the present paper, and I won't say anything about it. In fact I may occasionally use the term 'semantic' rather broadly, including under it concepts which can be taken to belong to syntax rather than to semantics. No significance should be attached to these real or apparent violations of established terminology.

[12] I am of course using the word 'semantic' here in a loose, pretheoretic sense.

[13] Actually the matter is a little more complicated than I make it appear. For there are indexical expressions such as 'now', of which it is not clear whether they could be replaced by variables. If we take 'now' to be a shorthand for 'at the present time' then of course we can replace it by 'at t', where t is a variable ranging over moments. It has been proposed however ([4], [5], [12]) that 'now' should be treated as a sentential operator, on a par with the operators 'it was the case that' and 'it will be the case that' which are traditionally considered in tense logics of the type first introduced by Prior. This proposal is, at least in the form in which it is available in the literature, incompatible with the replacements that the revised form of theory requires. I have reached the conviction however, that nothing compels us to a view of 'now' on which the substitution of 'at t' is inadmissible.

[14] I haven't yet stated this clause explicitly. From the discussion in Section I. it should be clear, however, that it should have some such form as:

$[\![$You may $\varphi]\!]_c^{Per} = \{w \in $ Pos (c): $(\exists t > t_c)$ $(B_c \in [\![\varphi]\!]_c(\langle w, t\rangle)$ & w belongs to the smallest member of Pos(c,B_c) which contains any worlds w' such that $(\exists t > t_c)(B_c \in [\![\varphi]\!]_c(\langle w',t\rangle))\}$

(here B_c is the addressee in c).

[15] This notation is a little misleading in that it conceals the fact that $[\![\varphi]\!]_c^{Per}$ is defined on only a small subset of the domain of $(\lambda\varphi)(\lambda c)[\![\varphi]\!]_c$.

[16] This requires in particular that we modify (15) in such a way that if

(19) x may take an apple or take a pear

is the representation of (3) then for any assignment s (of objects to variables)

(15') $[\![(19)]\!]_c(s) = \{\langle w,t\rangle : (\exists c')(w_{c'} = w$ & $t_{c'} = t$ & the addressee of c' $= s(x)$ & $[\![(19)]\!]_{c'}^{Per} \subseteq$ Per$(c',s(x))\}$

[17] See e.g. [2], [3].

[18] This assumption is fundamental to both model theoretic semantics, as it was established by Montague, and to truth theory as advocated by Davidson and his school. See in particular [1].

[19] See footnote on p. 29.
Once we accept that there are two distinct computations for $[\![(3)]\!]_c^{Per}$ and $[\![(3)]\!]_c$ the notation used so far becomes strictly speaking ambiguous. To proceed with full propriety we should make the notation dependent on the analysis. But let that pass.

[20] This is a problem generally with explanations in the theory of indirect speech acts, to which the present argument belongs. For the theory of indirect speech acts see e.g. [13].

[21] It may be noted at this point that the complications that arise in connection with examples such as (34) closely parallel a familiar problem in the theory of conditionals. In the very first presentations of the theory of conversational implicature it was proposed that the truth conditions of English conditionals are correctly represented by the truth table for material

implication; and that the intensional interpretations which hearers commonly associate with conditional sentences when they are actually used can be explained on the basis of these truth conditions by an appeal to the rules of conversation. This proposal looks promising enough as long as we restrict our attention to conditionals which are not embedded in larger linguistic units. But problems arise in connection with such embedded conditionals as

(35)   If aunt Emilia will disinherit us if we do not invite her then we will.

According to the truth functional account of 'if' the truth conditions (35) come out equivalent to those of

(36)   If aunt Emilia will disinherit us then we will invite her;

and this is not what somebody who utters (35) would naturally be understood as saying. Here too the problem is that the intended reading of (35) cannot be obtained simply by adding an implicature to the reading which is provided by the truth definition. This indeed is the main reason why such accounts of the conditional had to be abandoned.

²² As disjunctive permission sentences have two different readings (37) must operate alongside (9) and (29), which we already saw were needed to obtain the truth conditions corresponding to the weak readings of these sentences. This means that strictly speaking we must acknowledge two separate analyses for sentences such as (3), which correspond to the two different computations. Neither of these is a target however for the objections listed at the end of Section II.

BIBLIOGRAPHY

[1]   Davidson, D. (1967), 'Truth and Meaning', *Synthese* **17**.
[2]   Frege, G. (1960), 'On Sense and Denotation', in M. Black and P. Geach (eds.), *The Philosophical Writings of Gottlob Frege*, Oxford.
[3]   Frege, G. (1967), 'The Thought', in P. F. Strawson (ed.), *Philosophical Logic*, Oxford.
[4]   Gabbay, D. (1976), *Investigations into Tense Logic and Modal Logic with Applications to Linguistics and Philosophy*, D. Reidel Publ. Co., Dordrecht, Holland.
[5]   Kamp, H. (1971), 'Formal Properties of "Now"', *Theoria* **37**.
[6]   Kamp, H. (1973), 'Free Choice Permission', in *Proceedings of the Aristotelian Society*.
[7]   Kamp, H. (forthcoming), 'On Historical Necessity'.
[8]   Kaplan, D. (1978), 'Dthat', *Syntax and Semantics* **9**.
[9]   Kaplan, D. 'Demonstratives', (unpublished).
[10] Lewis, D. (1970), 'A Problem About Permission', to appear in E. Saarinen *et al.* (eds.), *Essays in Honour of Jaakko Hintikka*, D. Reidel Publ. Co., Dordrecht, Holland.
[11] Prior, A. (1968), 'Now', *Noûs* **2**.
[12] Searle, J. (1975), 'Indirect Speech Acts', *Syntax and Semantics* **3**.
[13] Stalnaker, R., 'Comments on Lewis's Problem about Permission', (unpublished).
[14] Thomason, R. (ed.) (1974), *Formal Philosophy: Selected Papers of Richard Montague*, New Haven.
[15] Morris, Ch. (1955), *Signs, Language and Behavior*, New York.

GILLES FAUCONNIER

IMPLICATION REVERSAL IN A
NATURAL LANGUAGE

Much recent work about language has been representational: the solution of particular problems and the account of linguistic distributions is often perceived as being the choice (or the discovery) of abstract representations (e.g., semantic, syntactic, logical . . .) which reflect directly, largely by means of their configurations, properties and generalizations only dimly apparent at the 'surface'. Of course, rules are necessary to relate these representations to the actually observed manifestations of language and the form of these rules, like that of the representations, is considered to be a question of crucial importance in linguistic theory.

It would seem that the unquestionable fruitfulness of this methodology in some areas of linguistics has had the tendency to make us believe that this is the only legitimate conception of a rigorous ('scientific') approach to the study of language; and so there are few theories on today's market which do not incorporate a level of logical form or semantic representation.[1]

In a series of previous papers,[2] I have called this type of assumption into question by demonstrating that abstract representations played no role in the understanding of the syntactic and semantic facts related to the question of 'polarity'; grammatical polarity was shown to be a special case of semantic (and/or pragmatic) polarization; and the intermediate concepts needed to give an explanatory account of this broader phenomenon include 'pragmatic scale' and 'implication reversal' which are not representational.

The present paper brings more evidence in favour of this general methodology by presenting two theorems relative to implication-reversing environments and showing their application to a range of linguistic phenomena wider than previously envisaged. We will begin by summarizing the results obtained in the earlier studies mentioned, before discussing the new material.

1. PRAGMATIC SCALES REVERSED

A scale of elements $(x_1, x_2, \ldots)$ is associated pragmatically with a propositional schema $R(x)$ if it is assumed that for any two elements on the scale, x_1 and x_2, x_2 higher than x_1, $R(x_1)$ entails[3] $R(x_2)$:

F. Guenthner and S. J. Schmidt (eds.), Formal Semantics and Pragmatics
for Natural Languages, 289–301. All Rights Reserved.
Copyright © 1978 by D. Reidel Publishing Company, Dordrecht, Holland.

$$\left[\begin{array}{l} M \\ \\ x_2 \\ \\ x_1 \\ \\ m \end{array}\right. \qquad R(x_1) \Rightarrow R(x_2)$$

For example, it is commonly assumed that the capacity to solve a difficult problem entails the capacity to solve a simpler one (although this is in no way a logical necessity); if so, a scale of decreasing complexity is associated with the propositional schema 'Max can solve x'.

$$\left[\begin{array}{l} M = \text{'the simplest problem'} \\ \\ x_2 \\ \\ x_1 \\ \\ m = \text{'the most difficult problem'} \end{array}\right.$$

$$R(x) = \text{'Max can solve } x\text{'} \qquad R(x_1) \Rightarrow R(x_2).$$

The extremities of such scales are typically denoted by grammatical superlatives[4] like m and M in example 1; no elements corresponding to these extremities need actually exist: the closure is conventional.

Given the type of implication which characterizes such scales, if m is the minimum point on the scale, then for any x:

$$R(m) \Rightarrow R(x)$$

and therefore

$$R(m) \Rightarrow \forall x R(x)$$

This implication mirrors the fact that a sentence like (2) can be understood to mean (3):

(2)   Max can solve the most difficult problem.
(3)   Max can solve any problem.

Negation reverses implication:

if $R(x_1) \Rightarrow R(x_2)$
then $\sim R(x_2) = \sim R(x_1)$

This means that if a scale S is associated with $R(x)$ then a scale S of opposite orientation to S will be associated with $\sim R(x)$: the maximum of S will be the minimum of S. In the example corresponding to (1) we have:

$R(x) = $ 'Max can solve x'
$\sim R(x) = $ 'Max cannot solve x'
$m = $ 'the most difficult problem'
$M = $ 'the simplest problem'
$R(m) \Rightarrow \forall x R(x)$
$R(M) \Rightarrow \forall x \sim R(x).$

We find that indeed M gives rise to a quantified reading in the negative counterpart of (2):

(4)   Max cannot solve *the simplest problem.*
        (= Max cannot solve any problem)

Superficially, then, evidence for scale reversal in these cases has the following form: a superlative gives rise to a quantified reading in a sentence but not in its negation, and the polar opposite of that superlative gives rise to the quantified reading only in the negative counterpart of the sentence:

(2)   Max can solve the most difficult problem.
(2′)   + Max cannot solve the most difficult problem.
(4)   Max cannot solve the simplest problem.
(4′)   + Max can solve the simplest problem.

('+' indicates the lack of a 'quantified' reading, one implicating *any* in place of the superlative).

A broader question which follows naturally from these observations is the following: what environments other than negation give rise to quantified readings for superlatives (when such readings are absent in the simple declarative counterparts)?

Environments having this property turn out to be quite varied; here are some examples:

–negative matrix (not think, not convince, not certain, doubt, . . .)

(5)   + Max can solve the simplest problem.
(6)   I don't think Max can solve the simplest problem.
(7)   You can't convince me that Max can solve the simplest problem.
(8)   It's not certain that Max can solve the simplest problem.

–if-clauses:

(9)   I'll be surprised if Max can solve the simplest problem.
(10)   If Max can solve the simplest problem, he will be rewarded.

–comparatives:

(11)   +It is hard to see the most distant stars with this telescope.

((11) has no quantified reading: it cannot be read to mean 'it is hard to see any stars with this telescope'.)

(12)   It is harder to see this planet than (it is) to see the most distant stars.

(quantified reading: it is harder to see this planet than to see any stars).

–too ... (for) ... to ...

(13)   Max is too stupid to solve the simplest problem.
(14)   Alex is too proud to accept the slightest criticism.

(compare: *Alex accepts the slightest criticism).

–universal statements:

(15)   Anybody who can solve the simplest problem is fit for this job.
(16)   We shall forgive anyone who shows the faintest sign of repentance.

–before:

(17)   He was executed before he could show the faintest sign of repentance.

–questions:

(18)   Can Max solve the simplest problem?
(19)   Did Max show the faintest sign of repentance?

–only, first:

(20)   Max was the only one to show the faintest sign of repentance.

Strikingly, these environments are the very same which reverse standard (grammatical) polarity; for example, with the negative polarity item 'ever', we have:

(21)   (a) *Max *ever* works.

negation:	(b) Max doesn't *ever* work.
negative matrix:	(c) You can't convince me that Max *ever* works.
if clause:	(d) If Max *ever* works he will be rewarded.
comparatives:	(e) Alex works more than Max *ever* worked (ellipsis: ... than Max *ever* did)
too ... to ...:	(f) Max is too lazy to *ever* work.
universals:	(g) Anybody who has *ever* worked enjoys doing nothing.
before:	(h) Before he *ever* works, Alex will try all other means of surviving.
questions:	(i) Did Max *ever* work?
only, first:	(j) Max was the $\left\{\begin{array}{l}\text{only}\\\text{first}\end{array}\right\}$ one to *ever* work for Rockefeller.

Why should superlatives give rise to quantified readings in some environments and not in others? When we conceptualize the problem in terms of pragmatic scales, there is an easy answer: given a propositional schema $T(x)$, a superlative 's' will produce a quantified reading in T (i.e., $T(s) \Rightarrow \forall x T(x)$) if it denotes the minimum of a scale associated with T; now assume that $T(x)$ is a complex schema containing $R(x)$:

$$T(x) = U \; R(x) \; V$$

and that $R(x)$ is associated with scale S:

$$S \begin{array}{|c} \begin{array}{l} \rule{0pt}{0pt} \\ M \\ \\ x_2 \\ \\ x_1 \\ \\ m \end{array} \end{array} \quad R(x_1) \Rightarrow R(x_2).$$

If the superlative 's' denotes M, the maximum of scale S, it will not produce any quantified reading in the simple schema R. But it will produce a quantified reading in the complex schema T if $T(x)$ is associated with scale $\tilde{S}$ (same elements as S but opposite orientation); that is if for x_1, x_2 on S we have:

$$T(x_2) \Rightarrow T(x_1)$$

Another way to put it is to say that the environment U_____V must reverse the orientation of scales:

$$\text{if} \quad R(x_1) \Rightarrow R(x_2)$$
$$\text{then} \quad U \ R(x_2) \ V \Rightarrow U \ R(x_1) \ V.$$

A sufficient condition for this reversal is that U____V should reverse implication in general:

$$\text{if} \quad P \Rightarrow Q$$
$$\text{then} \quad U \ Q \ V \Rightarrow U \ P \ V.$$

We have shown elsewhere[5] that polarity-reversal environments (as in (21)) do indeed share the property of reversing implicational scales and in most cases implication itself. For example, consider the case in which 'U____V' is the conditional 'if____ then Z'. '$U \ P \ V$' in this case would be:

'if P then Z'

which we can assimilate for the present purpose to:

'$P \Rightarrow Z$'.

In the same way:

'$U \ Q \ V$' = '$Q \Rightarrow Z$'.

Now from $P \Rightarrow Q$ it follows trivially that:

$$[Q \Rightarrow Z] \Rightarrow [P \Rightarrow Z]$$

(informally, because when Q entails Z and P entails Q, then by transitivity P entails Z).

In other words, for this particular U____V environment, whenever $P \Rightarrow Q$ holds, then the reverse implication $U \ Q \ V \Rightarrow U \ P \ V$ holds. Therefore, the environment 'if____ then Z' has the required property of reversing implication.

That comparative environments also reverse scales is a simple consequence of the scalarity involved in their semantics. The following sketch gives an informal idea of what is going on: assume that with

$$R(x) = \text{'x works'}$$

we associate pragmatically the scale:

$$S \left\{ \begin{array}{l} M = \text{Hercules} \\ x_2 \\ x_1 \end{array} \right.$$

on which x_2 works more than x_1, M ($=$ Hercules) being the one who works the hardest.[6] Now consider the environment:

'Max works more than _____'

($U = $ Max works more than, $V = \phi$)
We have, using the same notation as before:

$T(x) = $ Max works more than x works.

Obviously, if Max works more than x_2, he also works more than x_1:

$$\left\{ \begin{array}{l} M = \text{Hercules} \\ \xleftarrow{\hspace{2cm}} \text{Max} \\ x_2 \\ x_1 \end{array} \right.$$

So we have:

$$T(x_2) \Rightarrow T(x_1)$$

which shows that the scale S is indeed reversed with respect to the complex schema $T(x)$. In particular, M becomes a minimum as confirmed by the quantified reading of (22):

(22)   Max works more than even Hercules (does).

($= $ 'Max works more than anybody') (*even* in such sentences signals the end-point of a scale).

One consequence is that negation plays no special role in explaining these phenomena: it is simply one of the many scale-reversing environments (perhaps a statistically dominant one).[7] Another is that, contrary to previous claims, no special hypotheses about 'natural' logical forms or semantic representations are needed to account for polarity: in fact the type of induced quantification at work here and its syntactic reflexes[8] cast serious doubt on the existence of any single level at which scope relations might be represented.

2. TWO THEOREMS

2.1. *Existential extraction*

Let $U\underline{\qquad}V$ be an environment which reverses implication (and therefore scales, and polarity):

$$\text{if} \qquad P \Rightarrow Q$$
$$\text{then} \quad U\,Q\,V \Rightarrow U\,P\,V$$

Consider the schema $R(x)$ and the complex schema $T(x)$ obtained by embedding $R(x)$ in $U\underline{\qquad}V$:

$$T(x) = U\ R(x)\ V$$

For any constant a, Existential Generalization allows us to write:

(23) $R(a) \Rightarrow \exists x R(x)$

Since $U\underline{\qquad}V$ reverses implication, (23) yields:

(24) $U\ \exists x R(x)\ V \Rightarrow U\ R(a)\ V$

Since (24) is valid for any arbitrary constant a, we obtain, through Universal Generalization:

(25) $\boxed{U\ \exists x R(s)\ V \Rightarrow \forall x\ U\ R(x)\ V.}$

We shall call this property the *Existential Extraction Law*.

Hence, environments which reverse implication, and therefore scales, have the implicative property of Existential Extraction. We can check empirically that this is indeed the case; for example:

(26)   I would be surprised if there was a man who could lift this bus.

$$\Rightarrow$$

(26′)   For any man, I would be surprised if he could lift this bus.

(27)   This but is too heavy for there to be a man who can lift it.

$$\Rightarrow$$

(27′)   For any man, this bus is too heavy for him to lift it.

Notice that Existential Extraction is a generalization of the well-known law of Quantifier Negation is predicate calculus:[9]

(28) $\sim \exists x R(x) \Rightarrow \forall x \sim R(x)$

(28) is merely the expression of the general theorem (25) in the special case when 'U____V' is the negative environment '$\sim$____ϕ'. These observations make it possible to understand why there has been a widespread tendency to analyze polarity phenomena in terms of negation: any context which is negative or equivalent to a negation will have the properties of the more general implication-reversing environments U____V, among which (25). It casts a new light on the much debated issue of whether *any* is uniformly a universal quantifier (Reichenbach, Quine, Bolinger, Savin, Ehrenkranz-Legrand) or sometimes an existential quantifier (Klima, Horn). According to the former (29) corresponds to (30); according to the latter it corresponds to (31):

(29)   If anybody calls, I will answer the door.
(30) $\forall x$ (if x calls, I will answer the door).
(31)   If $\exists x$ (x calls), I will answer the door.

In our presentation, this type of problem disappears since *any* is not a quantifier but rather indicates the extremity of a scale: the equivalence of (30) and (31) is only a special case of *Existential Extraction* (theorem 25).

Some environments reverse intervals of pragmatic scales, but do not reverse implication in general; for them, theorem (25) is no longer valid: (32) does not imply (33):

(32)   'I wonder if $\exists x R(x)$'
(33)   '$\forall x$ (I wonder if $R(x)$).

In such environments, Quine's theory of the logic of *any* is inadequate even in the most simple cases; take (34):

(34)   I wonder if Susan married anybody.

According to Quine, *any* is always a universal quantifier with wide scope and (34) would then be logically analyzed as (35):

(35) $\forall x$ (I wonder if Susan married x).

But this is not the meaning of (34), since one may be sure that Susan did not marry Paul, Max, Gustave … and still wonder whether there was somebody that she did marry. Accordingly in (34) *any* has the force of an existential quantifier, but not of a universal quantifier. And this is predicted by a scalar analysis:[10] sentences like (36) have the same force as (34) (*mutatis mutandis*):

(36)   I wonder if Max can solve the simplest problem.

They do not induce universal, but only existential quantification. Likewise, (37) cannot be associated with (38):

(37)   John is the only man who did anything.

(38)   ∀x (John is the only man who did x).

(38), but not (37), entails that John did everything.

2.2. *De Morgan's Law generalized*

Inclusive *or* (like ∨ in Propositional Calculus) has the property that:

(39) $P \Rightarrow P$ or Q

(39′) $Q \Rightarrow P$ or Q

for any two propositions P and Q. Given an implication-reversing environment U_____V, the defining property of U_____V applied to (39) yields:

(40) U P or Q $V \Rightarrow U$ P V

and applied to (39′)

(41) U P or Q $V \Rightarrow U$ Q V

Taken together (40) and (41) are equivalent to (42):

(42) $\boxed{U \; P \text{ or } Q \; V \Rightarrow U \; P \; V \text{ and } U \; Q \; V.}$

This accounts for the often noted fact[11] that *or* has the force of a conjunction rather than a disjunction in negative, affective, comparative, implicative, etc., environments, since we have shown that these environments reverse implication:

(43)   I don't like tea *or* coffee.

(44)   I would be sorry to see Max *or* Bill fail.

(45)   Lucy is taller than Harriet *or* Christine.

(46)   If you mow the lawn *or* wash the windows, you will be rewarded.

(47)   This problem is too hard for you *or* me to solve.

(48)   I escaped before the FBI *or* the CIA could find me.

These examples entail the following respectively:

(43′)   I don't like tea *and* I don't like coffee.

(44′)   I would be sorry to see Max fail *and* I would be sorry to see Bill fail.

(45′) Lucy is taller than Harriet *and* Lucy is taller than Christine.

(46′) If you mow the lawn you will be rewarded *and* if you wash the windows you will be rewarded.

(47′) This problem is too hard for you to solve *and* this problem is too hard for me to solve.

(48′) I escaped before the FBI could find me *and* I escaped before the CIA could find me.

The success of this account is perhaps most striking in the case of the comparatives: if we take the logic of comparatives to be something like:

$$d°T > d°R$$

(the degree to which T holds is greater than the degree to which R holds) then if P and Q are on a scale such that $d°Q > d°P$ we have the implication $P \Rightarrow Q$ (if P holds then Q will hold also, and to a greater degree). This implication is reversed in a comparative environment '$d°T > \_\_\_\_$':

$$'d°T > d°Q' \Rightarrow 'd°T > d°P'.$$

And theorem (42) applies to such structures (cf. 45 and 45′):

(49) $d°T > d°(P \text{ or } Q) \Rightarrow d°T > d°P$ and $d°T > d°Q$.

But, strangely enough, the antecedent in (49) has no obvious independent meaning: what is $d°(P \text{ or } Q)$? That is, we understand (50) by itself but not (51):

(50) the degree to which Harriet is tall

(51) ∗the degree to which Harriet or Christine is tall.

This leads to the paradox that this antecedent acquires meaning only by virtue of the implication which theorem (42) allows for implication-reversing environments in general.

Theorem (42) is of course the general case of De Morgan's Law: we obtain De Morgan's Law for the special context '$U\_\_\_\_V$' = '$\sim\_\_\_\_\phi$' In that case (42) becomes:[12]

$$\sim(P \text{ or } Q) = \sim P \text{ and } \sim Q$$

The two theorems we have presented are not unrelated: just as Quantifier Negation can be viewed as an application of De Morgan's Law to an infinite disjunction, Existential Extraction can be viewed as an application of (42) to an infinite disjunction.

C.N.R.S., Paris

NOTES

[1] Notice that this is true of theoretical viewponts which are claimed to be conceptually opposed, e.g., 'Montague grammar', the 'extended standard theory' (cf. Chomsky, 1976), generative semantics, etc.

[2] Cf. references.

[3] This entailment can be (and usually is) pragmatic rather than purely logical.

[4] By 'grammatical' superlatives we mean expressions like 'the most Adj N' or 'the Adj +est N'. End points of scales can also be denoted by 'pragmatic' superlatives, e.g., *Hercules* in example (22).

[5] Cf. Fauconnier (1976).

[6] This scale is implicational: $R(x_1) \Rightarrow R(x_2)$, because if '$x_1$ works' and x_2 works harder than x_1, then 'x_2 works'.

[7] More rigorous proofs for these and other polarity-reversing environments are given in F-1976, 1977, together with a critique of previous treatments in 'representational' terms (Baker (1970) and Lakoff (1970)).

[8] The logical principles at work here are sensitive to syntactic 'island' constraints.

[9] The law of quantifier negation also includes the reverse implication:

(i) $\forall x \sim R(x) \Rightarrow \sim \exists x R(x).$

The generalization of this law to arbitrary implication-reversing U____V environments (which would be 'universal incorporation') cannot be proven, one reason being that there is no guarantee that if $U\ R(x)\ V$ is well-defined, $U\ \exists x R(x)\ V$ is well-defined (cf. the case of comparatives). But it can be proven for a number of particular implication-reversing environments, such as negation (case of (i)), or 'if ____ then____'.

[10] The interaction of pragmatic scales with interrogative environments and the corresponding induced quantification are studied in F-76.

[11] For example, facts similar to (45) and (46) are presented as a puzzle by Ehrenkranz (1973).

[12] Also: P and $Q \Rightarrow P$, therefore $U\ P\ V \Rightarrow U\ PandQ\ V$

         P and $Q \Rightarrow Q$, therefore $U\ Q\ V \Rightarrow U\ PandQ\ V.$

Hence: $U\ P\ V$ or $U\ Q\ V \Rightarrow U\ P$ and $Q\ V$. If U____$V = \sim$____ϕ this becomes: $\sim P$ or $\sim Q \Rightarrow \sim (P$ and $Q)$, another of De Morgan's laws.

BIBLIOGRAPHY

Baker, C. (1970), 'Double Negatives', *Linguistic Inquiry*, I.2.

Bolinger, D. (1960), 'Linguistic Science and Linguistic Engineering', *Word*, XVI.

Chomsky, N. (1976), 'Conditions on Rules', MIT mimeo.

Ehrenkranz LeGrand, J. (1973), 'Sometimes, or = and', *Linguistic Inquiry*, IV.2.

Ehrenkranz LeGrand, J. (1974), 'AND and OR; some SOMES and all ANYs', *CLS*, 10.

Fauconnier, G. (1975), 'Polarity and the Scale Principle', *CLS*, 11.

Fauconnier, G. (1976), 'Etude de certains aspects logiques et grammaticaux de la quantification et de l'anaphore en français et en anglais" doctorat d'Etat', Université de Paris VII.

Fauconnier, G. (1977), 'Polarité syntaxique et sémantique', *Linguisticae Investigationes*, I.1.

Horn, L. (1972), *On the Semantic Properties of Logical Operators in English*, UCLA dissertation.

Klima, E. (1964), 'Negation in English', in *The Structure of Language*.

Lakoff, G. (1970), 'Linguistics and Natural Logic', *Synthèse*, 21.

Quine, W. V. (1960), *Word and Object*, MIT Press.

Reichenbach (1947), *Elements of Symbolic Logic*, Macmillan, New York.

Savin, H. (1974), 'Every *Any* means Every', in *Current Problems in Psycholinguistics*, Editions du CNRS, Paris.

JÁNOS S. PETÖFI

STRUCTURE AND FUNCTION OF THE GRAMMATICAL COMPONENT OF THE TEXT-STRUCTURE WORLD-STRUCTURE THEORY

1. INTRODUCTORY REMARKS

The 'text-structure world-structure theory' (a formal semiotic text theory) has been conceived as an integrated theory, which is supposed to enable the analysis and description of all semiotic aspects of natural languages. (This text theory is henceforth referred to in this paper by the German abbreviation TeSWeST: 'Text-Struktur Welt-Struktur-Theorie).

1.1. With the general methodological principles of the TeSWeST I have dealt in Petöfi (1976). I included there the following outline of the structure of the theory (cf. Figure 1, where the direction of the analysis is indicated by arrows).

1.2. In this paper here I will not deal with questions of the general structure of the TeSWeST, I only aim at giving a description of the Text Grammatical Component and concentrate on the description of the Disambiguating Syntactic Formation Component (DiSynFC).[1]

The reason why our research until now focused on the DiSynFC is that it is of central importance for the Mapping Component (MC) as well as for the World Semantic Component (WSeC), because the structure of the MC and WSeC is dependent on the structure of the DiSynFC.[2]

2. THE STRUCTURE OF THE DISAMBIGUATING SYNTACTIC FORMATION COMPONENT

The formation rule system of the DiSynFC consists of communicative rules, canonical-syntactic rules, lexicon rules and inference rules.

The communicative rules (CR) and the canonical-syntactic rules (SR) operate with categories independent of natural languages. Intensional-semantic relations between the structures generated by communicative and canonical-syntactic rules and particular natural languages are established by means of the lexicon rules (LR). The application of the LR-s and SR-s results in the intensional-semantic representation (TInR) of the generated

303

F. Guenthner and S. J. Schmidt (eds.), Formal Semantics and Pragmatics for Natural Languages, 303–338. All Rights Reserved.
Copyright © 1978 by D. Reidel Publishing Company, Dordrecht, Holland.

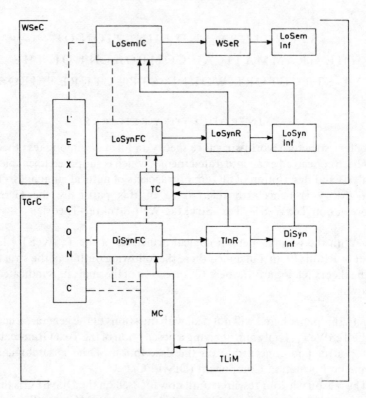

Fig. 1. Explanation of abbreviations used.

DiSynFC   Disambiguating Syntactic Formation Component
DiSynInf   Disambiguated syntactic inferences
LoSemIC   Logico-Semantic Interpretation Component
LoSemInf   Logico-semantic inferences
LoSynFC   Logico-Syntactic Formation Component
LoSynInf   Logico-syntactic inferences
LoSynR   Logico-syntactic representations
MC   Mapping Component
TC   Translation Component
TGrC   Text Grammatical Component
TInR   Intensional-semantic text representations
TLiM   Linear text manifestations
WSeC   World-Semantic Component
WSeR   World-semantic representations

text or of a particular reading of the natural language text under analysis. The task of the inference rules (IR) is to derive the intensional-semantic representations (DiSynInf-s) of admissible inferences from the intensional-semantic text representations (TInR-s). The inferences proper (inference utterances) are the results of the application of the MC on the DiSynInf-s.

The TInR-s must meet the following conditions:

(a)   The TInR-s must be canonical representations indifferent to the surface structure of actual utterances/discourses of the particular natural language; this is a precondition:

     (α) for a theoretically acceptable and optimal handling of paraphrasing (i.e., the replacement of utterances/discourses by semantically identical but structurally different utterances/discourses) which occur in all natural languages;

     (β) for carrying out optimally diachronic and synchronic (stylistic, dialectological, socio-linguistic) comparisons within a given natural language, and

     (γ) for fulfilling the theory's claim to (an at least limited) universality.

(b)   The TInR-s must be able to represent completely the syntactic relations contained explicitly or implicitly in natural language utterances.

(c)   The structure of the TInR-s must allow:

     (α) their easy construction,

     (β) an easy derivation of DiSynInf-s from them, and

     (γ) their systematic decomposition and the arrangement of the constituents into various kinds of classes while retaining the information where they originated from (this last requirement is, above all, indispensable for the semantic interpretation of discourses).

(d)   The TInR-s must contain all the information necessary to optimally carry out the semantic interpretation; this means that if possible nothing should happen in the WSeC but the assignment of the appropriate denotata to the individual elementary signs of the TInR and the construction of the interpretation of the utterance in question out of these denotata.

(e)   The TInR-s must allow the explication of 'coherent text in L'; this means that

     (α) in case of analysis they must contain all the information

necessary for deciding whether the TInR obtained as the
result of the analysis is a representation of a coherent
discourse of the natural language L or not,

(β) in case of synthesis the DiSynFC must only generate
representations of coherent discourses.

This kind of DiSynFC structure will on the one hand facilitate the
translation of the TInR-s into the language of a future complex logical
syntax and on the other hand it provides a suitable base for comparative
and contrastive grammatical research.

The complete formation rule system is presented in Chapter 2.5. I refer to
rules in this chapter using their numbers in the formation rule system.

2.1. *The system of canonical-syntactic rules*

The canonical-syntactic rules serve to construct syntactically well-formed
representations.

2.1.1. The presentation of the *inventory of the basic expressions* used in
the rule system can serve as a short introduction into the treatment of
the canonical-syntactic rules. (Examples for the application can be found in
the description of particular rules.)

Basic expressions:

(1) *argument variables* (α^σ)

    (a)   object variables (δ^σ)

    (aa)   proper-name variables (v)

    (aba) object-class variables

          individual-variables $(\xi \mathcal{N}_L | \mathcal{D} \{ \xi \mathcal{N}_L \})$

          mass-variables $(\xi \mathcal{N}_L | \mathcal{D} \{ \xi \mathcal{N}_L \})$

          Individual-variables and mass-variables have to be read as
follows: the class of those $\xi \mathcal{N}_L$-individuals or that $\xi \mathcal{N}_L$-
material which is defined in $\mathcal{D} \{ \xi \mathcal{N}_L \}$, where $\mathcal{D} \{ \xi \mathcal{N}_L \}$ is an
expression in the lexicon (of type L or $\pm$) of a natural
language.

    (abb) quantification components (constants, variables)

    (abba) quantifiers

          zero-quantifier (θ)

          ω-quantifier variables (ω)

          (an ω-quantifier represents a quantity between a
zero quantity and a universal quantity)

universal quantifier (A)
(abbb) quantifier-specifier variables (φ^ω)
(a quantifier-specifier represents a unit of measuring or counting)
(abc) identifiers
definitizer (U)
(indicates that the object is unambiguously determined in a particular text-subworld)
indefinitizer (V)
(indicates that the object is not determined unambiguously in a particular text-subworld)

(b) Text (T), proposition (Π^τ), and predicate frame variables ($\pi^{\tau n}$)
'τ' is a variable designating types, 'n' indicates the number of arguments (cf. (2)).

(c) Argument-role indicator variables (λ)
The role of the particular argument-expressions within an argument frame is indicated by argument-role indicators (canonical case-labels).

(2) *Predicate function frames (pff-s)*

(a) *n*-place pff-s with object arguments
$[\varphi^{\tau n}]\{\lambda_1: \delta_1^\sigma, \ldots, \lambda_n: \delta_n^\sigma\}$; these pff-s serve to form descriptions — there is no special type marker for them.

(b) *n* place pff-s containing at least one text, one proposition or one predicate frame as argument
$[\varphi^{\tau n}]\{\lambda_1: \delta_1^\sigma, \ldots, \lambda_i: T/\Pi^\tau/\pi^{\tau n}, \ldots, \lambda_n: \delta_n^\sigma\}$; when used directly these pff-s provide the world-specific or communication-specific characterization of a description (cf. the types below), or they serve to represent a speech act; when used *indirectly* they themselves serve to describe. In the enumeration of individual types below I only mention the functor part φ^τ of the pff-s, 'n' is dropped.

(ba) proposition-kernel forming pff-s
(baa) descriptive pff-s (with a φ-functor)
(bab) world-constitutive pff-s (with a φ^W-functor)
(bac) performative-modal pff-s (with a φ^P-functor)
(bad) communicative pff-s (with a φ^C-functor)
(bb) proposition forming pff-s
(bba) local pff-s ($[f]\{l:\underline{\quad} o:\underline{\quad}\}$)
(bbb) temporal pff-s ($[f]\{t:\underline{\quad} o:\underline{\quad}\}$)

The functor part of these pff-s is specified by 'f' in the rule system; f is a functor constant and has to be read as follows: 'it is the case' / 'it occurs (happens)'; the local or temporal character is marked by the argument-role indicators 'l' or 't'. In order to mark the local or temporal character explicitly, the role indicators can also be used as functor superscripts, e.g., f^l, f^t.)

    (bc)   performative-active pff-s (with a φ^{PA}-functor)

(3) *Modifier function frames (mff-s)*
    (a) mff-s with a functor-operand slot ($[[\varphi']\_]\{\mathscr{A}\}$)
    (b) mff-s with a modifier-operand slot ($[[[\varphi'']\_]\varphi]\{\mathscr{A}\}$
      '_' marks the slot for the operand, '$\mathscr{A}$' is a variable designating the argument frame.

(4) *Connective predicate function frames (connective pff-s)*
    (a) connective pff-s with object-expression argument places
      ($[\varphi^{Cn}]\{\lambda_1: \delta_1^\sigma, \ldots, \lambda_n: \delta_n^\sigma\}$)
    (b) connective pff-s with text or proposition argument places
      ($[\varphi^{Cn}]\{\lambda_1: T_1/\Pi_1^\tau, \ldots, \lambda_n: T_n/P_n^\tau\}$)

2.1.2. We start the *description of the canonical-syntactic rules* with SR 4.

SR 4 $\pi :=: [([([\varphi''])\varphi'])\varphi'']\{\mathscr{A}''\}$.

This rule allows us to construct, e.g., the following representations:

    (1) $p_1 :=: [[[\text{VERY}] \text{ QUICK}] \text{ EAT}] \{a: §\text{Peter}§ \, o': §\text{the apple}§\}$,
    (2) $p_2 :=: [[[\text{VERY}] \text{ CLEVER}] \text{ BOY}]\{o'': §\text{Peter}§\}$

The expressions between the '§' sign are not well-formed canonical representations.

The two examples show that the categories φ and φ' are independent of natural language categories. φ includes verbs as well as nouns, φ' adverbs as well as adjectives in languages where they are distinguished.

Here I do not want to go into the question whether it is necessary to use argument-role indicators.

Expressions of the kind referred to in (1) and (2) (with well-formed arguments) I call predicate frames — in contrast to predicate function frames.

These descriptive predicate frames form the kernel of atomic propositions, but do not constitute propositions themselves, as they are not specified for time (and place), world and performative-modality.

Once the kernels (1) and (2) are made arguments of proposition forming pff-s, they become atomic propositions. The formation rule for atomic propositions is SR 3b.

SR 3b $\quad \Pi := [f]\{l: \delta^l, o: [f]\{t: \delta^t, o: \pi\}\}.$

Using the proposition forming pff-s the following proposition can be constructed from (1):

$$(3) \qquad P_1 := [tCi]\{l: d^l_{P_1}\ o: [tCi]\{t: d^t_{P_1}\ o: p_1\}\}$$

This formula has to be read as follows: "It is the case at the place $d^l_{P_1}$ that it is the case at the point in time or in the period $d^t_{P_1}$ that p_1".

('*tCi*' is an abbreviation and stands for 'it is the case'.)

SR 2c $\quad \pi^W := [([([\varphi'']) \varphi']) \varphi^W]\{\lambda_1: \mathbb{C}_1/\mathbb{C}_2, (\lambda_2: \alpha_2^\sigma), o: \Pi^\diamond\}.$

Using this rule the kernel of an atomic world-constitutive proposition can be constructed from (3):

$$(4) \qquad p_1^W := [\text{KNOW}]\{e: \S\text{Anna}\S, o: P_1\}.$$

Further examples for world-constitutive functors are *to believe, to know, to hope, to see, to hear, to be convinced of, to regard as a fact,* etc.

The argument of the world-constitutive pff-s marked by λ_1 always refers to one of the persons communicating ($\mathbb{C}_1, \mathbb{C}_2$). Further research will have to clarify whether certain world-constitutive pff-s require also an argument λ_2 apart from argument λ_1. Also the world-constitutive elements can be modified by the $[[\varphi']\_]$ or $[[[\varphi'']\varphi']\_]$ mff-s.

SR 2c describes how the world-constitutive pff-s are used *directly*, but they can also be used *descriptively*. In the utterance "I believe that Peter knows when he travels to Paris", 'believe' is a directly used whereas 'knows' is a descriptively used world-constitutive functor. We can therefore speak of two classes of world-constitutive pff-s: φ^W pff-s and φ pff-s. (The iteration of world-constitutive elements should be analysed by considering both SR 2c and SR 4.)

SR 2b $\quad \Pi^W := [f]\{l: \delta^l_W, o: [f]\{t: \delta^t_W, o: \pi^W\}\}.$

Using this rule the following atomic world-constitutive proposition can be constructed from (4):

(5) $P_1^W :=: [tCi]\{l: d_{W1}^l, o: [tCi]\{t: d_{W1}^t, o: p_1^W\}\}.$

This formula has to be read as follows: "It is the case at the place d_{W1}^l that it is the case at the point in time or period d_{W1}^t that p_1^W".

The world-constitutive propositions play an important role in the world-semantic interpretation. Both the elements d_W^l and d_W^t of the world-constitutive propositions as well as the functor of the proposition kernel (of the world-constitutive predicate frame) with the argument λ_1 contribute to the partial 'labeling' and the partial definition of the type of subworlds which can be assigned as interpretation to a given text.

The complete label assignment to the subworlds and the complete definition of their type take place with the help of the atomic texts (performative-modal propositions).

SR $1c_1$ $\pi^P :=: [([([\varphi''])\varphi'])\varphi^P]\{s: \mathbb{C}_1, g: \mathbb{C}_2, o: \Pi^{W\diamond}\}.$

Using this rule the kernel of the following atomic performative-modal proposition (or in other words, atomic text) can be constructed from (5):

(6) $p_1^P :=: [\text{ASSERT}]\{s: \S\text{Anne}\S, g: \S\text{Paul}\S, o: P_1^W\}.$

Further examples for performative-modal functors are *to tell*, *to ask*, *to order*, *to promise*, etc., SR $1c_1$ also allows the modification of performative-modal functors by the $[[\varphi']\_\_]$ or $[[[\varphi'']\varphi']\_\_]$ mff-s. The performative pff-s can also be used directly or descriptively, my remark made in connection with SR 2c applies accordingly.

SR $1b$ $T_{\text{IND}} :=: [f] \left\{ l: \delta_P^l, o: [f]\{t: \delta_P^t, o: \left|\begin{matrix}\pi^P\\\pi^{PA}\end{matrix}\right|\}\right\}.$

Using this rule the following atomic text can be constructed from (6):

(7) $T_1 :=: [tCi]\{l: d_{P1}^l, o: [tCi]\{t: d_{P1}^t, o: p_1^P\}\}.$

This formula has to be read as follows: "It is the case at the place d_{P1}^l that it is the case at the point in time or at the period d_{P1}^t that p_1^P".

The d_P^l and the d_P^t elements of atomic texts (i.e., performative-modal propositions) as well as the functor of the performative-modal predicate frames with the arguments λ_1 and λ_2 complete the label assignment to a subworld and its definition. These elements operate, roughly speaking, on the (incomplete) subworld labels and the descriptive propositions: They reinforce the inclusion of a certain fact in a given subworld (e.g., 'A asserts to B that A knows that P'), or they predict the inclusion of a certain fact in a given subworld (e.g., '*A* promises to *B* that it will be a fact for *A* that *P*), or they ask whether a certain fact is included in a given subworld (e.g., '*A* asks *B* whether *B* believes that *P*', if this is no exam questioning), etc.

IND-operation

The T-constituent of the canonical representation (TInR) of a text is a tree structure; the nodes of this tree structure have to be indexed to represent unambiguously how structure parts/tree parts are related to each other. 'IND' indicates that such an indexing (an 'index guided substitution') has to take place.

SR 3a, SR 2a, SR 1a

3a $\quad \Pi^\diamond \quad :=: \left| \begin{array}{l} \Pi \\ [\varphi^{Cn}]\{\lambda_1 \colon \Pi_1^\diamond, \ldots, \lambda_n \colon \Pi_n^\diamond\} \end{array} \right|$

2a $\quad \Pi^{W\diamond} :=: \left| \begin{array}{l} \Pi^W \\ [\varphi^{Cn}]\{\lambda_1 \colon \Pi_1^{W\diamond}, \ldots, \lambda_n \colon \Pi_n^{W\diamond}\} \end{array} \right|$

1a $\quad T^\diamond \quad \underset{(*)}{:=:} \left| \begin{array}{l} T \\ [\varphi^{Cn}]\{\lambda_1 \colon T_1^\diamond, \ldots, \lambda_n \colon T_n^\diamond\} \end{array} \right| // (\kappa \mathscr{T}) \Theta \mathscr{T} (\neg \mathscr{T})$

These rules allow the construction of complex units (connexions) out of atomic units.

Using so-called connective pff-s complex propositions can be constructed out of atomic propositions (cf. SR 3a), complex world-constitutive propositions can be constructed out of atomic world-constitutive propositions (cf. SR 2a), and texts can be constructed out of atomic texts (cf. SR 1a). These rules are based on the hypothesis that connective pff-s connect elements on the same hierarchy level. Further research will have to show, whether the connective pff-s should only have elements of one type as their arguments or also elements of different types.

The term 'connective functor' designates those elements in the canonical structure which can be regarded as canonical correspondences of the object language connectives and of other language units fulfilling connective functions (e.g., certain verbs: '*p* implies *q*', '*p* entails *q*', '*p* follows from *q*', etc.).

All three rules are recursive and thus allow the construction of connexions with differently structured complex hierarchies. Due to the operations $(*)$, $\kappa \mathscr{T}$, $\Theta \mathscr{T}$, and $\neg \mathscr{T}$ rule SR 1a has also to be treated separately.

*-operation

The rules of the formation rule system guarantee the constructing of well-formed canonical representations. At the same time they must also allow the application of an analysing algorithm. But not all the elements necessary for the well-formedness of a $T^\diamond$ are always present in the text to be analysed. In case of elliptic texts the missing elements have to be selected interpretatively out of the elements admissible in the given context; '*' serves to mark the elements so selected.

$\kappa\mathcal{T}$ (canonical transformation)

If we select $a = \text{MiR}$ or $a = \text{SeR}$ when applying SR 0a, the resulting $T^\diamond$ tree is not well-formed. Well-formedness is only achieved by applying the canonical transformation. This can be illustrated by a simple example. Let us take

$$p_1 :=: [[[\text{VERY}] \text{ QUICK}] \text{ EAT}] \{: \S\text{Peter}\S, o': \S\text{the apple}\S\}$$

and let us assume that the elements in the argument places, the functor, the functor modifier, and the modifier of the modifier are all definienda in the lexicon. (In other words, this p_1 is a pLeR_1, a p_1 containing only 'lexical representations'.)

Each definiendum can be replaced by its definiens from the lexicon, if the world-constitutive and/or performative-modal pff-s dominating p_1 do not explicitly block the substitution. In the lexicon each definiendum is defined in accordance with its canonical syntactic category thus also allowing for the combination of definientia in accordance with their categories. This means that after combining the definiens of VERY with the definiens of QUICK, this complex unit has to be combined with the definiens of EAT; then the argument descriptions provided by the definientia in the lexicon have to be inserted into the argument places of this complex functor description. By means of these insertions and combinations we arrive at a representation consisting only of type SeR elements (i.e., a semantic representation). If not all elements are replaced by their definientia, we arrive at a 'mixed representation' (MiR).

$\Theta\mathcal{T}$ (theme-propositum transformation)

As we have already pointed out earlier, all TInR-s have to contain all the information necessary for the world-semantic representation. Information determining the theme-propositum structure is also part of this information. (The terms 'theme' and 'propositum' are used in a semantic sense here: 'Theme' designates the part of the structure which is talked about, whereas 'propositum' designates the part of the structure, which is said. Different theme-propositum structures of the same indifferent $T^\diamond$ *cause different sets of inferences.*[3] The theme-propositum structure is treated as follows:

The elements functioning as 'theme' (or as 'propositum') within a $T^\diamond$ have to be marked in the course of generation (or analysis). It can also occur that several elements function as themes of different rank within the same unit — in this case we can speak of several layers of a theme hierarchy. Once an atomic text, specified with respect to the theme part (the theme parts) is constructed, it has to be converted into a predicate-argument structure with the theme as the argument part; this conversion is carried out by the theme-propositum-transformation.

A simplified example of a theme-propositum assignment can serve as an illustration. Let us, e.g., look at (7) with all its constituents discussed in (6) to (3) and in (1).

(It has to be stressed once more that these examples are only illustrations they are 'quasi-terminal' units, their derivation is not indicated.)

In example (8) which is meant to show the theme-propositum structure I have also included the structure preceding structure (4).

(8) (7) $T_1 :=: [tCi]\{l: d^l_{P1}, o: [tCi]\{t: d^t_{P1}, o: p^P_1\}\}$

(6) $p^P_1 :=: [\text{ASSERT}]\{s: \S\text{Anna}\S, g: \S\text{Paul}\S, o: P^W_1\}$

(5) $P^W_1 :=: [tCi]\{l: d^l_{W1}, o: [tCi]\{t: d^t_{W1}, o: p^W_1\}\}$

(4') $\pi^W_1 :=: [\varphi^W_1]\{e: v, o: \Pi_1\}$

(4) $p^W_1 :=: [\text{KNOW}_\Phi]\{e: \S\text{Anna}\S, o: P_1\}$

(3) $P_1 :=: [tCi]\{l: d_1, o: [tCi]\{t: d^t_1, o: p_1\}\}$

(1) $p :=: [[[\text{VERY}] \text{ QUICK}] \text{ EAT}]\{a: \S\text{Peter}\S, o': \S\text{the apple}\S\}.$

'Φ' indicates that 'KNOW' is the (main) propositum in T_1. Example (9) presents T_1, which is a well-formed formula with respect to the theme-propositum structure but otherwise abbreviated:

(9) $T_{\Theta 1} :=: [\text{KNOW}]\{\lambda\varphi^W_1 T_1 \varphi^W_1\}.$

This formula has to be read as follows:

(a) As a kind of formula: The 'value' of the constituent φ^W_1 of T_1 is 'KNOW'.

(b) As a kind of text: "Anne asserts to Paul at the place d^l_{P1} at the time d^t_{P1} that what she does at the place d^l_{W1} at the time d^t_{W1} with respect to that Peter eats the apple very quickly at the place d_1^l at the time d_1^t, is, that she *knows* it".

$\neg T$ *(negation transformation)*

As to the negation it is established to talk about 'weak' and 'strong' negation. The 'logical negation' ('it is not the case that p') is called 'weak negation', because it is not specified which of p's constituents is subject to negation. An adequate description of natural languages requires the unambiguous representation of the 'strong negation'. In the framework of the TeSWeST this can be achieved as follows: In the course of generation (analysis) the elements to be negated have to be marked. The representation of negation in a well-formed $T^\diamond$ has to coincide with a corresponding theme-propositum transformation which converts the marked elements into the propositum, the adequate negation is the weak logical negation of the transformed structure. The transformation which forms the logical weak but adequately negated structure is called 'negation transformation'.

The following formula presents the negation of formula (9):

(10) $\neg[\text{KNOW}]\{\lambda_1\,\varphi_1^W\,T_1\,\varphi_1^W\}$

A simplified reading runs as follows: "Anne does not *know* that ...", she only 'believes' so.

SR lc_2

$$\pi^{\text{PA}} := : [([([\varphi''])\varphi'])\varphi^{\text{PA}n}]\,\{\mathscr{A}^n\}.$$

This rule describes how to use the performative-active pff-s, which serve to carry out 'an action with words' (and do not serve to define the modality of a descriptive proposition), e.g., "I hereby open this meeting".

(11) $p^{\text{PA}} := : [\text{OPEN}]\,\{a: \S I\S,\ o: \S\text{the meeting}\S\}$

The 'hereby' is expressed by a specially performative modal pff. It can be paraphrased by "(here and now) act communicatingly".

The rules discussed so far direct the construction of a global hierarchy (performative-modal proposition, world-constitutive proposition, descriptive proposition; due to possible further embeddings the descriptive proposition may be highly complex) as well as the construction of (possibly also hierarchically structured) connexions of any degree of complexity by using connective elements on the various levels of the global hierarchy.

In the following paragraphs I will now give short descriptions of the rules which direct the set-up of the argument structures.

SR 5a

$$\mathscr{A}^n := \lambda_1 \colon \alpha_1^\sigma, \ldots, \lambda_n \colon \alpha_n^\sigma.$$

This is a substitution rule referring to the argument-configuration variable ($\mathscr{A}^n$). The 'λ'-s symbolize the so-called 'argument-role indicators', the 'σ'-s symbolize the sortal specifications, which have to direct the insertion. The $\lambda_i \colon \alpha_i^\sigma$-tuples are entered in the lexicon together with the particular functors.[4] SR 5a makes possible that a $\lambda_i \colon \alpha_i^\sigma$-tuple is formed first and a functor (functor class) for which the tuple thus formed can serve as arguments is selected in the next stage.

SR 5b

$$\alpha^\sigma := \begin{vmatrix} \delta^{\sigma\diamond} \\ T^\diamond \\ \Pi^{\zeta\diamond} \\ \pi^\zeta \end{vmatrix}$$

An argument place of a pff can be filled by an object-argument, a text, a (performative/world-constitutive/descriptive) proposition or a (performative/world-constitutive/descriptive) predicate-frame. The corresponding variables are presented in SR 5b. In this sequence 'ζ' symbolizes different sorts of actions/states/processes, whereas the 'σ' stands for different sorts of objects. The σ-sorts contain the ζ-sorts, provided we include 'abstract objects' in the set of objects contained in the σ-sort. 'σ' below the ':=:' sign indicates sortally correct substitution.

SR 6a

$$\delta^{\sigma\diamond} := \begin{vmatrix} \delta^\sigma \\ [\varphi^{Cn}]\, \{\lambda_1 \colon \delta_1^{\sigma\diamond}, \ldots, \lambda_n \colon \delta_n^{\sigma}\}^\diamond \end{vmatrix}.$$

The object arguments can be either simple or complex. A complex object argument is formed by connecting simple object arguments by means of connective pff-s. Complex object arguments are necessary only in cases when a constituent of an utterance is complex in such a way that the utterance cannot be represented as a connexion of two propositions as, e.g., in example (12) compared with (13):

(12)   *Anne and Peter bought a house.* (Anne and Peter together.)

(13)   *Anne and Peter bought a house.* (Each of them separately, i.e., Anne bought a house and Peter bought a house.)

Rule 6a is recursive, similar to rules 3a, 2a and 1a.

SR 6b

$$\delta^{\sigma} := : \begin{vmatrix} N \mathcal{N}_T \\ I \mathcal{N}_T \\ M \mathcal{N}_T \end{vmatrix}.$$

An object argument is either a proper-name index, or an individual index or a mass index.

An index is a complex symbol, its first element is either an 'N', or an 'I' or an 'M', its second element is a text-specific natural number ($\mathcal{N}_T$). The indices stand for proper names or descriptions of objects, their task is to express co-referentiality within an intensional-semantic text representation (TInR).

SR 7a

$$N \mathcal{N}_T := : v^{\langle .., w, .. \rangle}$$

A proper name index has to be used in all those cases when in the course of construction of a text no defining units are assigned to an object apart from its proper name.

The symbols of those worlds in which objects named exist have to be assigned to the proper-name indices as a specification.

SR 7b, SR 7c

7b

$$I \mathcal{N}_T := : \begin{vmatrix} [[\omega_{(i)} \hat{} \varphi^{\omega} [[\xi \mathcal{N}_L | \mathscr{D} \{ \xi \mathcal{N}_L \{]]_{//L \mathscr{F}}]]^{\langle\langle .., U(\{\delta\})w, .. \rangle, \langle .., V(\{\delta\})w, .. \rangle\rangle} \\ [[\begin{vmatrix} \theta \\ A_{(i)} \end{vmatrix} \hat{} \varphi^{\omega} [[\xi \mathcal{N}_L | \mathscr{D} \{ \xi \mathcal{N}_L \}]]_{//L \mathscr{F}}]]^{\langle .., w, .. \rangle} \end{vmatrix}$$

7c

$$M \mathcal{N}_T := : \begin{vmatrix} [[\omega \hat{} \varphi^{\omega} [[\xi \mathcal{N}_L | \mathscr{D} \{ \xi \mathcal{N}_L \}]]_{//L \mathscr{F}}]]^{\langle\langle .., U(\{\delta\})w, .. \rangle, \langle .., V(\{\delta\})w, .. \rangle\rangle} \\ [[\begin{vmatrix} \theta \\ A \end{vmatrix} \hat{} \varphi^{\omega} [[^{\xi} \mathcal{N}_L | \mathscr{D} \{ \xi \mathcal{N}_L \}]]_{//L \mathscr{F}}]]^{\langle .., w, .. \rangle} \end{vmatrix}$$

Individual indices stand for descriptions of countable objects, mass indices stand for descriptions of uncountable objects 'occurring' in the text. The structure of an object description is presented in the following line:

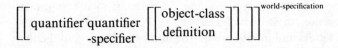

The set of quantifiers contains the universal quantifier (A), the zero-quantifier (θ), and all the other quantifiers (ω) including also such quantifiers as e.g., *some, few, many*, etc.

Apart from the zero-quantifier, all other quantifiers have two readings, a 'group reading' and an 'enumeration reading' if they quantify countable objects. (The difference between these two readings is analogous to the difference between the examples (12) and (13)). The enumeration reading is indicated by the 'i' subscript of the quantifier.

It is the function of the quantifier-specifier to specify the unit of measure applying for the particular objects, such as, e.g., *piece, meter, mile, ounce,* ... (and for multiples and fractions of these units) as well as such units as *bunch, flock, crowd, clutch,* etc.

The definition of an object class is represented as follows: $\xi \mathcal{N}_L | \mathcal{D}\{\xi \mathcal{N}_L\}$ and has to be read as "those $\xi \mathcal{N}_L$-s which are defined in $\mathcal{D}\{\xi \mathcal{N}_L\}$".

The world-specification has to indicate in what subworld of the world system manifested by the text the ω (or A) pieces/quantities of the object defined in $\mathcal{D}\{\xi \mathcal{N}_L\}$, measured by the φ^ω-unit are unique and in what subworld they are variables, i.e., non-unique. The object's uniqueness in world w is symbolized by Uw, non-uniqueness by Vw. In certain cases it is dependant on other objects whether an object is unique or non-unique in a subworld (cf. the different readings of "Each man loves a woman"). This possible dependency on other objects is expressed by the facultative '$\{\delta\}$'-symbols.

Simplified a complete individual-index and mass-index looks as follows:

(14) $[[1\widehat{\ }\text{bunch} [[x03|[\text{flower}]\{o: x03\}]]]]^{\langle Uw_1 \rangle}$

(15) $[[\text{few}\widehat{\ }\text{yards} [[x04|[\text{cloth}]\{o: x04\}]]]]^{\langle Vw_1 \rangle}$

In (14) there is "*the* one bunch of flower (unique in w_1)", whereas in (15) there are "a few yards of cloth (not exactly defined in w_1)".

$L\mathcal{T}$ (lexicon-index transformation)

The '$L\mathcal{T}$' sign besides the description for object-classes refers to the lexicon-index transformation. In a lexicon (of the type L or $\mathbf{\not{L}}$ the variables consist of a combination of letters and numbers, the numbers are numbers in the lexicon. (The combinations of letters and numbers provide the necessary number of variables.) When constructing δ-s relating to a text (under analysis or generation) these variables have to be restructured into a specific combination of letters and numbers with the numbers referring to the text in order to conserve unambiguous TInR-s. Exactly this is the purpose of the lexicon-index transformation.

SR 1a to SR 7c guarantee the well-formedness of a $T^\diamond$. If there is a so-called 'operation-symbol' below the ': = :'-sign, the validity of this operation stretches from this rule to SR 7c (cf. 'a', 'σ', '$*$', and 'IND').

SR 0 assigns the structures necessary for the world-semantic interpretation to a well-formed $T^\diamond$ (SR 0b), and the mapping information representing the relationship between the given $T^\diamond$ and its linear manifestation (SR 0a). ('a' indicates whether the given TInR belongs to type LeR, MiR, or SeR.)

SR 0a
$$TB_a := {:}\, \langle \text{TInR}_a, T\Omega \rangle.$$

The generation of a text or the analysis of a natural language text consists in the construction of $\langle \text{TInR}, T\Omega \rangle$ pairs. 'TInR' symbolizes an intensional-semantic text representation, '$T\Omega$' the mapping information mentioned above.

SR 0b
$$\text{TInR} := {:}\, \langle T^\diamond, \text{TWD} \rangle$$

An intensional-semantic text representation (TInR) consists of a text ($T^\diamond$) and a so-called 'text-world description' (TWD). The TWD represents the systems resulting from the restructuring of the $T^\diamond$ necessary for the world-semantic interpretation.

SR (0α) to SR (0γ)

(0α) $\text{TWD} := {:}\, \langle\!\langle ., w, . \rangle, \langle ., \text{TW}^w, . \rangle, \text{TWaN}, \underset{\text{CAT}}{U} [[., \text{TW}^w, .]] \rangle.$

(0β) $w\,\S = \S\, \langle d_P^l, d_P^t, p^p, d_W^l, d_W^t, p^W \rangle.$

(0γ) $\text{TW}^w \langle\!\langle ., d, . \rangle, \langle ., d^l, . \rangle, \langle ., d^t, . \rangle, \langle ., P^\diamond, . \rangle, \langle ., \text{ThN}, . \rangle,$
         $M_{RR} \rangle^w.$

These rules serve for the construction of the TWD. A TWD (cf. SR (0α)) consists (sequence as in rule) of the ordered set of the text-subworld definitions, the ordered set of the particular text-subworld representations, the representation of the so-called accessibility relations existing between the particular text-subworlds, and of the category-preserving amalgamation of the particular text-subworld representations.

The degree of complexity of the TWD can vary, because φ'' in SR 4 can be a descriptively used communicative functor allowing for a special kind of recursivity. Even though acceptability functions as limitation for recursive embedding in standard contexts, TInR-s (and consequently also $T^\diamond$-s and TWD-s) may contain several recursive embeddings. In case of such TInR-s so-called 'communicative nets' (CN) are needed to represent the communicative situations (who communicates what to whom) on the particular levels of embedding. In this case the TWD-s have to be constructed in accordance with the particular CN-s as descriptions of particular narrated text worlds.

In accordance with SR (0β) a text-subworld definition is an ordered 6-tuple. A partial interpretation of this subworld definition has been treated in SR 1b and SR 2b, but several questions are still unclear, e.g., does SR (0β) mean that all atomic texts represent a text-subworld (i.e., that all elements of the 6-tuple have the same subscript), or is it possible/necessary to have such an interpretation that keeps one of the elements (or a combination of the elements) of the 6-tuple constant and allows all the other elements to vary in accordance with the constant element(s)? In other words: Is it possible that only a place, or only a point in time, or only a person, or only a performative world-constitutive configuration (e.g., everything about which A asserts to B that he ($=A$) believes in it) define a text-subworld? ("§ . . . §" in SR (0β) shows that this rule is not really an unambiguous rule yet because this question has not been decided.)

A text-subworld representation (cf. SR (0γ)) consists of the following elements (sequence as in rule): the ordered set of indices of objects existing in the given text-subworld, the ordered set of indices of objects (local informations)/defining the topology of the given text-subworld, the ordered set of temporal informations defining the chronology of the given subworld, the ordered set of the descriptive propositions which describe the structure of the given text-subworld, the ordered set of the so-called 'thematic nets', and the matrix of the so-called 'referent-relations'. (Even though the topology and chronology of the subworlds are only implicitly provided in the descriptions of the objects of the type d^l or d^t, on demand it can also be provided explicitly. In this case also these explicit representations have to be assigned to the descriptions of particular text subworlds.)

Symbols occurring in SR (0α) to SR (0γ) but not yet treated are to be understood as follows:

Out of the predicate frames which contain a given δ as one of their arguments ordered sets have to be formed. These ordered sets are the so-called 'thematic nets' (ThN). Their number is identical with the number of the different δ-s.

For each thematic net it has to be specified, what other arguments, apart from the δ determining the specific net, occur in its predicate frames. These informations form a referent-relations matrix (M_{RR}).

Based on the w-s and the M_{RR} it has to be determined, what other text-subworld(s) can be reached by what text-subworld and how. These so-called 'accessibility-relations' existing between particular text-subworlds form the text-world accessibility net (TWaN).

The particular text-subworld description (cf. SR (0γ)) have to be amalgamated according to the categories occurring in these descriptions (CAT). This amalgamation will result in the complete (complex) text-world description ($\underset{CAT}{U}$ [[. , TW^w, .]].

Towards the end of these remarks on SR 0 I want to stress that the terms 'text-world' and 'text-subworld', which occur several times in these rules, are grammatic terms. The TWD is the product of grammatic operations only (of the syntactic and intensional-semantic interpretation). It is the task of the WSeC to decide whether a particular TWD can be regarded as the manifestation of a world-complex assignable to the given text as interpretation.

2.2. *The system of communicative rules*

The communicative rules serve to represent the communicative embedding of texts $(T^\diamond)$. In the context of embedding it is necessary to distinguish between communicative and metacommunicative situations.

CR 3a, CR 3b

3a $\quad \Pi^C := : [f] \{l: \delta^t_C, o: [f] \{t: \delta^t_C, o: \pi^C\}\}.$

3b $\quad \pi^C := : [([([\varphi''])\varphi'])\varphi^C] \{s: \mathbb{C}_1, g: \mathbb{C}_2, mo: \delta^C\}.$

Using these rules it is possible to represent a communicative situation. By allowing to describe place and point in time of the communication, the persons communicating and the objects of communication (message), the rules assign the parameters which control the world-semantic interpretation from a pragmatic point of view of the TB-s.

'δ^C' designates the description of the 'message-object' (*mo*); among other things the description contains either a TB or a TInR; TB and TInR are constructed in accordance with the SR-s.

The description of the message-object can contain/contains also information about the type of the communicated text and, consequently, a d^C selects/can select the lexicon or the definientia sections appropriate for the interpretation and the mode of interpretation.

In most cases place-object arguments and time-object arguments of CR 3a and SR 1b are identical. The arguments with the role-indicator 's' of CR 3b and SR $1c_1$ are always identical, and this also applies for the arguments with the role-indicator 'g'. Thus a semantic-pragmatic contact is established between the communicative and the semantic rules. I would also like to point out that as a consequence of the identity of the s-arguments and g-arguments, respectively, $\mathbb{C}_1$ and $\mathbb{C}_2$ in SR $1c_1$ and in SR 2c have to be read as 'I'/'we' and 'you'/'you'. Such a reading marks the direct use of the performative-modal and world-constitutive pff-s.

CR 1a to CR 2b

la $\quad \Sigma^{\mu P} :=: [f] \{l: \delta^l_{\mu P}, o: [f] \{t: \delta^t_{\mu P}, o: \pi^{\mu P}\}\}.$

1b $\quad \pi^{\mu P} :=: [([([\varphi''])\varphi'])\varphi^{\mu P}] \{s: \mathbb{C}_{\mu 1}, g: \mathbb{C}_{\mu 2}, o: \Pi^{\mu W}\}.$

2a $\quad \Pi^{\mu W} :=: [f] \{l: \delta^l_{\mu W}, o: [f] \{t: \delta^t_{\mu W}, o: \pi^{\mu W}\}\}.$

2b $\quad \pi^{\mu W} :=: [([([\varphi''])\varphi'])\varphi^{\mu W}] \{\lambda_1: \mathbb{C}_{\mu 1}/\mathbb{C}_{\mu 2}, (\lambda_2: \alpha_2^\sigma), o: \Pi^{\mathbb{C}}\}.$

These rules are so-called 'metacommunicative rules', they are especially important for the analysis of written natural language texts or of records of conversations.

CR 1a to CR 3b are formally analogous with SR 1b to SR 4. (With the exception of the SR-s marked with 'a', they are missing in the analogous communicative rules, but these recursive rules could easily be introduced if it should be necessary.)

The application of the communicative rules is illustrated by the following simplified example:

(16) (1a) $S_1^{\mu P} :=: [tCi] \{l: \S\text{München}, o: [tCi] \{t: \S 1965\S\ o{:}p_1^{\mu P}\}\}$
$\qquad\qquad$ Zürich$\S$

$\quad$ (1b) $p_1^{\mu P} :=: [\text{TELL}] \{s: \S\text{Droemersche} \quad \{g: X, o: P_1^{\mu W}\}\}.$
$\qquad\qquad$ Verlagsanstalt$\S$

$\quad$ (2a) $P_1^{\mu W} :=: [tCi] \{l: \S\text{München}/, o: [tCi] \{t: \S 1965\S, o: p_1^{\mu W}\}\}.$
$\qquad\qquad$ Zürich$\S$

$\quad$ (2b) $p_1^{\mu W} :=: [\text{FACT}] \{g: \S\text{Droemersche} \quad, o: P_1^{\mathbb{C}}\}.$
$\qquad\qquad$ Verlagsanstalt$\S$

$\quad$ (3a) $P_1^{\mathbb{C}} :=: [tCi] \{l: \S\text{Zürich}\S, o: [tCi] \{t: \S\text{Weihnachten } mo: p_1^{\mathbb{C}}\}\}.$
$\qquad\qquad$ 1949$\S$

$\quad$ (3b) $p_1^{\mathbb{C}} :=: [\text{COMMUNICATE}] \{s: \S\text{Max} \quad, g: X, mo: d_1^{\mathbb{C}}\}.$
$\qquad\qquad$ Frisch$\S$

$\quad$ (4) $d_1^{\mathbb{C}} :=: \S\text{TB}_1$, with the title 'Tagebuch 1946–1949'$\S$.

I only want to add three remarks to this example:

(a)   One can easily find examples to show in what cases the information contained in CR 1a to CR 3b can be relevant for the world-semantic interpretation the TB_1.

(b)   The book title given in the description of d_1^C is not necessarily an unambiguous instruction for the semantic interpretation. In spite of the title, TB_1 can still be a 'fictitious' text.

(c)   It is debatable whether the description of d_1^C need only contain a TB or a TB-connexion formed by means of 'special connectives'. These special connectives would not connect atomic texts to form texts but connect texts to form 'chains of texts'.

2.3. *The system of lexical rules*

The lexicon component consists of two subcomponents: the lexicon (in a narrow sense) which assigns definitions to the elements of the given language (words, phrases/idioms), and the so-called 'name register' which contains proper names (with linguistic and/or encyclopedic explication). The term 'definition' here comprises all types of explications used in the lexicon, i.e., it is used here as 'definition in the lexicon'. Only a part of these definitions is a 'definition' as understood in logic or philosophy of science. (I do not want to go into the question of how ordinary language, the language of different sciences or trades have to be treated within the lexicon component.)

In most cases, apart from the lexicon of a given language, we will also need a so-called 'text-specific lexicon' for the generation of texts or the analysis of natural language texts. This lexicon also contains the two subcomponents mentioned above: the lexicon of text-specific definitions and the register of text-specific proper names. I will henceforth use the symbols '*LDef*' and '*ŁDef*' for the two kinds of lexicons and the symbols '*LReg*' and '*ŁReg*' for the registers.

LR 0

$$ŁDef :=: [[TInR_{LeR} =_{Def} \cdots =_{Def} TInR_{SeR}]].$$
$$\underset{CAT}{}$$

This rule serves to construct the text-specific definitions. (The symbol 'CAT' indicates that TInR-s belonging to the category 'definition', i.e., representations of texts describing objects have to be constructed.)

If, e.g., the object ⌜the book Peter was given by his aunt⌝ occurs in a text, the expression "the book Peter was given by his aunt" has to be constructed. It can thus be regarded as a definiendum ($TInR_{LeR}$) and can be defined in such a way that the constituents 'book', 'give', etc. are replaced by their definientia from the lexicon.

First I want to make a general remark on the rules on which I am going to comment now: The system of SR (+CR) and the LR can be used in two different ways in the generation,

(a)   either the SR-s are applied first, and the LR-s after this (this corresponds with Chomsky's way of generating sentences), or

(b)   a definiendum is taken out of the lexicon right away and is systematically expanded.

In the TeSWest (b) becomes possible because predicate-function frames serve as basic elements of the lexicon, i.e., the lexicon component constitutes the lexicon of the TGrC in such a way that the TGrC is at the same time the grammar of the lexicon.

LR 1

$$\varphi^{Cn}\{\mathscr{A}^n\} :=: \left| \begin{array}{c} \text{LeR} \\ \text{MiR} \\ \text{SeR} \end{array} \right| \quad \mathscr{E} \quad LDef_{\pi}c.$$

This rule serves to replace the connective pff-s by canonical connectives or their definientia. The 'canonical connectives' need not be 'similar' to the words of the given natural language, they can also be constructs. The substitution of the 'object-language connectives' is guaranteed by the MC.

LR 2

$$\omega :=: \left| \begin{array}{c} \text{LeR} \\ \text{MiR} \\ \text{SeR} \end{array} \right| \quad \mathscr{E} \quad \left| \begin{array}{c} LDef \\ \textit{\pounds}Def \end{array} \right|_{\omega}.$$

This rule serves to replace the ω-quantifier. My comments on LR 1 apply analogously.

LR 3

$$\lambda :=: \imath \in R_{ABB}.$$

This rule serves to replace an argument-role indicator variable by an argument-role indicator abbreviation. (The set of role indicators and consequently also the set of role indicator abbreviations (R_{ABB}) is finite.)

Remark: Argument-role indicator variables and sortal specifications function as redundancy conventions. The indicators and sortal specification have to be regarded as definienda and can be replaced by their definientia. The replacement of definientia has to be directed by special rules.

LR 4

$$\varphi^{\Delta}[[\,.\,]] :=: \begin{vmatrix} \text{LeR} \\ \text{MiR} \\ \text{SeR} \end{vmatrix} \quad \mathcal{E} \quad \begin{vmatrix} LDef \\ \text{Ł}Def \end{vmatrix}_{\pi}, ; \varphi^{\Delta} = \varphi''/\varphi'/\varphi^{\tau}.$$

This rule serves to replace the predicate function frames and the modifier function frames. (As to the structure of the frames in question, cf. the rules of the SR systems. 'τ' marks particular classes of functors, including the particular sorts within particular classes.)

LR 5a

$$\mathcal{D}\!\{\xi\mathcal{N}\,\}:=: \begin{vmatrix} \text{LeR} \\ \text{MiR} \\ \text{SeR} \end{vmatrix} \quad \mathcal{E} \quad \begin{vmatrix} LDef \\ \text{Ł}Def \end{vmatrix}_{\text{Obj}}.$$

This rule serves to replace the 'defining part' of individual-variables and mass-variables. This defining part can be a definiendum in the lexicon (cf., e.g., (14) and (15) if 'flower' and 'cloth' are definienda in the lexicon), but it can also be a definiens of MiR or SeR type.

LR 5b

$$\varphi^{\omega} :=: \begin{vmatrix} \text{LeR} \\ \text{MiR} \\ \text{SeR} \end{vmatrix} \quad \mathcal{E} \quad \begin{vmatrix} LDef \\ \text{Ł}Def \end{vmatrix}_{\pi^{\cdot\cdot}}.$$

This rule serves to replace the quantifier-specifier variable, which is a special predicate function frame.

LR 6

$$v :=: n\varepsilon \begin{vmatrix} LReg \\ \text{Ł}Reg \end{vmatrix}.$$

This rule selects an element from the name register. The rule does not handle the case that these registers can also assign definientia to the names.

2.4. *The system of inference rules*

In general, the inference rules (IR) functioning within the TGrC can be divided into three classes:

(a)   IR-s allowing the derivation of linguistic-(canonical-) syntactic parallels to logical-syntactic inferences;

(b)   IR-s allowing the derivation of par-excellence linguistic-(canonical-) syntactic inferences;

(c)   IR-s allowing the derivation of linguistic-semantic/ encyclopedic inferences (implicatures).

The system of inference rules is not yet elaborated. The examples below are only supposed to give a general idea about the structure and functioning of the rules.

(a) When constructing the linguistic parallels to logical-syntactic inferences, a decisive role is played by the connective pff-s on the one hand, and the internal structure of the T-representations on the other hand. Let us first have a look, e.g., at the way how *modus ponens* can be represented by the rules of the DiSynFC

(17)   [IMPL] $\{$is: [AND] $\{o1$: [IMPL] $\{$is: A, im: $B\}$, $o2$: $A\}$, im: $B\}$.

(The abbreviations '*is*' and '*im*' stand for the argument-role indicators 'implicans' and 'implicatum', '*o1*' and '*o2*' mark indicators of equal rank.) This connection of connectives is read (starting with the inside) as follows:

((A implies B) and A) implies B.

As a second example let us look at the utterance

(18)   *Peter is writing a book.*

In the context of this utterance the inference that Peter and the book which Peter is writing exist in the same text subworld must be avoided. The descriptive proposition constituent of the intensional-semantic representation of (18) can be constructed as follows (cf. SR 3b and SR 4):

(19) $P := [tCi] \{l: d^l, o: [tCi]\{t: d^l, o: p\}\}.$
       $p := [\text{WRITE}] \{a: \S \text{Peter}\S, eo: \S \text{a book}\S\}.$

A possible general rule to exclude the above mentioned inadmissible inference runs as follows:

    "If d^t is the time-argument of a descriptive proposition, the existence of an object having the role of an effected object in the kernel of this proposition, cannot be asserted in d^t".

We arrive at a general rule of a different kind if we operate with the world-specifications of the object-arguments (cf. SR (0β)). By using a rule operating with world-specifications of the object-arguments it can be excluded that inadmissible inferences of the type discussed in (18) are drawn, on the other hand, problems connected with so-called 'intensional contexts' can also be solved. Let us, e.g., look at (20):

(20)   *Peter is looking for a unicorn.*

A possible partial $T^\diamond$-representation which can be assigned to (20) (with object-argument indices at those argument places which matter for the ruleo to be formulated) is presented in (21):

(21) $P^W := : [tCi]\{l: I01^{\langle Uw_j\rangle}, o: [tCi]\{t: d^t_W, o: p^W\}\}$
         $p^W := : [FACT]\{e: \mathbb{C} \ o: P\}$
         $P := : [tCi]\{t: d^t, o: [tCi]\{t: d^t, o: p\}\}$
         $p := : [LOOK\text{-}FOR] \ a: \S Peter\S, o: I02^{\langle Vw_j\rangle}$

(where $I01$ stands for the place in the world (w_j) at which it is a fact that P; $I02^{\langle Vw_j\rangle}$ stands for the looked-for unicorn; $\mathbb{C}$ stands for the communicating person).

Thus the rule can be formulated as follows: If w_j is not a subworld of w_i, the existence of $\delta^{Uw_j}/\delta^{Vw_j}$ cannot be asserted in w_i. The operation with (sub)worlds enables the very general (i.e., referring to any kind of worlds) treatment of 'intensional contexts'.

(b) We can speak about par-excellence linguistic-syntactic inferences, if inferences are derived by reducing an argument frame or a complex functor (or both). The inferences 23.4 to 23.9 can be drawn from (22) by reducing the argument frame:

(22)   *Peter is writing a letter to Paul.*

In a text-subworld where the utterance "Peter is writing a letter to Paul" is accepted as a true utterance, the following utterances must also be accepted as true:

(23)   23.1 *Peter exists.*
         23.2 *Paul exists.*
         23.3 *The letter does not exist yet.*
         23.4 *Peter is writing.*

23.5 *Peter is writing a letter.*
23.6 *Peter is writing to Paul.*
23.7 *A letter is being written.*
23.8 [Somebody] *is writing to Paul.*
23.9 *A letter is being written to Paul.*

If (22) is not regarded as one propositum but as a complex structure with an internal theme-propositum structure, some of the enumerated inferential utterances change or more syntactic inferences become possible.

The derivation of these inferences can be directed within the TGrC by laying down the standard way of forming argument-configurations for pff-s with n-place functors (apart from laying down how the existential inferences are derived).

The inferences 25.2 and 25.3 are drawn by reducing the complex functor of the representation of (24):

(24)   *Peter is running very quickly.*

In a text-subworld where the utterance "Peter is running very quickly" is accepted as a true utterance, the following utterances must be accepted as true also:

(25)   25.1 *Peter exists.*
         25.2 *Peter is running quickly.*
         25.3 *Peter is running.*

My remarks about the theme-propositum structure referring to (22) apply here analogously. The drawing of these inferences can be directed by taking the requirements of these reductions into account when assigning the categories φ' and φ'' to natural language elements.

(c) We speak about linguistic-semantic/encyclopedic inferences if we draw inferences from particular units of natural language utterances on the basis of our knowledge about the objects/actions/states/processes described by these units. The inferences 27.1 to 27.5 which can be drawn from (26) are such linguistic-semantic/encyclopedic inferences:

(26)   *Peter's son will go to Paris next year to begin his studies at the Sorbonne.*

In a text-subworld where the utterance (26) is accepted as a true utterance, the following utterances have to be accepted as true also:

(27)   27.1 *Normally Peter is older than 36 years.*

27.2 *Peter's son is older than 18 years.*

27.3 *Peter's son has already passed (or will pass) the necessary exams in school (next year).*

27.4 *Peter's son is not in Paris at present or not permanently.*

27.5 *Peter's son wants to go to university.*

My remarks about the theme-propositum structure referring to (22) apply here analogously.

We draw these inferences

(α) by regarding the elements in the TInR of (26) as definienda and by replacing them by their definientia from the lexicon,

(β) by applying the canonical transformation ($\kappa\mathcal{T}$) to the structure thus received, and

(γ) by determining the independent structure parts of the transformed structure (cf. the above discussed types of inferences).

2.5. *List of formation rules*

In the preceding chapters I have briefly commented on the rules of the DiSynFC, now I want to present these rules in the form of a list. All symbols occurring in these rules are presented in a list of symbols.

The list of rules contains the communicative rules (CR), the canonical-syntactic rules (SR), and the lexicon rules (LR). It does not contain inference rules (IR) as this system is not worked out yet. The list of symbols contains variables, constants and auxiliary symbols in the following sequence:

(a) variables (Greek letters and the symbols $\mathcal{A}^n$, $\mathbb{C}_1$, $\mathbb{C}_2$, $\mathbb{C}_{\mu 1}$, $\mathbb{C}_{\mu 2}$, T, $T^\diamond$);

(b) constants (Latin letters and the symbol θ):

(c) auxiliary symbols (includes all non-alphabetic signs and the symbols $\kappa\mathcal{T}$, $\Theta\mathcal{T}$, $L\mathcal{T}$, $\neg\mathcal{T}$, IND, a, ε, $\mathcal{E}$)

2.5.1. *List of rules*

CR 1a $\Sigma^{\mu P} :=: [f]\{l: \delta^l_{\mu P}, o: [f]\{t: \delta^t_{\mu P}, o: \pi^{\mu P}\}\}.$

1b $\pi^{\mu P} :=: [([([\varphi''])\varphi'])\varphi^{\mu P}]\{s: \mathbb{C}_{\mu 1}, g: \mathbb{C}_{\mu 2}, o: \Pi^{\mu W}\}.$

2a $\Pi^{\mu W} :=: [f]\{l: \delta^l_{\mu W}, o: [f]\{t: \delta^t_{\mu W}, o: \pi^{\mu W}\}\}.$

2b $\pi^{\mu W} :=: [([([\varphi''])\varphi'])\varphi^{\mu W}]\{\lambda_1: \mathbb{C}_{\mu 1}/\mathbb{C}_{\mu 2}, (\lambda_2: \alpha^\sigma_2), o: \Pi^\mathbb{C}\}.$

3a $\Pi^\mathbb{C} :=: [f]\{l: \delta\mathfrak{k}, o: [f]\{t: \delta\mathfrak{k}, o: \pi^\mathbb{C}\}\}.$

3b $\pi^\mathbb{C} :=: [([([\varphi''])\varphi'])\varphi^\mathbb{C}]\{s: \mathbb{C}_1, g: \mathbb{C}_2, mo: \delta^\mathbb{C}\}.$

SR 0a $\mathrm{TB}_{\shortparallel} :=: \langle \mathrm{TInR}_{\shortparallel}, T\Omega\rangle.$

'a' indicates whether the given units belong to type LeR, MiR, or SeR; $T\Omega$ contains the mapping information representing the relationship between the given TInR and its linear manifestation.

0b   TInR $:=: \langle T^\diamond, \text{TWD} \rangle$

(0a) TWD $:=: \langle\langle ., w, . \rangle, \langle ., \text{TW}^w, . \rangle, \text{TWaN}, \underset{\text{CAT}}{\text{U}} [[., \text{TW}^w, .]] \rangle.$

(0β) $w \; \S = \S \; \langle d_P^l, d_P^t, p^P, d_W^l, d_W^t, p^W \rangle.$

(0γ) $TW^w :=: \langle\langle ., d, . \rangle, \langle ., d^l, . \rangle, \langle ., d^t, . \rangle, \langle ., P^\diamond, . \rangle, \langle ., \text{ThN}, . \rangle,$
        $M_{RR} \rangle^w.$

(01) ThN: Out of the predicate frames which contain a given 'd' as one of their arguments ordered sets have to be formed. These ordered sets are the so-called 'thematic nets' (ThN). Their number is identical with the number of the different δ-s.

(02) M_{RR}: For each thematic net it has to be specified, what other arguments, apart from the 'd' determining the specific net, occur in its predicate frames. These informations form a referent-relations matrix (M_{RR}).

(03) TWaN: Based on the w-s and the M_{RR} it has to be determined, what other text-subworld(s) can be reached by what text-subworld and how. These so-called 'accessibility-relations' existing between particular text-subworld form the text-world accessibility net (TWaN).

(04) $\underset{\text{CAT}}{\text{U}} [[., \text{TW}^w, .]]$: The particular text-subworld description (cf. SR (0γ)) have to be amalgamated according to the categories occurring in these descriptions (CAT). This amalgamation will result in the complete (complex) text-world description ($\underset{\text{CAT}}{\text{U}} [[., \text{TW}^w, .]]$).

(The degree of complexity of the TWD can vary, because φ^n in SR 4 can be a descriptively used communicative functor allowing for a special kind of recursivity. Even though acceptability functions as limitation for recursive embedding in standard contexts, TInR-s (and consequently also $T^\diamond$-s and TWD-s) may contain several recursive embeddings. In case of such TInR-s so-called 'communicative nets' (CN) are needed to represent the communicative situations (who communicates what to whom) on the particular levels of embedding. In this case the TWD-s have to be constructed in accordance with the particular CN-s as descriptions of particular narrated text worlds.)

1a $\quad T^{\diamond} \underset{(*)}{:=:} \left| \begin{array}{l} T \\ [\varphi^{Cn}]\{\lambda_1: T_1^{\diamond}, \ldots, \lambda_n: T_n^{\diamond}\} \end{array} \right|_{//(\kappa\mathcal{F})\Theta\mathcal{F}(\neg\mathcal{F})}$

1b $\quad T_{\text{IND}} \underset{\text{IND}}{:=:} [f]\{l: \delta_P^l, o: [f]\{t: \delta_P^t, o: \left| \begin{array}{l} \pi^P \\ \pi^{PA} \end{array} \right| \}$.

$1c_1 \quad \pi^P :=: [([([\varphi''])\varphi'])\varphi^P]\{s: \mathbb{C}_1, g: \mathbb{C}_2, o: \Pi^{W\diamond}\}$.

$1c_2 \quad \pi^{PA} :=: [([([\varphi''])\varphi'])\varphi^{PAn}]\{\mathscr{A}^n\}\}$.

2a $\quad \Pi^{W\diamond} :=: \left| \begin{array}{l} \Pi^W \\ [\varphi^{Cn}]\{\lambda_1: \Pi_1^{W\diamond}, \ldots, \lambda_n: \Pi_n^{W\diamond}\} \end{array} \right|$.

2b $\quad \Pi^W :=: [f]\{l: \delta_W^l, o: [f]\{t: \delta_W^t, o: \pi^W\}\}$

2c $\quad \pi^W :=: [([([\varphi''])\varphi'])\varphi^W]\{\lambda_1: \mathbb{C}_1/\mathbb{C}_2, (\lambda_2: \alpha_2^\sigma), o: \Pi^\diamond\}$

3a $\quad \Pi^\diamond :=: \left| \begin{array}{l} \Pi \\ [\varphi^{Cn}]\{\lambda_1: \Pi_1^\diamond, \ldots, \lambda_n: \Pi_n^\diamond\} \end{array} \right|$.

3b $\quad \Pi :=: [f]\{l: \delta^l, o: [f]\{t: \delta^t, o: \pi\}\}$.

4 $\quad \pi :=: [([([\varphi''])\varphi'])\varphi^n]\{\mathscr{A}^n\}$

5a $\quad \mathscr{A}^n :=: \lambda_1: \alpha_1^\sigma, \ldots, \lambda_n: \alpha_n^\sigma$.

5b $\quad \alpha^\sigma \underset{\sigma}{:=:} \left| \begin{array}{l} \delta^{\sigma\diamond} \\ T^\diamond \\ \Pi^{\zeta\diamond} \\ \pi^\zeta \end{array} \right.$

6a $\quad \delta^{\sigma\diamond} :=: \left| \begin{array}{l} \delta^\sigma \\ [\varphi^{Cn}]\{\lambda_1: \delta_1^{\sigma\diamond}, \ldots, \lambda_n: \delta_n^{\sigma\diamond}\} \end{array} \right|$.

6b $\quad \delta^\sigma :=: \left| \begin{array}{l} N\mathcal{N}_T \\ I\mathcal{N}_T \\ M\mathcal{N}_T \end{array} \right|$.

7a $\quad N\mathcal{N}_T :=: v^{\langle \cdot \cdot, w, \cdot \cdot \rangle}$.

7b $\quad I\mathcal{N}_T :=:$

$$\left| \begin{array}{l} [[\omega_{(i)}{}^\smallfrown\varphi^\omega[[\xi\mathcal{N}_L|\mathscr{D}\{\xi\mathcal{N}_L\}]]]_{//L\mathcal{F}}]]^{\langle\langle \cdot\cdot, U(\{\delta\})w, \cdot\cdot\rangle, \langle \cdot\cdot, V(\{\delta\})w, \cdot\cdot\rangle\rangle} \\ \\ [[\left| \begin{array}{l} \theta \\ A_{(i)} \end{array} \right.{}^\smallfrown\varphi^\omega[[\xi\mathcal{N}_L|\mathscr{D}\{\xi\mathcal{N}_L\}]]]_{//L\mathcal{F}}]]^{\langle \cdot\cdot, w, \cdot\cdot\rangle} \end{array} \right|.$$

7c $M\mathcal{N}_T :=:$

$$\left| \begin{array}{l} [[\omega^\frown\varphi^\omega[[\xi\mathcal{N}_L|\mathcal{D}\{\xi\mathcal{N}_L\}]]_{//L\mathcal{F}}]]^{\langle\langle..U(\{\delta\})w,.\rangle,\langle..,V(\{\delta\})w,.\rangle\rangle} \\ [[\left|\begin{array}{c}\theta\\A\end{array}\right|^\frown\varphi^\omega[[\xi\mathcal{N}_L|\mathcal{D}\{\xi\mathcal{N}_L\}]]_{//L\mathcal{F}}]]^{\langle..,w,..\rangle} \end{array}\right|$$

LR 0 $\text{\L}Def :=: [[\text{TInR}_{\text{LeR}} =_{Def} .. =_{Def} \text{TInR}_{\text{SeR}}]].$
        $\underset{\text{CAT}}{}$

1    $\varphi^{Cn}\{\mathscr{A}^n\} :=: \left|\begin{array}{l}\text{LeR}\\\text{MiR}\\\text{SeR}\end{array}\right| \mathscr{E} \; LDef_{\pi^c}.$

2    $\omega :=: \left|\begin{array}{l}\text{LeR}\\\text{MiR}\\\text{SeR}\end{array}\right| \mathscr{E} \; \left|\begin{array}{l}LDef\\\text{\L}Def\end{array}\right|_\omega.$

3    $\lambda :=: \imath\varepsilon R_{ABB}.$

4    $\varphi^\Delta[[.]] :=: \left|\begin{array}{l}\text{LeR}\\\text{MiR}\\\text{SeR}\end{array}\right| \mathscr{E} \; \left|\begin{array}{l}LDef\\\text{\L}Def\end{array}\right|_{\pi^\Delta}; \; \varphi^\Delta = \varphi''/\varphi'/\varphi^\tau.$
        $\underset{\Delta}{}$

5a $\mathcal{D}\{\xi\mathcal{N}_L\} :=: \left|\begin{array}{l}\text{LeR}\\\text{MiR}\\\text{SeR}\end{array}\right| \mathscr{E} \; \left|\begin{array}{l}LDef\\\text{\L}Def\end{array}\right|_{\text{Obj}}.$

5b $\varphi^\omega :=: \left|\begin{array}{l}\text{LeR}\\\text{MiR}\\\text{SeR}\end{array}\right| \mathscr{E} \; \left|\begin{array}{l}LDef\\\text{\L}Def\end{array}\right|_{\pi^\omega}.$

6    $\nu :=: n\varepsilon \left|\begin{array}{l}LReg\\\text{\L}Reg\end{array}\right|.$

2.5.2. List of symbols

(a) Variables

$\mathscr{A}^n$	configuration of n-arguments
$\mathbb{C}_1, \mathbb{C}_2$	communicators (communicating persons)
$\mathbb{C}_{\mu1}, \mathbb{C}_{\mu2}$	meta-communicators
$\mathcal{D}\{\xi\mathcal{N}_L\}$	expression (definiendum or definiens) in the Lexicon (of type L or $\text{\L}$) of a natural language
α^σ	argument
δ^c	object-argument (object-argument of a communicative pff)
$\delta^{\text{\L}}$	object-argument (local-argument of a communicative position)

δ_P^l object-argument (local-argument of a performative-modal proposition)

δ_W^l object-argument (local-argument of a world-constitutive proposition)

$\delta_{\mu P}^l$ object-argument (local-argument of a meta performative-modal proposition)

$\delta_{\mu W}^l$ object-argument (local-argument of a meta world-constitutive proposition)

δ_C^t object-argument (temporal-argument of a communicative proposition)

δ_P^t object-argument (temporal-argument of a performative-modal proposition)

δ_W^t object-argument (temporal-argument of a world-constitutive proposition)

$\delta_{\mu P}^t$ object-argument (temporal-argument of a meta performative-modal proposition)

$\delta_{\mu W}^t$ object-argument (temporal-argument of a meta world-constitutive proposition)

δ^σ object-argument of type σ

$\delta^{\sigma\diamond}$ complex object-argument of type σ

φ^C functor of a communicative pff

φ^{Cn} functor of a connective pff

$\varphi^{Cn}\{\mathscr{A}^n\}$ connective pff

φ^n functor of a descriptive pff

φ^P functor of a performative-modal pff

φ^{PAn} functor of a performative-active pff

φ^W functor of a world-constitutive pff

$\varphi^{\mu P}$ functor of a meta performative-modal pff

$\varphi^{\mu W}$ functor of a meta world-constitutive pff

φ^ω quantifier-specifier (functor of a special descriptive pff)

$\varphi^\Delta[[\,.\,]]$ predicate function frame (metavariable; $\Delta = '/''/\tau/)$

φ^τ functor (metavariable; 'τ' stands for a syntactic and/or semantic type)

φ' modifier of a functor

φ'' modifier of a modifier

λ argument-role indicator

ν proper-name

ω quantifier of type ω with a group reading

$\omega_{(i)}$	quantifier of type ω with an enumeration reading
π	descriptive pff
π^C	connective pff
$\pi^{\mathbb{C}}$	communicative pff
π^P	performative-modal pff
π^{PA}	performative-active pff
π^W	world-constitutive pff
$\pi^{\mu P}$	meta performative-modal pff
$\pi^{\mu W}$	meta world-constitutive pff
π^ω	quantifier-specifier pff
π^ζ	pff belonging to the type ζ (metavariable)
π^Δ	mff (modifier-function frame) or pff; metavariable, $\Delta = '/''/\tau$)
Π	descriptive proposition
Π^C	communicative proposition
Π^W	world-constitutive proposition
$\Pi^{W\diamond}$	complex world-constitutive proposition
$\Pi^{\mu W}$	meta world-constitutive proposition
$\Pi^{\zeta\diamond}$	complex proposition belonging to the type ζ (metavariable)
$\Pi^\diamond$	complex descriptive proposition
σ	semantic type (sortal specification)
ζ	syntactic type and sortal specification
$\xi\mathcal{N}_L$	object-class variable
$\Sigma^{\mu P}$	meta performative-modal proposition
T	atomic text
$T^\diamond$	complex text

(b) *Constants*

A	universal quantifier with a group-reading
$A_{(i)}$	universal quantifier with an enumeration reading
CN	communicative net
d	object-argument (object-argument of a descriptive proposition)
d_P^l	object-argument (local-argument of a performative proposition)
d_W^l	object-argument (local-argument of a world-constitutive proposition)
d_P^l	object-argument (temporal-argument of a performative proposition)

d_W^t	object-argument (temporal-argument of a world constitutive proposition)
f	functor constant ('it is the case')
g	goal-object role (argument-role indicator)
$I\mathcal{N}_T$	individual-index (standing for an object-description)
l	local-object role (argument-role indicator)
LDef	definition in the lexicon of a natural language
ŁDef	definition in a text-specific lexicon
LeR	lexical representation (a definiendum or a representation containing definienda only)
mo	message-object role (argument-role indicator)
M_{RR}	matrix of referent-relations
MiR	mixed representation (a definiens or a representation containing LeR-s and SeR-s)
$M\mathcal{N}_T$	mass-index (standing for an object-description)
n	proper name
$N\mathcal{N}_T$	proper-name index
o	object-role (argument-role indicator)
p^P	performative-modal predicate frame
p^W	world-constitutive predicate frame
$P^\diamond$	complex (descriptive) proposition
$\imath$	argument-role indicator (an abbreviation)
R_{ABB}	set of argument-role indicator abbreviation
s	source-object role (argument-role indicator)
SeR	semantic representation (a definiens or a representation containing only semantic primitives)
t	temporal-object role (argument-role indicator)
TB	text basis
ThN	thematic net
TInR	intensional-semantic representation of a text
$T\Omega$	mapping information
TW^w	representation of the text-subworld w
$TWaN$	text-world accessibility net
TWD	text-world description
U	definitizer
V	indefinitizer
w	text-subworld label
θ	zero quantifier

(c) *Auxiliary symbols*

IND	index (in general a natural number)
$L\mathcal{T}$	lexicon-index transformation
$\neg\mathcal{T}$	negation transformation
$\kappa\mathcal{T}$	canonical transformation
$\Theta\mathcal{T}$	theme-proposition transformation
a	semantic type
$\in$	element of
$\mathscr{E}$	structural constituent (definiendum or definiens) of
U CAT	marks category-preserving amalgamation
$=_{Def}$	defined in Lexicon (definiendum $=_{Def}$ definiens)
$:=:$	bi-directional rewriting rule
$:=:_{''}$	marks semantic-type preserving bi-directional rewriting rule
$:=:$ IND	marks index-guided bi-directional rewriting rule
$:=:$ CAT	marks categorically correct bi-directional rewriting rule
$:=:_{\sigma}$	marks sortally correct bi-directional rewriting rule
$:=:_{(*)}$	marks interpretation-marking bi-directional rewriting rule
$:=:_{\Delta}$	marks syntactic-type preserving bi-directional rewriting rule
$\S=\S$	non well-formed bi-directional rewriting rule
$[-]\{-\}$	[functor] {argument-configuration}
$[[-]-]$	complex functor, [[modifier] functor]
$[[[-]-]-]$	complex functor, [[modifier-of-modifier]modifier]functor]
$[[\ ]]$	mark parts/units belonging together
$(\ )$	mark facultative units
$\{\ \}$	mark parts/units belonging together
$|$	connects a variable with its 'definition'
$/$	select one of the choices
$|\ |$	select one of the choices
$//$	assigns operation symbols to a rule
$\langle .,x,.\rangle$	$\langle$ordered set of x-s$\rangle$ ('x' is a metavariable)
$\widehat{\ }$	concatenation

3. REMARKS ON THE MAPPING COMPONENT (MC)

It is the task of the Mapping Component to determine unambiguously the admissible $\langle$TInR, TLiM$\rangle$-pairs. The MC must meet the following requirements:

(a)   In case of synthesis it must enable
   (α) the derivation of such TLiM-s that manifest the intension represented by the given TInR and only this;
   (β) the derivation of such TLiM-s that manifest the intension represented by the given TInR, but are ambiguous;
   (γ) the derivation of such TLiM-s that do not entirely manifest the intension represented by the given TInR, however, when analyzing these derived TLiM-s among the admissible TInR-s that can be assigned to these TLiM-s, the originally given TInR can also be reconstructed.
(b)   In case of analysis it must enable the determination of the appropriate TInR (or TInR-s) with respect to all TLiM-s enumerated in (a)
(c)   Apart from all that it must enable the derivation of those TLIM-s assignable to the given DiSynInf-s, which manifest the intension represented by the DiSynInf and only those.

The MC can meet these requirements only if

(a)   it has a rule system that based on the structural properties of the TInR-s can determine which information $(T\Omega)$ directs the derivation of the admissible TLiM-s (cf. (a) and (b)),
(b)   it has a rule system which can carry out the morphological and syntactic operations necessary for the synthesis of any $\langle$TInR, $T\Omega\rangle$-pair, based on the TInR (more exactly on the $T^{\diamond}$) (this not only applies for atomic texts but also for highly complex texts).
(c)   it has a rule system for analysis which can assign the admissible $\langle$TInR, $T\Omega\rangle$-pair(s) to the given TLiM-s.

It is obvious that the rule system referred to in (a) is the most important one because the rule systems referred to in (b) and (c) presuppose the existence of (a); but the construction of (a) presupposes substantial information about the structure of the TInR-s.

Whereas the rules directing the construction of TInR-s are independent of particular natural languages (or put otherwise: they can operate with the lexicon of any natural language having the structure required by the TGrC), the MC rules are natural language specific. The rule systems of the MC mentioned above have not yet been elaborated for any natural language.

4. CLOSING REMARKS

In this paper I have discussed the structure of the grammatical component of a (formal semiotic) text theory (TeSWeST), which consists of a grammatical, a world-semantic and a lexicon component. I would like to draw attention to the following points:

(a) the Grammatical Component (TGrC) can also function independently within the TeSWeST and provide a complete linguistic description of natural language texts. The exclusive task of the World-Semantic Component (WSeC) consists in assigning appropriate denotata ('worlds' as interpretations) to the representations constructed by the Grammatical Component.

(b) Even though the Disambiguating Syntactic Formation Component (DiSynFC) could construct formulae containing only canonical-syntactic symbols, in generation as well as in analysis it is normally the case that we use the canonical-syntactic and lexicon rules in any sequence. Within the TeSWeST it is therefore not really appropriate to talk about an independent syntactic component (in analogy with logical syntaxes). The Grammatical Component (TGrC) of the TeSWeST and the Lexicon of a natural language form a complex consisting of 'syntax plus intensional semantics', the representations constructed by the TGrC plus Lexicon are intensional-semantic text representations (TInR-s).

(c) It follows from (a) and (b) that the Grammatical Component requires a special constructed Logico-Syntactic Formation Component (LoSynFC) in the World-Semantic Component of the TeSWeST.

The LoSynFC must be able to represent all the information contained in the intensional-semantic text representations. Only if we have a so structured LoSynFC can we speak of a Translation Component (TC) which guarantees the functioning of the TeSWeST, i.e., the combination of the Grammatical Component with the World-Semantic Component (cf. Figure 1).

Universität Bielefeld

NOTES

[1] For information about the general structure and particular aspects of the TeSWeST, cf.
Petöfi (1973), Petöfi (1975a), Petöfi and Rieser (1974), and Rieser (1976).
[2] The first detailed description of the grammatical component of the TeSWeST is contained in
Petöfi (1973). The rule system was used to analyse several ordinary and scientific language
texts between 1973 and 1975 (within the project 'Colloquial language — scientific language',
financially supported by the Werner-Reimers-Stiftung, Bad Homburg v.d.H.). Rieser (1976)
constitutes one of the most detailed analyses. The experiences gained during this work within
the project contributed in the first place to a revision of the rule system. The revised version is
presented in this paper.
[3] For information about the theme-propositum structure in general and problems connected
with theme-propositum structure, negation, and inferences, cf. Petöfi (1975b).
[4] For information about the introduction of argument labels by definitions, cf. Heydrich
(1976).

BIBLIOGRAPHY

Heydrich, W. (1976), 'Zur Einführung von Argument-labels', in Petöfi and Bredemeier (eds.),
Das Lexikon in der Grammatik — die Grammatik im Lexikon, Papers in Textlinguistics,
Vol. 13, pp. 439–492, Buske, Hamburg, 1977.
Petöfi, J. S. (1973), 'Towards an Empirically Motivated Grammatical Theory of Verbal Texts',
in Petöfi and Rieser (eds.), *Studies in Text Grammar*, Reidel, Dordrecht, pp. 205–275.
Petöfi, J. S. (1975a), *Vers une théorie partielle du texte*, Papers in Textlinguistics, Vol. 9, Buske,
Hamburg.
Petöfi, J. S. (1975b), *"Modalité" et "topic-comment" dans une grammaire textuelle à base
logique*, Papers in Textlinguistics, Vol. 9, pp. 35–80, Buske, Hamburg.
Petöfi, J. S. (1976), 'A formal Semiotic Text Theory as an Integrated Theory of Natural
Language (Methodological Remarks)', in Dressler (ed.), *Current Trends in Textlinguistics*,
Research in Text Theory, Vol. 2, pp. 35–46, W. de Gruyter, Berlin and New York, 1978.
Petöfi, J. S. and Rieser, H. (1974), *Probleme der modelltheoretischen Interpretation von Texten*,
Papers in Textlinguistics, Vol. 7, Buske, Hamburg.
Rieser, H. (1976), *Aspekte einer partiellen Texttheorie*, Untersuchungen zur Textgrammatik
mit "nicht-linear" festgelegter Basis unter besonderer Berücksichtigung des Lexikon und
des Fachsprachenproblems, Manuscript, Bielefeld.

ROLAND HAUSSER AND DIETMAR ZAEFFERER

QUESTIONS AND ANSWERS IN A CONTEXT-DEPENDENT MONTAGUE GRAMMAR

0. INTRODUCTION

A successful formal reconstruction of a fragment of a natural language like the one presented in Montague (1973)[1] calls for extensions in various directions. Two of the most challenging ones among them are the inclusion of non-declarative sentence moods and a treatment of context-dependency beyond the interpretation of tense. The present paper advances some steps in both directions since we believe that dealing with context-dependency is a prerequisite for a satisfactory treatment of interrogatives. While transformationalists tend to regard interrogatives in isolation,[2] scholars interested in the semantics of natural language, both outside the Montague school (e.g., Keenan and Hull, 1973) and inside (e.g., Hamblin, 1973), have noted the relation that links up questions with their possible answers. Montague himself suggests[3] that a syntax and semantics of interrogatives should provide a characterization of the semantic content of a correct answer. Whether a certain expression counts as a correct answer, however, depends on the context in which it is uttered. An appropriate context has to contain an utterance of a corresponding interrogative expression. Therefore we shall tackle the problem from the rear. First we ask: What are the expressions that may serve as answers when uttered in an appropriate context and how are they interpreted? And then: How are interrogatives to be analysed in order to make sure that each corresponding answer is assigned a correct interpretation? Our attempt may thus be regarded as a first step toward a formal grammar of discourse.

1. TYPES OF QUESTIONS AND ANSWERS

Grammarians usually classify interrogatives into the following three main categories:

(A)   Yes–no questions
(B)   Alternative questions
(C)   WH-questions.

339

F. Guenthner and S. J. Schmidt (eds.), Formal Semantics and Pragmatics
for Natural Languages, 339–358. All Rights Reserved.

Category (C) may be subclassified according to what element of the sentence is asked for:

(C1)   the subject
(C2)   the direct object
(C3)   a subject complement
(C4)   an object complement
(C5)   an adverbial.

Category (C5) comprises again a number of subcategories we shall not enumerate here. In the following, we shall restrict ourselves to the most important types, namely (A) (yes–no questions), (C1) and (C2) (which we shall call term questions), and those subcategories of (C5) (adverbial questions) that use the question words *how, where, when,* and *why.*

Let us examine now the expressions that may serve as answers to these types of questions. Consider for example (1), an instance of a yes–no question:

(1)   Does John love Mary?

With respect to a context created by an utterance of (1), or, as we shall also say, in the context of (1), the following expressions may be used in giving an answer:

(1a)   Yes.
(1b)   He does.
(1c)   He does so.
(1d)   He loves her.
(1e)   He loves Mary.
(1f)   John loves her.
(1g)   John loves Mary.
(1h)   Yes, (1b).
...   ...
(1m)   Yes, (1g).

Neglecting the different degrees of acceptability of (1a)–(1m), we may state that they all have two features in common:

(i)   they commit the speaker (disregarding irony, etc.) to the truth of (1g), and
(ii)   they supply just the information required by the utterance of (1).

This contrasts them with answers like (1n) and (1o):

(1n)   Yes, certainly.

(1o)   Yes, probably.

which give more and less, respectively, information than required and which may therefore be called over- and under-answers, respectively. Since these will presumably have to be analysed on the basis of exact answers, we feel entitled not to treat them here.

Looking through our list of possible answers to (1) one can notice that there is an increase of redundancy and explicitness from (1a) to (1g) and again from (1h) to (1m). We may call therefore (1a) a minimal or non-redundant answer and (1g) a redundant answer. (1b)–(1f) are then partially redundant answers, and (1h)–(1m) combine each a non-redundant answer with a (partially) redundant one.

Regarding the semantics of (1a) through (1m), it is clear that they are equivalent only with respect to certain contexts, namely those produced by an utterance of (1). If we replace (1) by (2),

(2)   Does Bill love Mary?

(1a)–(1e) and (1h)–(1k) are still equivalent to each other, but not to (1f), (1g), (1l), and (1m). The former two still express the same proposition as they did with respect to the first context, but they have now a different illocutionary force insofar as they cannot count as answers anymore.[4] The latter two become somewhat odd in the new context.

Things are very similar with respect to term questions and their answers. Consider the following examples:

(3)   Who dates Mary?

(3a)   Bill.

(3b)   Bill does.

(3c)   Bill does so.

(3d)   Bill dates her.

(3e)   Bill dates Mary.

Again we may distinguish between a minimal, non-redundant answer like (3a), partially redundant answers like (3b)–(3d) and a (fully) redundant answer like (3e). There are, however, no answers to term questions corresponding to the (h)–(m) cases of example (1).

Concerning adverbial questions, the kinds of expressions that may play the rôle of an appropriate answer are demonstrated by the following example:

(4)   When will Mary meet John?
(4a)   At seven p.m.
(4b)   She will do so at seven p.m.
(4c)   She will meet him at seven p.m.
(4d)   She will meet John at seven p.m.
(4e)   Mary will do so at seven p.m.
(4f)   Mary will meet him at seven p.m.
(4g)   Mary will meet John at seven p.m.

Again, there is a scale of increasing redundancy from (4a) to (4g). And again the truth value of the answer expression will depend on the question in the context of which it is uttered, except for (4g). In this respect (4g) behaves like (3e) and (1g). This shows that redundant answers are not very interesting from a semantical point of view since their semantic representation is identical to that of ordinary declarative sentences. In fact, they are ordinary declarative sentences and the question with respect to which they are interpreted determines only the illocutionary force that they carry. Their answerhood depends on the relation between their intension and that of the question expression, and both can be established independently. The situation is different, as we have seen, with the other kinds of answers, where not only the illocutionary force depends on the meaning of the question expression but also the respective meaning the answer expression has. Since both, redundant and non-redundant answers are possible, and since non-redundant answers are generally much more natural, we hold that no serious theory of questions and answers should restrict itself to a treatment of redundant answers alone, and that it should be able to handle both. As shown above, redundant answers represent no problem with respect to semantic interpretation; the problems they pose concern only the theory of speech acts. The remaining answer-types, on the other hand, do present interesting problems concerning semantic interpretation. We may distinguish between the (a)-cases, which we called minimal answers, and the remaining ones, which share the feature of containing one or more unbound or exophoric pro-forms. But the problem of exophoric pro-forms is not limited to answer-expressions alone, it may be viewed as an instance of the general problem of determining the reference for pro-forms. We shall not go deeper into this matter here (cf. Hausser, 1977), but it seems that once this problem is solved, all partially redundant answers may be reduced to redundant ones. Therefore it is the phenomenon of minimal answers that represents the basic and crucial problem to be solved by a semantic theory of questions and answers. A final look at alternative questions and their answers may demonstrate now our reason for neglecting them in this context. Consider (5)–(5f):

(5)   Does Mary sleep or is John sick?
(5a)   Mary sleeps.
(5b)   John is sick.
(5c)   The former.
(5d)   The latter.
(5e)   Yes.
(5f)   No.

The example shows that with respect to alternative questions, only redundant answers (5a, b) or answers with exophoric proforms (5c, d) are possible, but not minimal answers of the yes–no type.

2. EXTENDING THE PTQ-LOGIC INTO A CONTEXT-DEPENDENT SYSTEM

While the fragment of English presented in 'English as a formal language' (Montague, 1974, Chapter 6) is given a direct semantic interpretation, the fragments contained in 'Universal grammar' (Montague, 1974, Chapter 7) and in PTQ are (for the sake of perspicuity) interpreted indirectly via auxiliary languages of typed intensional logic. The 'pragmatic'[5] aspect of the notion of truth defined in PTQ lies in the fact that it is made relative not only to a given model or interpretation, as usual in model theoretical semantics, but also to a so-called point of reference $\langle i, j \rangle$, consisting of a possible world and a moment of time. This will not suffice, however, for the interpretation of minimal answers, since, as we have pointed out in the preceding section, their truth value depends on the meaning of a previously uttered interrogative expression. Therefore we have to extend the PTQ-logic into a context-dependent system which specifies for each point of reference the meaning of the preceding utterance. We could do that, following a suggestion by D. Lewis (1970), by simply adding a further coordinate, a 'previous discourse coordinate', to the point of reference, but this approach would be exposed to M. J. Cresswell's objection that it leads to an inflation of coordinates: "why not a country, climate, religion, or 'previous drinks' coordinate?" (Cresswell, 1973, p. 111). We therefore prefer another way of extending the PTQ-logic[6] which comprises the following three steps.

First we replace the interpretation or intensional model by a context-model. We define a *context-model* as an ordered triple $\langle \mathscr{A}, C, ca \rangle$, where $\mathscr{A}$ is an interpretation having the form $\langle A, I, J, \leqslant, F \rangle$ and being defined as in PTQ (p. 258), C is the set of contexts, and ca is a function from $I \times J$ into C ('ca' stands for 'context-assignment function'). C in turn is defined as $\{c_0\} \cup \bigcup_{a \in \text{Type}} ME_a$, where ME_a or the set of meaningful expressions of type a is defined as in PTQ (p. 256f.) and c_0 stands for the empty context, i.e., a context without previous discourse. (We could, of course, give C a much more complex structure in order to account for other phenomena than immediate previous-discourse dependency, but the simple formulation given here will be sufficient for the restricted aims of this paper.)

The second step of our extension of the PTQ-logic introduces a new set of basic symbols, namely the union of the sets $C\text{-Var}_a$ ($a \in \text{Type}$) or the set of *context-variables*. If n is any natural number and $a \in \text{Type}$, then $c\text{-}v_{n,a}$ is the nth context-variable of type a. These additional basic expressions permit us to define a larger set of meaningful expressions for each type a, which we call ME_a'. The definition of ME_a' runs like that of ME_a (p. 256f.) with the following two differences:

(i) The first clause of the definition is replaced by (1'):

(1')   Every variable, constant, and context-variable of type a is in ME_a'.

(ii) In the remaining clauses, each occurrence of 'ME_a' is replaced by 'ME_a''. It follows that ME_a is a proper subset of ME_a' and that $ME_a' \backslash ME_a$[7] consists of those meaningful expressions which contain at least one context-variable. It may be called the set of context-dependent meaningful expressions.

In the third step of our extension, the respective definitions for extension and intension of a meaningful expression are now adjusted to ME_a'. Let $\mathscr{L}$ be a context-model having the form $\langle \mathscr{A}, C, ca \rangle$. Suppose further that g is an $\mathscr{A}$-assignment as defined in PTQ (p. 258). If $\alpha \in ME_a'$ and $\langle i, j \rangle \in I \times J$, then $\alpha^{\mathscr{L}, i, j, g}$ is to be the *extension* of α with respect to $\mathscr{L}, i, j$, and g, where $\alpha^{\mathscr{L}, i, j, g}$ is defined as follows:

(1)   If α is a constant, then $\alpha^{\mathscr{L}, i, j, g}$ is $F(\alpha)(\langle i, j \rangle)$.
(2)   If α is a variable, then $\alpha^{\mathscr{L}, i, j, g}$ is $g(\alpha)$.
(3)   If $\alpha \in C\text{-Var}_a$, then $\alpha^{\mathscr{L}, i, j, g}$ is $[ca(\langle i, j \rangle)]^{\mathscr{L}, i, j, g}$, in case $ca(\langle i, j \rangle) \in ME_a$, and $\alpha^{\mathscr{L}, i, j, g}$ is u else (u stands for undefined).

The following clauses (4)–(11) are systematic modifications of the clauses

(3)–(10) in PTQ, p. 258f. (including Thomason's amendments in fn. 10 on p. 259). We obtain our modified clauses from the corresponding original ones by (i) replacing each occurrence of 'ME' by 'ME'', (ii) replacing each superscript $^{\mathscr{A},i,j,g}$ or $^{\mathscr{A},i,j,g'}$ by $^{\mathscr{L},i,j,g}$ or $^{\mathscr{L},i,j,g'}$, respectively, and (iii) adding 'in case $\alpha^{\mathscr{L},i,j,g}$, $\beta^{\mathscr{L},i,j,g}$ are not u, and $\gamma^{\mathscr{L},i,j,g}$ is u else', where α, β, and γ are the meaningful expressions mentioned in the antecedens and consequens, respectively. If $\phi \in ME'_t$, then ϕ is an *interpretable formula* with respect to $\mathscr{L}$, i, and j if and only if $\phi^{\mathscr{L},i,j,g}$ is not u. If ϕ is an interpretable formula with respect to $\mathscr{L}$, i, and j, then ϕ is *true* with respect to that context-model and point of reference if and only if $\phi^{\mathscr{L},i,j,g}$ is 1 for every $\mathscr{A}$-assignment g. The *intension* $\alpha^{\mathscr{L},g}$ of α relative to $\mathscr{L}$ and g is then defined as that function h with domain $I \times J$ such that whenever $\langle i, j \rangle \in I \times J$, $h(\langle i, j \rangle) = \alpha^{\mathscr{L},i,j,g}$, in case $\alpha^{\mathscr{L},i,j,g}$ is not u, and $\alpha^{\mathscr{L},g}$ is u else.

The fact that our system allows for the case that the extension of a meaningful expression is undefined has obviously somewhat tedious technical consequences and calls for a justification. We included this feature in order to account for the fact that a minimal answer is interpretable only with respect to an appropriate context, i.e., a context built up by a suitable question. In particular, all minimal answers are uninterpretable with respect to the empty context c_0.

3. TERM QUESTIONS AND THEIR MINIMAL ANSWERS

As we have demonstrated in Section 1, the minimal answer to a term question consists in an utterance of a term phrase. Consider the following example:

(6)   What does Mary imagine?

(6a)   A dragon.[8]

But we have stated also that an expression like (6a), when uttered in a context like (6), denotes a truth value. It is true exactly in case Mary does imagine a dragon and false if she does not. How can these observations be combined in a formally consistent way? Note that there is a small but important difference between the term 'a dragon' and the expression (6a): The latter ends with a full stop, which indicates a falling tone and makes the utterance count as a declarative one. We shall therefore assign expressions like (6a) the category t (declarative sentence), and translate them into expressions of type t (formulas). Since the intension of (6a) depends partly on the intension of the term 'a dragon' and partly on the context, we have to translate it, according to the principle of compositionality, into a context-dependent meaningful expression containing the translation of 'a dragon'. The simplest way of doing this is adding a context-variable of fitting type to the intensionalized term-translation. We translate thus the minimal answer (6a) into (6a'):

(6a') $\Gamma(\hat{P} \vee x[\text{dragon}'(x) \wedge P\{x\}])$.

Assuming that Γ is a context-variable of type $\langle\langle s, f(T)\rangle, t\rangle$, (6a') as a whole turns out to be an element of ME'_t, as desired. It is easy to state now the properties an appropriate translation (6') of (6) has to show: First, it has to be of the same type as Γ, and second, if (7') is the translation of the redundant answer (7),

(7)   Mary imagines a dragon

then the extension of (6a') with respect to a context-model and a point of reference such that $ca(\langle i, j\rangle)$ is (6') has to be the same as the extension of (7') with respect to that model and point of reference. In other words, minimal and redundant answers have to be equivalent with respect to the same question. We meet this requirement formally on the basis of the principle of functional application by abstracting a function from an appropriate open formula such that it may be applied to arguments like that of Γ in (6a'). Thus a translation of (6) would be (6'):

(6') $\hat{\mathscr{P}}m^*(\hat{}\text{imagine}'(\mathscr{P}))$.

According to clause (3) of our definition, the extension of (6a') with respect to a context-model and a point of reference of the kind specified above, is the same as that of (6a''):

(6'') $\hat{\mathscr{P}}m^*(\hat{}\text{imagine}'(\mathscr{P}))\,(\hat{P} \vee x[\text{dragon}'(x) \wedge P\{x\}])$.

According to some valid PTQ-principles, (6a'') is equivalent with (6a'''):

(6''') $m^*(\hat{}\text{imagine}'(\hat{P} \vee x[\text{dragon}'(x) \wedge P\{x\}]))$.

This, in turn, is exactly the result of translating (7), which shows that the desired equivalence of minimal and redundant answer is met. So far we have been loosely speaking of the translation of, e.g., (7). This is not quite correct, however, since there are two semantically different translations of (7), usually referred to as its referential and non-referential reading. Above we have treated only the latter one. It is not difficult, however, to derive the referential reading of (6a) as well:

(6b) $F_{10,0}$(a dragon, he$_0$.)

(6b) is surface-identical with (6a), but it translates differently:

(6b′) $\hat{P} \vee x[\text{dragon}'(x) \wedge P\{x\}](\hat{x}_0 \Gamma(\hat{P}P\{x_0\}))$.

After some reformulations we get:

(6b″) $\hat{P} \vee x[\text{dragon}'(x) \wedge P\{x\}](\hat{x}_0 m^* (\hat{\,}\text{imagine}'(\hat{P}P\{x_0\}))),$

which is the result of translating the referential reading of (7).

There are, however, some phenomena our analysis doesn't account for yet. Consider for example (8) and (8a):

(8)   Whom does Mary kiss?
(8a)   A fish.

(8a) is not uninterpretable with respect to the context created by (8), but it does not give the information required. (8) doesn't just ask for any object of Mary's kissing but for a human one. As fishes never are human, (8a) is an implicitly contradictory and hence always false answer with respect to (8). With respect to (9), on the other hand,

(9)   What does Mary kiss?

(8a) might well be a true answer (provided Mary is a little queer). The following two steps are necessary in order to handle these facts adequately: We have to assign different translations to *what* and *who(m)* on the basis of the features *human* and *not human*, respectively, and we have to add two meaning postulates ensuring that in all possible worlds and at any moment of time, e.g., John is a human and a fish is not.[9]

Next consider (10)–(11a):

(10)   Whom will Bill meet?
(11)   Which girl will Bill meet?
(11a)   The drum-major.

While (11a) may be a true answer to (10) as well as to (11), the conditions for its being true are not the same in both cases. Suppose the drum-major is a man. Then (11a) may be true with respect to (10), but never with respect to (11), since in the latter context, but not in the former, (11a) implies that the drum-major is a girl.[10] Our analysis of which-questions will have to account for this fact.

Finally consider (12)–(13a):

(12)   Who sleeps?
(13)   What does John eat?
(12a)   Nobody.
(13a)   Nothing.

The fact that (12a) becomes nonsensical in the context of (13) and that the same holds for (13a) with respect to (12) shows again the effects of the semantic difference between *what* and *who*. Note, however, the complete naturalness of (12a) with respect to (12) and of (13a) with respect to (13), which suggests that *what* and *who* questions do not presuppose the existence of a thing or person having the specified property. Therefore we translate *who* and *what* without existential quantifier. The data seem to be a little less convincing regarding *which* questions but we believe that (14), (14a) is also a natural question–answer pair:[11]

(14)   Which man will Mary kiss?
(14a)   No one.

Hence we propose to regard the existence of some man whom Mary will kiss as an invited inference rather than a logically valid one[12] and we introduce no existential quantifier into the translation of *which* neither.

As a kind of summary of our investigations in this section, we shall give now translations for several of our examples according to the rules stated in the appendix. ('(n/m)' stands for '(n) in the context of (m)'.)

(9)   What does Mary kiss?
(9′) $\hat{\mathscr{P}}_1 m^*(\text{kiss}'(\hat{P}\,\mathscr{P}_1\{\hat{x}[\neg\,\text{human}'(x) \wedge P\{x\}]\}))$.
(8a)   A fish.
(8a′) $\Gamma(\hat{P} \vee x[\text{fish}'(x) \wedge P\{x\}])$.
(8a′/9′) $\vee u[\text{fish}'_*(u) \wedge \text{kiss}'_*(m, u)]$.
(10)   Whom will Bill meet?
(10′) $\hat{\mathscr{P}}_1 W\,b^*(\text{meet}'(\hat{P}\,\mathscr{P}_1\{\hat{x}[\text{human}'(x) \wedge P\{x\}]\}))$.
(11)   Which girl will Bill meet?
(11′) $\hat{\mathscr{P}}_1 W\,b^*(\text{meet}'(\hat{P}\,\mathscr{P}_1\{\hat{x}[\text{girl}'(x) \wedge P\{x\}]\}))$.
(11a)   The drum-major.
(11a′) $\Gamma(\hat{P} \vee y[\wedge x[\text{drum-major}'(x) \leftrightarrow x = y] \wedge P\{x\}])$.
(11a′/10′)
         $W \vee v[\wedge u[\text{drum-major}'_*(u) \leftrightarrow u = v] \wedge \text{meet}'_*(b, v)]$

(11a'/11')

$$W \vee v[\wedge u[\text{drum-major}'_*(u) \leftrightarrow u = v] \wedge \text{girl}'_*(v)$$
$$\wedge \text{meet}'_*(b, v)].$$

(12)   Who sleeps?

(12') $\mathscr{P}_1 \hat{P} \mathscr{P}_1 \{\hat{x}[\text{human}'(x) \wedge P\{x\}]\} (\hat{\ } \text{sleep}')$

(12a)   Nobody.

(12a') $\Gamma(\hat{P} \neg \vee x[\text{human}'(x) \wedge P\{x\}])$

(12a'/12')

$$\neg \vee u[\text{human}'_*(u) \wedge \text{sleep}'_*(u)]$$

(13)   What does John eat?

(13') $\mathscr{P}_1 j*(\hat{\ } \text{eat}'(\hat{P} \mathscr{P}_1 \{\hat{x}[\neg \text{human}'(x) \wedge P\{x\}]\}))$

(13a)   Nothing.

(13a') $\Gamma(\hat{P} \neg \vee x[\neg \text{human}'(x) \wedge P\{x\}])$

(13a'/13')

$$\neg \vee u[\neg \text{human}'_*(u) \wedge \text{eat}'_*(j, u)]$$

4. YES–NO QUESTIONS AND THEIR MINIMAL ANSWERS

The analysis of yes–no questions seems to be very simple. The set of minimal answer expressions contains just those two members which gave the whole category its name. The interrogative expressions themselves are derivable from ordinary declarative sentences in a rather simple way. This coincides with the fact that they do not contain characteristic question words. There are, however, some particularities to be accounted for. First compare (15), (16), and (15a):

(15)   Will John leave?

(16)   Won't John leave?

(15a)   No.

What are the conditions for (15a) to be true? With respect to (15), (15a) is true just in case John will not leave. The same holds, however, with respect to (16). It follows that the negative form in (16) is not a truth functional component of the whole expression. It rather has the function of an attitudinal disjunct, telling us something about the expectation the speaker had: "Oh, I thought he would." would be a natural continuation.

Secondly, consider (17) and (17a):

(17)   Will Mary talk or does the dragon sleep?

(17a)   Yes.

It is very improbable that (17a) will serve as a natural answer to (17). This is due to the fact that (17) can hardly be anything else than an alternative question. Compare, however, (18):

(18)   Does Bill drink or smoke?

Here the alternative as well as the yes–no reading are possible and therefore (17a) is a possible answer to (18).

We account for these facts by deriving yes–no interrogatives not from declarative sentences, but from terms and intransitive verb phrases, excluding thus negation and sentential conjunction and disjunction.

The further requirements an adequate analysis of yes–no questions and their minimal answers must meet are quite obvious: If ϕ? is a yes–no interrogative and ϕ is the corresponding declarative sentence, then the extension of *Yes.* with respect to ϕ? has to be truth exactly in case the extension of ϕ is truth and the extension of *No.* with respect to ϕ? has to be truth if and only if ϕ is not true. The following translations have the desired properties: $\hat{p}[\check{\ } p]$ (for *yes*) and $\hat{p}[\neg\check{\ } p]$ (for *no*) denote complementary sets of propositions. $\Gamma(\hat{p}[\check{\ } p])$ (representing *Yes.*) and $\Gamma(\hat{p}[\neg\check{\ } p])$ (representing *No.*) denote truth values, provided the context-variable Γ denotes sets of properties of propositions. The context-variable stands again for the translation of an appropriate question, e.g., (15):

(15′) $\hat{q}q\{\check{\ }W\, j*(\check{\ }\text{leave}')\}.$
(15a′) $\Gamma(\hat{p}[\neg\check{\ } p]).$

If we interpret (15a′) with respect to (15′), we may read it roughly as follows: The set of properties of the proposition that John will leave contains the property of not being the case. The reduction shows the desired equivalence with the redundant answer (19):

(19)   John won't leave.
(19′) $\neg W \text{ leave}'_*(j)$
(15a′/15′)
           $\neg W \text{ leave}'_*(j)$

5. ADVERBIAL QUESTIONS AND THEIR MINIMAL ANSWERS

Our general approach works for adverbial questions as well as for term and yes–no questions. We shall therefore restrict our discussion to two special points. First it is obvious that an adverbial question determines not only the syntactic category of the expression which, together with the full stop, makes up a minimal answer, but also part of its semantic content. The following examples may serve as an illustration:

(20)　　How does Bill walk?
(20a)　　Rapidly.
(20b)　　Slowly.
(20c)　　At seven p.m.
(20d)　　At the corner.
(20e)　　Into the park.
(20f)　　Because of Mary.

Only (20a) and (20b) make sense in the context of (20), (20c)–(20f) don't. The data are similar to those which concern the difference between *what*, *who*, and *which* plus a common noun phrase, and therefore we account for them in an analogous way: We introduce a feature into the translation of the adverbial question word (e.g., MANNER in the case of *how* — we use upper case letters in order to avoid confusion with the common noun translation *manner'*) and we ensure by a meaning postulate that this feature turns out to be redundant if the answer is suitable. But there is another phenomenon to be noticed which has no counterpart among the term questions. Compare (21), (22), and the answers (21a)–(22a):

(21)　　Where does John walk?
(22)　　Where will John meet the blonde?
(21a)　　In the park.
(21b)　　Into the park.
(22a)　　At the party.

(21a)–(22a) do all make sense in the context of (21), but only (21a) and (22a) do so in the context of (22). The consequence is clear: (21) has to be assigned two readings, due to the lexical ambiguity of the question word *where*. The following translations, derived according to the rules stated in the Appendix, show our proposal for dealing with that phenomenon:

(21′)　　$\lambda a_1 j^*(\lambda P \hat{x}[\text{PLACE}(a_1) \wedge a_1\{x, P\}](\hat{\ }\text{walk}'))$.
(21″)　　$\lambda a_1 j^*(\lambda P \hat{x}[\text{DIRECTION}(a_1) \wedge a_1\{x, P\}](\hat{\ }\text{walk}'))$.

Using MP(14) and MP(15) (cf. the appendix, 8.4) we get the following translations for (21a) and (21b) in the context of the place- and the direction-reading of (21), respectively:

(21a'/21')

$$in'(\hat{j}, \hat{\ }walk', \hat{P} \lor v[\land u[park'_*(u) \leftrightarrow u = v] \land P\{v\}]).$$

(21b'/21'')

$$into'(\hat{j}, \hat{\ }walk', \hat{P} \lor v[\land u[park'_*(u) \leftrightarrow u = v] \land P\{v\}]).$$

Again, we have equivalence with the redundant answers (23) and (24):

(23)   John walks in the park.
(24)   John walks into the park.

6. MULTIPLE QUESTIONS

Thus far we have been considering only questions that ask for one and only one item. With respect to them, a minimal answer consists in the declarative utterance of one expression of the corresponding category. There are, however, interrogative sentences like (25) which ask for more than one item:

(25)   Who kisses whom?

A suitable minimal answer is, e.g., (25a):

(25a)   Mary Bill.

We may call questions like (25) two-term questions. A somewhat different example is the following:

(26)   When will John meet Mary where?
(26a)   At seven p.m. at the corner.

Questions of this kind may be called two-adverbial questions. But the items asked for in a multiple question need not be of the same category, as the following example demonstrates:

(27)   Who seeks the dragon where?
(27a)   Mary in the park.

Note, however, that the degree of acceptability of the question and especially of the minimal answer diminishes as the number of questioned items increases:

(28)   Who kisses whom where when how?
(28a)   Mary Bill at the corner in the evening rapidly.

But since, apart from acceptability, there is no principled reason against a question–answer pair like (28), (28a), our rules account also for cases like this.

The situation is different with expressions like the following:

(29)   *Does John leave when?
(29a)   *Yes in the evening.

The reason for rejecting (29) is not a low degree of acceptability but sheer ungrammaticality: A yes–no question cannot contain any additional questioned item. We therefore restrict the possibility of generating multiple questions to term and adverbial questions (cf. rule S19.(d) in the Appendix).

7. CONCLUDING REMARKS

In conclusion we shall point out briefly some of the most important respects in which our approach differs from other recent proposals concerning the formal semantics of questions. We differ from Keenan and Hull (1973) mainly in three points: (a) We provide explicit and separate rules for translating question and answer expressions from natural into logical language, (b) we do not restrict ourselves to which and yes–no questions, and (c) we do not exclude answers of the nobody/nothing type from the class of natural answers. We differ from Hamblin (1973) in that our approach does not make it necessary to 'lift' the whole semantics in type, letting, e.g., the intension of a formula be the unit set of a proposition instead of the proposition itself. While Hamblin proposes to let questions denote uniformly sets of propositions, we propose to let questions denote different types of sets according to the type of that expression which is the critical one in any kind of answer. Finally, in contrast to Karttunen (1976), we do not believe that an adequate analysis of direct questions can be given by supplementing a grammar of embedded questions with the remark that direct questions can be derived from a deleted performative 'I ask you to tell me' plus the corresponding embedded questions. Apart from other problems concerning the performative analysis we see no way such a proposal could be amended in order to account for the phenomenon of minimal answers which we showed to be the crucial semantic problem in connection with direct questions.

8. APPENDIX

An extension of the PTQ-fragment of English including direct questions and minimal answers

8.1. *Additional categories*

(a) *Categories for direct questions*

$t/(t//t)$ is the category of direct yes–no questions.

t/T is the category of direct one-term questions.

t/IAV is the category of direct one-adverbial questions.

If $A, B \in \{T, IAV\}$, then $(\ldots(t/A)/\ldots)/B$ are the categories of direct multiple questions, in particular

$(t/T)/T$ is the category of direct two-term questions, and

$(t/IAV)/IAV$ is the category of direct two-adverbial questions.

(b) *Primed categories*

If A is a category, then $(A)'$ is also a category (parentheses will be omitted if no ambiguity can arise). In particular, t' is the category of open sentences.

8.2. *Additional basic expressions*

$B_{IV} = B_{IV}^{\mathrm{PTQ}} \cup \{\text{sleep, leave}\}$

$B_{T} = B_{IV}^{\mathrm{PTQ}} \cup \{\text{seven p.m., nobody, nothing}\}$

$B_{T'} = \{\text{who, what}\}$

$B_{TV} = B_{TV}^{\mathrm{PTQ}} \cup \{\text{meet, kiss, imagine}\}$

$B_{IAV'} = \{\text{how, when, where}_1, \text{where}_2, \text{why}\}$

$B_{CN} = B_{CN}^{\mathrm{PTQ}} \cup \{\text{blonde, girl, drum-major, human, dragon, evening, corner, party}\}$

$B_{IAV/T} = B_{IAV/T}^{\mathrm{PTQ}} \cup \{\text{into, at, because of}\}$

$B_{t//t} = \{\text{yes, no}\}.$

8.3. *Additional S- and T-rules*

Let s be an additional distinct member of Con_e, MANNER, TIME, PLACE, DIRECTION, and REASON be particular distinct members of $\mathrm{Con}_{\langle\langle s, f(IAV)\rangle\rangle, t\rangle}$, and a be the variable $v_{0,\langle s, f(IAV)\rangle}$.

(a) *Basic rules*

  T1.(d)$'$ *John, Mary, Bill, ninety, seven p.m.* translate into j^*, m^*, b^*, n^*, s^* respectively.

   (f)   *nobody* and *nothing* translate into $\hat{P}\neg \vee x[\text{human}'(x) \wedge P\{x\}]$ and $\hat{P}\neg \vee x[\neg\text{human}'(x) \wedge P\{x\}]$ respectively.

   (g)   *who* and *what* translate into $\hat{P}\mathscr{P}\{\hat{x}[\text{human}'(x) \wedge P\{x\}]\}$ and $\hat{P}\mathscr{P}\{\hat{x}[\neg\text{human}'(x) \wedge P\{x\}]\}$ respectively.

   (h)   *how, when, where*$_1$, *where*$_2$, *why* translate into
$\lambda P \, \hat{x}[\text{MANNER } (a) \wedge a\{x, P\}]$, $\lambda P \, \hat{x}[\text{TIME } (a) \wedge a\{x, P\}]$,
$\lambda P \, \hat{x}[\text{PLACE} \quad (a) \wedge a\{x, P\}]$, $\lambda P \, \hat{x}[\text{DIRECTION} (a) \wedge a\{x, P\}]$,
$\lambda P \, \hat{x}[\text{REASON } (a) \wedge a\{x, P\}]$ respectively.

(i)   *yes, no* translate into $\hat{p}[\check{}p]$, $\hat{p}[\neg\check{}p]$ respectively.

S2a.   If $\xi \in P_{CN}$, then $F_{2a}(\xi) \in P_{T'}$, where $F_{2a}(\xi) = which\ \xi$.

T2a.   If $\xi \in P_{CN}$ and ξ translates into ξ', then $F_{2a}(\xi)$ translates into
$\hat{P}\mathscr{P}\{\hat{x}[\xi'(x) \wedge P\{x\}]\}$.

(b) *Rules of functional application*

S4.–S10. apply to normal categories as well as to their primed variants. If
one of the input expressions is of a primed category, the category of the
output expression has to be replaced by its primed variant.

S5'.   If $\delta \in P_{IV/T}$ and $\beta \in P_T$, then $F_5(\delta, \beta) \in P_{IV}$, where $F_5(\delta, \beta) = \delta\beta$
if β does not have the form he_n or who and $F_5(\delta, he_n) = \delta\ him_n$ and
$F_5(\delta, who) = \delta\ whom$.

(c) *Formation rules for direct questions*

(Since our main concern here is not syntax and for the sake of brevity we
give only a rough outline of rule S19, an explicit statement of which would
require the definition of several auxiliary notions.)

S18.   If $\alpha \in P_T$ and $\delta \in P_{IV}$, then $F_{16}(\alpha, \delta)$, $F_{17}(\alpha, \delta)$, $F_{18}(\alpha, \delta) \in P_{t'}$,
$F_{16}(\alpha, \delta) = whether\ \alpha\delta'$, $F_{17}(\alpha, \delta) = whether\ \alpha\delta''$, $F_{18}(\alpha, \delta)$
$= whether\ \alpha\delta'''$, and δ', δ'', δ''' come from δ by replacing the first
verb in δ by its third person singular present, future, or present
perfect, respectively.

T18.   If $\alpha \in P_T$, $\delta \in P_{IV}$, and α, δ translate into α', δ' respectively, then
$F_{16}(\alpha, \delta)$ translates into $q\{\hat{}\alpha'(\hat{}\delta')\}$,
$F_{17}(\alpha, \delta)$ translates into $q\{\hat{}W\alpha'(\hat{}\delta')\}$,
$F_{18}(\alpha, \delta)$ translates into $q\{\hat{}H\alpha'(\hat{}\delta')\}$.
q is to be the variable $v_{0,\langle s, f(t//t)\rangle}$.

S19.   If $\phi \in P_{t'}$ and α, α', ..., β, β', ... are the first, second, ...
members of $P_{T'}$ and $P_{IAV'}$ respectively that occur in ϕ, then
either:

(a)   there is no such α or β and $F_{19}(\phi) \in P_{t/(t//t)}$, $F_{19}(\phi) = \phi'$?,
where ϕ' comes from ϕ by first replacing the first verb in ϕ
by its do-supported form (the do-supported form of *is* being
is, of course, etc.) and then substituting the auxiliary for the
initial *whether*; or

(b)   there is exactly one $\alpha \in P_{T'}$ as required and $F_{20}(\phi) \in P_{t/T}$,
where either $\alpha = who$ and $F_{20}(\phi) = \phi$?, or $\alpha = whom$ and
$F_{20}(\phi) = whom\ \phi'$?, where ϕ' comes from ϕ by deleting

whom in ϕ, replacing the first verb in ϕ by its do-supported form, and preposing the auxiliary; or

(c) there is exactly one $\beta \in P_{IAV'}$ as required and $F_{21}(\phi) \in P_{t/IAV}$, $F_{21}(\phi) = \beta\phi'$?, where ϕ' comes from, ϕ by deleting β in ϕ, replacing the first verb in ϕ by its do-supported form, and preposing the auxiliary; or

(d) there are $n(n>1)$ α or β as required and $F_{22,n}(\phi) \in P_{(...(t/A)/...)/B}(A, B \in \{T, IAV\})$, $F_{22,n}(\phi) = \phi$?.

T19.   If $\phi \in P_{t'}$, ϕ translates into ϕ', and $\alpha^1, \ldots, \alpha^n$, in that order, are the free occurrences, from left to right, of variables in ϕ', then $F_{19}(\phi)$, $F_{20}(\phi)$, $F_{21}(\phi)$, and $F_{22,n}(\phi)$ translate into $\lambda v_1 \ldots \lambda v_n \phi''$, where $v_i (1 \leqslant i \leqslant n)$ is the i-th variable of the same type as α^i and ϕ'' comes from ϕ' by replacing each α^i in ϕ' by the i-th variable of the same type.

(d) *Formation rules for minimal answers*

S20a.   If $A \in \{t//t, T, IAV\}$ and $\alpha \in P_A$, then $F_{23}(\alpha) \in P_t$, where $F_{23}(\alpha) = \alpha$. .

T20a.   If $\alpha \in P_A$ $(A \in \{t//t, T, IAV\})$ and α translates into α', then $F_{23}(\alpha)$ translates into $\Gamma(\alpha')$.
Γ is to be the context-variable $c\text{-}v_{0,\,\langle \langle s, f(A) \rangle, t \rangle}$.

S20b.   If $\alpha_1 \in P_{A_1}, \ldots, \alpha_n \in P_{A_n}$ $(A_i \in \{T, IAV\}, 1 \leqslant i \leqslant n)$, then $F_{24,n}(\alpha_1, \ldots, \alpha_n) \in P_t$ and $F_{24,n}(\alpha_1, \ldots, \alpha_n) = \alpha_1 \ldots \alpha_n$. .

T20b.   If $\alpha_1 \in P_{A_1}, \ldots, \alpha_n \in P_{A_n}$ $(A_i \in \{T, IAV\}, 1 \leqslant i \leqslant n)$, and $\alpha_1, \ldots, \alpha_n$ translate into $\alpha_1', \ldots, \alpha_n'$ respectively, then $F_{24,n}(\alpha_1, \ldots, \alpha_n)$ translates into $\Delta_{A_1,\ldots,A_n}(\alpha_n') \ldots (\alpha_1')$, where $\Delta_{A_1,\ldots,A_n}$ is the context-variable $c\text{-}v_{0,\,\langle \langle \ldots \langle s, f(A_1) \rangle, \ldots \rangle, \langle \langle s, f(A_n) \rangle, t \rangle \rangle}$.

8.4. *Additional meaning postulates*

(10) $\square \alpha(\,\text{human}')$, where α is j^*, m^*, b^*, or $F_n(\xi)$ $(0 \leqslant n \leqslant 2)$, and ξ translates *man, woman, blonde,* or *girl.*

(11) $\square \alpha(\neg\,\text{human}')$, where α is n^*, s^*, or $F_n(\xi)$ $(0 \leqslant n \leqslant 2)$, and ξ translates any member of B_{CN} except *human* and those mentioned in MP(10).

(12) $\square \text{MANNER}(\,\delta)$, where δ translates *rapidly* or *slowly.*

(13) $\Box$ TIME(δ), where δ translates *in the evening* or *at seven p.m.*.

(14) $\Box$ PLACE$(\delta(\beta))$, where δ translates *in* or *at* and β is $F_n(\xi)$ $(0 \leqslant n \leqslant 2)$, where ξ translates *park, corner,* or *party*.

(15) $\Box$ DIRECTION$(\delta(\beta))$, where δ translates *into* and β translates any member of P_T except *ninety, seven p.m.,* $F_n(price)$, or $F_n(temperature)$ $(0 \leqslant n \leqslant 2)$.

(16) $\Box$ REASON$(\delta(\beta))$, where δ translates *because of* and β translates any member of P_T except *ninety* and *seven p.m.*.

Universität München

NOTES

The present paper developed out of many discussions the authors had with each other as well as with many colleagues. For commenting on and criticizing earlier versions of this paper we are indebted especially to Max Cresswell, Edward Keenan, Godehard Link, Richmond Thomason, Theo Vennemann, and the members of his seminar on problems of the theory of grammar in the summer of 1976. Remaining shortcomings and mistakes are, of course, entirely our own.

[1] 'The proper treatment of quantification in ordinary English', henceforth abbreviated as PTQ. This article has been reprinted as Chapter 8 of Montague (1974), to which we refer.

[2] Cf., e.g., Bach (1970).

[3] PTQ, p. 248, fn. 3.

[4] According to one view, answers constitute an illocutionary type (a subcategory of assertions) since they may be defined in terms of the specific change in the interactional situation they produce: They fulfill the commitment established by the previous question and they commit the speaker to the truth of their propositional content.

[5] Like Hamblin (1973, p. 47) we do not accept Montague's identifying 'pragmatics' with 'indexical semantics'. The central problems of pragmatics, as we understand this notion, are those of a theory of speech acts. For an analysis of the speech acts of asking a question see Zaefferer (in preparation).

[6] The basic idea of this approach has been outlined in Chapter 5 of Hausser (1974).

[7] As usual we understand by $A \backslash B$, A and B being any sets, the complement of the intersection of A and B with respect to A.

[8] We apologize for being fed up a little with unicorns.

[9] Remember that PTQ treats proper names as rigid designators, i.e., as referring to the same individual at all points of reference. Therefore, if *Bill jn.* refers to a steamboat, *Bill jn.* is necessarily non-human.

[10] This fact has been pointed out also by Keenan and Hull (1973, p. 448f.).

[11] In this respect we subscribe to Marga Reis' critique of Keenan and Hull (1973) in Reis (1974), fn. 17.

[12] For the notion of an invited inference see Geis and Zwicky (1971).

BIBLIOGRAPHY

Bach, Emmon (1970), 'Questions', *Linguistic Inquiry* **2**, 153–166.

Cresswell, Max J. (1973), *Logics and Languages*, Methuen, London.

Geis, Michael L. and Zwicky, Arnold M. (1971), 'On Invited Inferences', *Linguistic Inquiry* **2**, 561–566.

Hamblin, C. L. (1973), 'Questions in Montague English', *Foundations of Language* **10**, 41–53.

Hausser, Roland R. (1974), 'Quantification in an Extended Montague Grammar, Unpublished doctoral dissertation, University of Texas at Austin.

Hausser, Roland R. (1977), 'How do Pronouns Denote?, to appear in F. Heny and H. Schnelle (eds.), *Syntax and Semantics*, Vol. 10, Academic Press, New York.

Karttunen, Lauri (1976), 'Syntax and Semantics of Questions', *Linguistics and Philosophy* **1**, 3–44.

Keenan, Edward L. and Hull, Robert D. (1973), 'The Logical Presuppositions of Questions and Answers, in J. S. Petöfi and D. Franck (eds.), *Presuppositions in Philosophy and Linguistics*, Athenäum, Frankfurt/Main, pp. 441–466.

Lewis, David K. (1972), 'General Semantics', in D. Davidson and G. Harman (eds.), *Semantics of Natural Language*, Reidel, Dordrecht, pp. 169–218.

Montague, Richard (1974), *Formal Philosophy*, Yale University Press, New Haven.

Reis, Marga (1974), Rezension zu: Petöfi/Franck (1973). *Deutsche sprache* **4**, 287–304.

Wunderlich, Dieter (1976), 'Fragesätze und Fragen', in *Dieter Wunderlich, Studien zur Sprechakttheorie*, Suhrkamp, Frankfurt/Main, pp. 181–250.

Zaefferer, Dietmar (In preparation), Frageausdrücke und Fragen im Deutschen. Ihre Syntax, Semantik und Pragmatik.

WALTHER KINDT

THE INTRODUCTION OF TRUTH PREDICATES
INTO
FIRST-ORDER LANGUAGES*

0. This paper is a shortened and slightly changed version of my 1976 paper. In the present paper I will only deal with the question in which way it might be possible to extend first-order languages to languages with truth predicates.[1] The problems of the Liar paradox and of the introduction of truth predicates have often been treated and different solutions have been proposed. But such proposals are not very useful unless they are developed within a precise theory of language and, what is more important, within a theory of language extensions. It is astonishing that there were for a long time no serious systematic attempts to answer the questions: what type of language extension should the introduction of a truth predicate be regarded as, and under which conditions can such a predicate be introduced in a unique way.[2] Only if one tries to answer these questions is it possible to find a complete and adequate solution to the problems under discussion. But if one does try to do it then in my opinion it is not too difficult to give what looks like an intuitively acceptable solution.[3]

1. First-order languages (without equality symbol and without function symbols) are given relative to a set of logical symbols (we will take $\neg$, $\vee$, $\bigvee$ as primitive symbols), a countable set V of variables (denoted by $v, v', \ldots$) and a class of constants among which individual constants (denoted by $a, a', \ldots$) must be distinguished from relation constants, also called predicates (denoted by $P, P', \ldots$). If K is a set of constants, then I will designate by $T(K)$ the set of K-terms, i.e., the set which contains the individual constants of K and the variables. Formulas (denoted by $\varphi, \psi, \ldots$) are constructed in the usual manner. A formula φ is called a K-formula if the only constants which occur in φ belong to K. The set of K-formulas is denoted by $F(K)$. A formula φ is called a statement if no variable occurs free in φ; the set of K-statements is denoted by $A(K)$. A K-structure is an ordered pair $S = \langle X, I \rangle$, where $X \neq 0$ and I is a mapping which interprets each constant of K in the usual manner. Elements of X^V are called assignment functions and are denoted by $\alpha, \alpha', \ldots$. I shall write $S \underset{\alpha}{\vDash} \varphi$ for: φ is valid under α in S (see e.g., Bell and Slomson, 1974); specifically $S \vDash \varphi$ means that φ is a statement and that φ is valid in S (i.e., $S \underset{\alpha}{\vDash} \varphi$ for any α). A

359

F. Guenthner and S. J. Schmidt (eds.), Formal Semantics and Pragmatics
for Natural Languages, 359–371. All Rights Reserved.

first-order language L (of classical type) consists of a set $K(L)$ of constants and a set of $K(L)$-structures. These structures are also called L-structures and instead of $A(K(L))$, $F(K(L))$ and $T(K(L))$ I shall write $A(L)$, $F(L)$ and $T(L)$ respectively.

1.1. DEFINITION: Let L and L' be first-order languages. L' is an extension of L iff

(1) $K(L) \subset K(L')$,
(2)   there is a bijective mapping f from the set of L-structures to the set of L'-structures such that $f(S) \restriction K(L) = S$ for any L-structure S.[4]

1.2. DEFINITION: Let L' be a first-order language, and let W be a monadic predicate of $K(L')$.
W is a truth predicate in L' iff for every L'-structure $S' = \langle X', I' \rangle$ and for every $\varphi \in A(L')$:

(A_1) if $\varphi \in I'(W)$ then $S' \vDash \varphi$;
(A_2) if $S' \vDash \varphi$ and $\varphi \in X'$ then $\varphi \in I'(W)$.

I call (A_1) the correctness condition and (A_2) the completeness condition for W with respect to S'. If W satisfies (A_1) but not necessarily (A_2) for each S', W is called a partial truth predicate in L'.

In a wider sense it follows from Tarski (1935) that it is impossible in general to extend a first-order language L to a first-order language with a truth predicate $W \notin K(L)$. For instance, if there is any L-structure $S = \langle X, I \rangle$ and any individual constant $a \in K(L)$ such that $I(a) = \neg Wa$ ($\neg Wa$ corresponds to the Liar sentence), then such an extension cannot be defined. Conversely, it is clear that such an extension exists if, for example, the only statements which lie in the universe X of any L-structure $S = \langle X, I \rangle$ belong to $A(L)$. It is a remarkable fact that in the latter case it is not always exactly one extension that is allowed by 1.2. For instance, if every L-structure $S = \langle X, I \rangle$ has the property that Wa is the only statement which belongs to X and that $I(a) = Wa$, then, with respect to each structure of the extended language, it is possible both to regard Wa as true and to regard Wa as not true.

Apart from the problem of whether L can be extended to a first-order language with a truth predicate or only with a partial one, it is an important question whether there is a natural way of defining such an extension.

Before dealing with this question I will consider an example. Let $S = \langle X, I \rangle$ be a L-structure, $\varphi \in A(L)$, $S \vDash \varphi$ and $a \in K(L)$. In order to extend S to a $K(L) \cup \{W\}$-structure $S' = \langle X', I' \rangle$ one has to specify how W is interpreted by I'. In the case of $I(a) = \varphi$ it seems to be quite natural to set $Wa \in I'(W)$. On the other hand, in the case of $I(a) = Wa$ it is not yet clear whether one should assume $Wa \in I'(W)$ or not. The difference between the two cases demonstrates the crucial point concerning an intuitively adequate interpretation of W. In the first case, the decision on $Wa \in I'(W)$ can be reduced to $S \vDash \varphi$ with (A_1). In the second case, on the other hand, the decision on $Wa \in I'(W)$ is not reducible. Indeed, the attempt to reduce this decision leads back to the initial condition $Wa \in I'(W)$. According to this it seems to be obvious that an interpretation of W by I' is adequate only if for every φ which belongs to $I'(W)$ the decision for $\varphi \in I'(W)$ is reducible in some way or other to validity properties of S. For if one wishes to have W as a truth predicate it is not admissible to regard arbitrary statements as true in S', but only such statements for which this can be justified by recourse to certain validity properties of S.

With the notion of reducibility it will be possible to characterize certain extensions of L as natural. But first of all it is necessary to give this notion a precise definition.

In the following let L be a first-order language, and let W be a monadic predicate such that $W \notin K(L)$. Let $K' = K(L) \cup \{W\}$ and suppose that $S = \langle X, I \rangle$ is any L-structure.

1.3. DEFINITION: The two-place relation $R(S)$ is defined by: For every $\varphi, \psi \in F(K')$, $\alpha \in X^V$, $t \in T(L)$, $v \in V$ and $x \in X$:

   (1)   if $\varphi \in A(K')$ and $(I \cup \alpha)(t) = \varphi$ then
         $\langle Wt, \alpha \rangle \, R(S) \, \{\langle \varphi, \alpha \rangle\}$ and $\langle \neg Wt, \alpha \rangle \, R(S) \, \{\langle \neg \varphi, \alpha \rangle\}$;
   (2)   if $\varphi \notin F(L)$ then $\langle \neg \neg \varphi, \alpha \rangle \, R(S) \, \{\langle \varphi, \alpha \rangle\}$;
   (3)   if $\varphi \vee \psi \notin F(L)$ then $\langle \varphi \vee \psi, \alpha \rangle \, R(S) \, \{\langle \varphi, \alpha \rangle\}$,
         $\langle \varphi \vee \psi, \alpha \rangle \, R(S) \, \{\langle \psi, \alpha \rangle\}$ and
         $\langle \neg(\varphi \vee \psi), \alpha \rangle \, R(S) \, \{\langle \neg \varphi, \alpha \rangle, \langle \neg \psi, \alpha \rangle\}$;
   (4)   if $\bigvee v\varphi \notin F(L)$ then $\langle \bigvee v\varphi, \alpha \rangle \, R(S) \, \{\langle \varphi, \alpha_v^x \rangle\}$
         and $\langle \neg \bigvee v\varphi, \alpha \rangle \, R(S) \, \{\langle \neg \varphi, \alpha_v^y \rangle; y \in X\}$,
         where α_v^y is defined by
         $\alpha_v^y(v') = (v')$ for $v' \neq v$ and $\alpha_v^y(v) = y$.

$R(S)$ is called the reduction relation with respect to S.
$\langle \varphi, \alpha \rangle \, R(S) \, \{\langle \varphi_j, \alpha_j \rangle; j \in J\}$ means that the decision on the validity of φ under α can be reduced to all the decisions on the validity of φ_j under α_j

for all $j \in J$. It should be remarked here that $R(S)$ is not the only reduction relation which might be defined. For instance, instead of 1.3(3) it would also be reasonable to define $\langle \varphi \vee \psi, \alpha \rangle$ $R(S)$ $\{\langle \varphi, \alpha \rangle, \langle \psi, \varphi \rangle\}$, $\langle \varphi \vee \psi, \alpha \rangle$ $R(S)$ $\{\langle \varphi, \alpha \rangle, \langle \neg \psi, \alpha \rangle\}$, $\langle \varphi \vee \psi, \alpha \rangle$ $R(S)$ $\{\langle \neg \varphi, \alpha \rangle, \langle \psi, \alpha \rangle\}$ and $\langle \neg (\varphi \vee \psi), \alpha \rangle R(S) \{\langle \neg \varphi, \alpha \rangle, \langle \neg \psi, \alpha \rangle\}$ for $\varphi \vee \psi \notin F(L)$. But in this case one gets a relation which leads to an interpretation of W that is weaker than the one which is obtained by the proposed definition. One can show, however, that 1.3 yields the best possible compatibility with the validity concept of first-order languages.

1.4. DEFINITION: An ordered pair $\langle B, m_0 \rangle$ is a tree with the initial point m_0 iff:

(1) B is a two-place relation,
(2)   for each element m of the field of B (i.e., the union of the range and the domain of B) there is a finite B-chain[5] which leads from m_0 to m.

A point m of the tree $\langle B, m_0 \rangle$ (i.e., $m = m_0$ or m belongs to the field of B) is called an end point if there is no m' such that $m \ B \ m'$. $\langle B, m_0 \rangle$ is said to be finite if there does not exist an infinite B-chain.

1.5. DEFINITION: Let $M(S)$ be the set of ordered pairs $\langle \varphi, \alpha \rangle$ such that $\varphi \in F(K')$ and $\alpha \in X^V$.
A tree $\langle B, m_0 \rangle$, with $B \subset M(S) \times M(S)$ and $m_0 \in M(S)$, is called a $R(S)$-tree if for each element m of the range of B there is an $M' \subset M(S)$ such that for each m':
$m \ B \ m'$ iff $m' \in M'$ and $m \ R(S) \ M'$.

1.6. DEFINITION: The set $G(S) \subset M(S)$ is defined by:
$\langle \varphi, \alpha \rangle \in G(S)$ iff there is a finite $R(S)$-tree with the initial point $\langle \varphi, \alpha \rangle$ such that $S \underset{\alpha'}{\vDash} \psi$ for every end point $\langle \psi, \alpha' \rangle$ of the tree.

1.7. DEFINITION: Let φ be a statement of $A(K')$. The decision regarding the truth of φ with respect to S is reducible iff there is an α such that $\langle \varphi, \alpha \rangle \in G(S)$. φ is called grounded with respect to S if the decision regarding the truth of φ, or the truth of $\neg \varphi$ with respect to S, is reducible.[6]

It is now clear that the adequateness condition proposed above can be formulated as follows: an adequate extension $S' = \langle X, I' \rangle$ of S must satisfy the condition that for each $\varphi \in I'(W)$ the decision regarding the truth of φ with respect to S is reducible. Therefore the optimal extension which can be defined must also fulfill the condition that each $\varphi \in X$ for which the decision regarding the truth of φ with respect to S is reducible belongs to $I'(W)$.

1.8. THEOREM: Let L be a first-order language, and let W be a monadic predicate, with $W \notin K(L)$. Let L' be defined by:
$K(L') = K(L) \cup \{W\}$;
$S' = \langle X', I' \rangle$ is a L'-structure iff $S' \upharpoonright K(L)$ is an L-structure and $I'(W) = \{\varphi \in X'; \langle \varphi, \alpha \rangle \in G(S)$ for some $\alpha\}$. Then W is a partial truth predicate in L' and furthermore the following conditions hold:

(1)   For every L'-structure $S' = \langle X', I' \rangle$ and for every statement φ which is grounded with respect to $S' \upharpoonright K(L)$ the conditions (A_1) and (A_2) in 1.2 are fulfilled.

(2)   Let L'' be an extension of L such that $K(L'') = K(L')$ and that (A_1) and (A_2) are satisfied for every L''-structure $S' = \langle X'', I'' \rangle$ and for every statement φ which is grounded with respect to $S'' \upharpoonright K(L)$. Then for all L'-structures $S' = \langle X', I' \rangle$ and for all L''-structures $S'' = \langle X'', I'' \rangle$, if $S' \upharpoonright K(L) = S'' \upharpoonright K(L)$ then $I'(W) \subset I''(W)$.

This theorem says in particular that L' is in a sense the weakest extension of L such that (1) is satisfied. A proof of 1.8 is sketched out in my 1976.

The definition of $G(S)$ which is given by 1.6 starts from the intuitive idea that a statement should be regarded as true with respect to the extension of S if this decision can be reduced to validity properties of S. Besides this characterisation of the interpretation of W, it is plausible that for the $G(S)$ which determines the interpretation of W there must exist a recursive definition which is based on the repeated application of (A_2). In fact, it is easy to prove the following result.

1.9. THEOREM: $G(S)$ is equal to the set $G'(S)$ defined, under the assumptions of definition 1.3, by:

if $S \underset{\alpha}{\models} \psi$ then $\langle \varphi, \alpha \rangle \in G'(S)$;

if $\{\langle \varphi_j, \alpha_j \rangle; j \in J\} \subset G'(S)$;   and
$\langle \varphi, \alpha \rangle \, R(S) \, \{\langle \varphi_j, \alpha_j \rangle; j \in J\}$ then $\langle \varphi, \alpha \rangle \in G'(S)$.

2. In the preceding section the question has been discussed of whether there is a natural way of defining an extension L' with a truth predicate or at

least with a partial truth predicate $W \notin K(L)$ for each first-order language L. I have argued that such an extension L' is adequate only if L' satisfies the condition:

(C)   For every L'-structure $S' = \langle X', I' \rangle$ and for every statement $\varphi \in I'(W)$ the decision regarding the truth of φ with respect to $S' \upharpoonright K(L)$ is reducible.

However, in my opinion this condition does not suffice for characterizing L' as adequate. It seems to be necessary to postulate that instead of (C) L' fulfills the following condition.

(C')   For every L'-structure $S' = \langle X', I' \rangle$ and for every ordered pair $\langle \varphi, \alpha \rangle$, if $S' \underset{\alpha}{\vDash} \varphi$ then $\langle \varphi, \alpha \rangle \in G(S' \upharpoonright K(L))$.

(C') is a more general condition than (C) (it is easy to show that (C') and (A_1) imply (C)). What (C') postulates is that — intuitively speaking — each validity property of a given structure of the extended language L' must be justified by recourse to validity properties of the underlying structure of the restricted language L. The requirement to give such a justification is in my opinion necessary because the introduction of a truth predicate should not have the effect that in any structure of the extended language some statements become valid by accident and the validity is not based on properties of the underlying structure. If one accepts this argument one has to ask under which conditions an extension L' of L which satisfies (C') can be defined.

It is clear that it is not in general possible to define a first-order extension L' which satisfies (C'). If there are, for instance, an L-structure $S = \langle X, I \rangle$ and an individual constant $a \in K(L)$ such that $I(a) = Wa$ then Wa is not grounded with respect to S. On the other hand either $S' \vDash Wa$ or $S' \underset{\alpha}{\vDash} \neg Wa$ is fulfilled for any suitable extension S' of S.

I think that the only conclusion which can be drawn from these facts is that first-order languages of classical type don't give an appropriate frame for a theory of languages with truth predicates. For in an adequate extension L' of L it must be admissible, if necessary, that for some L'-structures $S' = \langle X, I' \rangle$ and for some statements φ neither $S' \vDash \varphi$ nor $S' \vDash \neg \varphi$. More exactly, it follows from (C') that $S' \vDash \varphi$ or $S' \vDash \neg \varphi$ can be fulfilled only if φ is grounded with respect to $S' \upharpoonright K(L)$. Therefore, in the case of $\alpha(v) = \varphi$, $S' \underset{\alpha}{\vDash} Wv$ or $S' \underset{\alpha}{\vDash} \neg Wv$ must be satisfied only if φ is grounded with respect to $S' \upharpoonright K(L)$. This means, in other words, that it seems to be inadequate to postulate generally that a truth predicate W is defined for every statement of the extended language. Instead of this one should only demand that W is defined for every grounded statement. But if one wants to satisfy the latter postulate one must leave the frame of first-order languages of classical type and proceed to consider first-order languages with partially defined predicates (called PDP-languages in the following).

First I shall generalize the hitherto used notions of structure and validity for the case of PDP-languages.

2.1. DEFINITION: Let K be a set of constants. $S = \langle X, I \rangle$ is a K-structure iff

(1) $X \neq 0$,
(2) I is a function with range K,
(3) I assigns to each individual constant of K an element of X,
(4) I assigns to each n-ary predicate of K an n-place partial relation on X, i.e., an ordered pair $\langle Z_0, Z_1 \rangle$ such that $Z_i \subset X^n$ for $i < 2$ and $Z_0 \cap Z_1 = 0$.[7]

2.2. DEFINITION: Let K be a set of constants, and let $S = \langle X, I \rangle$ be a K-structure. For any n-ary $P \in K$, for $t_0, \ldots, t_{n-1} \in T(K)$, $\alpha \in X^V$, φ, $\psi \in F(K)$, $v \in V$ and for $x \in X$ we set:

(1)   if $\langle (I \cup \alpha)(t_0), \ldots, (I \cup \alpha)(t_{n-1}) \rangle \in (I(P))_1$ then $S \underset{\alpha}{\models} Pt_0 \ldots t_{n-1}$;
       if $\langle (I \cup \alpha)(t_0), \ldots, (I \cup \alpha)(t_{n-1}) \rangle \in (I(P))_0$ then
       $S \underset{\alpha}{\models} \neg Pt_0 \ldots t_{n-1}$;
(2)   if $S \underset{\alpha}{\models} \varphi$ then $S \underset{\alpha}{\models} \neg \neg \varphi$;
(3)   if $S \underset{\alpha}{\models} \varphi$ or $S \underset{\alpha}{\models} \psi$ then $S \underset{\alpha}{\models} \varphi \vee \psi$;
       if $S \underset{\alpha}{\models} \neg \varphi$ and $S \underset{\alpha}{\models} \neg \psi$ then $S \underset{\alpha}{\models} \neg(\varphi \vee \psi)$;
(4)   if $S \underset{\alpha_v^x}{\models} \varphi$ then $S \underset{\alpha}{\models} \vee v\varphi$;
       if $S \underset{\alpha_v^y}{\models} \neg \varphi$ for each $y \in X$ then $S \underset{\alpha}{\models} \neg \vee v\varphi$.

In 2.2 I have chosen Kleene's strong interpretation of the logical symbols (see Kleene, 1952, p. 334), the only one which is compatible with 1.3.

2.3. DEFINITION: A PDP-language L consists of a set $K(L)$ of constants and a set of K-structures in the sense of 2.1.

First-order languages of classical type can be regarded as special PDP-languages.

2.4. DEFINITION: A PDP-language is a first-order language of classical type iff for every L-structure $S = \langle X, I \rangle$ and for every n-ary predicate $P \in K(L)$:
$(I(P))_0 \cup (I(P))_1 = X^n$.

In the following I shall use, as far as possible, the notations and definitions which I have introduced in Section 1 also for PDP-languages.

At first glance the logic of PDP-languages seems to have the disadvantage that the completeness theorem does not hold any longer with respect to the classical predicate calculus.[8] However, it is easy to see that this theorem holds if one generalize the notion of logical consequence as follows.

2.5. DEFINITION: Let K be a set of constants, $\varphi \in A(K)$ and $\Phi \subset A(K)$. φ is a logical consequence of Φ iff $S \vDash \varphi$ for every K-structure $S = \langle X, I \rangle$ and for every $\alpha \in X^V$ with the property that S is defined for φ and α (i.e., $S \underset{\alpha}{\vDash} \varphi \vee \neg \varphi$) and that $S \underset{\alpha}{\vDash} \psi$ for every $\psi \in \Phi$.

2.6. THEOREM: Let K be a set of constants, $\varphi \in A(K)$ and $\Phi \subset A(K)$. φ is deducible from Φ iff φ is a logical consequence of Φ.

For the proof of the nontrivial 'only if' part one uses a calculus without cut rule.

In the following we deal with the problem of introducing truth predicates into PDP-languages. For this we must first generalize the definition 1.2 and, in particular, decide under which conditions a statement φ should belong to $(I'(W))_0$ for any L'-structure $S' = \langle X', I' \rangle$. I will choose the generalisation which best preserves the properties of truth predicates in first-order languages of classical type.

2.7. DEFINITION: Let L' be a PDP-language, and let W be a monadic predicate such that $W \in K(L')$.
W is a truth predicate in L' iff for every L'-structure $S' = \langle X', I' \rangle$ and for every $\varphi \in A(L')$:

(B_1) if $\varphi \in (I'(W))_0$ then $S' \vDash \neg \varphi$;
          if $\varphi \in (I'(W))_1$ then $S' \vDash \varphi$;

(B_2) if $S' \vDash \neg \varphi$ and $\varphi \in X'$ then $\varphi \in (I'(W))_0$;
          if $S' \vDash \varphi$ and $\varphi \in X'$ then $\varphi \in (I'(W))_1$.

2.8. DEFINITION: Let L, L' and L'' be PDP-languages such that $K(L') = K(L'')$ and such that L' and L'' are extensions of L.

L' is a weaker extension of L than L'' iff for every L'-structure $S' = \langle X', I' \rangle$ and for every L''-structure $S'' = \langle X'', I'' \rangle$, if $S' \upharpoonright K(L) = S'' \upharpoonright K(L)$ then:

(1) $I'(a) = I''(a)$ for each individual constant $a \in K(L')$;

(2) $(I'(P))_i \subset (I''(P))_i$ for each predicate $P \in K(L')$ and for each $i < 2$.

2.9. THEOREM: Let L be a PDP-language, and let W be a monadic predicate such that $W \notin K(L)$.

Then there is exactly one PDP-language L' such that

(1) L' is an extension of L and $K(L') = K(L) \cup \{W\}$,

(2) W is a truth predicate in L',

(3) L' fulfills the condition (C').

The language guaranteed by 2.9 is called the natural extension of L with respect to the introduction of W as truth predicate. There are some other characterisations of L' which I will now state.

2.10. THEOREM: Let L and L' be PDP-languages, and let W be a monadic predicate such that $W \notin K(L)$. Suppose that L' is an extension of L, with $K(L') = K(L) \cup \{W\}$.

Then the following conditions are equivalent:

(1) L' is the natural extension of L with respect to the introduction of W as truth predicate.

(2)   For every L'-structure $S' = \langle X', I' \rangle$, for every $\varphi \in F(L')$ and for every $\alpha \in X'^V$,

$\langle \varphi, \alpha \rangle \in G(S' \upharpoonright K(L))$ iff $S' \models_\alpha \varphi$.

(3)   For every L'-structure $S' = \langle X', I' \rangle$,

$(I'(W))_0 = \{\varphi \in X'; \langle \neg \varphi, \alpha \rangle \in G(S' \upharpoonright K(L))$ for some $\alpha\}$,

$(I'(W))_1 = \{\varphi \in X'; \langle \varphi, \alpha \rangle \in G(S' \upharpoonright K(L))$ for some $\alpha\}$.

(4) L' is the weakest extension of L such that W is a truth predicate in L'.

For proofs of 2.9 and 2.10 see my 1976 paper. Finally I will present a characterisation of L' which gives a rather simple and plausible construction for L'.[9] It should be remarked, however, that this construction and the determination of the interpretation of W defined thereby are based essentially on the generalized concept of structure introduced in 2.1. In contrast to this, the determination of W defined via $G(S)$ is independent of this concept.

2.11. THEOREM: Let L be a PDP-language, and let W be a monadic predicate such that $W \notin K(L)$. Let L' be the extension of L defined as follows (for sets Φ of formulas let $\bar{\phi} = \{\neg \varphi; \varphi \in \Phi\}$):

(1) $K(L') = K(L) \cup \{W\}$.
(2)   To each L-structure $S = \langle X, I \rangle$ is assigned an L'-structure S' via
         $S' = \langle X, I \cup \{\langle W, \langle Z_0, Z_1 \rangle\rangle\}\rangle$, where $Z_0 = \overline{Z_1}$ and Z_1 is
         recursively defined by:
         if $\varphi \in A(L') \cap X, \Phi \subset Z_1$ and $\langle X, I \cup \{\langle W, \langle \bar{\Phi}, \Phi \rangle\rangle\}\rangle \vDash \varphi$ then
         $\varphi \in Z_1$.

Then L' is the natural extension of L with respect to the introduction of W as truth predicate.

The construction of L' given in this theorem follows closely the idea of how — I suppose — one would intuitively say that a language extension with the aim of introducing a truth predicate W must proceed: For a given structure S of the underlying language one defines successively the extension and the anti-extension of W in the extended structure in such a way that they are closed under (B_2).

3. I will conclude this paper with a few general remarks about some of the consequences of the above discussion. This discussion may have made clear why the problems of the Liar paradox and of the introduction of truth predicates could have been controversial for such a long time. In my opinion, this was because the problems of language extensions had not been analyzed strictly enough. There are, however, different types of language extensions. For example, no difficulties attach to the case where a new n-ary predicate Q is introduced into a PDP-language L relative to the variables $v_0, \ldots, v_{n-1}$ and to the formula $\psi \in F(L)$ as follows.
    Each L-structure $S = \langle X, I \rangle$ is extended to a $K(L) \cup \{Q\}$-structure $S' = \langle X, I' \rangle$ such that:

(B)   for every $\alpha \in X^V$,
         $S' \underset{\alpha}{\vDash} Q v_0 \ldots v_{n-1}$ iff $S' \underset{\alpha}{\vDash} \psi$,
         $S' \underset{\alpha}{\vDash} \neg Q v_0 \ldots v_{n-1}$ iff $S' \underset{\alpha}{\vDash} \neg \psi$.

S' is uniquely determined by this condition and hence the definition of the extended language L' can be represented concisely by postulating that (B) holds for each L'-structure. In the special case where L is of classical type it is possible to replace (B) by the condition

$$S' \vDash \bigwedge v_0 \dots \bigwedge v_{n-1}(Qv_0 \dots v_{n-1} \leftrightarrow \psi).$$

Therefore the definition of L' can be represented in this case by postulating that $\bigwedge v_0 \dots \bigwedge v_{n-1}(Qv_0 \dots v_{n-1} \leftrightarrow \psi)$ is valid in L'. In other words, Q is definable in L and the language extension considered here is of the well known type of extensions by definitions, where $\bigwedge v_0 \dots \bigwedge v_{n-1}(Qv_0 \dots v_{n-1} \leftrightarrow \psi)$ is the defining axiom.

In contrast to this the language extensions for introducing truth predicates are of a more general type which can be described as follows.

A new n-ary predicate Q is introduced into a PDP-language L relative to the variables $v_0, \dots, v_{n-1}$ and to the function $f: Y^n \to F(K(L) \cup \{Q\})$ so that each L-structure $S = \langle X, I \rangle$ is extended to a $K(L) \cup \{Q\}$-structure $S' = \langle X, I' \rangle$ which satisfies the condition

(B')   for all $\varphi \in F(K(L) \cup \{Q\})$, for all $y_0, \dots, y_{n-1} \in Y$ and for all $\alpha \in X^V$, if $f(y_0, \dots, y_{n-1}) = \varphi$ and $\alpha(v_i) = y_i$ for each $i < n$ then: $S' \underset{\alpha}{\vDash} Qv_0 \dots v_{n-1}$ iff $S' \underset{\alpha}{\vDash} \varphi$, $S' \underset{\alpha}{\vDash} \neg Qv_0 \dots v_{n-1}$ iff $S' \underset{\alpha}{\vDash} \neg\varphi$.

In general, (B') does not determine uniquely one extension S' and hence it is not sufficient for a characterisation of an extension L' of L to postulate that (B') holds for every L'-structure. According to the results of our discussion in Section 2 it seems to be reasonable, however, to regard the weakest extension L' of L such that every L'-structure fulfills (B') as the natural extension.

An important difference between the two types of language extensions is the fact that the first, but not the second, type has the following elimination property:

There is a function $e: F(L') \to F(L)$ which can be defined in a natural way with respect to (B) such that for every L'-structure $S' = \langle X', I' \rangle$, for every $\varphi \in F(L')$ and for every $\alpha \in X'^V$, $S' \underset{\alpha}{\vDash} \varphi$ iff $S' \upharpoonright K(L) \underset{\alpha}{\vDash} e(\varphi)$.

The second type has instead only the following reduction property:

For every L-structure S there is a relation $R(S)$ which can be

defined in a natural way with respect to (B′) such that for every
L'-structure $S' = (X', I')$, for every $\varphi \in F(L')$ and for every
$\alpha \in X'^V$,
$S' \underset{\alpha}{\models} \varphi$ iff there is a finite $R(S' \upharpoonright K(L))$-tree with the initial point
$\langle \varphi, \alpha \rangle$ such that $S' \upharpoonright K(L) \underset{\alpha}{\models} \psi$ for every end point $\langle \psi, \alpha' \rangle$ of the
tree.

The loss of the elimination property for the second type is compensated by
an essential gain in expressibility. For the example of a truth predicate this
gain consists, e.g., in the possibility of expressing the proposition that there
are true statements, a proposition which could not be expressed otherwise,
not even by an infinite disjunction of statements. I think it is an important
task to investigate which theoretically or empirically relevant predicates
can be introduced after the second type of language extension (the predicate
'heterological', e.g., on which the antinomy of Grelling is based can be
introduced correctly in this way). In addition to this a more general
discussion of the problem of language extensions seems to be necessary.
Two questions, in particular, should be dealt with:

First, what types of language extensions can or should be distinguished
on empirical or theoretical grounds?

Second, what problems arise if several language extensions are carried
out successively, especially with regard to the compatibility and
extendibility of the respective new notions?

These questions will have to await further investigation; my aim in this
section of the present paper has simply been to point out the need for such
research.

Fakultät für Linguistik und Literaturwissenschaft
Universität Bielefeld

NOTES

* I would like to thank M. Pätzold and D. Segal for helping with the English.
[1] The basic ideas underlying my investigations were first presented in a talk on the occasion of
a conference at the University of Bielefeld, December 1974. Kripke's research in this field and
his paper, November 1975, and also the article of Martin and Woodruff 1976 were unknown to
me during my work on the first draft of my 1976. Kripke's approach is based on the same idea
and reaches the same main results. There are, however, several differences in matters of
presentation, explicitness, emphasis and in some particular results.
[2] Meanwhile I have learned from Feferman (1976) that — besides the approaches of Kripke
and Martin and Woodruff — there are also investigations which deal with related problems
concerning type-free mathematical theories and propose similar solutions. By the way, the

method of truth and validity definition described in this paper is not essentially new. In particular, I have already applied this method in a general form to the theory of dialogue games although I did not explicitly handle the case of languages with truth predicates (cf. Kindt, 1972).

[3] In contrast to Kripke I am convinced that the given solution is the best justifiable one.

[4] If $S = \langle X, I \rangle$ is a K-structure, then $S \upharpoonright K'$ is defined by $S \upharpoonright K' := \langle X, I \upharpoonright K' \rangle$, where $I \upharpoonright K'$ is the restriction of I to K'.

[5] A sequence f is a B-chain iff $f_j B f_{j+1}$ whenever j and $j+1$ belong to the range of f.

[6] For the notion of groundedness see also Kripke (1975, p. 706). In contrast to Kripke I have defined this notion in a way which is based directly on the idea of reducibility and which is independent of the later discussion dealing the question of what type of languages gives an appropriate frame for the introduction of truth predicates. This way has in my opinion the advantage of showing more clearly why it is natural to restrict the application of truth predicates exactly to the set of grounded statements.

[7] In the terminology of Kripke Z_1 is called the extension and Z_0 the anti-extension of the predicate.

[8] More exactly, this calculus seems to be complete but not correct.

[9] Cf. Kripke (1975, pp. 702–705); the construction of L' given by Kripke is based on a definition by transfinite induction. It is, however, not necessary to make use of the theory of ordinals and the method of transfinite induction if one does not have the need to discriminate different levels in the construction of L'.

BIBLIOGRAPHY

Bell, J. L. and Slomson, A. B. (1974), *Models and Ultraproducts*, Amsterdam.

Feferman, S. (1976), 'Comparison of some Type-Free Semantic and Mathematical Theories', Ms. University of Stanford (to appear in *JSL*).

Kindt, W. (1972), *Eine Abstrakte Theorie von Dialogspielen*, Dissertation, University of Freiburg.

Kindt, W. (1976), 'Über Sprachen mit Wahrheitsprädikat', Ms. University of Bielefeld, to appear in Ch. Habel and S. Kanngießer (eds.), *Sprachdynamik und Sprachstruktur*, Tübingen.

Kleene, S. C. (1952), *Introduction to Metamathematics*, Amsterdam.

Kripke, S. (1975), 'Outline of a Theory of Truth', *Journal of Philosophy* **72**, 690–716.

Martin, R. L. and Woodruff, P. W. (1976), 'On Representing "True in L" in L', in, A. Kasher (ed.), *Language in Focus*, Reidel, Dordrecht.

Tarski, A. (1935), 'Der Wahrheitsbegriff in den formalisierten Sprachen', *Studia Philosophica* **1**.

LIST OF PARTICIPANTS

Bad Homburg Workshop   June 14–18, 1976

1. Prof. Lennart Åqvist   Universität Stuttgart
                                7 Stuttgart 1, F.R.G.

2. Prof. Robin Cooper   University of Massachusetts
                                Amherst, MA 01002, U.S.A.

3. Prof. M. J. Cresswell   Victoria University
                                Wellington, New Zealand

4. Dr Lauri Carlson   University of Helsinki
                                Helsinki, Finland

5. Dr Jerrold Edmondson   Technische Universität Berlin
                                1 Berlin, F.R.G.

6. Prof. Gilles Fauconnier   CRNS
                                Paris 75004, France

7. Dr Franz Guenthner   Universität Stuttgart
                                7 Stuttgart 1, F.R.G.

8. Dr Roland Hausser   Universität München
                                8 München, F.R.G.

9. Prof. Hans Kamp   Bedford College
                                London, Great Britain

10. Prof. Edward Keenan   UCLA
                                Los Angeles, CA 90018, U.S.A.

11. Dr Uwe Mönnich   Universität Tübingen
                                74 Tübingen, F.R.G.

12. Prof. Janos Petöfi   Universität Bielefeld
                                48 Bielefeld, F.R.G.

13. Dr Tanya Reinhart   University of Tel Aviv
                                Tel Aviv, Israel

14. Dr Hannes Rieser   Universität Bielefeld
                                48 Bielefeld, F.R.G.

15. Dr Walther Kindt   Universität Bielefeld
                                48 Bielefeld, F.R.G.

16. Prof. Christian Rohrer   Universität Stuttgart
                                7 Stuttgart 1, F.R.G.

17. Prof. S. J. Schmidt   Universität Bielefeld
                                48 Bielefeld, F.R.G.

18. Prof. Richard Smaby   University of Pennsylvania
                                Philadelphia, PA 19104, U.S.A.

19. Prof. Richmond Thomason   University of Pittsburgh
                                Pittsburgh, PA 15213, U.S.A.

INDEX

375

SYNTHESE LANGUAGE LIBRARY

Texts and Studies
in Linguistics and Philosophy

Managing Editors:

JAAKKO HINTIKKA

Academy of Finland, Stanford University, and Florida State University (Tallahassee)

STANLEY PETERS

The University of Texas at Austin

Editors:

EMMON BACH (University of Massachusetts at Amherst)
JOAN BRESNAN (Massachusetts Institute of Technology)
JOHN LYONS (University of Sussex)
JULIUS M. E. MORAVCSIK (Stanford University)
PATRICK SUPPES (Stanford University)
DANA SCOTT (Oxford University)